W9-CBC-555

Handbook of Prayers

Handbook of Prayers

Reverend James Socías
General Editor

SCEPTER PUBLISHERS
MIDWEST THEOLOGICAL FORUM

Published in the United States of America by

SCEPTER PUBLISHERS, INC.
20 Nassau St.
Princeton, New Jersey 08542

and

MIDWEST THEOLOGICAL FORUM
712 S. Loomis St.
Chicago, Illinois 60607

With Ecclesiastical Approval

Published by the authority of the Bishop's Committee
on the Liturgy, National Conference of Bishops
(United States of America)

Fourth American Edition 1997

ISBN 0-933932-60-X

ACKNOWLEDGMENTS

The English translation, original texts, general introduction, pastoral notes, arrangement, and design of *Order of Christian Funeral* © 1989, 1985, International Committee on English in the Liturgy, Inc. (ICEL); excerpts from the English translation of *The Roman Missal* © 1973, ICEL; excerpts from the English translation of *Holy Communion and Worship of the Eucharist outside Mass* © 1974, ICEL; excerpts from the English translation of *The Liturgy of the Hours* © 1982, ICEL; excerpts from the English translation of *Book of Blessings* © 1987, ICEL. All rights reserved.

Additional Blessings for Use in the United States of America © 1988, United States Catholic Conference (USCC). All rights reserved.

Scripture readings from *The New American Bible with Revised New Testament*, copyright © 1986, Confraternity of Christian Doctrine, Washington D.C., and used by license of copyright owner: All rights reserved.

Psalm texts from *The Psalms: A New Translation* © The Grail (England) 1963. The complete psalms first published in 1963 by and available through Wm. Collins Sons & Company Ltd; in North America available through the Paulist Press, Inc. and Collins + World.

Text for the *Stations of the Cross* and for the "Consideration" of the *Ten-Day Devotion to the Holy Spirit* (text of the homily "The Great Unknown"), both by Blessed Josemaría Escrivá de Balaguer in *The Way of the Cross* and *Friends of God* respectively. Excerpts from *Holy Rosary* also by Blessed Josemaría Escrivá.

   © Originals—Scriptor, S.A. (Madrid)

   © Translations—Scepter Ltd., London 1981

Latin text of the Order of Mass from *Missale Romanum*, ed. typ. alt. © 1975, Typis Polyglottis Vaticanis.

Full-page illustrations were taken, by kind permission, from the book *My Forgotten Prayers and My Forgotten Saints*, by the Benziger Sisters, Publishers. Used by permission.

To Jesus, Mary, and Joseph,
the Holy Family of Nazareth,
that from them we may learn to pray
so that our family may become
a truly Christian one.

CONTENTS

The Eucharistic Sacrifice

Prayers After Mass

Devotions to the Blessed Virgin Mary

Devotions to St. Joseph

Various Prayers

Prayers at the Time of Death

LORD, TEACH US TO PRAY

"The year 2000 marks a kind of challenge. We must look at the *immensity of good* that has sprung from the mystery of the Incarnation of the Word and, at the same time, not lose sight of the *mystery of sin*, which is continually expanding. Saint Paul writes that *'where sin increased . . . , grace overflowed all the more . . . .'*

"This profound truth presents a perennial challenge for prayer. It shows how necessary prayer is for the world and for the Church, because in the end it constitutes *the easiest way of making God and his redeeming love present in the world.* God entrusted to men their own salvation; He entrusted to them the Church and, in the Church, the redeeming work of Christ. God entrusted this to all, both to individuals and to humanity as a whole. *He entrusted all to one and one to all.* The prayer of the Church, and especially the prayer of the pope, must constantly reflect this awareness."[1]

And what is the best way to pray? The disciples knew our Lord Jesus Christ very well in this detail: he prayed often, in their midst or alone. Moved by our Lord's dedication to prayer, they once asked him: "Lord, teach us to pray." In answer, our Lord gave them the model of all prayer: "When you pray, say: 'Our Father, who art in heaven . . . .'" Buoyed by this confidence, we pray. We begin with the prayers that we learned in childhood. They are very much a part of Christian tradition.

---

1. John Paul II, *Crossing the Threshold of Hope* (=CTH), 23-24, New York: Alfred A. Knopf, 1994.

Through our vocal prayers, we learn the life of Jesus Christ and we gain his confidence in talking to our Father God. Then our conversations with God become sincere and true, face to face, heart to heart.

Through our vocal prayers, we begin this conversation with God. *"Prayer is a search for God,* but it is also *a revelation of God.* Through prayer God reveals himself as Creator and Father, as Redeemer and Savior, as the Spirit who 'scrutinizes everything, even the depths of God' (1 Cor 2:10), and above all 'the secrets of human hearts' (cf. Ps 43[44]:22). *Through prayer God reveals himself above all as Mercy*—that is, Love that goes out to those who are suffering, Love that sustains, uplifts, and invites us to trust. The victory of good in the world is united organically with this truth. A person who prays professes such a truth and in a certain sense makes God, who is *merciful Love,* present in the world."[2]

This handbook is a compilation of prayers that will help us talk to God in a confident and intimate way. Most of these prayers are traditional and are thus grounded in the piety of the communion of saints. Some are the fruit of meditations of Blessed Josemaría Escrivá from his book The Way of the Cross and from his various homilies that deal with devotion to Jesus, Mary, and Joseph—*the trinity on earth.*

We entrust this treasury of prayers to the Blessed Virgin Mary. May she, who needed only to embrace her Son to make her prayer heard, teach us to pray as she prays—with the utmost confidence, not rooted in our own worth, merit or devotion, but rather in the love and mercy of our Lord Jesus Christ.

---

2. CTH, 25-26.

HOW TO BE A BETTER CATHOLIC

UNIVERSAL CALL TO HOLINESS

"All Christians in any state or walk of life are called to the fullness of Christian life and to the perfection of charity."[1] "Be perfect, as your heavenly Father is perfect."[2] God wants us to be holy. One must try to sanctify oneself in one's place within the Church of Christ.

"[Lay Christians] live in the ordinary circumstances of family and social life, from which the very web of their existence is woven."[3]

"By their very vocation, they seek the Kingdom of God by engaging in temporal affairs and by ordering them according to the plan of God. They live in the world, that is, in each and in all of the secular professions and occupations."[4]

"Hence the laity, dedicated as they are to Christ and anointed by the Holy Spirit, are marvelously called and prepared, so that even richer fruits of the Spirit may be produced in them. For all their works, prayers, and apostolic undertakings, family and married life, daily work, relaxation of mind and body, if they are accomplished in the Spirit—indeed even the hardships of life, if patiently borne—all

---

1. Vatican Council II, *Lumen Gentium* (=LG), 31.
2. Matthew 5:48.
3. LG, 31.
4. Ibidem.

these become spiritual sacrifices acceptable to God through Jesus Christ. In the celebration of the Eucharist these may most fittingly be offered to the Father along with the body of the Lord. And so, worshiping everywhere by their holy actions, the laity consecrate the world itself to God, everywhere offering worship by the holiness of their lives."[5]

"Priests will acquire holiness in their own distinctive way by exercising their functions sincerely and tirelessly in the Spirit of Christ.

"Since they are ministers of the Word of God, they read and hear every day the Word of God, which they must teach to others. If they strive at the same time to make it part of their own lives, they will become daily more perfect disciples of the Lord. . . ."[6]

In order to sanctify ourselves in the ordinary circumstances of our life, we need to grow in our spiritual life, especially through prayer, self-denial, and work.

Life of Prayer

"We learn to pray at certain moments by hearing the Word of the Lord and sharing in his paschal mystery, but his Spirit is offered us at all times, in the events of *each day,* to make prayer spring up from us."[7]

"Prayer in the events of each day and each moment is one of the secrets of the kingdom revealed to 'little children,' to the servants of Christ, to the poor of the Beatitudes. It is right and good to pray so that the coming of the kingdom of justice and peace may influence the march of history, but it is just as important to bring the help of prayer into humble, every-

---

5. *Catechism of the Catholic Church* (=CCC), 901, Libreria Editrice Vaticana, 1994; cf. LG 10, 34; I Peter 2:5.

6. Vatican Council II, *Presbyterorum Ordinis* (=PO), 20; cf. 1 Timothy 4:15-16.

7. CCC, 2659; cf. Matthew 6:11, 34.

day situations; all forms of prayer can be the leaven to which the Lord compares the kingdom."[8]

"But do not imagine that prayer is an action to be carried out and then forgotten. The just man 'delights in the law of the Lord and meditates on his law day and night. Through the night, I meditate on you' and 'my prayer comes to you like incense in the evening.' Our whole day can be a time of prayer—from night to morning and from morning to night."[9]

Life of Self-Denial

"The way of perfection passes by way of the cross. There is no holiness without renunciation and spiritual battle. Spiritual progress entails the ascesis and mortification that gradually lead to living in the peace and joy of the Beatitudes."[10] "Without mortification there is no happiness on earth."[11]

"Let us listen to our Lord: 'He who is faithful in a very little thing is faithful also in much; and he who is dishonest in a very little thing is dishonest also in much.' It is as if he were saying to us: 'Fight continuously in the apparently unimportant things which are to my mind important; fulfill your duty, punctually; smile at whoever needs cheering up, even though there is sorrow in your soul; devote the necessary time to prayer, without haggling; go to the help of anyone who looks for you; practice justice, and go beyond it with the grace of charity.'"[12]

---

8. CCC, 2660; cf. Luke 13:20-21.

9. Blessed Josemaría Escrivá, *Christ is Passing By* (=CPB), 119, Princeton, N.J.: Scepter Publishers, 1974.

10. CCC, 2015; cf. 2 Timothy 2:4.

11. Blessed Josemaría Escrivá, *Furrow* (=FW), 983, Princeton, N.J.: Scepter Publishers, 1988.

12. CPB, 77.

Self-denial will be more precious if it is united to charity according to the teaching of St. Leo the Great: "Let us give to virtue what we refuse to self-indulgence. Let what we deny ourselves by fast be the refreshment of the poor."

Life of Work

"*Human work* proceeds directly from persons created in the image of God and called to prolong the work of creation by subduing the earth, both with and for one another. Hence work is a duty: 'If any one will not work, let him not eat.' Work honors the Creator's gifts and the talents received from him. It can also be redemptive. By enduring the hardship of work in union with Jesus, the carpenter of Nazareth and the one crucified on Calvary, man collaborates in a certain fashion with the Son of God in his redemptive work. He shows himself to be a disciple of Christ by carrying the cross, daily, in the work he is called to accomplish. Work can be a means of sanctification and a way of animating earthly realities with the Spirit of Christ."[13]

"In work, the person exercises and fulfills in part the potential inscribed in his nature. The primordial value of labor stems from man himself, its author and its beneficiary. Work is for man, not man for work.

"Everyone should be able to draw from work the means of providing for his life and that of his family, and of serving the human community."[14]

---

13. CCC, 2427; cf. *Gaudium et Spes* (=GS), 34; Genesis 1:28, 9:14-18; *Centessimus Annus* (=CA), 31; 2 Thessalonians 3:10, 4:11; *Laborem Exercens* (=LE), 27.
14. CCC, 2428; cf. LE, 6.

SUMMARY OF CHRISTIAN BELIEFS

We are required to know and to believe:

- That there is one supreme, eternal, infinite God, the Creator of heaven and earth.
- That the good will be rewarded by him for ever in heaven, and that the wicked who die unrepentant will be punished for ever in hell.
- That in the Holy Trinity there are three Persons, coeternal, coequal: God the Father, God the Son, and God the Holy Spirit.
- That the Second Person of the Holy Trinity became man and died on the cross to save us.
- The tenets of the *Apostles' Creed*.
- In the *Commandments of God and of the Church*.
- That the *seven sacraments* were instituted by Christ to give us grace; especially, that Baptism is necessary and that the Eucharist is a pledge of our future glory.
- That *Sacred Tradition* and *Sacred Scripture*, which together form one sacred deposit of the Word of God, are entrusted to the Church.
- Whatever God teaches us by his Church, who in her teaching cannot deceive us or be deceived.

    "'The Roman Pontiff, head of the college of bishops, enjoys [this] infallibility in virtue of his office, when, as supreme pastor and teacher of all the faithful, he proclaims by a definitive act a doctrine pertaining to faith or morals. . . . The infallibility promised to the Church is also present in the body of bishops when, together with Peter's successor, they exercise the supreme 'Magisterium,' above all in an Ecumenical Council. When the Church through its supreme Magisterium proposes a doctrine 'for belief as being divinely revealed' and as the teaching of Christ, the definitions 'must be adhered to with the obedience of faith.'"[15]

---

15. Cf. CCC, 891.

SPIRITUAL GAME PLAN

Do you want to be a really good Christian? The first of your battles will be to enter into and remain in the state of grace, to avoid any mortal sin. And, then, because you want to love God above all things, you will also try not to commit venial sins.

The practice of some acts of piety throughout the day will help you to have a divine contemplative life in the midst of the daily routine. The habitual performance of these acts will also be the foundation for growing in Christian virtues. Most important is to be consistent in your daily schedule, in your spiritual game plan, so that you will live as a child of God.

Daily

- *Get up at a fixed time*, as early as possible. Eight hours of sleep should be enough. More than this or less than six hours of sleep may is usually not healthy.

- *Offer your day* to God through the intercession of our Lady.

- *Work with order and intensity* during the day as a way of serving God. Set goals and establish priorities in order to develop a practical schedule. Sanctifying ordinary work is the goal of our life.

- *Try to attend Mass, receiving holy Communion*, as often as possible. This is the best sacrifice we can offer to God. Prepare yourself for the Mass by spending some time in prayer.

- *Spend some time in mental prayer* before the Blessed Sacrament (15 minutes, if possible).

- Pray the *Angelus* at noontime. (During Easter-time, we say the *Regina Cæli* instead.)

- Pray the *Rosary*, if possible, with your family, of-fering each decade for a specific intention.

- Do some other *spiritual reading*. Start with the New Testament or some well-known spiritual book. Ten to fifteen minutes is sufficient.

- Make a short *examination of conscience* at the end of the day before going to bed. Two or three min-utes is enough. Follow these steps: Humble your-self in the presence of God. Tell him, "Lord, if you will, you can make me clean." Ask for light to acknowledge your defects and virtues and to see the dangers and opportunities of the day. Ask for repentance, amendment, and encouragement.

Weekly

- Center all activities around the *holy Mass* on *Sun-day*, the Lord's day. It is also a family day—for rest and spiritual growth.

- If you do not receive holy Communion every day, receive at least on Sundays and holy days of obli-gation.

- Saturday is traditionally dedicated to the Blessed Virgin Mary. Honor her and say some special prayer, such as the *Hail Holy Queen.*

Monthly

- Go to *Confession* at least once a month. It is the sacrament of joy. Pope John Paul II says: "God is always the one who is principally offended by sin—'I have sinned against You'—and God alone can forgive. He does so through the ministry of the priest in the sacrament of Penance, which is the ordinary way of obtaining forgiveness and remission of mortal sins. Every mortal sin must always be stated with its determining circumstances in an individual confession."[16]

- Seek and follow the *spiritual guidance* of a wise, prudent, and knowledgeable priest.

- *Spend a few hours in recollection*, best done before the Blessed Sacrament. Consider how you are directing your life toward God.

Yearly

- *Spend two or three days each year in silence*, speaking with God only. A few days of *retreat* are necessary for the soul in the same way that the body needs a vacation. It is a yearly opportunity for conversion.

Always

- Stay in the *presence of God:* be aware that he is always close to you. Try to please him in everything as a child tries to please his/her parents.

- *Thank God* for the graces that he constantly gives you.

- Do everything *for the love of God:* this is purity of intention. Always purify your intention. Make *acts of contrition* and *atonement* for your sins and sins of others.

- Try to *live as you would like to die*. We shall die as we have lived.

---

16. John Paul II, *Reconciliation and Penance* (=RP), Libreria Editrice Vaticana, 1984.

THE SEVEN SACRAMENTS

"The [seven] sacraments are efficacious signs of grace, instituted by Christ and entrusted to the Church, by which divine life is dispensed to us. The visible rites by which the sacraments are celebrated signify and make present the graces proper to each sacrament. They bear fruit in those who receive them with the required dispositions."[17]

Baptism[18]

By which we are born into the new life in Christ

The fruits of this sacrament are:

- Remission of original sin.

- Birth into the new life by which man becomes an adoptive son of the Father, a member of Christ, and a temple of the Holy Spirit.

- Incorporation into the Church, the body of Christ, and participation in the priesthood of Christ.

- The imprinting, on the soul, of an indelible spiritual sign, the *character*, which consecrates the baptized person for Christian worship. Because of this *character*, Baptism cannot be repeated.

Confirmation[19]

By which we are more perfectly bound to the Church and enriched with a special strength of the Holy Spirit

The fruits of this sacrament are:

- An increase and deepening of baptismal grace.

---

17. CCC, 1131.
18. Cf. CCC, 1277-1279.
19. Cf. CCC, 1303-1316.

- A deepening of one's roots in the divine filiation, which makes one cry, "Abba, Father!"

- A firming of one's unity with Christ.

- An increase of the gifts of the Holy Spirit.

- A strengthening of one's bond with the Church and closer association with her mission.

- Special strength of the Holy Spirit to spread and defend the faith by word and action as a true witnesses of Christ, to confess the name of Christ boldly, and to never be ashamed of the cross.

- The imprinting, as in Baptism, of a spiritual mark or indelible *character* on the Christian's soul. Because of this *character*, one can receive this sacrament only once in one's life.

The Holy Eucharist[20]

By which Christ associates his Church
and all her members with the sacrifice of the cross

The fruits of this sacrament are:

- An increase in the communicant's union with Christ.

- Forgiveness of venial sins.

- Preservation from grave sins.

- A strengthening of the bonds of charity between the communicant and Christ.

- A strengthening of the unity of the Church as the Mystical Body of Christ.

---

20. Cf. CCC, 1407, 1413, 1416. The holy Eucharist is really, truly, and substantially the Body, Blood, Soul, and Divinity of Jesus Christ, under the appearances of bread and wine. The holy Eucharist is not only a sacrament; it is also a sacrifice—the holy sacrifice of the Mass.

Reconciliation or Penance[21]

By which sins after Baptism are forgiven

The fruits of this sacrament are:

- Reconciliation with God: the penitent recovers sanctifying grace.
- Reconciliation with the Church.
- Remission of the eternal punishment incurred by mortal sins.
- Remission, at least in part, of temporal punishments resulting from sin.
- Peace and serenity of conscience, and spiritual consolation.
- An increase of spiritual strength for the Christian battle.

Anointing of the Sick[22]

By which a special grace is conferred during grave illness or old age

The fruits of this sacrament are:

- Unity with the passion of Christ, for the sick person's own good and that of the whole Church.
- Strength, peace, and courage to endure as a Christian the sufferings of illness or old age.
- Forgiveness of sins, if the sick person was not able to obtain it through the sacrament of Penance.
- Restoration of health, if it is conducive to the salvation of the soul.
- Preparation for entering eternal life.

---

21. Cf. CCC, 1486, 1497. Individual and integral confession of grave sins followed by absolution remains the only ordinary means of reconciliation with God and with the Church.

22. Cf. CCC, 1527, 1532.

Holy Orders[23]

*By which the task of serving
in the name and in the person of Christ is conferred*

The fruits of this sacrament are:

- *The mission* and *faculty* ("the sacred power") to act *in persona Christi.*
- Configuration to Christ as Priest, Teacher, and Pastor.
- The imprinting, as in Baptism, of an indelible *character* that cannot be repeated or conferred temporarily.

Matrimony[24] (See Church Laws Concerning Marriage on p. 20.)

*By which a man and a woman form
with each other an intimate communion of life and love*

The fruits of this sacrament for the spouses are:

- The grace to love each other with the love with which Christ has loved his Church.
- A perfecting of their human love.
- A strengthening of their indissoluble unity.
- Sanctification on their way to heaven.
- The grace to "help one another to attain holiness in their married life and in welcoming and educating their children."
- An integration into God's covenant with man: *Authentic married love is caught up into divine love.*

---

23. Cf. CCC, 1536, 1591, 1598. It is bishops who confer the sacrament of Holy Orders in the three degrees: episcopate, presbyterate, and diaconate. In the Latin Church, the sacrament of Holy Orders for the presbyterate is normally conferred on only those candidates who are ready to embrace celibacy freely and who publicly manifest their intention of staying celibate for the love of God's kingdom and the service of others.
24. Cf. CCC, 1638, 1639, 1641, 1660, 1664. The *marriage* bond has been established by God himself in such a way that a marriage concluded and consummated between baptized persons can never be dissolved.

THE TEN COMMANDMENTS OF GOD

"What good deed must I do, to have eternal life?"
"If you would enter into life, keep the Commandments."[25]

Christ—through the example of his own life and by
his preaching—attested to the permanent validity
of the Ten Commandments.

The Decalogue contains a privileged expression of
the natural law. It is made known to us by divine
revelation and by human reason.[26]

1. **I am the Lord your God.**
   You shall not have strange gods before me. You
   shall not make to thyself any graven thing; nor
   the likeness of anything that is in heaven above,
   or in the earth beneath, nor of those things that
   are in the waters under the earth. You shall not
   adore them nor serve them.
2. **You shall not take the name of the Lord your God
   in vain.**
3. **Remember to keep holy the Sabbath day.**
4. **Honor your father and your mother.**
5. **You shall not kill.**
6. **You shall not commit adultery.**
7. **You shall not steal.**
8. **You shall not bear false witness against your
   neighbor.**
9. **You shall not covet your neighbor's wife.**
10. **You shall not covet your neighbor's goods.**

25. Cf. Matthew 19:16-17.
26. Cf. CCC, 2075, 2076, 2080.

THE SIX PRECEPTS OF THE CHURCH [27]

The obligatory character of these positive laws decreed by the pastoral authorities is meant to guarantee to the faithful the indispensable minimum in the spirit of prayer and moral effort, in the growth in love of God and neighbor:

1. **"You shall attend Mass on Sundays and holy days of obligation."**

   This precept requires to participate in the Eucharistic celebration, when the Christian community gathers together on the day commemorating the resurrection of the Lord.

2. **"You shall confess your sins at least once a year."**

   This precept ensures preparation for the Eucharist by the reception of the sacrament of Reconciliation, which continues Baptism's work of conversion and forgiveness.

3. **"You shall humbly receive your Creator in holy Communion at least during the Easter season."**

   This precept guarantees as a minimum the reception of the Lord's body and blood in connection with the Paschal feasts, the origin and center of the Christian liturgy.

4. **"You shall keep holy the holy days of Obligation."**

   This precept requires the completion of the Sunday observance by participation in the principal liturgical feasts that honor the mysteries of the Lord, the Virgin Mary, and the saints. It requires, also, abstinence from those labors and business concerns that impede the worship to be rendered to God, the joy that is proper to the Lord's day, or the proper relaxation of mind and body.

5. **"You shall observe the prescribed days of fasting and abstinence."**

   This precept ensures the times of ascesis and penance that prepare us for the liturgical feasts; they help us acquire freedom of heart and mastery over our instincts.

6. **"You shall provide for the material needs of the Church."**

   This precept requires the faithful to contribute to the Church according to their own abilities.

HOLY DAYS OF OBLIGATION

Holy days of obligation in addition to all the Sundays of the year.	In the Universal Church	In Australia	In Malaysia & Singapore	In Canada	In England and Wales	In Ireland	In Kenya	In New Zealand	In Nigeria	In the Philippines	In Scotland	In the U. S. A.
Jan. 1. Mary, Mother of God	•			•					E		•	C
Jan. 6. Epiphany	•	A	A	A	C	•	A	E	A	A	A	B
March 17. St. Patrick						•						
March 19. St. Joseph	•								E			
Ascension	•	•	•	B	•	•	•	•	E	B	D	•
Holy Body and Blood of Christ	•	B	B	B	•	•		B	E	B	B	B
June 29. Ss. Peter and Paul	•	B			C			B	E		D	
Aug. 15. Assumption	•	C	•		C	•	•	•	E		D	C
Nov. 1. All Saints	•	C	•		C	•	•		E		D	C
Dec. 8. Immaculate Conception	•					•			E	•		•
Dec. 25. Christmas	•	•	•	•	•	•	•	•	•	•	D	•

A = Transferred to the Sunday between January 2 and January 8.

B = Transferred to the following Sunday.

C = When the date falls on a Saturday or a Monday, no obligation is attached for that year.

D = When the date falls on a Saturday, no obligation is attached for that year.

E = The precept of attending Mass is transferred to the following or preceding Sunday.

DAYS OF PENANCE

"Conversion is accomplished in daily life by gestures of reconciliation, concern for the poor, the exercise and defense of justice and right, by the admission of faults to one's brethren, fraternal correction, revision of life, examination of conscience, spiritual direction, acceptance of suffering, endurance of persecution for the sake of righteousness. Taking up one's cross each day and following Jesus is the surest way of penance." "The *seasons and days of penance* in the course of the liturgical year (Lent, and each Friday in memory of the death of the Lord) are intense moments of the Church's penitential practice."[28]

All members of the Christian faithful are, in their own way, bound to do penance in virtue of divine law. In order that all may be joined in a common observance of penance, penitential days are prescribed in which the Christian faithful, in a special way, pray; exercise works of piety and charity; and deny themselves by fulfilling their responsibilities more faithfully, and especially by observing fast and abstinence according to the following:[29]

- The time of Lent and all Fridays of the year are, throughout the universal Church, days and times especially appropriate for spiritual exercises; penitential liturgies; pilgrimages as signs of penance; voluntary self-denial, such as fasting and almsgiving.
- Abstinence from meat (or some other food) or another penitential practice, according to the prescriptions of the conference of bishops, is to be observed on each Friday of the year unless it is a solemnity. Fast and abstinence from meat are to be observed on Ash Wednesday and on Good Friday.

28. CCC, 1435, 1438; cf. Luke 9:23.
29. Cf. *Codex Iuris Canonici* (=CIC), 1244-1245, 1249-1253.

- All persons who have completed their fourteenth year are bound by the law of abstinence. All adults (eighteen years or older) are bound by the law of fast up to the beginning of their sixtieth year. Pastors and parents are to see to it that minors who are not bound by a law of fast or abstinence are educated nevertheless in an authentic sense of penance.
- It is for the conference of bishops to determine more precisely the observances of fast and abstinence and to substitute in whole or in part for fast or abstinence other forms of penance, especially works of charity and exercises of piety and missionary works.
- Diocesan bishops can proclaim special days of penance for their own dioceses or territories, but only for individual occasions (*per modum actus*).

WORKS OF MERCY [30]

The *works of mercy* are charitable actions by which we come to the aid of our neighbor's spiritual and bodily necessities. Giving alms to the poor is one of the chief witnesses to fraternal charity; it is also a work of justice pleasing to God.

Corporal	Spiritual
• Feeding the hungry.	• Counseling the doubtful.
• Giving drink to the thirsty.	• Instructing the ignorant.
• Clothing the naked.	• Admonishing sinners.
• Sheltering the homeless.	• Comforting the afflicted.
• Visiting the sick.	• Forgiving offenses.
• Visiting the imprisoned.	• Bearing wrongs patiently.
• Burying the dead.	• Praying for the living and the dead.

---

30. Cf. CCC, 2447.

CHURCH LAWS
CONCERNING MARRIAGE [31]

Matrimony—defined as the *marriage covenant by which a man and woman establish between themselves a partnership of the whole of life—is by its nature ordered towards the good of the spouses and the procreation and education of offspring.* For a baptized couple, this covenant has been raised by Christ to the dignity of a sacrament.

Because Christ instituted this sacrament, he also gives a man and a woman their vocation to marriage. The covenant thus involves not only a man and a woman, but also Christ. In establishing marriage as a vocation in life, God gave it the characteristics that enable human love to achieve its perfection and allow family life to be full and fruitful. Outside marriage, or without a proper realization of its nature, the right conditions for the fruitfulness of human love and for a successful family life do not exist.

The Catholic Church has the right to establish laws regarding the validity of marriages, since marriage for the baptized is both a covenant and a sacrament. And it is only the Catholic Church that has jurisdiction over those marriages, with due regard for the competence of civil authority concerning the merely civil effects. No one other than the Church has the power or authority to change ecclesiastical laws.

Unity and Indissolubility

Unity of marriage signifies that the *covenant* established is between one man and one woman: the hus-

---

31. This section (pp. 20-25) is excerpted from James Socías, *Marriage Is Love Forever*, Princeton, N.J.: Scepter Publications, 1994.

band cannot marry another woman during the lifetime of his wife, nor can the wife marry another man
during the lifetime of her husband. *Polygamy*—having more than one spouse at the same time—is contrary to the equal personal dignity of men and
women, who in Matrimony give themselves with a
love that is total and, therefore unique and exclusive.
Indissolubility refers to the fact that the bond of sacramental marriage cannot be broken except by the
death of either the husband or the wife.

Consent

Matrimonial consent is an act of the will by which a
man and a woman, in an irrevocable covenant, mutually give and accept each other, declaring their
willingness to welcome children and to educate
them. Consent must be a free act of the will of each
of the contracting parties, without coercion or serious fear arising from external circumstances. To be
free means:

- *To be acting without constraint.*
- *To be unimpeded by natural or ecclesiastical law.*

Only those capable of giving valid matrimonial consent can get married: Matrimony is created through
the consent of the parties—consent legitimately
manifested between persons who, according to law,
are capable of giving that consent.

Conditions for a Valid Marriage

1. The contracting parties must be capable, according to Church law, of giving matrimonial consent. Before Matrimony is celebrated, it must be
   evident that no impediment stands in the way of
   its valid and licit (lawful) celebration.

2. The consent given by the parties must be deliberate, fully voluntary, free, mutual, and public. Therefore, the following are incapable of contracting marriage:

   • Persons who lack sufficient use of reason.

   • Persons who suffer from grave lack of discretion of judgment concerning essential matrimonial rights and duties that are to be mutually given and accepted.

   • Persons who, because of serious psychic illness, cannot assume the essential obligations of Matrimony.

3. The consent must be *legitimately manifested in canonical form*, in the presence of an authorized priest or deacon and two witnesses. Canonical form does not oblige non-Catholics when they marry other non-Catholics, but only Catholics—even if only one of the two parties is Catholic—who have not left the Church by a formal act. *The priest or deacon who assists at the celebration of a marriage receives the consent of the spouses in the name of the Church and gives them the blessing of the Church. The presence of the Church's minister, as well as that of the witnesses, visibly expresses the fact that marriage is an ecclesial reality.*

Age Requirement

As a condition for marriage, the Church requires that a man has completed his sixteenth year (one's sixteenth year is completed the day after one's sixteenth birthday) and that a woman has completed her fourteenth year of age (one's fourteenth year of age is completed the day after one's fourteenth birthday). These ages are the minima for validity. There may be civil laws, as well, regulating the minimum age for each state and country, but failure to comply with these laws does not invalidate marriage in the eyes of the Church.

Invalid Marriages

Marriage is permanent, because God established it so from the very beginning. The indissolubility of marriage is for the good of husband and wife, their children, and human society as a whole. The civil government has no power to dissolve a valid marriage—even if the marriage is between non-Catholics.

The government can dissolve only the civil aspects of marriage, such as ownership of property, custody of the children, etc. *Even when civil divorce is allowed by the country's law*, marriage, in God's eyes, still exists.

The Church does not have the power to dissolve a valid, sacramental marriage that has been *consummated*. She may declare a marriage *null and void* only upon investigation and on evidence that the marriage did not exist from the very beginning. The reasons could be one of the following:

- Lack of fully *voluntary and free consent*.
- Some deficiency in the *form of the marriage celebration*.
- The presence of an *impediment* that makes a marriage invalid.

The *declaration of nullity* (so-called *annulment*) is a very important decision of an ecclesiastical court. A very careful investigation has to be made by the court before that conclusion can be reached, ensuring that no valid marriage is declared *null and void* by mistake.

Mixed Marriages

Marriages between a Catholic and a baptized Christian who is not in full communion with the Catholic Church are called *mixed marriages*. For *mixed marriages*, permission (not dispensation) from the local ordinary (usually the bishop) is required for validity. Marriages between Catholics and unbaptized persons (*disparity of cult*) are invalid unless a dispensation from the local ordinary is granted. All this presupposes that these marriages are celebrated with all other necessary conditions fulfilled.

The local bishop may grant permission or dispensation for such marriages on the following conditions:

- The Catholic party declares that he or she is prepared to remove dangers of falling away from the faith and makes a sincere promise to do all in his or her power to have all the children baptized and brought up in the Catholic Church.

- The other party is to be informed at an appropriate time of these promises that the Catholic person has to make. It is important that the other person be truly aware of the commitments and obligations of the Catholic spouse.

- Both persons are to be instructed with respect to the essential ends and properties of marriage, which are not to be excluded by either party.

- The man and woman should *marry in the Catholic Church*. The canonical form (Church ceremony with an authorized Catholic priest or deacon and at least two other witnesses present) is to be followed. When there are serious difficulties, the local bishop may give a dispensation and allow another form which is public (such as a civil ceremony) to be followed. It is never allowed, however, to have the Catholic priest or deacon and a non-Catholic minister, rabbi, or public official, each performing his or her own rite, asking for the consent of the parties. Likewise, it is forbidden to have another religious marriage ceremony before or after the Catholic ceremony for giving or receiving the matrimonial consent. Marriage consent is given only once.

Worthy Reception of the Sacrament of Matrimony

Once these requirements for a valid marriage are fulfilled, some other conditions are needed for the *worthy* reception of the *sacrament* of Matrimony:

- *Baptism.* Both parties must be baptized persons.
- *Rectitude of intention.* Being carried away by emotions or momentary passions should be avoided. Premarital pregnancy is not a sufficient reason to marry someone, as that could involve an added mistake.
- *Spiritual preparation.* One should be in the state of grace. The sacraments of Penance and holy Eucharist are strongly recommended as immediate preparation.
- *Confirmation.* Catholics should have previously received the sacrament of Confirmation. This sacrament should be received before marriage, unless grave difficulties stand in the way.
- *Knowledge of the duties of married life.* Such duties include mutual fidelity of the spouses until death, and care for the bodily and spiritual welfare of the children sent by God.
- *Obedience to the marriage laws of the Church.*

INDULGENCES [32]

Definition

- "An indulgence is a remission before God of the temporal punishment due to sins whose guilt has already been forgiven, which the faithful Christian who is duly disposed gains under certain prescribed conditions through the action of the Church which, as the minister of redemption, dispenses and applies with authority the treasury of the satisfactions of Christ and the saints."

- "An indulgence is obtained through the Church who, by virtue of the power of binding and loosing granted her by Christ Jesus, intervenes in favor of individual Christians and opens for them the treasury of the merits of Christ and the saints to obtain from the Father of mercies the remission of the temporal punishments due for their sins. Thus the Church does not want simply to come to the aid of these Christians, but also to spur them to works of devotion, penance, and charity."

Explanation

- An indulgence is partial or plenary according as it removes either part or all of the temporal punishment due to sin. It may be applied to the living or the dead: *through indulgences the faithful can obtain— for themselves and also for the souls in purgatory—the remission of temporal punishment resulting from sin* . Because we and the faithful departed now being purified are members of the same communion of saints, one way in which we can help them is to obtain indulgences for them, so that the temporal punishments due to their sins may be remitted.

---

32. Cf. CCC, 1471-1479; CIC, 992-997; Paul VI, *Indulgentiarum Doctrina,1967*, Librerìa Editrice Vaticana.

Requirements

Only one plenary indulgence, with the exception of the plenary indulgence applicable at the moment of death, may be gained on any one day. Several plenary indulgences may be gained on the basis of a single sacramental confession; only one may be gained, however, on the basis of a single Communion and prayer for the pope's intentions.

If we are not properly disposed to receive a plenary indulgence when it is granted to us, we receive only a partial indulgence, according to the degree of perfection of our dispositions.

To gain an indulgence one must:

- Be baptized, not excommunicated, and in the state of grace at least at time of completion of the prescribed works.
- Have at least the intention of receiving the indulgence and fulfill the enjoined works at the stated time and according to the tenor of the grant.

The *usual conditions* for gaining a plenary indulgence are, in addition to the good work to which it is attached:

- *Confession* and *holy Communion* on the day of the performance of the good work itself, or within a few days before or after.
- *Prayer for the intentions of the pope.* For this, recitation of one *Our Father* and one *Hail Mary* suffices, though the faithful may say any other prayer, according to their personal devotion.
- *Exclusion of all attachment to sin, even the slightest venial sin.*
- *Reception of holy Communion* and prayer for the pope's intentions are should take place on the same day as the good work.

Plenary Indulgence

One may gain a *plenary indulgence* by:

• Visiting the Blessed Sacrament for half an hour.
• Visiting any parish church:
  – On the day of the titular feast of the church.
  – On August 2, the day of the "Portiuncula indulgence," or on another suitable day to be fixed by the local ordinary (usually the bishop.)
  – On November 2 (applicable to the dead only).

  On these visits one should recite the *Our Father* and the *Creed* and fulfill the three requirements (Confession, Communion, and prayer for the pope's intentions).

• Reading the Bible for at least half an hour.
• Making the Stations of the Cross.
• Praying the Rosary (five decades) in a church or with one's family.
• Receiving the Apostolic Blessing at the hour of death.

Partial Indulgence

One of the faithful who, being at least inwardly contrite, performs a work carrying with it a partial indulgence receives through the Church the remission of temporal punishment. A *partial indulgence* is granted to the faithful who:

• In the performance of their duties and in bearing the trials of life *raise their minds with humble confidence to God, adding*—even if only mentally—*some pious invocation.*
• In a spirit of faith and mercy *give of themselves or of their goods* to serve others in need.

- In a spirit of penance voluntarily *deprive themselves* of what is licit and pleasing to them.
- *Devoutly use religious articles* (crucifixes, rosaries, scapulars, medals) properly blessed by a priest.

SACRAMENTALS [33]

Sacramentals are sacred signs by which spiritual effects, especially, are signified and are obtained by the intercession of the Church. "They prepare the faithful to receive the fruit of the sacraments and sanctify various circumstances of life."

"Among the sacramentals, blessings occupy an important place. They include praise of God for his works and gifts, as well as the Church's intercession for people, that they may be able to use God's gifts according to the spirit of the Gospel." Besides blessings, other sacramentals are: the Sign of the Cross, use of holy water and the religious articles mentioned above.

CARDINAL VIRTUES [34]

A virtue is a habitual disposition to do good. Among all the virtues, there are four that play a pivotal role and accordingly are called cardinal.

- *Prudence*, which disposes the practical reason to discern in every circumstance one's true good and to choose the right means for achieving it.
- *Justice*, which consists in the firm and constant will to give God and neighbor their due.
- *Fortitude*, which ensures firmness in difficulties and constancy in the pursuit of the good.
- *Temperance*, which moderates the attraction of the pleasures of the senses and provides balance in the use of created goods.

33. Cf. CCC, 1677-1678.
34. Cf. CCC, 1805-1807, 1835-1837.

THEOLOGICAL VIRTUES [35]

The theological virtues dispose Christians to live in a close relationship with the Holy Trinity. These virtues have God for their origin, their motive, and their object—God known by faith, God hoped in and loved for his own sake.

Faith

- "Faith is the theological virtue by which we believe in God and believe all that he has said and revealed to us and that holy Church proposes for our belief because he is truth itself."

- "The gift of faith remains in one who has not sinned against it. But "faith apart from works is dead": when it is deprived of hope and love, faith does not fully unite the believer to Christ and does not make him a living member of his body."

- "The disciple of Christ must not only keep the faith and live it, but also profess it, confidently bear witness to it, and spread it. . . . Service of and witness to the faith are necessary for salvation."

Hope

- "Hope is the theological virtue by which we desire the kingdom of heaven and eternal life as our happiness, placing our trust in Christ's promises and relying not on our own strength, but on the help of the grace of the Holy Spirit."

- "The virtue of hope responds to the aspiration to happiness that God has placed in the heart of every man; it takes up the hopes that inspire a men's activities and purifies them, so as to order

---

35. Cf. CCC, 1814-1829, 1842-1844.

them to the Kingdom of heaven; it keeps man from discouragement; it sustains him during times of abandonment; it opens up his heart in expectation of eternal beatitude. Buoyed up by hope, he is preserved from selfishness and led to the happiness that flows from charity."

- "Christian hope unfolds from the beginning of Jesus' preaching in the proclamation of the Beatitudes."

Charity

- "Charity is the theological virtue by which we love God above all things for his own sake, and our neighbor as ourselves for the love of God."

- "Jesus makes charity the *new commandment*. . . . 'This is my commandment, that you love one another as I have loved you.' The Lord asks us to love as he does, even our *enemies*, to make ourselves the neighbor of those farthest away, and to love children and the poor as Christ himself."

- "Charity is superior to all the virtues. It is the first of the theological virtues. The practice of all the virtues is animated and inspired by charity, which 'binds everything together in perfect harmony.'"

- "The practice of the moral life animated by charity gives to the Christian the spiritual freedom of the children of God. He no longer stands before God as a slave, in servile fear, or as a mercenary looking for wages, but as a son, as children responding to the love of him who 'first loved us'".

GIFTS OF THE HOLY SPIRIT [36]

The gifts of the Holy Spirit belong in their fullness to Christ, the Son of David. They complete and perfect the virtues of those who receive them. They make the faithful docile in readily obeying divine inspirations.

The gifts of the Holy Spirit are:

- Wisdom
- Understanding
- Counsel
- Fortitude
- Knowledge
- Piety
- Fear of the Lord

FRUITS OF THE HOLY SPIRIT [37]

The fruits of the Spirit are perfections that the Holy Spirit forms in us as the first fruits of eternal glory.

The apostolic tradition of the Church lists twelve fruits:

- Charity
- Joy
- Peace
- Patience
- Kindness
- Goodness
- Generosity
- Gentleness
- Faithfulness
- Modesty
- Self-control
- Chastity

---

36. Cf. CCC, 768, 798-801, 1830.
37. Cf. CCC, 1832; cf. Galatians 5:22-23.

MORTAL AND VENIAL SINS [38]

"Sins are rightly evaluated according to their gravity. The distinction between mortal and venial sin, already evident in the Scripture, became part of the apostolic tradition of the Church. It is corroborated by human experience."

"*Mortal sin* destroys charity in the heart" of the sinner. It requires "a new initiative of God's mercy and a conversion of heart which is normally accomplished within the sacrament of Reconciliation. For a sin to be mortal, three conditions must together be met".

- *Grave matter* is specified by divine law (Ten Commandments) and the ultimate end of man.

- "*Full knowledge* [is] knowledge of the sinful character of the act, of its opposition to God's law. . . . Unintentional ignorance can diminish or even remove the imputability of a grave offense. But no one is deemed to be ignorant of the principles of the moral law, which are written in the conscience of every man."

- "*Complete consent* [is] a consent sufficiently deliberate to be a personal choice. Feigned ignorance and hardness of heart do not diminish, but rather increase, the voluntary character of a sin. . . . The promptings of feelings and passions can diminish the voluntary and free character of the offense, as can external pressures or pathological disorders. Sin committed through malice, by deliberate choice of evil, is the gravest."

"*Venial sin* allows charity to subsist, even though it offends and wounds it."

---

38. Cf. CCC, 1854-1860; cf. 1 John 16-17.

CAPITAL SINS AND OPPOSED VIRTUES [39]

The Capital Sins can be classified according to the virtues they oppose. They are called "capital" because they engender other sins, other vices.

Capital Sins	Virtues Opposed
• Pride	• Humility
• Covetousness	• Liberality
• Lust	• Chastity
• Anger	• Meekness
• Gluttony	• Temperance
• Envy	• Brotherly love
• Sloth	• Diligence

SINS AGAINST THE HOLY SPIRIT [40]

"'Whoever *blasphemes against the Holy Spirit* never has forgiveness, but is guilty of an eternal sin.' There are no limits to the mercy of God, but anyone who deliberately refuses to accept his mercy by repenting, rejects the forgiveness of his sins and the salvation offered by the Holy Spirit. Such hardness of heart can lead to final impenitence and eternal loss." This sin blocks the person's route to Christ, and the sinner puts himself outside the range of God's forgiveness. In this sense, the sins against the Holy Spirit cannot be forgiven.

SINS THAT CRY TO HEAVEN [41]

Catechetical tradition recalls that there are *"sins that cry to heaven"*: the blood of Abel; the sin of the Sodomites; ignoring the cry of the people oppressed in Egypt and that of the foreigner, the widow, and the orphan; injustice to the wage earner.

---

39. Cf. CCC, 1866-1867.
40. Cf. CCC, 1864, 1866.
41. Cf. CCC, 1867.

BEATITUDES [42]

"The Beatitudes respond to the natural desire for happiness. This desire is of divine origin: God has placed it in the human heart in order to draw us to the One who alone can fulfill it." They "teach man the final end to which God calls us: the Kingdom, the vision of God, participation in the divine nature, eternal life, filiation, rest in God." They are the heart of Jesus' preaching. "They continue the promises made to the Chosen People from the time of Abraham to the time of Christ, fulfilling the promises by ordering them no longer merely to the possession of a territory, but also to the Kingdom of heaven:

- Blessed are the poor in spirit, for theirs is the kingdom of heaven.
- Blessed are those who mourn, for they shall be comforted.
- Blessed are the meek, for they shall inherit the earth.
- Blessed are those who hunger and thirst for righteousness, for they shall be satisfied.
- Blessed are the merciful, for they shall obtain mercy.
- Blessed are the pure in heart, for they shall see God.
- Blessed are the peacemakers, for they shall be called sons of God.
- Blessed are those who are persecuted for righteousness' sake, for theirs is the kingdom of heaven.
- Blessed are you when men revile you and persecute you and utter all kinds of evil against you falsely on my account. Rejoice and be glad, for your reward is great in heaven."

42. Cf. CCC, 1716, 1718, 1725-1726; cf. Matthew 5: 3-12..

CHRISTIAN PRAYER

Prayer is the raising of one's mind and heart to God or the requesting of good things from God.[43] *Prayer* and *Christian life* are *inseparable*, for they concern the same love and the same renunciation, proceeding from love.[44]

What is prayer?

"[Prayer] is commonly held to be a conversation. In a conversation there are always an 'I' and a 'thou' or 'you.' In this case the 'Thou' is with a capital 'T'. If at first the 'I' seems to be the most important element in prayer, prayer teaches that the situation is actually different. *The 'Thou' is more important, because our prayer begins with God.* . . .

"*In prayer, then, the true protagonist is God.* The protagonist is *Christ,* who constantly frees creation from slavery to corruption and leads it toward liberty, for the glory of the children of God. The protagonist is the *Holy Spirit,* who 'comes to the aid of our weakness.' We begin to pray, believing that it is our own initiative that compels us to do so. Instead, we learn that it is always God's initiative within us, just as Saint Paul has written. *This initiative restores in us our true humanity; it restores in us our unique dignity.*"[45]

Christian prayer tries above all to meditate on the mysteries of Christ: to get to know him, love him, and being united to him. We learn what prayer is by reviewing the life of Christ. He taught us how to pray. When Jesus prayed to his Father, he was already teaching us how to pray.[46]

---

43. St. John Damascene, *De fide orth.* 3, 24; in J. P. Migne, ed., *Patrologia Græca* (=PG), 94, 1089C, Paris, 1857-1866.
44. Cf. CCC, 2745.
45. CTH, 16-17.
46. Cf. CCC, 2607, 2708.

"The Church invites the faithful to regular prayer: daily prayers, the Liturgy of the Hours, Sunday Eucharist, the feasts of the liturgical year."[47]

Types of Prayer

"Prayer in the events of each day and each moment is one of the secrets of the kingdom revealed to 'little children,' to the servants of Christ, to the poor of the Beatitudes. It is right and good to pray so that the coming of the kingdom of justice and peace may influence the march of history, but it is just as important to bring the help of prayer into humble, everyday situations; all forms of prayer can be the leaven to which the Lord compares the kingdom."[48]

"The Christian tradition comprises three major expressions of the life of prayer:

- *"Vocal prayer*, founded on the union of body and soul in human nature, associates the body with the interior prayer of the heart, following Christ's example of praying to his Father and teaching the Our Father to his disciples.

- *"Meditation* is a prayerful quest engaging thought, imagination, emotion, and desire. Its goal is to make our own, in faith, the subject considered, by confronting it with the reality of our own life.

- *"Contemplative prayer* is the simple expression of the mystery of prayer. It is a gaze of faith fixed on Jesus, an attentiveness to the Word of God, a silent love. It achieves real union with the prayer of Christ to the extent that it makes us share in his mystery."[49]

---

47. CCC, 2720.
48. CCC, 2660.
49. Cf. CCC, 2721-2724.

The Battle of Prayer[50]

The battle of prayer is inseparable from the necessary "spiritual battle" to act habitually according to the Spirit of Christ: we pray as we live, because we live as we pray.

The principal difficulties that we find are:

* We "don't have the time." Prayer is considered as an occupation incompatible with all the other things we have to do.

  The remedy: "Make the time" for your personal prayer, knowing that nothing could excuse your failing to do so.

* We "get distracted." Concentration becomes really difficult and we easily give up.

  The remedy: Turn your heart back to God, offering him the distractions with humility, without discouragement.

* We "feel dry." It seems that the heart is separated from God, with no taste for thoughts, memories, and feelings, even spiritual ones.

  The remedy: Remember that "unless the grain of wheat falls into the earth and dies, it remains alone; but if it dies, it bears much fruit."

There are also two frequent temptations that threaten prayer:

* Lack of faith. Prayer is not the first priority.

  The remedy: Ask our Lord with a humble heart, "Lord, increase my faith."

* Acedia. A form of depression stemming from lax ascetical practice, that leads to discouragement.

  The remedy: Trust God more and hold fast in constancy.

---

50. Cf. CCC, 2752, 2755.

BASIC PRAYERS

A certain memorization of some essential prayers, far from opposing the dignity of young Christians, or obstructing personal dialogue with the Lord, constitutes an answer to a real need. That which is memorized must at the same time be absorbed and gradually understood in depth in order to become a source of Christian life.[1]

THE SIGN OF THE CROSS

Christians begin their day, their prayers, and their activities with the Sign of the Cross. The Sign of the Cross strengthens us in temptations and difficulties.

In nómine Patris, et Fílii, et Spíritus Sancti. Amen.
Per signum crucis de inimícis nostris líbera nos, Deus noster. In nómine Patris, . . .

In the name of the Father, and of the Son, and of the Holy Spirit. Amen.
By the sign of the cross deliver us from our enemies, you who are our God. In the name . . .

THE LORD'S PRAYER

"In the Our Father, the object of the first three petitions is the glory of the Father: the sanctification of his name, the coming of the kingdom, and the fulfillment of his will. The four others present our wants to him: they ask that our lives be nourished, healed of sin, and made victorious in the struggle of good over evil. By the final 'Amen,' we express our *'fiats'* concerning the seven petitions: 'So be it.'"[2]

---

1. John Paul II, *Catechesis Tradendæ* 55.
2. *Catechism of the Catholic Church* (=CCC), 2857, 2865, Libreria Editrice Vaticana,1994.

Pater noster, qui es in cælis: sanctificétur nomen
tuum; advéniat regnum
tuum; fiat volúntas tua,
sicut in cælo, et in terra.

Our Father, who art in
heaven, hallowed be thy
name. Thy kingdom come;
thy will be done on earth
as it is in heaven.

Panem nostrum coti-
diánum da nobis hódie;
et dimítte nobis débita
nostra, sicut et nos dimíttimus debitóribus nos-
tris; et ne nos indúcas in
tentatiónem; sed líbera
nos a malo. Amen.

Give us this day our
daily bread; and forgive
us our trespasses as we
forgive those who tres-
pass against us; and lead
us not into temptation,
but deliver us from evil.
Amen.

THE HAIL MARY

The greeting of the angel Gabriel opens this prayer.
It is God himself who, through his angel as interme-
diary, greets Mary. The grace with which Mary is
filled is the presence of him who is the source of all
grace.

Mary is Mother of God and our mother. We can entrust all our cares and petitions to her. She prays for
us as she prayed for herself: "Let it be done to me
according to your word."

By entrusting ourselves to her prayer, we abandon
ourselves to the will of God together with her. Our
trust broadens further to surrender "the hour of our
death" wholly to her care. May she be there as she
was at her Son's death on the cross. May she welcome us as our mother at the hour of our passing to
lead us to her son, Jesus, in paradise.[3]

---

3. Cf. CCC 2676-2677.

Ave, María, grátia plena, Dóminus tecum; benedícta tu in muliéribus, et benedíctus fructus ventris tui, Iesus.

Hail, Mary, full of grace, the Lord is with thee; blessed art thou among women, and blessed is the fruit of thy womb, Jesus.

Sancta María, Mater Dei, ora pro nobis peccatóribus, nunc et in hora mortis nostræ. Amen.

Holy Mary, Mother of God, pray for us sinners, now and at the hour of our death. Amen.

THE GLORY BE (THE DOXOLOGY)

The Glory Be, perhaps derived from Christ's command to the apostles to baptize "in the Name of the Father, and of the Son and of the Holy Spirit," has been prayed since the first centuries of Christianity.

This hymn of praise to the triune God joins us with the heavenly hosts in glorifying God. With the Glory Be we also profess, in a formula against the heresies of Arius (who denied the divinity of the Son) and of Macedonius (who denied the divinity of the Holy Spirit), our faith in the most fundamental and basic mystery of revelation: the mystery of the Holy Trinity.

Glória Patri, et Fílio, et Spirítui Sancto.

Glory be to the Father, and to the Son, and to the Holy Spirit.

Sicut erat in princípio et nunc et semper et in sǽcula sæculórum. Amen.

As it was in the beginning, is now, and ever shall be, world without end. Amen.

MORNING OFFERING

O Jesus, through the Immaculate Heart of Mary, I offer you my prayers, works, joys, and sufferings of this day for all the intentions of your Sacred Heart, in union with the holy sacrifice of the Mass throughout the world, in thanksgiving for your favors, in reparation for my sins, for the intentions of all my relatives and friends, and in particular for the intentions of the Holy Father. Amen.

CONSECRATION TO THE BLESSED VIRGIN

My Queen and my Mother, I give myself entirely to you, and, in proof of my affection, I give you my eyes, my ears, my tongue, my heart, my whole being without reserve. Since I am your own, keep me and guard me as your property and possession. Amen.

ACT OF FAITH

O my God, I firmly believe that you are one God in three divine Persons, Father, Son and Holy Spirit; I believe that your divine Son became man and died for our sins, and that he shall come to judge the living and the dead. I believe these and all the truths that the holy Catholic Church teaches, because you have revealed them, who can neither deceive nor be deceived.

ACT OF HOPE

O my God, relying on your almighty power and infinite mercy and promises, I hope to obtain pardon for my sins, the help of your grace, and life everlasting, through the merits of Jesus Christ, my Lord and Redeemer.

ACT OF CHARITY

O my God, I love you above all things, with my whole heart and soul, because you are all-good and worthy of all love. I love my neighbor as myself for the love of you. I forgive all who have injured me and ask pardon of all whom I have injured.

PRAYER BEFORE A DAY'S WORK

Direct, we beg you, O Lord, our actions by your holy inspirations, and grant that we may carry them out with your gracious assistance, that every prayer and work of ours may begin always with you, and through you be happily ended. Amen.

ACCEPTANCE OF GOD'S WILL

In all things may the most holy, the most just, and the most lovable will of God be done, praised, and exalted above all for ever. Your will be done, O Lord, your will be done. The Lord has given, the Lord has taken away; blessed be the name of the Lord.

PRAYER TO KEEP THE PRESENCE OF GOD

Lord, God Almighty, you have brought us safely to the beginning of this day. Defend us today by your mighty power, so that we may not fall into any sin, and that all our words may so proceed and all our thoughts and actions be so directed as to be always just in your sight. Through Christ our Lord. Amen.

ANGELE DEI

Angele Dei, qui custos es mei, me tibi commissum
pietates superna illumina, custodi, rege et guberna.
Amen.

SYMBOLUM APOSTOLORUM

Credo in Deum, Patrem omnipoténtem,
Creatórem cæli et terræ.
Et in Iesum Christum, Fílium eius únicum,
Dóminum nostrum:
qui concéptus est de Spíritu Sancto,
natus ex María Vírgine,
passus sub Póntio Piláto,
crucifíxus, mórtuus, et sepúltus;
descéndit ad ínferos;
tértia die resurréxit a mórtuis;
ascéndit ad cælos;
sedet ad déxteram Dei Patris omnipoténtis;
inde ventúrus est iudicáre vivos et mórtuos.
Credo in Spíritum Sanctum,
sanctam Ecclésiam Cathólicam,
Sanctórum communiónem,
remissiónem peccatórum, carnis resurrectiónem,
vitam ætérnam. Amen.

ORATIO PRO PONTÍFICE

V. Oremus pro Pontífice nostro N.

R. **Dóminus conservet eum et vivíficet eum, et
beatum faciat eum in terra, et non tradat eum in
ánimam inimicórum eius.**

PRAYER TO ONE'S GUARDIAN ANGEL

Angel of God, my guardian dear, to whom God's love commits me here, ever this day (or night) be at my side, to light and guard, to rule and guide. Amen.

THE APOSTLES' CREED

The *Apostles' Creed* is rightly considered to be a faithful summary of the apostles' teaching. It is the ancient baptismal symbol of the Church of Rome.[4]

I believe in God, the Father almighty,
    creator of heaven and earth.
I believe in Jesus Christ, his only Son, our Lord.
    He was conceived by the power of the Holy Spirit
        and born of the Virgin Mary.
    He suffered under Pontius Pilate,
        was crucified, died, and was buried.
    He descended into hell.
    On the third day he rose again.
    He ascended into heaven,
        and is seated at the right hand of the Father.
    He will come again to judge the living
        and the dead.
I believe in the Holy Spirit,
    the holy Catholic Church,
    the communion of saints,
    the forgiveness of sins, the resurrection of the body,
    and the life everlasting. Amen.

PRAYER FOR THE POPE

V. Let us pray for our Sovereign Pontiff N.
R. **The Lord preserve him and give him life, and make him blessed upon the earth, and deliver him not to the will of his enemies.**

4. Cf. CCC 184.

PSALMUS 94 (95)

Veníte, exsultémus Dómino;
　iubilémus Deo salutári nostro.
Præoccupémus fáciem eius in confessióne et
　in psalmis iubilémus ei.
Quóniam Deus magnus Dóminus
　et rex magnus super omnes deos.
Quia in manu eius sunt profúnda terræ,
　et altitúdines móntium ipsíus sunt.
Quóniam ipsíus est mare, et ipse fecit illud,
　et siccam manus eius formavérunt.
Veníte, adorémus et procidámus et
　génua flectámus ante Dóminum, qui fecit nos,
quia ipse est Deus noster,
　et nos pópulus páscuæ eius et oves manus eius.
Utinam hódie vocem eius audiátis:
　"Nolíte obduráre corda vestra,
　　sicut in Meríba secúndum diem Massa in desérto,
　ubi tentavérunt me patres vestri:
　　probavérunt me, etsi vidérunt ópera mea.
Quadragínta annis tæduit me generatiónis illíus, ·
et dixi: Pópulus errántium corde sunt isti.
Et ipsi non cognovérunt vias meas;
　ídeo iurávi in ira mea:
　　Non introíbunt in réquiem meam."

Glória Patri . . .

PSALM 94 (95)

This hymn of adoration to God was an introduction to the Sabbath liturgy of the synagogue. The Church has placed it at the beginning of each day's divine office.

Come, let us sing to the Lord
  and shout with joy to the Rock who saves us.
Let us approach him with praise and thanksgiving
  and sing joyful songs to the Lord.
The Lord is God, the mighty God,
  the great king over all the gods.
He holds in his hands the depths of the earth
  and the highest mountains as well.
He made the sea; it belongs to him,
  the dry land, too, for it was formed by his hands.
Come, then, let us bow down and worship,
  bending the knee before the Lord, our maker.
For he is our God and we are his people,
  the flock he shepherds.
Today, listen to the voice of the Lord:
Do not grow stubborn, as your fathers did
  in the wilderness, when at Meribah and Massah
  they challenged me and provoked me,
Although they had seen all of my works.
Forty years I endured that generation.
  I said, "They are a people whose hearts go astray
  and they do not know my ways."
So I swore in my anger,
  "They shall not enter into my rest."

Glory Be.

LITURGY OF THE HOURS

The mystery of Christ, his Incarnation and Passover, which we celebrate in the Eucharist especially at Sunday Mass, permeates and transfigures the time of each day, through the celebration of the Liturgy of the Hours, "the divine office." This celebration, faithful to the apostolic exhortations to "pray constantly," is "so devised that the whole course of the day and night is made holy by the praise of God." In this "public prayer of the Church," the faithful (clergy, religious, and lay people) exercise the royal priesthood of the baptized. The Liturgy of the Hours, which is like an extension of the Sacrifice of the Mass, does not exclude—but rather, in a complementary way, calls forth—the various devotions of the People of God, especially adoration of the Blessed Sacrament.

The Psalms constitute the masterwork of prayer in the Old Testament. They present two inseparable qualities: the personal and the communal. They extend to all dimensions of history, recalling God's promises already fulfilled and looking for the coming of the Messiah.[5]

Gatherings of the laity—for prayer, apostolic work or any other purpose—are encouraged to fulfill the Church's office by celebrating part of the Liturgy of the Hours.[6]

Morning Prayer

Morning Prayer, celebrated as the light of a new day is dawning, recalls the resurrection of the Lord Jesus, the true light enlightening all mankind and "the Sun of justice", "rising from on high."[7]

---

5. Cf. CCC 1174, 1178, 2596.
6. Cf. *General Instruction of the Liturgy of the Hours* (=GILH) 27.
7. Cf. GILH, 37.

God, come to my assistance.
R. Lord, make haste to help me.
Glory Be.

> The day is filled with splendor
> When God brings light from light,
> And all renewed creation
> Rejoices in his sight.

> The Father gives his children
> The wonder of the world
> In which his power and glory
> Like banners are unfurled.

> With every living creature,
> Awaking with the day,
> We turn to God our Father,
> Lift up our hearts and pray:

> O Father, Son, and Spirit,
> Your grace and mercy send,
> That we may live to praise you
> Today and to the end.

PSALMODY

Ant. 1 It is you whom I invoke, O Lord. In the morning you hear me.

Morning prayer for help   Psalm 5:2-10,12-13

> *Those who have received the Word of God which*
> *dwells within will rejoice for ever.*

To my words give ear, O Lord, *
  give heed to my groaning.
Attend to the sound of my cries, *
  my King and my God.
It is you whom I invoke, O Lord. *
  In the morning you hear me;

in the morning I offer you my prayer, *
  watching and waiting.
You are no God who loves evil; *
  no sinner is your guest.
The boastful shall not stand their ground *
  before your face.
You hate all who do evil; *
  you destroy all who lie.
The deceitful and bloodthirsty man *
  the Lord detests.
But I, through the greatness of your love, *
  have access to your house.
I bow down before your holy temple, *
  filled with awe.
Lead me, Lord, in your justice, +
  because of those who lie in wait; *
  make clear your way before me.
No truth can be found in their mouths, *
  their heart is all mischief,
their throat a wide-open grave, *
  all honey their speech.
All those you protect shall be glad *
  and ring out their joy.
You shelter them; in you they rejoice, *
  those who love your name.
It is you who bless the just man, Lord: *
  you surround him with favor as with a shield.
Glory Be.
Ant. It is you whom I invoke, O Lord. In the morning you hear me.
Ant. 2 We praise your glorious name, O Lord, our God.

Canticle

Glory and honor are due to God alone   1 Chronicles 29:10-13

Blessed be the God and Father of our
Lord Jesus Christ (Eph 1:3)

Blessed may you be, O Lord, +
  God of Israel our father, *
  from eternity to eternity.
Yours, O Lord, are grandeur and power, *
  majesty, splendor, and glory.
For all in heaven and on earth is yours; +
  yours, O Lord, is the sovereignty: *
  you are exalted as head over all.
Riches and honor are from you, *
  and you have dominion over all.
In your hands are power and might; *
  it is yours to give grandeur and strength to all.
Therefore, our God, we give you thanks *
  and we praise the majesty of your name.
Glory Be.
Ant. We praise your glorious name, O Lord, our
God.

Ant. 3 Adore the Lord in his holy court.

A tribute of praise to the Word of God   Psalm 29

A voice was heard from heaven, saying,
'This is my beloved Son' (Mt 3:17)

O give the Lord, you sons of God, *
  give the Lord glory and power;
give the Lord the glory of his name. *
  Adore the Lord in his holy court.
The Lord's voice resounding on the waters, *
  the Lord on the immensity of waters;
the voice of the Lord, full of power, *
  the voice of the Lord, full of splendor.

The Lord's voice shattering the cedars, *
  the Lord shatters the cedars of Lebanon;
he makes Lebanon leap like a calf *
  and Sirion like a young wild-ox.
The Lord's voice flashes flames of fire. +
  The Lord's voice shaking the wilderness. *
  The Lord shakes the wilderness of Kadesh;
the Lord's voice rending the oak tree *
  and stripping the forest bare.
The God of glory thunders. *
  In his temple they all cry: "Glory!"
The Lord sat enthroned over the flood; *
  the Lord sits as king for ever.
The Lord will give strength to his people, *
  the Lord will bless his people with peace.
Glory Be.
Ant.   Adore the Lord in his holy court.

Scripture Reading   2 Thes 3:10-13
We gave you a rule when we were with you: not to
let anyone have any food if he refused to do any
work. Now we hear that there are some of you who
are living in idleness, doing no work themselves but
interfering with everyone else's. In the Lord Jesus
Christ, we order and call on people of this kind to go
on quietly working and earning the food that they
eat. My brothers, never grow tired of doing what is
right.

Responsory

R. **Blessed be the Lord our God, * blessed from
    age to age.** Repeat R.
His marvelous works are beyond compare,* blessed
from age to age. Glory Be. R.

CANTICLE OF ZECHARIAH

Ant.   Blessed be the Lord our God.

Blessed be the Lord, the God of Israel; *
  he has come to his people and set them free.

He has raised up for us a mighty savior, *
  born of the house of his servant David.

Through his holy prophets he promised of old +
  that he would save us from our enemies, *
  from the hands of all who hate us.

He promised to show mercy to our fathers *
  and to remember his holy covenant.

This was the oath he swore to our father Abraham: +
  to set us free from the hands of our enemies, *
  free to worship him without fear,

  holy and righteous in his sight *
  all the days of our life.

You, my child, shall be called the prophet
    of the Most High; *
  for you will go before the Lord
    to prepare his way,
  to give his people knowledge of salvation *
  by the forgiveness of their sins.

In the tender compassion of our God *
  the dawn from on high shall break upon us,
  to shine on those who dwell in darkness
  and the shadow of death, *
  and to guide our feet into the way of peace.

Glory Be.

Ant.   Blessed be the Lord our God.

INTERCESSIONS

As the new day begins let us praise Christ, in whom
is the fullness of grace and the Spirit of God.

R. *Lord, give us your Spirit.*

We praise you, Lord,
—and we thank you for all your blessings. **R.**
Give us peace of mind and generosity of heart;
—grant us health and strength to do your will. **R.**
May your love be with us during the day;
—guide us in our work. **R.**
Be with all those who have asked our prayers,
—and grant them all their needs. **R.**
Our Father.

PRAYER

Father,
may everything we do
begin with your inspiration
and continue with your saving help.
Let our work always find its origin in you
and through you reach completion.
We ask this through our Lord Jesus Christ, your Son,
who lives and reigns with you and the Holy Spirit,
one God, for ever and ever.
R. Amen.

DISMISSAL

If a priest or deacon presides, he dismisses the people as at Mass.

Otherwise, Morning Prayer concludes:

May the Lord bless us,
protect us from all evil
and bring us to everlasting life.
R. Amen.

MIDDAY PRAYERS

ANGELUS

For centuries the Church has recited the *Angelus*, especially at noon, in honor of the Incarnation.

V. Angelus Dómini, nun tiávit Maríæ.

V. The angel of the Lord declared unto Mary;

R. **Et concépit de Spíritu Sancto.**

R. **And she conceived by the Holy Spirit.**

Ave María.

Hail Mary.

V. Ecce ancílla Dómini.

V. Behold the handmaid of the Lord.

R. **Fiat mihi secúndum verbum tuum.**

R. **Be it done unto me according to your word.**

Ave María.

Hail Mary.

V. Et Verbum caro factum est.

V. And the Word was made flesh,

R. **Et habitávit in nobis.**

R. **And dwelt among us.**

Ave María.

Hail Mary.

V. Ora pro nobis, sancta Dei Génetrix.

V. Pray for us, O holy Mother of God,

R. **Ut digni efficiámur promissiónibus Christi.**

R. **That we may be made worthy of the promises of Christ.**

Orémus.

Let us pray.

Grátiam tuam, quaésumus, Dómine, méntibus nostris infúnde; ut qui, ángelo nuntiánte, Christi Fílii tui incarnatiónem cognóvimus, per passió-

Pour forth, we beseech you, O Lord, your grace into our hearts, that we, to whom the incarnation of Christ, your Son, was made known by the mes-

nem eius et crucem, ad
resurrectiónis glóriam
perducámur. Per eúndem
Christum Dóminum nos-
trum.

R. **Amen.**

sage of an angel, may by
his passion and cross be
brought to the glory of his
resurrection, through the
same Christ our Lord.

R. **Amen.**

REGINA CÆLI (for Easter Time) By Gregory V (+998)

V. Regína cæli, lætáre.
Allelúia.

R. **Quia quem meruísti
portáre. Allelúia.**

V. Resurréxit, sicut
dixit. Allelúia.

R. **Ora pro nobis,
Deum. Allelúia.**

V. Gaude et lætáre,
Virgo María. Allelúia.

R. **Quia surréxit Dómi-
nus vere. Allelúia.**

Orémus.

Deus, qui per resurrec-
tiónem Fílii tui, Dómini
nostri Iesu Christi, mun-
dum lætificáre dignátus
es: præsta, quǽsumus;
ut, per eius Genitrícem
Vírginem Maríam, per-
pétuæ capiámus gáudia
vitæ. Per eúndem Chris-
tum Dóminum nostrum.

R. **Amen.**

V. Queen of heaven, re-
joice! Alleluia.

R. **For he whom you
did merit to bear.
Alleluia.**

V. Has risen, as he said.
Alleluia.

R. **Pray for us to God.
Alleluia.**

V. Rejoice and be glad, O
Virgin Mary. Alleluia.

R. **For the Lord is truly
risen. Alleluia.**

Let us pray.

O God, who gave joy to
the world through the
resurrection of your Son
our Lord Jesus Christ,
grant, we beseech you,
that through the intercession of the Virgin Mary,
his Mother, we may ob-
tain the joys of everlasting life, through the
same Christ our Lord.

R. **Amen.**

EVENING PRAYERS

BRIEF EXAMINATION AT NIGHT

Make a brief examination of conscience before going to bed at night. Two or three minutes will suffice.

- **Place yourself in the presence of God,** recognizing his strength and your weakness. Tell him: "Lord, if you will, you can make me clean."

- **Ask your guardian angel for light** to acknowledge your defects and virtues: *What have I done wrong? What have I done right? What could I have done better?*

- **Examine your conscience** with sincerity:
  Did I often consider that God is my Father? Did I offer him my work? Did I make good use of my time? Did I pray slowly and with attention? Did I try to make life pleasant for other people? Did I criticize anyone? Was I forgiving? Did I pray and offer some sacrifices for the Church, for the pope, and for those around me? Did I allow myself to be carried away by sensuality? By pride?

- **Make an act of contrition** (p. 62), sorrowfully asking our Lord's pardon.

- **Make a specific resolution** for tomorrow:
  — *To stay away from certain temptations.*
  — *To avoid some specific faults.*
  — *To exert special effort to practice some virtue.*
  — *To take advantage of occasions for improvement.*

- **Pray three Hail Marys** to the Virgin Mary, asking for purity of heart and body.

CONFITEOR

Confíteor Deo omnipoténti,
beátæ Maríæ semper Vírgini,
beáto Michaéli Archángelo,
beáto Ioánni Baptístæ,
sanctis apóstolis Petro et Paulo,
ómnibus Sanctis, et vobis, fratres:
quia peccávi nimis cogitatióne,
verbo et ópere:
mea culpa, mea culpa,
   mea máxima culpa.
Ideo precor beátam Maríam semper Vírginem,
beátum Michaélem Archángelum,
beátum Ioánnem Baptístam,
sanctos apóstolos Petrum et Paulum,
omnes Sanctos, et vos, fratres,
oráre pro me ad Dóminum, Deum nostrum.

PSALMUS 50 (51)

Miserére mei, Deus, *
   secúndum misericórdiam tuam;
et secúndum multitúdinem miseratiónum tuárum *
   dele iniquitátem meam.
Amplius lava me ab iniquitáte mea *
   et a peccáto meo munda me.
Quóniam iniquitátem meam ego cognósco, *
et peccátum meum contra me est semper.
Tibi, tibi soli peccávi *
   et malum coram te feci,

I CONFESS

I confess to almighty God,
to blessed Mary ever Virgin,
to blessed Michael the archangel,
to blessed John the Baptist,
to the holy apostles Peter and Paul,
and to all the saints,
that I have sinned exceedingly in thought,
word and deed,
through my fault, through my fault,
   through my most grievous fault.
Therefore, I beseech blessed Mary ever Virgin,
blessed Michael the archangel,
blessed John the Baptist,
the holy apostles Peter and Paul,
and all the saints,
to pray for me to the Lord our God.

PSALM 50 (51)

David the contrite king, model of repentance, con-
fesses his sins. He asks for forgiveness with true
contrition and for the continuance of the friendship
of God. He promises to show his gratitude by serving God and teaching others to do his will.

Have mercy on me, God, in your kindness. *
In your compassion blot out my offense.
O wash me more and more from my guilt *
and cleanse me more from sin.

My offenses truly I know them; *
my sin is always before me.
Against you, you alone, have I sinned; *
what is evil in your sight I have done.

That you may be justified when you give sentence *
and be without reproach when you judge.

ut iustus inveniáris in senténtia tua *
   et æquus in iudício tuo.

Ecce enim in iniquitáte generátus sum, *
   et in peccáto concépit me mater mea.

Ecce enim veritátem in corde dilexísti *
   et in occúlto sapiéntiam manifestásti mihi.

Aspérges me hyssópo, et mundábor; *
   lavábis me, et super nivem dealbábor.

Audíre me fácies gáudium et lætítiam ,*
   et exsultábunt ossa, quæ contrivísti.

Avérte fáciem tuam a peccátis meis *
   et omnes iniquitátes meas dele.

Cor mundum crea in me, Deus, *
   et spíritum firmum ínnova in viscéribus meis.

Ne proícias me a fácie tua*
   et spíritum sanctum tuum ne áuferas a me.

Redde mihi lætítiam salutáris tui*
   et spíritu promptíssimo confírma me.

Docébo iníquos vias tuas,*
   et ímpii ad te converténtur.

Líbera me de sanguínibus, Deus, Deus salútis meæ,*
   et exsultábit lingua mea iustítiam tuam.

Dómine, lábia mea apéries, *
   et os meum annuntiábit laudem tuam.

Non enim sacrifício delectáris, *
   holocáustum, si ófferam, non placébit.

Sacrifícium Deo spíritus contribulátus, *
   cor contrítum et humiliátum, Deus, non despícies.

Benígne fac, Dómine, in bona voluntáte tua Sion, *
   ut ædificéntur muri Ierúsalem.

Tunc acceptábis sacrifícium iustítiæ,
     oblatiónes et holocáusta; *
   tunc impónent super altáre tuum vítulos.

O see, in guilt I was born, *
a sinner was I conceived.
Indeed you love truth in the heart; *
then in the secret of my heart teach me wisdom.
O purify me, then I shall be clean; *
O wash me, I shall be whiter than snow.
Make me hear rejoicing and gladness, *
that the bones you have crushed may revive.
From my sins turn away your face *
and blot out all my guilt.
A pure heart create for me, O God, *
put a steadfast spirit within me.
Do not cast me away from your presence, *
nor deprive me of your Holy Spirit.
Give me again the joy of your help; *
with a spirit of fervor sustain me,
that I may teach transgressors your ways *
and sinners may return to you.
O rescue me, God, my helper, *
and my tongue shall ring out your goodness.
O Lord, open my lips, *
and my mouth shall declare your praise.
For in sacrifice you take no delight, *
burnt offering from me
    you would refuse.
My sacrifice, a contrite spirit, *
A humbled, contrite heart
    you will not spurn.
In your goodness, show favor to Zion: *
rebuild the walls of Jerusalem.
Then you will be pleased with lawful sacrifice,
burnt offerings wholly consumed, *
then you will be offered young bulls on your altar.

ACT OF CONTRITION

O my God, I am heartily sorry for having offended you, and I detest all my sins, because I dread the loss of heaven and the pains of hell; but most of all because they offend you, my God, who are all good and deserving of all my love. I firmly resolve, with the help of your grace, to confess my sins, to do penance, and to amend my life. Amen.

PRAYER FOR VOCATIONS

Lord Jesus Christ, shepherd of souls, who called the apostles to be fishers of men, raise up new apostles in your holy Church. Teach them that to serve you is to reign: to possess you is to possess all things. Kindle in the hearts of our young people the fire of zeal for souls. Make them eager to spread your Kingdom upon earth. Grant them courage to follow you, who are the Way, the Truth and the Life; who live and reign for ever and ever. Amen.

ACCEPTANCE OF DEATH

O Lord, my God, from this moment on I accept with a good will, as something coming from your hand, whatever kind of death you want to send me, with all its anguish, pain and sorrow.

JESUS, MARY, AND JOSEPH

V. Jesus, Mary, and Joseph,
R. **I give you my heart and my soul.**
V. Jesus, Mary, and Joseph,
R. **Assist me in my last agony.**
V. Jesus, Mary, and Joseph,
R. **May I sleep and take my rest in peace with you.**

LITURGY OF THE HOURS *(Evening Prayer)*

Evening Prayer is celebrated in order that we may give thanks for what has been given us or what we have done well during the day. We also recall our redemption and that evening sacrifice of the Lord's Supper with the apostles. There he instituted the most holy sacrament of the Eucharist. He was anticipating the sacrifice he was to offer to the Father on the next day. We ask Christ to give us the grace of eternal light, which knows no setting.[1]

God, come to my assistance.

R. **Lord, make haste to help me.**

Glory Be. Alleluia.

HYMN

Christ be near at either hand,
Christ behind, before me stand,
Christ with me where'er I go,
Christ around, above, below.
Christ be in my heart and mind,
Christ within my soul enshrined,
Christ control my wayward heart,
Christ abide and ne'er depart.
Christ my life and only way,
Christ my lantern night and day,
Christ be my unchanging friend,
Guide and shepherd me to the end.

PSALMODY

Ant. 1 The Lord is my light and my salvation; whom shall I fear?

Trust in time of affliction   Psalm 26 (27)

God now truly dwells with me (Rev 21:3)

The Lord is my light and my help; *
  whom shall I fear?

_____
1. Cf. GILH, 37

The Lord is the stronghold of my life; *
  before whom shall I shrink?
When evil-doers draw near *
  to devour my flesh,
it is they, my enemies and foes, *
  who stumble and fall.
Though an army encamp against me *
  my heart would not fear.
Though war break out against me *
  even then would I trust.
There is one thing I ask of the Lord, *
  for this I long,
to live in the house of the Lord, *
  all the days of my life,
to savor the sweetness of the Lord, *
  to behold his temple.
For there he keeps me safe in his tent *
  in the day of evil.
He hides me in the shelter of his tent, *
  on a rock he sets me safe.
And now my head shall be raised *
  above my foes who surround me
and I shall offer within his tent +
  a sacrifice of joy. *
I will sing and make music for the Lord.
Glory Be.
Ant.   The Lord is my light and my salvation; whom
shall I fear?
Ant. 2I long to look on you, O Lord; do not turn
your face from me.

> *Some rose to present lies and false evidence*
> *against Jesus (Mk 14:57)*

O Lord, hear my voice when I call; *
  have mercy and answer.

Of you my heart has spoken: *
  "Seek his face."
It is your face, O Lord, that I seek; *
  hide not your face.
Dismiss not your servant in anger; *
  you have been my help.
Do not abandon or forsake me, *
  O God my help!
Though father and mother forsake me, *
  the Lord will receive me.
Instruct me, Lord, in your way; *
  on an even path lead me.
When they lie in ambush protect me *
  from my enemy's greed.
False witnesses rise against me, *
  breathing out fury.
I am sure I shall see the Lord's goodness *
  in the land of the living.
Hope in him, hold firm and take heart. *
  Hope in the Lord!
Glory Be.

Ant. I long to look on you, O Lord; do not turn
your face from me.

Ant. 3 He is the firstborn of all creation; he is supreme over all creatures.

Canticle   Colossians 1:12-20
        *Christ, the firstborn of all creation and
              the firstborn from the dead*

Let us give thanks to the Father, +
  who has qualified us to share *
    in the inheritance of the saints in light.
He has delivered us from the dominion of darkness *
  and transferred us to the kingdom
    of his beloved Son,

in whom we have redemption, *
  the forgiveness of sins.
He is the image of the invisible God, *
  the firstborn of all creation,
for in him all things were created,
    in heaven and on earth, *
  visible and invisible.
All things were created *
  through him and for him.
He is before all things, *
  and in him all things hold together.
He is the head of the body, the Church; *
  he is the beginning,
the firstborn from the dead, *
  that in everything he might be preeminent,
For in him all the fullness of God was pleased to dwell, *
  and through him to reconcile to himself all things,
whether on earth or in heaven, *
  making peace by the blood of his cross.
Glory Be.
Ant. He is the firstborn of all creation; he is supreme over all creatures.

SCRIPTURE READING   Jas 1:22,25

You must do what the Word tells you, and not just
listen to it and deceive yourselves. But the man who
looks steadily at the perfect law of freedom and
makes that his habit—not listening and then forget-
ting, but actively putting it into practice—will be
happy in all that he does.

RESPONSORY

R. Claim me once more as your own, Lord, *
  and have mercy on me. Repeat R.
Do not abandon me with the wicked; * have mercy on
me. Glory Be. R.

CANTICLE OF MARY

Ant. The Almighty has done great things for me, and holy is his Name.

My soul proclaims the greatness of the Lord, *
my spirit rejoices in God my Savior,
for he has looked with favor on his lowly servant. *
From this day all generations will call me blessed:
the Almighty has done great things for me, *
and holy is his Name.

He has mercy on those who fear him *
in every generation.

He has shown the strength of his arm, *
he has scattered the proud in their conceit.

He has cast down the mighty from their thrones, *
and has lifted up the lowly.

He has filled the hungry with good things, *
and the rich he has sent away empty.

He has come to the help of his servant Israel *
for he has remembered his promise of mercy,
the promise he made to our fathers, *
to Abraham and his children for ever.

Glory Be.

Ant. The Almighty has done great things for me, and holy is his Name.

INTERCESSIONS

Let us praise God, our almighty Father, who wished that Mary, his Son's mother, be celebrated by each generation. Now in need we ask:

R. **Mary, full of grace, intercede for us.**

You made Mary the mother of mercy;
— may all who are faced with trials feel
  her motherly love. R.

You wished Mary to be the mother of the family
    in the home of Jesus and Joseph;
—may all mothers of families foster love
    and holiness through her intercession. **R.**
You gave Mary strength at the foot of the cross
    and filled her with joy at the resurrection
    of your Son;
—lighten the hardships of those who are burdened
    and deepen their sense of hope. **R.**
You made Mary open to your word
    and faithful as your servant;
—through her intercession make us servants
    and true followers of your Son. **R.**
You crowned Mary queen of heaven;
—may all the dead rejoice in your kingdom
    with the saints for ever. **R.**

Our Father.

PRAYER

Stay with us, Lord Jesus,
for evening draws near,
and be our companion on our way
to set our hearts on fire with new hope.
Help us to recognize your presence among us
in the Scriptures we read,
and in the breaking of bread,
for you live and reign with the Father
    and the Holy Spirit,
one God for ever and ever. **R. Amen.**

DISMISSAL

If a priest or deacon presides, he dismisses the people as if at
Mass. Otherwise, Evening Prayer concludes:

May the Lord bless us,
protect us from all evil
and bring us to everlasting life. **R. Amen.**

PREPARATION FOR MASS

INTRODUCTION

"When our Lord instituted the Eucharist during the Last Supper, night had already fallen. This indicated, according to St. John Chrysostom, that 'the times had run their course.' The world had fallen into darkness, for the old rites, the old signs of God's infinite mercy to mankind, were going to be brought to fulfillment. The way was opening to a new dawn—the new pasch. The Eucharist was instituted during that night, preparing in advance for the morning of the resurrection.

"We too have to prepare for this new dawn. Everything harmful, worn out or useless has to be thrown away—discouragement, suspicion, sadness, cowardice. The holy Eucharist gives the sons of God a divine newness and we must respond in 'the newness of your mind,' renewing all our feelings and actions. We have been given a new principle of energy, strong new roots grafted onto our Lord. We must not return to the old leaven, for now we have the bread that lasts for ever.

"Think of the human experience of two people who love each other and yet are forced to part. They would like to stay together for ever, but duty—in one form or another—forces them to separate. They are unable to fulfill their desire of remaining close to each other, so human love—which, great as it may be, is limited—seeks a symbolic gesture. People who make their farewells exchange gifts or perhaps a photograph with a dedication so ardent that it seems almost enough to burn that piece of paper. They can do no more, because a creature's power is not as great as its desire.

"What we cannot do, our Lord is able to do. Jesus Christ, perfect God and perfect man, leaves us not a symbol, but a reality. He himself stays with us. He will go to the Father, but he will also remain among men. He will leave us not simply a gift that will make us remember him, not an image that becomes blurred with time, like a photograph that soon fades and yellows, and has no meaning except for those who were contemporaries. Under the appearances of bread and wine, He is really present, with his body and blood, with his soul and divinity."[1]

Our Lord told us: "I tell you most solemnly, if you do not eat the flesh of the Son of Man and drink his blood, you will not have life in you."

Sacramental communion increases the communicant's union with the Lord, forgives one's venial sins, and preserves one from grave sins. Since receiving this sacrament strengthens the bonds of charity between the communicant and Christ, it also reinforces the unity of the Church as the Mystical Body of Christ. The Church warmly recommends that the faithful receive holy Communion each time they participate in the celebration of the Eucharist; she obliges them to do so at least once a year.[2]

In order to receive holy Communion worthily, we must first confess any mortal sin we may remember. Venial sins are forgiven with a fervent communion, works of mercy, acts of sorrow, etc.

---

1. Blessed Josemaría Escrivá, *Christ is Passing By* (=CPB), 155, 183, Princeton, N. J.: Scepter Publishers, 1974.
2. *Catechism of the Catholic Church* (=CCC), 1416-1417, Libreria Editrice Vaticana, 1994.

"Anyone who desires to receive Christ in communion must be in the state of grace. Anyone aware of having sinned mortally must not receive communion without having received absolution in the sacrament of Penance."[3]

"Sometimes, indeed quite frequently, everybody participating in the Eucharistic assembly goes to Communion; and on some such occasions, as experienced pastors confirm, there has not been due care to approach the sacrament of Penance so as to purify one's conscience. This can of course mean that those approaching the Lord's table find nothing on their conscience, according to the objective law of God, to keep them from this sublime and joyful act of being sacramentally united with Christ. But there can also be, at least at times, another idea behind this: the idea of the Mass as only a banquet in which one shares by *receiving the body of Christ in order to manifest, above all else, fraternal communion*. It is not hard to add to these reasons a certain human respect and mere *conformity*.

"This phenomenon demands from us watchful attention and a theological and pastoral analysis guided by a sense of great responsibility. We cannot allow the life of our communities to lose the good quality of sensitiveness of Christian conscience, guided solely by respect for Christ, who, when He is received in the Eucharist, should find in the heart of each of us a worthy abode. This question is closely linked not only with the practice of the sacrament of Penance but also with a correct sense of responsibility for the whole deposit of moral teaching and for the precise distinction between good and evil, a distinction which then becomes for each person sharing

_____
3. CCC 1415.

in the Eucharist the basis for a correct judgment of self to be made in the depths of the personal conscience. St. Paul's words, 'Let a man examine himself,' are well known; this judgment is an indispensable condition for a personal decision whether to approach Eucharistic Communion or to abstain."[4]

We must fast one hour before Communion. Water and medicines do not break the fast. The elderly and those who are sick, as well as those caring for them, may receive holy Communion even if they have consumed something within the preceding hour.[5]

One should receive holy Communion with utmost reverence and devotion, bearing in mind that Christ himself, and not just an ordinary piece of bread, is being received. In some countries where the Holy See has confirmed the consultation of the Bishops' Conference, Holy Communion may be taken in the hand. Every communicant, however, always has the right to receive Holy Communion in the mouth.

Internal Preparation

To celebrate and to offer the holy Mass with greater fruit, we may consider that:

- The Eucharistic sacrifice is the most important event that happens each day.
- The Eucharistic sacrifice is the center of Christian life. All the sacraments, prayers, visits to the Blessed Sacrament, devotions, mortifications offered to God, as well as the apostolate, have the Mass as their central point of reference. If the center were to disappear and if attendance at Mass were consciously abandoned, then the whole Christian life would collapse.

---

4. John Paul II, *On the Mystery and Worship of the Eucharist*, no. 11, 1980.
5. Cf. *Codex Iuris Canonici* (=CIC), 919.

- The Eucharistic sacrifice is the most pleasing reality we can offer to God. Every member of the Mystical Body of Christ receives at Baptism the right and duty of taking part in the sacrifice of the Head of that Body. Our Mother the Church wants us to assist at the Mass, not as strangers or passive spectators, but with the effort to understand it better each time. We are to participate in the Mass in a conscious, pious, and active manner, with right dispositions and cooperating with divine grace.

- It is a good habit to pray on the way to Mass. Whether you drive or walk, turn your attention to the coming celebration. Pray for the priest, that he will minister to the needs of the parish. Pray for the congregation, that they will open their minds and hearts to what is being taught at the Mass.

- We offer this sublime sacrifice in union with the Church. Live the holy Mass feeling part of the Church, the Mystical Body of Christ, the people of God. Be united to the bishop of the diocese where the Mass is being offered and to the pope, the vicar of Christ for the universal Church.

- We must be united to the Sacrifice of Jesus, who is the only victim. Through him, we also offer to God the Father with the Holy Spirit all the sacrifices, sufferings, self-denials, and tribulations of each day.

- To receive holy Communion, we need—besides being in the state of grace—to have the right intention and keep the Eucharistic fast.

As immediate preparation, excite in your soul lively sentiments of faith, humility, and desire. Ask yourself: *Who becomes present? To whom does He becomes present? Why does He become present?*

ORATIO S. AMBROSII

Ad mensam dulcíssimi convívii tui,
   pie Dómine Iesu Christe,
ego peccátor de própriis meis méritis
   nihil præsúmens,
sed de tua confídens misericórdia et bonitáte,
accédere véreor et contremísco.
Nam cor et corpus hábeo
   multis crimínibus maculátum,
mentem et linguam non caute custodítam.
Ergo, o pia Déitas, o treménda maiéstas,
ego miser, inter angústias deprehénsus,
ad te fontem misericórdiæ recúrro,
ad te festíno sanándus,
sub tuam protectiónem fúgio;
et, quam Iúdicem sustinére néqueo,
Salvatórem habére suspíro.
Tibi, Dómine, plagas meas osténdo,
tibi verecúndiam meam détego.
Scio peccáta mea multa et magna,
   pro quibus tímeo:
spero in misericórdias tuas,
   quarum non est númerus.
Réspice ergo in me óculis misericórdiæ tuæ,
Dómine Iesu Christe, Rex ætérne, Deus et homo,
crucifíxus propter hóminem.
Exáudi me sperántem in te:
miserére mei pleni misériis et peccátis,
tu qui fontem miseratiónis
   numquam manáre cessábis.
Salve, salutáris víctima,
pro me et omni humáno génere
   in patíbulo Crucis obláta.

PRAYER OF ST. AMBROSE

Lord, Jesus Christ,
I approach your banquet table
in fear and trembling,
for I am a sinner,
and dare not rely on my own worth
but only on your goodness and mercy.
I am defiled by many sins
   in body and soul,
and by my unguarded thoughts and words.
Gracious God of majesty and awe,
I seek your protection,
I look for your healing;
Poor troubled sinner that I am,
I appeal to you, the fountain of all mercy.
I cannot bear your judgment,
but I trust in your salvation.
Lord, I show my wounds to you
and uncover my shame before you.
I know my sins are many and great,
and they fill me with fear,
but I hope in your mercies,
for they cannot be numbered.
Lord Jesus Christ, eternal king, God and man,
crucified for mankind,
look upon me with mercy and hear my prayer,
for I trust in you.
Have mercy on me,
full of sorrow and sin,
for the depth of your compassion never ends.
Praise to you, saving sacrifice,
offered on the wood of the cross for me
   and for all mankind.

Salve, nóbilis et pretióse Sanguis,
de vulnéribus crucifíxi
    Dómini mei Iesu Christi prófluens,
et peccáta totíus mundi ábluens.
Recordáre, Dómine, creatúræ tuæ,
quam tuo Sánguine redemísti.
Pǽnitet me peccásse,
cúpio emendáre quod feci.
Aufer ergo a me, clementíssime Pater,
omnes iniquitátes et peccáta mea,
ut, purificátus mente et córpore,
digne degustáre mérear Sancta sanctórum.
Et concéde, ut hæc sancta prælibátio
    Córporis et Sánguinis tui,
quam ego indígnus súmere inténdo,
sit peccatórum meórum remíssio,
sit delictórum perfécta purgátio,
sit túrpium cogitatiónum effugátio
ac bonórum sénsuum regenerátio,
operúmque tibi placéntium salúbris efficácia,
ánimæ quoque et córporis
contra inimicórum meórum
    insídias firmíssima tuítio. Amen.

ORATIO S. THOMÆ DE AQUINO

Omnípotens sempitérne Deus,
ecce accédo ad sacraméntum unigéniti Fílii tui,
Dómini nostri Iesu Christi:
accédo tamquam infírmus ad médicum vitæ,
immúndus ad fontem misericórdiæ,
cæcus ad lumen claritátis ætérnæ,
pauper et egénus ad Dóminum
    cæli et terræ.

Praise to the noble and precious blood,
flowing from the wounds of my crucified
     Lord Jesus Christ
and washing away the sins of the whole world.
Remember, Lord, your creature,
whom you have redeemed with your blood.
I repent my sins,
and I long to put right what I have done.
Merciful Father, take away
     all my offenses and sins;
purify me in body and soul,
and make me worthy to taste the holy of holies.
May your body and blood,
which I intend to receive,
     although I am unworthy,
be for me the remission of my sins,
the washing away of my guilt,
     the end of my evil thoughts,
and the rebirth of my better instincts.
May it incite me to do the works pleasing to you
and profitable to my health in body and soul,
and be a firm defense
     against the wiles of my enemies. Amen.

PRAYER OF ST. THOMAS AQUINAS

Almighty and ever-living God,
I approach the sacrament of your only-begotten son,
our Lord Jesus Christ.
I come sick to the doctor of life,
unclean to the fountain of mercy,
blind to the radiance of eternal light,
and poor and needy to the Lord
     of heaven and earth.

Rogo ergo imménsæ largitátis tuæ abundántiam,
quátenus meam curáre dignéris infirmitátem,
laváre fœditátem, illumináre cæcitátem,
ditáre paupertátem, vestíre nuditátem,
ut panem Angelórum,
    Regem regum et Dóminum dominántium,
tanta suscípiam reveréntia et humilitáte,
tanta contritióne et devotióne,
tanta puritáte et fide,
tali propósito et intentióne,
sicut éxpedit salúti ánimæ meæ.
Da mihi, quæso, domínici Córporis et Sánguinis
non solum suscípere sacraméntum,
sed étiam rem et virtútem sacraménti.
O mitíssime Deus,
da mihi Corpus unigéniti Fílii tui,
    Dómini nostri Iesu Christi,
quod traxit de Vírgine María, sic suscípere,
ut córpori suo mýstico mérear incorporári
et inter eius membra connumerári.
O amantíssime Pater,
concéde mihi diléctum Fílium tuum,
quem nunc velátum in via suscípere propóno,
reveláta tandem fácie perpétuo contemplári:
Qui tecum vivit et regnat
in sǽcula sæculórum. Amen.

ORATIO AD BEATAM MARIAM VIRGINEM

(FOR PRIESTS)

O Mater pietátis et misericórdiæ,
    beatíssima Virgo María,
ego miser et indígnus peccátor
ad te confúgio toto corde et afféctu,
et precor pietátem tuam,

Lord, in your great generosity,
heal my sickness, wash away my defilement,
enlighten my blindness, enrich my poverty,
and clothe my nakedness.
May I receive the bread of angels,
the King of kings and Lord of lords,
with humble reverence,
with the purity and faith,
the repentance and love,
and the determined purpose
that will help to bring me to salvation.
May I receive the sacrament
    of the Lord's body and blood,
and its reality and power.
Kind God,
may I receive the body of your only begotten Son,
    our Lord Jesus Christ,
born from the womb of the Virgin Mary,
and so be received into his mystical body
and numbered among his members.
Loving Father,
as on my earthly pilgrimage
I now receive your beloved Son
under the veil of a sacrament,
may I one day see him face to face in glory,
who lives and reigns with you for ever. Amen.

PRAYER TO THE VIRGIN MARY
(FOR PRIESTS)

Mother of mercy and love,
blessed Virgin Mary,
I am a poor and unworthy sinner,
and I turn to you
    in confidence and love.

ut, sicut dulcíssimo Fílio tuo
  in Cruce pendénti astitísti,
ita et mihi, mísero peccatóri,
  et sacerdótibus ómnibus,
hic et in tota sancta Ecclésia hódie offeréntibus
cleménter assístere dignéris
ut, tua grátia adiúti,
dignam et acceptábilem hóstiam
in conspéctu summæ et indivíduæ Trinitátis
  offérre valeámus. Amen.

FORMULA INTENTIONIS
(FOR PRIESTS)

Ego volo celebráre Missam,
et confícere Corpus et Sánguinem
  Dómini nostri Iesu Christi,
iuxta ritum sanctæ Románæ Ecclésiæ,
ad laudem omnipoténtis Dei
  totiúsque Cúriæ triumphántis,
ad utilitátem meam totiúsque Cúriæ militántis,
pro ómnibus qui se commendavérunt
  oratiónibus meis
in génere et in spécie,
et pro felíci statu sanctæ Románæ Ecclésiæ.

Gáudium cum pace,
emendatiónem vitæ, spátium veræ pæniténtiæ,
grátiam et consolatiónem Sancti Spíritus,
perseverántiam in bonis opéribus,
tríbuat nobis omnípotens et miséricors Dóminus.
Amen.

You stood by your Son
as he hung dying on the cross.
Stand by me, also, a poor sinner,
and by all the priests
who are offering Mass today
here and throughout the entire Church.
Help us to offer a perfect and acceptable sacrifice
in the sight of the holy and undivided Trinity,
our most high God.
Amen.

STATEMENT OF INTENTION
(FOR PRIESTS)

My purpose is to celebrate Mass
and to make present the body and blood
    of our Lord Jesus Christ
according to the rite of the holy Roman Church
to the praise of our all-powerful God
and all his assembly in the glory of heaven,
for my good and the good
    of all his pilgrim Church on earth,
and for all who have asked me to pray for them
in general and in particular,
and for the good of the holy Roman Church.
May the almighty and merciful Lord
grant us joy and peace,
amendment of life, room for true repentance,
the grace and comfort of the Holy Spirit,
and perseverance in good works.
Amen.

PRECES AD S. IOSEPH
(FOR PRIESTS)

O felícem virum,
beátum Ioseph,
cui datum est Deum
quem multi reges voluérunt vidére et non vidérunt,
audíre et non audiérunt,
non solum vidére et audíre,
sed portáre, deosculári, vestíre et custodíre!

V. Ora pro nobis, beáte Ioseph.

R. **Ut digni efficiámur promissiónibus Christi.**

Orémus.
Deus, qui dedísti nobis regale sacerdótium,
præsta, quaésumus,
ut sicut beátus Ioseph unigénitum Fílium tuum,
natum ex María Vírgine,
suis mánibus reverénter
   tractáre méruit et portáre,
ita nos fácias cum cordis mundítia
   et óperis innocéntia
tuis sanctis altáribus deservíre,
ut sacrosánctum Fílii tui Corpus et Sánguinem
hódie digne sumámus,
et in futuro saéculo praémium habére
   mereámur ætérnum.
Per eúndem Christum Dóminum nostrum. Amen.

PRAYER TO ST. JOSEPH
(FOR PRIESTS)

O blessed Joseph,
happy man whose privilege it was,
not only to see and hear that God
whom many a king had longed to see, yet saw not,
longed to hear, yet heard not;
but also to carry him in your arms and kiss him,
to clothe him and watch over him!

V. Pray for us, blessed Joseph.

R. **That we may be made worthy of the promises of Christ.**

Let us pray.

God, who has conferred upon us a royal priesthood,
we pray to you to give us grace to minister
    at your holy altars
with hearts as clean and lives as blameless
as those of blessed Joseph,
who was found worthy to hold in his arms
and with all reverence to carry
    your only-begotten Son,
born of the virgin Mary.
Enable us this day to receive worthily
the sacred body and blood of your Son,
and make us fit to win an everlasting reward
    in the world to come;
Through the same Christ our Lord. Amen.

VESTING PRAYERS (FOR PRIESTS)

"The vestment common to ministers of every rank is the alb, tied at the waist with the cincture, unless it is made to fit without a cincture. An amice should be put on first if the alb does not completely cover the street clothing at the neck. Unless otherwise indicated, the chasuble, worn over the alb and stole, is the vestment proper to the priest celebrant at Mass and other rites immediately connected with Mass."[6]

The following prayers are suggested.

The celebrant washes his hands and asks for the grace of purity.

Da, Dómine, virtútem mánibus meis ad abstergéndam omnem máculam; ut sine pollutióne mentis et córporis váleam tibi servíre.	Give virtue, O Lord, to my hands, that every stain may be wiped away; that I may be enabled to serve you without defilement of mind or body.

The amice, a rectangular piece of white cloth, is the helmet of salvation and a sign of resistance against temptation. The priest usually kisses it and passes it over his head before putting it across his shoulders and tying it around the waist.

Impóne, Dómine, cápiti meo gáleam salútis, ad expugnándos diabólicos incúrsus.	Place, O Lord, on my head the helmet of salvation, that I may overcome the assaults of the devil.

The alb, a white linen tunic which covers the priest's whole body, signifies perfect integrity.

Deálba me, Dómine, et munda cor meum; ut, in	Purify me, O Lord, from all stain and cleanse my

---

6. *General Instruction of the Roman Missal* (=GIRM), nos. 298-299, 1975.

sánguine Agni dealbátus gáudiis pérfruar sempitérnis.

heart, that, washed in the blood of the Lamb, I may enjoy eternal delights.

The cincture, a cord which fastens the alb at the waist, stands for purity.

Præcínge me, Dómine cíngulo puritátis, et extíngue in lumbis meis humórem libídinis; ut máneat in me virtus continéntiæ et castitátis.

Gird me, O Lord, with the cincture of purity, and quench in my heart the fire of concupiscence, that the virtue of continence and chastity may remain in me.

The stole, the long band that fits around the neck, is a symbol of immortality and the sign of the dignity of the ministerial priesthood.

Redde mihi, Dómine, stolam immortalitátis, quam pérdidi in prævaricatióne primi paréntis: et, quamvis indígnus accédo ad tuum sacrum mystérium, mérear tamen gáudium sempitérnum.

Restore to me, O Lord, the state of immortality which was lost to me by my first parents, and, although I am unworthy to approach your sacred mysteries, grant me nevertheless eternal joy.

The chasuble, the outermost vestment worn by the celebrant at Mass, is the emblem of charity, which makes the yoke of Christ light and agreeable.

Dómine, qui dixísti: Iugum meum suáve est et onus meum leve: fac, ut istud portáre sic váleam, quod cónsequar tuam grátiam. Amen.

O Lord, who said, "My yoke is sweet and my burden light," grant that I may carry it so as to obtain your grace.
Amen.

THE EUCHARISTIC SACRIFICE

This Is the Mass

The Mass, the memorial of the death and resurrection of the Lord—in which the sacrifice of the cross is perpetuated over the centuries—is the summit and source of all Christian worship and life; it signifies and effects the unity of the people of God and achieves the building up of the body of Christ. It is an action of Christ himself and the Church; in it Christ the Lord, by the ministry of a priest, offers himself, substantially present under the forms of bread and wine, to God the Father and gives himself as spiritual food to the faithful who are associated with his offering.[1]

The Mass: Christ on the Cross

We are born to live. Christ, however, was born to die. On the night of the Last Supper, Christ instituted the Mass in order to leave a memorial to his beloved Spouse, the Church. He offered his body and blood under the species of bread and wine to God the Father.

Taking bread, Christ said: "This is my body, which will be given up for you." Also taking the chalice with wine, he said: "This is the cup of my blood, the blood of the new and everlasting covenant. It will be shed for you and for all so that sins may be forgiven." Christ then commanded his apostles: "Do this in me-

1. Cf. *Codex Iuris Canonici* (=CIC), 897-898.

mory of me," making them priests of the New Testament. This rite anticipated the bloody sacrifice that Christ accomplished on the cross once and for all on Good Friday for the redemption of the world.

The Church continues to offer the sacrifice of the cross, but in a bloodless manner. The Mass is neither a repetition of nor a substitute for the cross, but the merit we gain from the Mass is the same merit that we would have gained had we actually been present at the foot of the cross on Calvary.

The historical event of Calvary does not, however, repeat itself, nor is it continued in each Mass. The sacrifice of Christ is perfect and, therefore, does not need to be repeated. Glorious in heaven, Christ does not die again. His sacrifice is not repeated; rather, the presence of the singular sacrifice of the cross is multiplied, overcoming time and space.

The Mass: The Sacrifice of the New Covenant

Of the sacrifice of Christ, the main sign or figure of the sacrifice of Christ in the Old Testament is the paschal lamb. At every Passover, the Jews recalled and renewed their covenant with God by sacrificing a lamb. This sacrificial lamb once spared the firstborn of the Jews from the exterminating angel who came to slay the firstborn of every family in Egypt.

Our Lord anticipates his sacrifice on the cross in the Last Supper, within the Jewish ritual celebration of the Passover. In the Cenacle as on Calvary, the essential elements of the sacrifice are there: the immolation and self-offering (body and blood) to God the Father. Christ is the unspotted Lamb. He sets all people free from the slavery of sin and establishes the eternal alliance between creature and Creator, the New Covenant. More than that, what had been only a foreshadowing in sign is now fully realized: the communion of blood and of life between God and us.

When the faithful are said to offer Mass together with the priest, this does not mean that all the members of the Church, like the priest himself, perform the visible liturgical rite. This is done by the celebrant only. He has been divinely appointed for this purpose through the sacrament of Holy Orders.

The principal victim of the sacrifice, is Jesus Christ. But the faithful, in order to exercise their common priesthood fully, should unite their sacrifice to his and thus offer themselves, also, to God the Father: "I exhort you . . . to present your bodies as a sacrifice, living, holy, pleasing to God—your spiritual service," wrote St. Paul to the Romans.[2]

The Mass "requires all Christians, so far as human power allows, to reproduce in themselves the sentiments that Christ had when he was offering himself in sacrifice: sentiments of humility, adoration, praise and thanksgiving to the divine Majesty. It requires them also to become victims, as it were, cultivating a spirit of self-denial according to the precepts of the Gospel, willingly doing works of penance, detesting and expiating their sins. It requires us all, in a word, to die mystically with Jesus Christ on the cross, so that we may say with the same apostle: 'With Christ, I hang upon the cross.'"[3]

---

2. Romans 12:1.
3. Pius XII, *Mediator Dei*, Nov 20, 1942.

The Mass: The Sacrifice of the Church

Christ bequeathed his sacrifice to the Church, not just to each individual believer. God wants to save us, not in an isolated manner, prescinding from any relationship among them, but as a people. Each Mass presupposes union among the faithful and of the faithful with their bishop, the pope, and the universal Church. Moreover, that solid union is made stronger with the celebration of the Eucharist and is a consequence of it. The Second Vatican Council states it in this manner: "In the sacrament of the eucharistic bread, the unity of believers, who form one body in Christ,[4] is both expressed and brought about."[5]

Both on the cross and in the Mass, the priest and victim are one and the same: Christ himself. He is both the one who offers and the one who is offered. No longer is there separation between priests and victims.

The words of Jesus Christ at the Last Supper—"Do this in memory of me"—command the continuation of his sacrifice on the cross in every holy Mass celebrated anywhere in the world until the end of time. This was announced in the Old Testament with these words of the prophet Malachi: "From the rising of the sun to its setting my name is great among the nations, and in every place there is a sacrifice and there is offered to my name a clean oblation."[6]

Following Christ's command, the priest offers the Mass acting as the representative of Christ. That is why he does not say, "This is the body and blood of Christ," but rather, "This is my body" and "This is my

---

4. Cf. 1 Corinthians 10-17.
5. Vatican Council II, *Lumen Gentium* (=LG), 3.
6. Malachi 1:11.

blood." The priest is the chosen instrument of Christ in the same manner that the brush is the painter's tool. In the Mass, Christ is no longer alone on the cross. As in any other sacrament, the Mass is an action of Christ and also of the Church. At the moment of the preparation of the gifts the entire Church presents itself for sacrifice with Christ.

We have testimonies from the very beginning of the life of the Church that the Christians had the celebration of the holy Mass on Sunday, the Lord's day, when the victory and triumph of the Lord's death became present.

In the Old Testament, the Jews rested on Saturday, giving thanks to God for the gift of creation. In the New Testament, we celebrate a new creation, to the life of grace: a supernatural creation far superior to the material creation of the world. No wonder, then, that the Church requires under pain of mortal sin that we to go to Mass at least on Sunday.

"The holy Mass cheers the heavenly court; it alleviates the poor souls in purgatory; it attracts all sorts of blessings to the earth; it gives more glory to God than all the sufferings of the martyrs put together, the penances of all the monks, all the tears shed by them since the beginning of the world and all their deeds until the end of time."[7]

The Mass: The Life of Each Christian

Because the Mass is the same sacrifice as Calvary, sacramentally renewed, with all its strength and sanctifying power, the Church considers it the center of its life and the life of each of the faithful.

---

7. St. John M. Vianney, *Sermon on the holy Mass.*

"The Eucharistic sacrifice is the 'source and summit of all Christian life'. It is a single sacrifice that embraces everything. It is the greatest treasure of the Church. It is her life."[8]

The Mass is also the center of the life and mission of each priest, who finds in it the direction and goal of his ministry.

"The holy Mass brings us face to face with one of the central mysteries of our faith, because it is the gift of the Blessed Trinity to the Church. It is because of this that we can consider the Mass the center and the source of a Christian's spiritual life.

"It is the aim of all the sacraments. The life of grace, into which we are brought by Baptism, and which is increased and strengthened by Confirmation, grows to its fullness in the Mass."[9]

"The more perfect form of participation in the Mass whereby the faithful, after the priest's Communion, receive the Lord's body from the same sacrifice is warmly recommended to those who are duly prepared and in the state of grace."[10]

Since the sacrifice of the Mass is the same as the sacrifice of Calvary, their purpose is the same:

- To adore the Blessed Trinity. The sacrifice of the cross was first of all a sacrifice of adoration and praise of God. Although the Mass is sometimes offered "in honor and in memory of the saints, the Church teaches us that the Mass is not offered

---

8. John Paul II, Prayer on Holy Thursday, 1982.
9. Blessed Josemaría Escrivá, *Christ Is Passing By* (=CPB), 87, Princeton, N. J.: Scepter Publishers, 1974.
10. Vatican Council II, *Sacrosanctum Concilium*, 55.
11. Council of Trent, Session 22, chapter 3.

to the saints but to God alone who has given them their crown."[11]

- To give thanks for the many benefits we receive from God, including those of which we are not aware. The second aim of the Mass is thanksgiving. Only Christ our Lord can offer God a worthy hymn of thanksgiving. He did so at the Last Supper when he gave thanks and when, hanging on the cross, he continued to give thanks; our Lord continues to thank God the Father for us in the holy sacrifice of the Mass.

- To ask pardon for our sins and for the many times we have not loved God as we should. This desire for expiation and atonement should lead us to make a good confession. The same Christ who died on the cross for our sins is present and offered in the Mass "so that sins may be forgiven."

- To ask for the spiritual and material things we need. The fourth purpose of the Mass is petition. Jesus Christ on the cross died "offering prayers and supplications and was heard because of his reverent obedience" and now in heaven "lives always to make intercession for us."[12] These graces benefit those present at holy Mass and the persons for whom it is offered.

The Mass: External Participation

We should participate in the Mass externally, taking care of some details.

- Attend the Mass with a spirit of prayer, praying as the Church teaches us to pray, avoiding dis-

---

12. Hebrews 5:7; 7:25.

tractions. Be one with the words, actions, and gestures of the celebrant, who acts in the person of Christ. Give up personal preferences; accept the option that the celebrant, considering the circumstances of the people in each community, has chosen from among the legitimate possibilities that the liturgy offers to us.

- Listen, respond, acclaim, sing, or keep opportune silence, in order to facilitate union with God and to deepen your reflection on the word of God.

- Stand, sit and kneel—and be serene—even if you see someone who does not do so.

- Be punctual. This is a considerate detail for Christ our Lord, himself, and for others who are attending Mass. Arrive before the priest goes to the altar. Leave only after the priest has left.

- Use your missal, or the missalette available in the church. By following the prayers of the priest, you can avoid distractions. The more complete missals for the faithful have the prayers of the Mass distributed in three main sections: Fixed Prayers of the Order of Mass, Proper Prayers, and Readings. The missalettes for the use of the faithful usually contain some of the variable prayers for each day's Mass and most of the fixed parts of the Order of Mass arranged in their usual sequence.

- Dress properly as for an important meeting and not, for instance, as if you were going to participate in a sport. Dress ought to convey the respect, solemnity and joy of the Mass.[13]

---

13. *Catechism of the Catholic Church* (=CCC), 1387, Librería Editrice Vaticane, 1994.

The Mass: Communion and Thanksgiving

Having the right intention in receiving Communion means having these good purposes: to please God, to achieve greater union with him through charity, and to apply this divine remedy to one's moral weaknesses. The sacrament should not be received out of routine, vainglory, or human respect.

We are bound, under serious obligation, to receive holy Communion at least once a year—ordinarily during Easter time—and when we are in danger of death.

Holy Communion may be received a second time on a given day, when and if one attends holy Mass, or when one in danger of death receives the Blessed Sacrament as Viaticum.

- Complete the Mass with an intense thanksgiving. Devote a few minutes to private prayer. In this way, your Mass will have direct influence on your work, your family life, your dealings with others, and the manner in which you will spend the rest of your day. In short, the Mass should not be an isolated event of the day; rather, it should be the inspiration and the dynamo for all your actions.

- Turn the whole day into a continuous preparation for the holy sacrifice of the Mass—working and praying—and, at the same time, into a never-ending act of thanksgiving. For a Christian, all honest activities can be turned into prayer.

- Imitate the piety of the Blessed Virgin Mary and ask it of her. While our Lord offered and immolated his flesh, Mary offered and immolated her spirit. Participate in each Mass as if it were your last.

Guidelines for Receiving Holy Communion

For Catholics: As Catholics, we fully participate in the celebration of the Eucharist when we receive Holy Communion. In order to be properly disposed to receive communion, participants should not be conscious of grave sin and normally should have fasted for one hour. A person who is conscious of grave sin is not to receive the Body and Blood of the Lord without prior sacramental confession except for a grave reason where there is no opportunity for confession. In this case the person is to be mindful of the obligation to make an act of perfect contrition, including the intention of confessing as soon as possible (CIC 916). A frequent reception of the Sacrament of Penance is encouraged for all.

For our fellow Christians: We welcome our fellow Christians to this celebration of the Eucharist as our brothers and sisters. We pray that our common baptism and the action of the Holy Spirit in this Eucharist will draw us closer to one another and begin to dispel the sad divisions which separate us. We pray that these will lessen and finally disappear, in keeping with Christ's prayer for us "that they may all be one" (Jn. 17:21).

Because Catholics believe that the celebration of the Eucharist is a sign of the reality of the oneness of faith, life and worship, members of those churches with whom we are not yet fully united are ordinarily not admitted to Holy Communion. Eucharistic sharing in exceptional circumstances by other Christians requires permission according to the directives of the diocesan bishop and the provisions of canon law (CIC 844.4). Members of the Orthodox churches, the Assyrian Church of the East and the Polish National Catholic Church are urged to respect the discipline of their own churches. According to Roman Catholic discipline, the Code of Canon Law does not object to reception of communion by Christians of these churches (CIC 844.3).

For those not receiving Holy Communion: All who are not receiving Holy Communion are encouraged to express in their hearts a prayerful desire for unity with the Lord Jesus and with one another.

For non-Christians: We also welcome to this celebration those who do not share in our faith in Jesus Christ. While we cannot admit them to Holy Communion, we ask them to offer their prayers for the peace and unity of the human family.

(NCCB; "Guidelines on Communion Reception,"1996)

ORDO MISSÆ
cum populo

RITUS INITIALES

RITUS INITIALES

1. Populo congregato, sacerdos cum ministris ad altare accedit, dum cantus ad introitum peragitur.
2. Cum ad altare pervenerit, facta cum ministris debita reverentia, osculo altare veneratur et, pro opportunitate, illud incensat. Postea cum ministris sedem petit.

SALUTATIO

Cantu ad introitum absoluto, sacerdos et fideles, stantes, signant se, dum sacerdos, ad populum conversus, dicit:

In nómine Patris, et Fílii,
  et Spíritus Sancti.

Populus respondet: **Amen.**

Deinde sacerdos, manus extendens, populum salutat, dicens:

A.

V. Grátia Dómini nostri Iesu Christi, et cáritas Dei, et communicátio Sancti Spíritus sit cum ómnibus vobis.

R. **Et cum spíritu tuo.**

B. Vel:

V. Grátia vobis et pax a Deo Patre nostro et Dómino Iesu Christo.

Populus respondet:

R. **Benedíctus Deus et Pater Dómini nostri Iesu Christi.**

ORDER OF MASS
with a congregation

INTRODUCTORY RITES

ENTRANCE SONG   **stand**

After the people have assembled, the priest and the ministers go to the altar while the entrance song is being sung.

When the priest comes to the altar, he makes the customary reverence with the ministers, kisses the altar, and (if incense is used) incenses it. Then, with the ministers, he goes to the chair.

GREETING

After the entrance song, the priest and the faithful remain standing and make the sign of the cross, as the priest says:

In the name of the Father, and of the Son, and of the Holy Spirit.

The people answer: **Amen.**

Then the priest, facing the people, extends his hands and greets all present with one of the following greetings:

A.

The grace of our Lord Jesus Christ and the love of God and the fellowship of the Holy Spirit be with you all.

The people answer: **And also with you.**

B. Or the priest says:

The grace and peace of God our Father and the Lord Jesus Christ be with you.

The people answer:

Blessed be God, the Father of our Lord Jesus Christ.

Vel:

R. Et cum spíritu tuo.

C. Vel:

Dóminus vobíscum.

Episcopus, loco **Dóminus vobíscum**, in hac prima salutatione dicit: **Pax vobis**.

Populus respondet: **Et cum spíritu tuo.**

3.   Sacerdos, vel diaconus vel alius minister idoneus, potest brevissimis verbis introducere fideles in Missam illius diei.

Ritus benedictionis et aspersionis aquæ benedictæ fieri potest in omnibus Missis dominicæ, iis etiam quæ horis vespertinis sabbati anticipantur, in omnibus ecclesiis et oratoriis.

A.   ORDO AD FACIENDAM ET ASPERGENDAM AQUAM BENEDICTAM

Huiusmodi ritus locum tenet actus pænitentialis initio Missæ peragendi.

Post salutationem, sacerdos, stans ad sedem, ad populum conversus, habens ante se vas cum aqua benedicenda, populum ad orandum invitat his vel similibus verbis:

Dóminum Deum nostrum,
fratres caríssimi, supplíciter deprecémur,
ut hanc creatúram aquæ benedícere dignétur,
super nos aspergéndam in nostri memóriam baptísmi.
Ipse autem nos adiuváre dignétur,
ut fidéles Spirítui, quem accépimus, maneámus.

Et post brevem pausam silentii prosequitur, manibus iunctis:

A.   **Omnípotens sempitérne Deus,**
qui voluísti ut per aquam, fontem vitæ
     ac purificatiónis princípium,
étiam ánimæ mundaréntur
ætérnaéque vitæ munus excíperent,

or:

And also with you.

C. Or the priest says:

The Lord be with you.

(Instead of the greeting, **The Lord be with you**, a bishop says: **Peace be with you**.)

The people answer: **And also with you.**

The priest, or deacon, or other suitable minister may very briefly introduce the Mass of the day.

A. The rite of blessing and sprinkling holy water may be celebrated in all churches and chapels at all Sunday Masses celebrated on Sunday or on Saturday evening.

or:

B. The penitential rite follows.

or:

C. If the Mass is preceded by some part of the Liturgy of the Hours, the penitential rite is omitted, and the Kyrie may be omitted. (See *General Instruction on the Liturgy of the Hours*, nos. 94-96.)

A. RITE OF BLESSING AND SPRINKLING HOLY WATER

When this rite is celebrated, it takes the place of the penitential rite at the beginning of Mass. The Kyrie is also omitted.

After greeting the people, the priest remains standing at his chair. A vessel containing the water to be blessed is placed before him. Facing the people, he invites them to pray, using these or similar words:

Dear friends,
this water will be used
to remind us of our baptism.
Let us ask God to bless it,
and to keep us faithful
to the Spirit he has given us.

After a brief silence, he joins hands and continues:

A. God our Father,
your gift of water
brings life and freshness to the earth;
it washes away our sins
and brings us eternal life.

dignáre, quǽsumus, hanc aquam ✠ benedícere,
qua vólumus hac die tua,
    Dómine, communíri.
Fontem vivum in nobis tuæ grátiæ renovári
et ab omni malo spíritus et córporis
per ipsam nos deféndi concédas,
ut mundis tibi córdibus propinquáre
tuámque digne salútem
    valeámus accípere.

Per Christum Dóminum nostrum. **R. Amen.**

B. Vel:

Dómine Deus omnípotens,
qui es totíus vitæ córporis et ánimæ fons et orígo,
hanc aquam, te quǽsumus, ✠ benedícas,
qua fidénter útimur
    ad nostrórum implorándam véniam peccatórum
et advérsus omnes morbos inimicíque insídias
tuæ defensiónem grátiæ consequéndam.

Præsta, Dómine, ut,
misericórdia tua interveniénte,
aquæ vivæ semper nobis sáliant in salútem,
ut mundo tibi corde
    appropinquáre possímus,
et omnis córporis animǽque
    perícula devitémus.

Per Christum Dóminum nostrum. **R. Amen.**

C. Vel, tempore paschali:

Dómine Deus omnípotens,
précibus pópuli tui adésto propítius;
et nobis, mirábile nostræ creatiónis opus,
sed et redemptiónis nostræ mirabílius, memorántibus,
hanc aquam ✠ benedícere tu dignáre.
Ipsam enim tu fecísti,
ut et arva fecunditáte donáret,
et levámen corpóribus nostris munditiámque præbéret.
Aquam étiam tuæ minístram misericórdiæ condidísti;
nam per ipsam solvísti tui pópuli servitútem,
illiúsque sitim in desérto sedásti;

We ask you now
to bless ✠ this water
and to give us your protection on this day,
which you have made your own.
Renew the living spring of your life within us
and protect us in spirit and body,
that we may be free from sin
and come into your presence
to receive your gift of salvation.

We ask this through Christ our Lord. **R. Amen.**

B. Or:

Lord God almighty,
creator of all life, of body and soul,
we ask you to bless ✠ this water:
as we use it in faith
forgive our sins
and save us from all illness
and the power of evil.

Lord,
in your mercy
give us living water,
always springing up as a fountain of salvation:
free us, body and soul, from every danger,
and admit us to your presence
in purity of heart.

Grant this through Christ our Lord. **R. Amen.**

C. Or (during the Easter season):

Lord God almighty,
hear the prayers of your people:
we celebrate our creation and redemption.
Hear our prayers and bless ✠ this water,
which gives fruitfulness to the fields
and refreshment and cleansing to man.
You chose water to show your goodness
when you led your people to freedom
through the Red Sea
and satisfied their thirst in the desert
with water from the rock.

per ipsam novum fœdus nuntiavérunt prophétæ,
quod eras cum homínibus initúrus;
per ipsam dénique,
    quam Christus in Iordáne sacrávit,
corrúptam natúræ nostræ substántiam
in regeneratiónis lavácro renovásti.
Sit ígitur hæc aqua nobis suscépti baptísmatis memória,
et cum frátibus nostris, qui sunt in Páscate baptizáti,
gáudia nos tríbuas sociáre.

Per Christum Dóminum nostrum. **R. Amen.**

Ubi locorum condicio aut populi traditio suadet ut salis commixtio in
benedictione aquæ servetur, sacerdos sal benedicit, dicens:

Súpplices te rogámus, omnípotens Deus,
ut hanc creatúram salis
benedícere ✠ tua pietáte dignéris,
qui per Eliséum prophétam in aquam
mitti eam iussísti,
ut sanarétur sterílitas aquæ.
Præsta, Dómine, quǽsumus,
ut, ubicúmque hæc salis et aquæ commíxtio
fúerit aspérsa, omni impugnatióne inimíci depúlsa,
præséntia Sancti tui Spíritus
nos iúgiter custódiat.

Per Christum Dóminum nostrum. **R. Amen**.

Deinde sal immittit in aquam, nihil dicens.

Postea, accepto aspersorio, sacerdos aspergit se et ministros, deinde clerum
et populum, pro opportunitate transeundo per ecclèsiam.

Interim peragitur unus e cantibus qui sequuntur, vel alius cantus aptus.

Ad sedem reversus, et cantu expleto, sacerdos, stans versus ad populum,
manibus iunctis, dicit:

Deus omnípotens, nos a peccátis puríficet,
et per huius Eucharístiæ celebratiónem
    dignos nos reddat,
qui mensæ regni sui partícipes efficiámur.

R. Amen.

Deinde, quando præscribitur, cantatur vel dicitur hymnus **Gloria in excélsis
Deo**.

Water was the symbol used by the prophets
to foretell your new covenant with man.
You made the water of baptism holy
by Christ's baptism in the Jordan:
by it you give us a new birth
and renew us in holiness.
May this water remind us of our baptism,
and let us share the joy
of all who have been baptized at Easter.

We ask this through Christ our Lord. R. **Amen.**

Where it is customary, salt may be mixed with the holy water. The priest
blesses the salt, saying:

Almighty God,
we ask you to bless ✠ this salt
as once you blessed
the salt scattered
  over the water
by the prophet Elisha.
Wherever this salt
  and water are sprinkled,
drive away the power of evil,
and protect us always
by the presence of your Holy Spirit.

Grant this through Christ our Lord. R. **Amen.**

Then he pours the salt into the water in silence.

Taking the sprinkler, the priest sprinkles himself and his ministers, then the
rest of the clergy and the congregation. He may move through the church
for the sprinkling of the people. Meanwhile, an antiphon or another appropriate song is sung.

When he returns to his place and the song is finished, the priest faces the
people and, with joined hands, says:

May almighty God cleanse us of our sins,
and through the eucharist we celebrate
make us worthy to sit at his table
in his heavenly kingdom.

The people answer: **Amen.**

When it is prescribed, the Gloria is then sung or said.

B. ACTUS PÆNITENTIALIS

Deinde sequitur actus pænitentialis. Sacerdos fideles invitat ad
pænitentiam:

Fratres, agnoscámus peccáta nostra,
ut apti simus ad sacra mystéria celebránda.

Fit brevis pausa silentii. Postea omnes simul faciunt confessionem:

A.

Confíteor Deo omnipoténti et vobis, fratres,
quia peccávi nimis
cogitatióne, verbo, ópere et omissióne:

et, percutientes sibi pectus, dicunt:

mea culpa, mea culpa, mea máxima culpa.

Deinde prosequuntur:

Ideo precor beátam Maríam semper Vírginem,
omnes Angelos et Sanctos,
et vos, fratres, oráre pro me
ad Dóminum Deum nostrum.

Sequitur absolutio sacerdotis:

B.   PENITENTIAL RITE

After the introduction to the day's Mass, the priest invites the people to recall their sins and to repent of them in silence. He may use these or similar words:

As we prepare to celebrate
the mystery of Christ's love,
let us acknowledge our failures
and ask the Lord for pardon and strength.

or:

Coming together as God's family,
with confidence let us ask the Father's forgiveness,
for he is full of gentleness and compassion.

or:

My brothers and sisters,[2]
to prepare ourselves to celebrate the sacred
mysteries, let us call to mind our sins.

A pause for silent reflection follows.

After the silence, one of the following three forms is chosen:

A. All say:

I confess to almighty God,
and to you, my brothers and sisters,
that I have sinned through my own fault

They strike their breast:

in my thoughts and in my words,
in what I have done,
and in what I have failed to do;
and I ask blessed Mary, ever virgin,
all the angels and saints,
and you, my brothers and sisters,
to pray for me to the Lord our God.

The priest says the absolution:

---

2. At the discretion of the priest, other words that seem more suitable under the circumstances, such as **friends, dearly beloved, brethren,** may be used. This also applies to parallel instances in the liturgy.

Misereátur nostri omnípotens Deus
et, dimíssis peccátis nostris,
perdúcat nos ad vitam ætérnam.

Populus respondet: **Amen.**

B.   Sacerdos fideles invitat ad pænitentiam::

Fratres, agnoscámus peccáta nostra,
ut apti simus ad sacra mystéria celebránda.

Postea sacerdos dicit:

Miserére nostri, Dómine.

Populus respondet: **Quia peccávimus tibi.**

Sacerdos:

Osténde nobis, Dómine, misericórdiam tuam.

Populus: **Et salutáre tuum da nobis.**

Sequitur absolutio sacerdotis:

Misereátur nostri omnípotens Deus
et, dimíssis peccátis nostris,
perdúcat nos ad vitam ætérnam.

Populus respondet: **Amen.**

C.   Deinde sacerdos, vel alius minister idoneus, sequentes, vel alias,
      invocationes cum **Kýrie, eléison** profert:

Qui missus es sanáre contrítos corde:
Kýrie, eléison.

Populus respondet: **Kýrie, eléison.**

Sacerdos:

Qui peccatóres vocáre venísti:
Christe, eléison.

Populus: **Christe, eléison.**

May almighty God have mercy on us,
forgive us our sins,
and bring us to everlasting life.

The people answer: **Amen.**

B. The priest says:

Lord, we have sinned against you:
Lord, have mercy.

The people answer: **Lord, have mercy.**

Priest:

Lord, show us your mercy and love.

People: **And grant us your salvation.**

The priest says the absolution:

May almighty God have mercy on us,
forgive us our sins,
and bring us to everlasting life.

The people answer: **Amen.**

C. The priest (or other suitable minister) makes the following or other invocations:

i

Priest:

You were sent to heal the contrite:
Lord, have mercy.

The people answer: **Lord, have mercy.**

Priest:

You came to call sinners:
Christ, have mercy.

Populus: **Christe, eléison.**

Sacerdos:

Qui ad déxteram Patris sedes,
ad interpellándum pro nobis: Kýrie, eléison.

Populus: **Kýrie, eléison.**

Sequitur absolutio sacerdotis:

Misereátur nostri omnípotens Deus
et, dimíssis peccátis nostris,
perdúcat nos ad vitam ætérnam.

Populus respondet: **Amen.**

People: **Christ, have mercy.**

Priest:

You plead for us at the right hand of the Father:
Lord, have mercy.

People: **Lord, have mercy.**

The priest says the absolution:

May almighty God have mercy on us,
forgive us our sins,
and bring us to everlasting life.

The people answer: **Amen.**

ii

Priest:

Lord Jesus, you came to gather the nations
into the peace of God's kingdom:
Lord, have mercy.

The people answer: **Lord, have mercy.**

Priest:

You come in word and sacrament to strengthen us in
holiness: Christ, have mercy.

People: **Christ, have mercy.**

Priest:

You will come in glory with salvation for your people:
Lord, have mercy.

People: **Lord, have mercy.**

The priest says the absolution:

May almighty God have mercy on us,
forgive us our sins,
and bring us to everlasting life.

The people answer: **Amen.**

iii

Priest:

Lord Jesus, you are mighty God and Prince of peace:
Lord, have mercy.

The people answer: **Lord, have mercy.**

Priest:

Lord Jesus, you are Son of God and Son of Mary:
Christ, have mercy.

People: **Christ, have mercy.**

Priest:

Lord Jesus, you are Word made flesh
    and splendor of the Father:
Lord, have mercy.

People: **Lord, have mercy.**

The priest says the absolution:

May almighty God have mercy on us,
forgive us our sins,
and bring us to everlasting life.

The people answer: **Amen.**

iv

Priest:

Lord Jesus, you came to reconcile us to one another and
    to the Father:
Lord, have mercy.

The people answer: **Lord, have mercy.**

Priest:

Lord Jesus, you heal the wounds of sin and division:
Christ, have mercy.

People: **Christ, have mercy.**

Priest:

Lord Jesus, you intercede for us with your Father:
Lord, have mercy.

People: **Lord, have mercy.**

The priest says the absolution:

May almighty God have mercy on us,
forgive us our sins,
and bring us to everlasting life.

The people answer: **Amen.**

---

v

Priest:

You raise the dead to life in the Spirit:
Lord, have mercy.

The people answer: **Lord, have mercy.**

Priest:

You bring pardon and peace to the sinner:
Christ, have mercy.

People: **Christ, have mercy.**

Priest:

You bring light to those in darkness:
Lord, have mercy.

People: **Lord, have mercy.**

The priest says the absolution:

May almighty God have mercy on us,
forgive us our sins,
and bring us to everlasting life.

The people answer: **Amen.**

vi

Priest:

Lord Jesus, you raise us to new life:
Lord, have mercy.

The people answer: **Lord, have mercy.**

Priest:

Lord Jesus, you forgive us our sins:
Christ, have mercy.

People: **Christ, have mercy.**

Priest:

Lord Jesus, you feed us with your body and blood:
Lord, have mercy.

People: **Lord, have mercy.**

The priest says the absolution:

May almighty God have mercy on us,
forgive us our sins,
and bring us to everlasting life.

The people answer: **Amen.**

vii

Priest:

Lord Jesus, you have shown us the way to the Father:
Lord, have mercy.

The people answer: **Lord, have mercy.**

Priest:

Lord Jesus, you have given us the consolation of the truth:
Christ, have mercy.

People: **Christ, have mercy.**

Priest:

Lord Jesus, you are the Good Shepherd,
leading us into everlasting life:
Lord, have mercy.

People: **Lord, have mercy.**

The priest says the absolution:

May almighty God have mercy on us,
forgive us our sins,
and bring us to everlasting life.

The people answer: **Amen.**

viii

Priest:

Lord Jesus, you healed the sick:
Lord, have mercy.

The people answer: **Lord, have mercy.**

Priest:

Lord Jesus, you forgave sinners:
Christ, have mercy.

People: **Christ, have mercy.**

Priest:

Lord Jesus, you give us yourself to heal us
     and bring us strength:
Lord, have mercy.

People: **Lord, have mercy.**

The priest says the absolution:

May almighty God have mercy on us,
forgive us our sins,
and bring us to everlasting life.

The people answer: **Amen.**

KYRIE ELEISON

4.   Sequuntur invocationes Kýrie, eléison, nisi iam præcesserint in aliqua formula actus pænitentialis.

V. Kýrie, eléison.   R. Kýrie, eléison.
V. Christe, eléison.   R. Christe, eléison.
V. Kýrie, eléison.   R. Kýrie, eléison.

GLORIA

5.   Deinde, quando præscribitur, cantatur vel dicitur hymnus:

Glória in excélsis Deo
et in terra pax homínibus bonæ voluntátis.
Laudámus te,
benedícimus te,
adorámus te,
glorificámus te,
grátias ágimus tibi propter magnam glóriam tuam,
Dómine Deus, Rex cæléstis,
Deus Pater omnípotens.
Dómine Fili unigénite, Iesu Christe,
Dómine Deus, Agnus Dei, Fílius Patris,
qui tollis peccáta mundi, miserére nobis;
qui tollis peccáta mundi,
     súscipe deprecatiónem nostram.
Qui sedes ad déxteram Patris, miserére nobis.
Quóniam tu solus Sanctus,
     tu solus Dóminus,
     tu solus Altíssimus,
Iesu Christe, cum Sancto Spíritu:
     in glória Dei Patris. Amen.

KYRIE

The invocations, **Lord, have mercy,** follow, unless they have already been
used in one of the forms of the act of penance.

V. Lord, have mercy.   R. **Lord, have mercy.**
V. Christ, have mercy.   R. **Christ, have mercy.**
V. Lord, have mercy.   R. **Lord, have mercy.**

or:

V. Kýrie, eléison.   R. **Kýrie, eléison.**
V. Christe, eléison.   R. **Christe, eléison.**
V. Kýrie, eléison.   R. **Kýrie, eléison.**

GLORIA

This hymn is said or sung on Sundays outside Advent and Lent, and solemnities and feasts, and in solemn local celebrations.[3]

Glory to God in the highest,
and peace to his people on earth.
Lord God, heavenly King,
almighty God and Father,
   we worship you, we give you thanks,
   we praise you for your glory.
Lord Jesus Christ, only Son of the Father,
Lord God, Lamb of God,
you take away the sin of the world:
   have mercy on us;
you are seated at the right hand of the Father:
   receive our prayer.
For you alone are the Holy One,
you alone are the Lord,
you alone are the Most High,
   Jesus Christ,
   with the Holy Spirit,
   in the glory of God the Father. Amen.

---

3. Cf. GIRM, 31.

COLLECTA

6.   Quo hymno finito, sacerdos, manibus iunctis, dicit:

Orémus.

Et omnes una cum sacerdote per aliquod temporis spatium in silentio orant.

Tunc sacerdos, manibus extensis, dicit orationem; qua finita, populus acclamat:

Amen.

LITURGIA VERBI

sit

PRIMA LECTIO

7.   Deinde lector ad ambonem pergit, et legit primam lectionem, quam omnes sedentes auscultant. Ad finem lectionis significandam, lector subdit:

Verbum Dómini.

Omnes acclamant: **Deo grátias.**

PSALMUS RESPONSORIUS

8.   Psalmista, seu cantor, psalmum dicit, populo responsum proferente.

SECUNDA LECTIO

9.   Postea, si habenda sit secunda lectio, lector eam in ambone legit, ut supra. Ad finem lectionis significandam, lector subdit:

Verbum Dómini.

Omnes acclamant: **Deo grátias.**

ALLELUIA VEL CANTUS

10.   Sequitur Allelúia, vel alter cantus.

OPENING PRAYER

Afterwards the priest, with hands joined, sings or says:

Let us pray.

Priest and people pray silently for a while.

Then the priest extends his hands and sings or says the opening prayer, at the end of which the people respond:

Amen.

LITURGY OF THE WORD

sit

FIRST READING

The reader goes to the lectern for the first reading. All sit and listen. To indicate the end, the reader adds:

The Word of the Lord.

All respond: **Thanks be to God.**

RESPONSORIAL PSALM

The cantor of the psalm sings or recites the psalm, and the people respond.

SECOND READING

When there is a second reading, it is read at the lectern as before. To indicate the end, the reader adds:

The Word of the Lord.

All respond: **Thanks be to God.**

ALLELUIA OR GOSPEL ACCLAMATION   **stand**

The alleluia or other chant follows. It is to be omitted if not sung.[4]

---

4. GIRM, 39; *Introduction to the Lectionary*, 23, 1981.

V. Allelúia.   R. Allelúia.
V. (Versus)   R. Allelúia.

Tempore quo allelúia non est dicendum.

Laus tibi, Christe, Rex ætérnæ glóriæ!

Laus et honor tibi, Dómine Iesu!
Glória et laus tibi, Christe!
Glória tibi, Christe, Verbo Dei!

EVANGELIUM

11.   Interim sacerdos incensum, si adhibetur, imponit. Postea diaconus,
Evangelium prolaturus, ante sacerdotem inclinatus, benedictionem petit,
submissa voce dicens:

Iube, domne, benedícere.

Sacerdos submissa voce dicit:

Dóminus sit in corde tuo et in lábiis tuis: ut digne et
competénter annúnties Evangélium suum: in nómine
Patris, et Fílii, ✠ et Spíritus Sancti.

Diaconus respondet: **Amen.**

Si vero non adest diaconus, sacerdos ante altare inclinatus secreto dicit:

Munda cor meum ac lábia mea, omnípotens Deus,
ut sanctum Evangélium tuum digne váleam nuntiáre.

12.   Postea diaconus, vel sacerdos, ad ambonem pergit, ministris pro
opportunitate cum incenso et cereis eum comitantibus, et dicit:

Dóminus vobíscum.

Populus respondet: **Et cum spíritu tuo.**

Diaconus, vel sacerdos:

Léctio sancti Evangélii secúndum N.,

et interim signat librum et seipsum in fronte, ore et pectore.

Populus acclamat: **Glória tibi, Dómine.**

Deinde diaconus, vel sacerdos, librum, si incensum adhibetur, thurificat, et
Evangelium proclamat.

V. Alleluia.   **R. Alleluia.**

V. (Verse)   **R. Alleluia.**

Lenten acclamation: Any of the following lines may be used.

Praise to you, Lord Jesus Christ,
   king of endless glory!

Praise and honor to you, Lord Jesus Christ!

Glory and praise to you, Lord Jesus Christ!

Glory to you, Word of God, Lord Jesus Christ!

GOSPEL

Meanwhile, if incense is used, the priest puts some in the censer. Then the deacon who is to proclaim the gospel bows before the priest and in a low voice asks the blessing:

Father, give me your blessing.

The priest says in a low voice:

The Lord be in your heart and on your lips that you may worthily proclaim his gospel. In the name of the Father, and of the Son, ✠ and of the Holy Spirit.

The deacon answers: **Amen.**

If there is no deacon, the priest bows before the altar and says inaudibly:

Almighty God, cleanse my heart and my lips that I may worthily proclaim your gospel.

Then the deacon (or the priest) goes to the lectern. He may be accompanied by ministers with incense and candles. He sings or says:

The Lord be with you.

The people answer: **And also with you.**

The deacon (or priest) sings or says:

A reading from the holy gospel according to N.

He makes the sign of the cross on the book, and then on his forehead, lips, and breast.

The people respond: **Glory to you, Lord.**

Then, if incense is used, the deacon (or priest) incenses the book and proclaims the gospel.

13. Finito Evangelio, diaconus, vel sacerdos dicit:

Verbum Dómini,

Omnibus acclamantibus: **Laus tibi, Christe.**

Deinde librum osculatur dicens secreto:

Per evangélica dicta deleántur nostra delícta.

HOMILIA

14. Deinde fit homilia, quæ habenda est omnibus diebus dominicis et
festis de præcepto; aliis diebus commendatur.

CREDO

15. Homilia expleta, fit, quando præscribitur, professio fidei:

Credo in unum Deum,
Patrem omnipoténtem,
 factórem cæli et terræ,
visibílium ómnium et invisibílium.

Et in unum Dóminum Iesum Christum,
Fílium Dei unigénitum,
et ex Patre natum, ante ómnia sæcula.
Deum de Deo, lumen de lúmine,
 Deum verum de Deo vero,
génitum, non factum, consubstantiálem Patri:
per quem ómnia facta sunt.
Qui propter nos hómines et propter nostram salútem
descéndit de cælis.

 Ad verba quæ sequuntur, usque ad factus est, omnes se inclinant.

Et incarnátus est de Spíritu Sancto
ex María Vírgine, et homo factus est.
Crucifíxus étiam pro nobis sub Póntio Piláto;
passus et sepúltus est,

At the end of the gospel, the deacon (or priest) adds:

The gospel of the Lord.

All respond: **Praise to you, Lord Jesus Christ.**

Then he kisses the book, saying inaudibly:

May the words of the gospel wipe away our sins.

HOMILY   **sit**

A homily shall be given on all Sundays and holy days of obligation; it is recommended for other days.

PROFESSION OF FAITH   **stand**

After the homily, the profession of faith is said on Sundays and solemnities; it may also be said in solemn local celebrations.[5]

We believe in one God,
   the Father, the Almighty,
   maker of heaven and earth,
   of all that is seen and unseen.
We believe in one Lord, Jesus Christ,
   the only Son of God,
   eternally begotten of the Father,
   God from God, Light from Light,
   true God from true God,
   begotten, not made, one in Being with the Father.
   Through him all things were made.
   For us men and for our salvation
      he came down from heaven:

All bow during these two lines:

by the power of the Holy Spirit
   he was born of the Virgin Mary,
      and became man.
For our sake he was crucified under Pontius Pilate;
   he suffered, died, and was buried.

---

5. Cf. GIRM, 44.

et resurréxit tértia die,
   secúndum Scriptúras,
et ascéndit in cælum,
   sedet ad déxteram Patris.
Et íterum ventúrus est cum glória,
iudicáre vivos et mórtuos,
cuius regni non erit finis.

Et in Spíritum Sanctum,
   Dóminum et vivificántem:
qui ex Patre Filióque procédit.
Qui cum Patre et Fílio simul adorátur
   et conglorificátur:
qui locútus est per prophétas.
Et unam, sanctam, cathólicam
   et apostólicam Ecclésiam.
Confíteor unum baptísma
   in remissiónem peccatórum.
Et exspécto resurrectiónem mortuórum,
et vitam ventúri sǽculi. Amen.

ORATIO UNIVERSALIS

16.   Deinde fit oratio universalis, seu oratio fidelium.

R. **Te rogámus audi nos.**

R. **Kýrie, eléison.**

On the third day he rose again
   in fulfillment of the Scriptures;
he ascended into heaven
   and is seated at the right hand of the Father.
He will come again in glory to judge the living
      and the dead,
   and his kingdom will have no end.
We believe in the Holy Spirit,
   the Lord, the giver of life,
   who proceeds from the Father and the Son.
   With the Father and the Son he is worshiped
      and glorified.
   He has spoken through the prophets.
We believe in one holy catholic
   and apostolic Church.
We acknowledge one baptism
   for the forgiveness of sins.
We look for the resurrection of the dead,
   and the life of the world to come. Amen.

In celebrations of Masses with children, the Apostles' Creed may be said after the homily.[6] See next page.

GENERAL INTERCESSIONS

Then follow the general intercessions (prayer of the faithful). The priest presides at the prayer. With a brief introduction, he invites the people to pray; after the intentions he says the concluding prayer.

It is desirable that the intentions be announced by the deacon, cantor, or other person.[7]

---

6. *Directory for Masses With Children*, 49.
7. Cf. GIRM, 47.

PROFESSION OF FAITH (CREED) for UK, Australia, etc.

We believe in one God,
   the Father, the Almighty,
   maker of heaven and earth,
   of all that is seen and unseen.
We believe in one Lord, Jesus Christ,
   the only son of God,
   eternally begotten of the Father,
   God from God, Light from Light,
   true God from true God,
   begotten, not made,
   of one Being with the Father.
   Through him all things were made.
For us men and for our salvation
   he came down from heaven:

All bow down during these two verses:

   by the power of the Holy Spirit
     he became incarnate from the Virgin Mary,
     and was made man.
For our sake he was crucified under Pontius Pilate;
   he suffered death, and was buried.
   On the third day he rose again
     in accordance with the Scriptures;
   he ascended into heaven and is seated
     at the right hand of the Father.
He will come again in glory to judge
   the living and the dead,
   and his kingdom will have no end.

We believe in the Holy Spirit, the Lord,
   the giver of life,
   who proceeds from the Father and the Son.
   With the Father and the Son he is worshiped
   and glorified.
   He has spoken through the prophets.
   We believe in one holy catholic
   and apostolic Church.
   We acknowledge one baptism
   for the forgiveness of sins.
   We look for the resurrection of the dead,
   and the life of the world to come. Amen.

APOSTLES' CREED

For use only in countries where approved for Mass. It may be said in the U.S. in celebrations of Masses with children.

I believe in God, the Father almighty,
   creator of heaven and earth.
I believe in Jesus Christ, his only Son, our Lord.
   He was conceived by the power of
      the Holy Spirit and born of the Virgin Mary.
   He suffered under Pontius Pilate,
      was crucified, died, and was buried.
   He descended to the dead.
   On the third day he rose again.
   He ascended into heaven,
      and is seated at the right hand of the Father.
   He will come again to judge
      the living and the dead.
I believe in the Holy Spirit,
   the holy catholic Church,
   the communion of saints,
   the forgiveness of sins,
   the resurrection of the body,
   and the life everlasting. Amen.

LITURGIA EUCHARISTICA

PRÆPARATIO DONORUM

17. His absolutis, incipit cantus ad offertorium. Interim ministri corporale, purificatorium, calicem et missale in altari collocant.

18. Expedit ut fideles participationem suam oblatione manifestent, afferendo sive panem et vinum ad Eucharistiæ celebrationem, sive alia dona, quibus necessitatibus Ecclesiæ et pauperum subveniatur.

19. Sacerdos, stans ad altare, accipit patenam cum pane, eamque aliquantulum elevatam super altare tenet, secreto dicens:

Benedíctus es, Dómine, Deus univérsi,
quia de tua largitáte accépimus panem,
quem tibi offérimus,
fructum terræ et óperis mánuum hóminum:
ex quo nobis fiet panis vitæ.

Deinde deponit patenam cum pane super corporale.

Si vero cantus ad offertorium non peragitur, sacerdoti licet hæc verba elata voce proferre; in fine populus acclamare potest:

Benedíctus Deus in sǽcula.

20. Diaconus, vel sacerdos, infundit vinum et parum aquæ in calicem, dicens secreto:

Per huius aquæ et vini mystérium
eius efficiámur divinitátis consórtes,
qui humanitátis nostræ fíeri dignátus est párticeps.

21. Postea sacerdos accipit calicem, eumque aliquantulum elevatum super altare tenet, secreto dicens:

Benedíctus es, Dómine, Deus univérsi,
quia de tua largitáte accépimus vinum,
quod tibi offérimus,
fructum vitis et óperis mánuum hóminum,
ex quo nobis fiet potus spiritális.

LITURGY OF THE EUCHARIST

PREPARATION OF THE ALTAR AND THE GIFTS
sit

After the liturgy of the word, the offertory song is begun. Meanwhile the ministers place the corporal, the purificator, the chalice, and the missal on the altar.

Sufficient hosts (and wine) for the communion of the faithful are to be prepared. It is most important that the faithful should receive the body of the Lord in hosts consecrated at the same Mass and should share the cup when it is permitted. Communion is thus a clearer sign of sharing in the sacrifice which is actually taking place.[8]

It is desirable that the participation of the faithful be expressed by members of the congregation bringing up the bread and wine for the celebration of the eucharist or other gifts for the needs of the Church and the poor.

The priest, standing at the altar, takes the paten with the bread and, holding it slightly raised above the altar, says inaudibly:

Blessed are you, Lord, God of all creation.
Through your goodness we have this bread to offer,
which earth has given and human hands
    have made.
It will become for us the bread of life.

Then he places the paten with the bread on the corporal.

If no offertory song is sung, the priest may say the preceding words in an audible voice; then the people may respond:

Blessed be God for ever.

The deacon (or the priest) pours wine and a little water into the chalice, saying inaudibly:

By the mystery of this water and wine may we come
to share in the divinity of Christ, who humbled himself
to share in our humanity.

Then the priest takes the chalice, and holding it slightly raised above the altar, says inaudibly:

Blessed are you, Lord, God of all creation.
Through your goodness we have this wine to offer,
fruit of the vine and work of human hands.
It will become our spiritual drink.

---

8. GIRM, 56h.

Deinde calicem super corporale deponit.

Si vero cantus ad offertorium non peragitur, sacerdoti licet hæc verba elata voce proferre; in fine populus acclamare potest:

Benedíctus Deus in sǽcula.

22.   Postea sacerdos, inclinatus, dicit secreto:

In spíritu humilitátis et in ánimo contríto
suscipiámur a te, Dómine;
et sic fiat sacrifícium nostrum in conspéctu tuo hódie,
ut pláceat tibi, Dómine Deus.

23.   Et, pro opportunitate, incensat oblata et altare. Postea vero diaconus vel minister incensat sacerdotem et populum.

24.   Deinde sacerdos, stans ad latus altaris, lavat manus, dicens secreto:

Lava me, Dómine, ab iniquitáte mea,
et a peccáto meo munda me.

25.   Stans postea in medio altaris, versus ad populum, extendens et iungens manus, dicit:

Oráte, fratres:
ut meum ac vestrum sacrifícium
acceptábile fiat apud Deum Patrem omnipoténtem.

Populus respondet:

Suscípiat Dóminus sacrifícium de mánibus tuis
ad laudem et glóriam nóminis sui,
ad utilitátem quoque nostram
totiúsque Ecclésiæ suæ sanctæ.

ORATIO SUPER OBLATA

26.   Deinde, manibus extensis, sacerdos dicit orationem super oblata; qua finita, populus acclamat:

Amen.

Then he places the chalice on the corporal.

If no offertory song is sung, the priest may say the preceding words in an audible voice; then the people may respond:

Blessed be God for ever.

The priest bows and says inaudibly:

Lord God, we ask you to receive us and be pleased with the sacrifice we offer you with humble and contrite hearts.

He may now incense the offerings and the altar. Afterwards the deacon or a minister incenses the priest and the people.

Next the priest stands at the side of the altar and washes his hands, saying inaudibly:

Lord, wash away my iniquity; cleanse me from my sin.

Standing at the center of the altar, facing the people, he extends and then joins his hands, saying:

Pray, brethren,[9] that our sacrifice
may be acceptable to God, the almighty Father.

The people respond:

**May the Lord accept the sacrifice at your hands
for the praise and glory of his name,
for our good, and the good of all his Church.**

PRAYER OVER THE GIFTS

With hands extended, the priest sings or says the prayer over the gifts, at the end of which the people respond:

Amen.

---

9. At the discretion of the priest, other words which seem more suitable under the circumstances, such as friends, dearly beloved, my brothers and sisters, may be used.

PREX EUCHARISTICA*

27. Tunc sacerdos incipit Precem eucharisticam. Manus extendens, dicit:

Dóminus vobíscum.

Populus respondet: **Et cum spíritu tuo.**

Sacerdos, manus elevans, prosequitur:

Sursum corda.

Populus: **Habémus ad Dóminum.**

Sacerdos, manibus extensis, subdit:

Grátias agámus Dómino Deo nostro.

Populus:

Dignum et iustum est.

PRÆFATIO

Sacerdos prosequitur præfationem manibus extensis.

ACCLAMATIO

In fine autem præfationis iungit manus et, una cum populo, ipsam præfationem concludit, cantans vel clara voce dicens:

**Sanctus, Sanctus, Sanctus Dóminus Deus Sábaoth.
Pleni sunt cæli et terra glória tua.**
     Hosánna in excélsis.
Benedíctus qui venit in nómine Dómini.
     Hosánna in excélsis.

28. In omnibus Missis licet sacerdoti celebranti illas partes Precis eucharisticæ cantare, quæ in Missis concelebratis cantari possunt.

In Prece eucharistica prima, seu Canone Romano, ea quæ inter parentheses includuntur omitti possunt.

---

* For concelebrations: 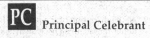 **Principal Celebrant**

EUCHARISTIC PRAYER

stand

The priest begins the eucharistic prayer. With hands extended, he sings or says:

The Lord be with you.

The people answer: **And also with you.**

He lifts up his hands and continues:

Lift up your hearts.

The people: **We lift them up to the Lord.**

With hands extended, he continues:

Let us give thanks to the Lord our God.

The people:

It is right to give him thanks and praise.

PREFACE

The priest continues the preface with hands extended.

ACCLAMATION

At the end of the preface, he joins his hands and, together with the people, concludes it by singing or saying aloud:

Holy, holy, holy Lord, God of power and might,
heaven and earth are full of your glory.
   Hosanna in the highest.
Blessed is he who comes in the name of the Lord.
   Hosanna in the highest.

In all Masses, the priest may say the eucharistic prayer in an audible voice. In sung Masses, he may sing those parts of the eucharistic prayer which may be sung in a concelebrated Mass.

In the first eucharistic prayer (the Roman canon), the words in brackets may be omitted.

 **CC** Concelebrants

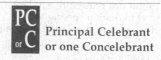 **PC** or **C** Principal Celebrant or one Concelebrant

I DE ADVENTU

DE DUOBUS ADVENTIBUS CHRISTI

29. Sequens præfatio dicitur in Missis de tempore a prima dominica
Adventus usque ad diem 16 decembris; in ceteris Missis, quæ celebrantur
eodem tempore et præfatione propria carent.

Vere dignum et iustum est, æquum et salutáre,
nos tibi semper et ubíque grátias ágere:
Dómine, sancte Pater, omnípotens ætérne Deus:
per Christum Dóminum nostrum.

Qui, primo advéntu in humilitáte carnis assúmptæ,
dispositiónis antíquæ munus implévit,
nobísque salútis perpétuæ trámitem reservávit:
ut, cum secúndo vénerit in suæ glória maiestátis,
manifésto demum múnere capiámus,
quod vigilántes nunc audémus exspectáre promíssum.

Et ídeo cum Angelis et Archángelis,
cum Thronis et Dominatiónibus,
cumque omni milítia cæléstis exércitus,
hymnum glóriæ tuæ cánimus, sine fine dicéntes:

Sanctus, Sanctus, Sanctus . . .

II DE ADVENTU

DE DUPLICI EXSPECTATIONE CHRISTI

30. Sequens præfatio dicitur in Missis de tempore a die 17 ad diem 24
decembris; in ceteris Missis, quæ celebrantur eodem tempore et præfatione
propria carent.

Vere dignum et iustum est, æquum et salutáre,
nos tibi semper et ubíque grátias ágere:
Dómine, sancte Pater, omnípotens ætérne Deus:
per Christum Dóminum nostrum.

Quem prædixérunt cunctórum præcónia prophetárum,
Virgo Mater ineffábili
    dilectióne sustínuit,
Ioánnes cécinit affutúrum
    et adésse monstrávit.

Qui suæ nativitátis mystérium
tríbuit nos præveníre gaudéntes,
ut et in oratióne pervígiles
et in suis invéniat láudibus exsultántes.

ADVENT I P1

THE TWO COMINGS OF CHRIST

This preface is said in the Masses of the season from the first Sunday of Advent to December 16 and in other Masses celebrated during this period which have no preface of their own.

Father, all-powerful and ever-living God,
we do well always and everywhere
    to give you thanks
through Jesus Christ our Lord.
When he humbled himself to come among us as a man,
he fulfilled the plan you formed long ago
and opened for us the way to salvation.
Now we watch for the day,
hoping that the salvation promised us will be ours
when Christ our Lord will come again in his glory.
And so, with all the choirs of angels
    in heaven
we proclaim your glory
and join in their unending hymn of praise:

Holy, holy, holy Lord, . . .

ADVENT II P2

WAITING FOR THE TWO COMINGS OF CHRIST

This preface is said in the Masses of the season from December 17 to December 24 inclusive and in other Masses celebrated during this period which have no preface of their own.

Father, all-powerful and ever-living God,
we do well always and everywhere
    to give you thanks
through Jesus Christ our Lord.
His future coming was proclaimed by all the prophets.
The virgin mother bore him in her womb with love
    beyond all telling.
John the Baptist was his herald
and made him known when at last he came.
In his love Christ has filled us with joy
as we prepare to celebrate his birth,
so that when he comes he may find us watching in prayer,
our hearts filled with wonder and praise.

Et ídeo cum Angelis et Archángelis,
cum Thronis et Dominatiónibus,
cumque omni milítia cæléstis exércitus,
hymnum glóriæ tuæ cánimus, sine fine dicéntes:

Sanctus, Sanctus, Sanctus . . .

I DE NATIVITATE DOMINI

DE CHRISTO LUCE

31.   Sequens præfatio dicitur in Missis de Nativitate Domini et de eiusdem
octava; infra octavam Nativitatis Domini, etiam in Missis, quæ secus
præfationem propriam haberent, exceptis iis Missis quæ præfationem
propriam de divinis mysteriis vel Personis habent; et in feriis temporis
Nativitatis.

Quando adhibetur Canon Romanus, dicitur Communicántes proprium, ut
infra.

In Missa quæ celebratur in Vigilia et in nocte Nativitatis Domini dicitur: et
noctem sacratíssimam celebrántes, qua, etc.; deinde semper dicitur: et diem
sacratíssimum celebrántes, quo, etc., usque ad octavam Nativitatis Domini
inclusive.

V̇ere dignum et iustum est, æquum et salutáre,
nos tibi semper et ubíque grátias ágere:
Dómine, sancte Pater, omnípotens ætérne Deus:
Quia per incarnáti Verbi mystérium
nova mentis nostræ óculis
    lux tuæ claritátis infúlsit:
ut, dum visibíliter Deum cognóscimus,
per hunc in invisibílium amórem rapiámur.
Et ídeo cum Angelis et Archángelis,
cum Thronis et Dominatiónibus,
cumque omni milítia cæléstis exércitus,
hymnum glóriæ tuæ cánimus, sine fine dicéntes:

Sanctus, Sanctus, Sanctus . . .

II DE NATIVITATE DOMINI

DE RESTAURATIONE UNIVERSA IN INCARNATIONE

32.   Sequens præfatio dicitur in Missis de Nativitate Domini et de eiusdem
octava; infra octavam Nativitatis Domini, etiam in Missis, quæ secus
præfationem propriam haberent, exceptis iis Missis quæ præfationem de
divinis mysteriis vel Personis habent; et inferiis temporis Nativitatis.

Quando adhibetur Canon Romanus, dicitur Communicántes proprium, ut
infra.

And so, with all the choirs of angels
   in heaven
we proclaim your glory
and join in their unending hymn of praise:

Holy, holy, holy Lord, . . .

CHRISTMAS I   P3

CHRIST THE LIGHT

This preface is said in Masses of Christmas and its octave; in Masses within
the Christmas octave even if they have their own preface, with the exception of Masses with a proper preface of the divine mysteries or Persons; and
on weekdays of the Christmas season.

When Eucharistic Prayer I is used, the special form of In union with the
whole Church is said.

Vigil Mass and Mass at midnight: we celebrate that night. . . . In other
Masses up to the octave of Christmas inclusive: we celebrate that day. . . .

Father, all-powerful and ever-living God,
we do well always and everywhere to give you thanks
through Jesus Christ our Lord.
In the wonder of the incarnation
your eternal Word has brought to the eyes of faith
a new and radiant vision of your glory.
In him we see our God made visible
and so are caught up in love of the God we cannot see.
And so, with all the choirs
   of angels in heaven
we proclaim your glory
and join in their unending hymn of praise:

Holy, holy, holy Lord, . . .

CHRISTMAS II   P4

CHRIST RESTORES UNITY TO ALL CREATION

This preface is said in Masses of Christmas and its octave; in Masses within
the Christmas octave even if they have their own preface, with the exception of Masses with a proper preface of the divine mysteries or Persons; and
on weekdays of the Christmas season.
When Eucharistic Prayer I is used, the special form of In union with the
whole Church is said.

In Missa quæ celebratur in Vigilia et in nocte Nativitatis Domini dicitur: et
noctem sacratíssimam celebrántes, qua, etc.; deinde semper dicitur: et diem
sacratíssimum celebránte, quo, etc., usque ad octavam Nativitatis Domini
inclusive.

Vere dignum et iustum est, æquum et salutáre,
nos tibi semper et ubíque grátias ágere:
Dómine, sancte Pater, omnípotens ætérne Deus:
per Christum Dóminum nostrum.
Qui, in huius venerándi festivitáte mystérii,
invisíbilis in suis,
    visíbilis in nostris appáruit,
et ante témpora génitus esse
cœpit in témpore;
ut, in se érigens
    cuncta deiécta,
in íntegrum restitúeret univérsa,
et hóminem pérditum
    ad cæléstia regna revocáret.
Unde et nos, cum ómnibus Angelis te laudámus,
iucúnda celebratióne clamántes:

Sanctus, Sanctus, Sanctus . . .

III DE NATIVITATE DOMINI

DE COMMERCIO IN INCARNATIONE VERBI

33. Sequens præfatio dicitur in Missis de Nativitate Domini et de eiusdem
octava; infra octavam Nativitatis Domini, etiam in Missis, quæ secus
præfationem propriam haberent, exceptis iis Missis quæ præfationem
propriam de divinis mysteriis vel Personis habent; et in feriis temporis
Nativitatis.
Quando adhibetur Canon Romanus, dicitur Communicántes proprium, ut
infra.
In Missa quæ celebratur in Vigilia et in nocte Nativitatis Domini dicitur: et
noctem sacratíssimam celebrántes, qua, etc.; deinde semper dicitur: et diem
sacratíssimum celebránte, quo, etc. usque ad octavam Nativitatis Domini
inclusive.

Vere dignum et iustum est, æquum et salutáre,
nos tibi semper et ubíque grátias ágere:
Dómine, sancte Pater, omnípotens ætérne Deus:
per Christum Dóminum nostrum.
Per quem hódie commércium
    nostræ reparatiónis effúlsit,
quia, dum nostra fragílitas

Vigil Mass and Mass at midnight: we celebrate that night. . . . In other
Masses up to the octave of Christmas inclusive: we celebrate that day. . . .

Father, all-powerful and ever-living God,
we do well always and everywhere
    to give you thanks
through Jesus Christ our Lord.
Today you fill our hearts with joy
as we recognize in Christ the revelation of your love.
No eye can see his glory as our God,
yet now he is seen as one like us.
Christ is your Son before all ages,
yet now he is born in time.
He has come to lift up all things to himself,
to restore unity to creation,
and to lead mankind from exile
    into your heavenly kingdom.
With all the angels of heaven
we sing our joyful hymn of praise:

Holy, holy, holy Lord, . . .

CHRISTMAS III   P5

DIVINE AND HUMAN EXCHANGE
IN THE INCARNATION OF THE WORD

This preface is said in Masses of Christmas and its octave; in Masses within
the Christmas octave even if they have their own preface, with the exception of Masses with a proper preface of the divine mysteries or Persons; and
on weekdays of the Christmas season.

When Eucharistic Prayer I is used, the special form of **In union with the
whole Church** is said.
Vigil Mass and Mass at midnight: we celebrate that night. . . . In other
Masses up to the octave of Christmas inclusive: we celebrate that day. . . .

Father, all-powerful and ever-living God,
we do well always and everywhere
    to give you thanks
through Jesus Christ our Lord.
Today in him a new light has dawned upon the world:
God has become one with man,
and man has become one again with God.

a tuo Verbo suscípitur,
humána mortálitas non solum
    in perpétuum transit honórem,
sed nos quoque, mirándo consórtio,
    reddit ætérnos.
Et ídeo, choris angélicis sociáti,
te laudámus
    in gáudio confiténtes:

Sanctus, Sanctus, Sanctus . . .

DE EPIPHANIA DOMINI

DE CHRISTO LUMINE GENTIUM

34. Sequens præfatio dicitur in Missis de sollemnitate Epiphaniæ. Dici potest, una cum præfationibus de Nativitate, etiam diebus post Epiphaniam usque ad sabbatum, quod præcedit festum Baptismi Domini. In sollemnitate Epiphaniæ, quando adhibetur Canon Romanus dicitur Communicántes proprium, ut infra.

Vere dignum et iustum est, æquum et salutáre,
nos tibi semper et ubíque grátias ágere:
Dómine, sancte Pater, omnípotens ætérne Deus:
Quia ipsum in Christo salútis nostræ mystérium
hódie ad lumen géntium revelásti,
et, cum in substántia
    nostræ mortalitátis appáruit,
nova nos immortalitátis eius glória reparásti.
Et ídeo cum Angelis et Archángelis,
cum Thronis et Dominatiónibus,
cumque omni milítia cæléstis exércitus,
hymnum glóriæ tuæ cánimus, sine fine dicéntes:

Sanctus, Sanctus, Sanctus . . .

DE BAPTISMATE DOMINI

Vere dignum et iustum est, æquum et salutáre,
nos tibi semper et ubíque grátias ágere:
Dómine, sancte Pater, omnípotens ætérne Deus:
Qui miris signásti mystériis novum
    in Iordáne lavácrum,
ut, per vocem de cælo delápsam,
habitáre Verbum tuum
    inter hómines crederétur;

Your eternal Word has taken upon himself
    our human weakness,
giving our mortal nature immortal value.
So marvelous is this oneness between God and man
that in Christ man restores to man
    the gift of everlasting life.
In our joy we sing to your glory
with all the choirs of angels:

Holy, holy, holy Lord, ...

EPIPHANY   P6

CHRIST THE LIGHT OF THE NATIONS

This preface is said in Masses on the Epiphany. It may be said, as may the
Christmas prefaces, on the days between the Epiphany and the Baptism of
the Lord.
When Eucharistic Prayer I is used, the special form of In union with the
whole Church is said.

Father, all-powerful and ever-living God,
we do well always and everywhere
    to give you thanks.
Today you revealed in Christ
    your eternal plan of salvation
and showed him as the light of all peoples.
Now that his glory has shone among us
you have renewed humanity in his immortal image.
Now, with angels and archangels,
and the whole company of heaven,
we sing the unending hymn
    of your praise:

Holy, holy, holy Lord, ...

BAPTISM OF THE LORD   P7

CONSECRATION AND MISSION OF CHRIST

Father, all-powerful and ever-living God,
we do well always and everywhere
    to give you thanks.
You celebrated your new gift of baptism
by signs and wonders at the Jordan.
Your voice was heard from heaven
to awaken faith in the presence among us
of the Word made man.

et, per Spíritum in colúmbæ spécie
    descendéntem,
Christus Servus tuus óleo perúngi lætítiæ
ac mitti ad evangelizándum paupéribus
    noscerétur.
Et ídeo cum cælórum virtútibus
in terris te iúgiter celebrámus,
maiestáti tuæ sine fine clamántes:

Sanctus, Sanctus, Sanctus . . .

I DE QUADRAGESIMA

DE SPIRITALI SIGNIFICATIONE QUADRAGESIMÆ

35. Sequens præfatio dicitur tempore Quadragesimæ, præsertim vero in dominicis, quando non est dicenda alia præfatio magis propria.

V ere dignum et iustum est, æquum et salutáre,
nos tibi semper et ubíque grátias ágere:
Dómine, sancte Pater, omnípotens ætérne Deus:
per Christum Dóminum nostrum.
Quia fidélibus tuis dignánter concédis
quotánnis paschália sacraménta
in gáudio purificátis méntibus exspectáre:
ut, pietátis offícia et ópera caritátis
    propénsius exsequéntes,
frequentatióne mysteriórum, quibus renáti sunt,
ad grátiæ filiórum plenitúdinem perducántur.

Et ídeo cum Angelis et Archángelis,
cum Thronis et Dominatiónibus,
cumque omni milítia cæléstis exércitus,
hymnum glóriæ tuæ cánimus, sine fine dicéntes:

Sanctus, Sanctus, Sanctus . . .

II DE QUADRAGESIMA

DE SPIRITALI PÆNITENTIA

36. Sequens præfatio dicitur tempore Quadragesimæ, præsertim vero in dominicis, quando non est dicenda alia præfatio magis propria.

V ere dignum et iustum est, æquum et salutáre,
nos tibi semper et ubíque grátias ágere:
Dómine, sancte Pater, omnípotens ætérne Deus:

Your Spirit was seen as a dove,
revealing Jesus as your servant,
and anointing him with joy as the Christ,
sent to bring to the poor
the good news of salvation.

In our unending joy we echo on earth
the song of the angels in heaven
as they praise your glory for ever:

Holy, holy, holy Lord, . . .

LENT I   P8

THE SPIRITUAL MEANING OF LENT

This preface is said in the Masses of Lent, especially on Sundays which
have no preface of their own.

Father, all-powerful and ever-living God,
we do well always and everywhere
    to give you thanks
through Jesus Christ our Lord.
Each year you give us this joyful season
when we prepare to celebrate the paschal mystery
with mind and heart renewed.
You give us a spirit of loving reverence for you,
    our Father,
and of willing service to our neighbor.
As we recall the great events that gave us new life in Christ,
you bring the image of your Son to perfection within us.
Now, with angels and archangels,
and the whole company of heaven,
we sing the unending hymn of your praise:

Holy, holy, holy Lord, . . .

LENT II   P9

THE SPIRIT OF PENANCE

This preface is said in the Masses of Lent, especially on Sundays which
have no preface of their own.

Father, all-powerful and ever-living God,
we do well always and everywhere
    to give you thanks.

Qui fíliis tuis ad reparándam méntium puritátem,
tempus præcípuum
    salúbriter statuísti,
quo, mente ab inordinátis afféctibus
    expedíta,
sic incúmberent transitúris
ut rebus pótius perpétuis inhærérent.
Et ídeo, cum Sanctis et Angelis univérsis,
te collaudámus, sine fine dicéntes:

Sanctus, Sanctus, Sanctus . . .

III DE QUADRAGESIMA

DE FRUCTIBUS ABSTINENTIÆ

37. Sequens præfatio dicitur de feriis Quadragesimæ et in diebus ieiunii.

Vere dignum et iustum est, æquum et salutáre,
nos tibi semper et ubíque grátias ágere:
Dómine, sancte Pater, omnípotens ætérne Deus:
Qui nos per abstinéntiam tibi grátias reférre voluísti,
ut ipsa et nos peccatóres ab insoléntia mitigáret,
et, egéntium profíciens aliménto,
imitatóres tuæ benignitátis effíceret.
Et ídeo, cum innúmeris Angelis ,
una te magnificámus laudis voce, dicéntes:

Sanctus, Sanctus, Sanctus . . .

IV DE QUADRAGESIMA

DE FRUCTIBUS IEIUNII

38. Sequens præfatio dicitur de feriis Quadragesimæ et in diebus ieiunii.

Vere dignum et iustum est, æquum et salutáre,
nos tibi semper et ubíque grátias ágere:
Dómine, sancte Pater, omnípotens ætérne Deus:
Qui corporáli ieiúnio vítia cómprimis,
    mentem élevas,
virtútem largíris et præmia:
per Christum Dóminum nostrum.
Per quem maiestátem tuam laudant Angeli
adórant Dominatiónes, tremunt Potestátes.
Caeli cælorúmque Virtútes, ac beáta Séraphim,
sócia exsultatióne concélebrant.

This great season of grace is your gift to your family
to renew us in spirit.
You give us strength to purify our hearts,
to control our desires,
and so to serve you in freedom.
You teach us how to live in this passing world
with our heart set on the world that will never end.
Now, with all the saints and angels,
we praise you for ever:

Holy, holy, holy Lord, . . .

LENT III   P10

THE FRUITS OF SELF-DENIAL

This preface is said in the Masses of the weekdays of Lent and on fast days.

Father, all-powerful and ever-living God,
we do well always and everywhere
    to give you thanks.
You ask us to express our thanks by self-denial.
We are to master our sinfulness and conquer our pride.
We are to show to those in need
    your goodness to ourselves.
Now, with all the saints and angels,
we praise you for ever:

Holy, holy, holy Lord, . . .

LENT IV   P11

THE REWARD OF FASTING

This preface is said in the Masses of the weekdays of Lent and on fast days.

Father, all-powerful and ever-living God,
we do well always and everywhere
    to give you thanks.
Through our observance of Lent
you correct our faults and raise our minds to you,
you help us grow in holiness,
and offer us the reward of everlasting life
through Jesus Christ our Lord.
Through him the angels and
    all the choirs of heaven
worship in awe before your presence.

Cum quibus et nostras voces ut admítti iúbeas,
    deprecámur,
súpplici confessióne dicéntes:

Sanctus, Sanctus, Sanctus . . .

DE DOMINICA I IN QUADRAGESIMA

DE TENTATIONE DOMINI

Vere dignum et iustum est, æquum et salutáre,
nos tibi semper et ubíque grátias ágere:
Dómine, sancte Pater, omnípotens ætérne Deus:
per Christum Dóminum nostrum.
Qui quadragínta diébus,
        terrénis ábstines aliméntis,
formam huius observántiæ ieiúnio dedicávit,
et, omnes evértens antíqui serpéntis insídias,
ferméntum malítiæ nos dócuit superáre,
ut, paschále mystérium
        dignis méntibus celebrántes,
ad pascha demum perpétuum transeámus.
Et ídeo cum Angelórum atque Sanctórum turba
hymnum laudis tibi cánimus, sine fine dicéntes:

Sanctus, Sanctus, Sanctus . . .

DE DOMINICA II IN QUADRAGESIMA

DE TRANSFIGURATIONE DOMINI

Vere dignum et iustum est, æquum et salutáre,
nos tibi semper et ubíque grátias ágere:
Dómine, sancte Pater, omnípotens ætérne Deus:
per Christum Dóminum nostrum.
Qui, própria morte prænuntiáta discípulis,
in monte sancto suam eis
        apéruit claritátem,
ut per passiónem,
        étiam lege prophetísque testántibus,
ad glóriam resurrectiónis perveníri constáret.
Et ídeo cum cælórum virtútibus
in terris te iúgiter celebrámus,
maiestáti tuæ sine fine clamántes:

Sanctus, Sanctus, Sanctus . . .

May our voices be one with theirs
as they sing with joy the hymn
    of your glory:

Holy, holy, holy Lord, . . .

FIRST SUNDAY OF LENT   P12

THE TEMPTATION OF THE LORD

Father, all-powerful and ever-living God,
we do well always and everywhere
    to give you thanks
through Jesus Christ our Lord.
His fast of forty days
makes this a holy season of self-denial.
By rejecting the devil's temptations
he has taught us
to rid ourselves of the hidden corruption of evil,
and so to share his paschal meal in purity of heart,
until we come to its fulfillment
in the promised land of heaven.
Now we join the angels and the saints
as they sing their unending hymn of praise:

Holy, holy, holy Lord, . . .

SECOND SUNDAY OF LENT   P13

TRANSFIGURATION

Father, all-powerful and ever-living God,
we do well always and everywhere
    to give you thanks
through Jesus Christ our Lord.
On your holy mountain he revealed himself in glory
in the presence of his disciples.
He had already prepared them for his approaching death.
He wanted to teach them through the Law and the Prophets
that the promised Christ had first to suffer
and so come to the glory of his resurrection.
In our unending joy we echo on earth
the song of the angels in heaven
as they praise your glory for ever:

Holy, holy, holy Lord, . . .

DE DOMINICA III IN QUADRAGESIMA
DE SAMARITANA
Quando legitur Evangelium de Samaritana, dicitur sequens præfatio:

Vere dignum et iustum est, æquum et salutáre,
nos tibi semper et ubíque grátias ágere:
Dómine, sancte Pater, omnípotens ætérne Deus:
per Christum Dóminum nostrum.
Qui, dum aquæ sibi pétiit potum a Samaritána præbéri,
iam in ea fídei donum ipse creáverat,
et ita eius fidem sitíre dignátus est,
ut ignem in illa divíni amóris accénderet.
Unde et nos tibi grátias ágimus,
et tuas virtútes cum Angelis prædicámus,
    dicéntes:

Sanctus, Sanctus, Sanctus . . .

DE DOMINICA IV IN QUADRAGESIMA
DE CÆCO NATO.
Quando legitur Evangelium de cæco nato dicitur sequens præfatio:

Vere dignum et iustum est, æquum et salutáre,
nos tibi semper et ubíque grátias ágere:
Dómine, sancte Pater, omnípotens ætérne Deus:
per Christum Dóminum nostrum.
Qui genus humánum,
    in ténebris ámbulans,
ad fídei claritátem per mystérium incarnatiónis addúxit,
et, qui servi peccáti véteris nascebántur,
per lavácrum regeneratiónis in fílios adoptiónis assúmpsit.
Propter quod cæléstia tibi atque terréstria
cánticum novum cóncinunt adorándo,
et nos, cum omni exércitu Angelórum,
proclamámus, sine fine dicéntes:

Sanctus, Sanctus, Sanctus . . .

DE DOMINICA V IN QUADRAGESIMA
DE LAZARO
Quando legitur Evangelium de Lazaro, dicitur sequens præfatio:

THIRD SUNDAY OF LENT   P14
THE WOMAN OF SAMARIA

This preface is said when the gospel about the Samaritan woman is read;
otherwise one of the prefaces of Lent is said.

Father, all-powerful and ever-living God,
we do well always and everywhere
to give you thanks
through Jesus Christ our Lord.
When he asked the woman of Samaria for water to drink,
Christ had already prepared for her the gift of faith.
In his thirst to receive her faith
he awakened in her heart the fire of your love.
With thankful praise,
in company with the angels,
we glorify the wonders of your power:

Holy, holy, holy Lord, . . .

FOURTH SUNDAY OF LENT   P15
THE MAN BORN BLIND

This preface is said when the gospel about the man born blind is read; otherwise one of the prefaces of Lent is said.

Father, all-powerful and ever-living God,
we do well always and everywhere
    to give you thanks
through Jesus Christ our Lord.
He came among us as a man,
to lead mankind from darkness
into the light of faith.
Through Adam's fall we were born as slaves of sin,
but now through baptism in Christ
we are reborn as your adopted children.
Earth unites with heaven
to sing the new song of creation,
as we adore and praise you for ever:

Holy, holy, holy Lord, . . .

FIFTH SUNDAY OF LENT   P16
LAZARUS

This preface is said when the gospel about Lazarus is read; otherwise, one
of the prefaces of Lent is said.

Vere dignum et iustum est, æquum et salutáre,
nos tibi semper et ubíque grátias ágere:
Dómine, sancte Pater, omnípotens ætérne Deus:
per Christum Dóminum nostrum.
Ipse enim verus homo Lázarum flevit amícum,
et Deus ætérnus e túmulo suscitávit,
qui, humáni géneris miserátus,
ad novam vitam sacris mystériis nos addúcit.
Per quem maiestátem tuam adórat exércitus Angelórum,
ante conspéctum tuum in æternitáte lætántium.
Cum quibus et nostras voces ut admítti iúbeas, deprecámur,
sócia exsultatióne dicéntes:

Sanctus, Sanctus, Sanctus . . .

I DE PASSIONE DOMINI

DE VIRUTE CRUCIS

39. Sequens præfatio dicitur infra hebdomadam quintam Quadragesimæ,
et in Missis de mysteriis Crucis et Passionis Domini.

Vere dignum et iustum est, æquum et salutáre,
nos tibi semper et ubíque grátias ágere:
Domine, sancte Pater, omnípotens ætérne Deus:
Quia per Fílii tui salutíferam passiónem
totus mundus sensum confiténdæ
    tuæ maiestátis accépit,
dum ineffábili crucis poténtia
iudícium mundi et potéstas émicat Crucifíxi.
Unde et nos, Dómine, cum Angelis et Sanctis univérsis,
tibi confitémur, in exsultatióne dicéntes:

Sanctus, Sanctus, Sanctus . . .

II DE PASSIONE DOMINI

DE VICTORIA PASSIONIS

40. Sequens præfatio dicitur in feriis II, III et IV Hebdomadæ sanctæ.

Vere dignum et iustum est, æquum et salutáre,
nos tibi semper et ubíque grátias ágere:
Domine, sancte Pater, omnípotens ætérne Deus:
per Christum Dóminum nostrum.
Cuius salutíferæ passiónis
    et gloriósæ resurrectiónis dies

Father, all-powerful and ever-living God,
we do well always and everywhere to give you thanks
through Jesus Christ our Lord.
As a man like us, Jesus wept for Lazarus his friend.
As the eternal God, he raised Lazarus from the dead.
In his love for us all, Christ gives us the sacraments
to lift us up to everlasting life.
Through him the angels of heaven
offer their prayer of adoration
as they rejoice in your presence for ever.
May our voices be one with theirs
in their triumphant hymn of praise:

Holy, holy, holy Lord, . . .

PASSION OF THE LORD I   P17

THE POWER OF THE CROSS

This preface is said during the fifth week of Lent and in Masses of the mysteries of the cross and the passion of the Lord.

Father, all-powerful and ever-living God,
we do well always and everywhere
    to give you thanks.
The suffering and death of your Son
brought life to the whole world,
moving our hearts to praise your glory.
The power of the cross reveals your judgment on this world
and the kingship of Christ crucified.
We praise you, Lord,
with all the angels and saints in their song of joy:

Holy, holy, holy Lord, . . .

PASSION OF THE LORD II   P18

THE VICTORY OF THE PASSION

This preface is said on Monday, Tuesday, and Wednesday of Holy Week.

Father, all-powerful and ever-living God,
we do well always and everywhere
    to give you thanks
through Jesus Christ our Lord.
The days of his life-giving death
    and glorious resurrection are approaching.

appropinquáre noscúntur,
quibus et de antíqui hostis supérbia triumphátur,
et nostræ redemptiónis recólitur sacraméntum.
Per quem maiestátem tuam
    adórat exércitus Angelórum,
ante conspéctum tuum in æternitáte lætántium.
Cum quibus et nostras voces ut admítti iúbeas,
    deprecámur, sócia exsultatióne dicéntes:

Sanctus, Sanctus, Sanctus . . .

DE DOMINICA IN PALMIS DE PASSIONE DOMINI

DE PASSIONE DOMINI

Vere dignum et iustum est, æquum et salutáre,
nos tibi semper et ubíque grátias ágere:
Dómine, sancte Pater, omnípotens ætérne Deus:
per Christum Dóminum nostrum.
Qui pati pro ímpiis dignátus est ínnocens,
et pro scelerátis indébite condemnári.
Cuius mors delícta nostra detérsit,
et iustificatiónem nobis resurréctio comparávit.
Unde et nos cum ómnibus Angelis te laudámus,
iucúnda celebratióne clamántes:

Sanctus, Sanctus, Sanctus . . .

DE MISSA CHRISMATIS

DE SACERDOTIO CHRISTI ET DE MINISTERIO SACERDOTUM

Vere dignum et iustum est, æquum et salutáre,
nos tibi semper et ubíque grátias ágere:
Dómine, sancte Pater, omnípotens ætérne Deus:
Qui Unigénitum tuum Sancti Spíritus unctióne
novi et ætérni testaménti constituísti Pontíficem,
et ineffábili dignátus es dispositióne sancíre,
ut únicum eius sacerdótium in Ecclésia servarétur.
Ipse enim non solum regáli sacerdótio
pópulum acquisitiónis exórnat,
sed étiam fratérna hómines éligit bonitáte,
ut sacri sui ministérii fiant mánuum
    impositióne partícipes.

This is the hour when he triumphed over Satan's pride,
the time when we celebrate
    the great event of our redemption.
Through Christ
the angels of heaven offer their prayer of adoration
as they rejoice in your presence for ever.
May our voices be one with theirs
in their triumphant hymn of praise:

Holy, holy, holy Lord, . . .

PASSION SUNDAY
(PALM SUNDAY)   P19

THE REDEEMING WORK OF CHRIST

Father, all-powerful and ever-living God,
we do well always and everywhere
to give you thanks
through Jesus Christ our Lord.
Though he was sinless, he suffered willingly for sinners,
Though innocent, he accepted death to save the guilty.
By his dying he has destroyed our sins.
By his rising he has raised us up to holiness of life.
We praise you, Lord, with all the angels
in their song of joy:

Holy, holy, holy Lord, . . .

PRIESTHOOD (CHRISM MASS)   P20

THE PRIESTHOOD OF CHRIST AND THE MINISTRY OF PRIESTS

This preface is said in the Chrism Mass on Holy Thursday.

Father, all-powerful and ever-living God,
we do well always and everywhere
    to give you thanks.
By your Holy Spirit you anointed your only Son
High Priest of the new and eternal covenant.
With wisdom and love you have planned
that this one priesthood should continue in the Church.
Christ gives the dignity of a royal priesthood
to the people he has made his own.
From these, with a brother's love,
he chooses men to share his sacred ministry
by the laying on of hands.

Qui sacrifícium rénovent, eius nómine,
　　redemptiónis humánæ,
tuis apparántes fíliis paschále convívium,
et plebem tuam sanctam caritáte prævéniant,
verbo nútriant,
　　refíciant sacraméntis.

Qui, vitam pro te fratrúmque
　　salúte tradéntes,
ad ipsíus Christi nitántur imáginem conformári,
et constántes tibi fidem
　　amorémque testéntur.

Unde et nos, Dómine, cum Angelis et Sanctis univérsis
tibi confitémur, in exsultatióne dicéntes:

Sanctus, Sanctus, Sanctus . . .

PASCHALIS I

DE MYSTERIO PASCHALI

41.　Sequens præfatio dicitur tempore paschali.

In Missa Vigiliæ paschalis dicitur: in hac potíssimum nocte; a die Paschæ
et per totam octavam: in hac potíssimum die; alias: in hoc potíssimum.

Quando adhibetur Canon Romanus, dicuntur Communicántes et Hanc
ígitur propria, ut infra.

In Missa Vigiliæ paschalis dicitur: et noctem sacratíssimam celebrántes.

Vere dignum et iustum est, æquum et salutáre:
Te quidem, Dómine, omni témpore confitéri,
sed in hac potíssimum nocte (die)
　　gloriósius prædicáre,
(sed in hoc potíssimum gloriósius prædicáre,)
cum Pascha nostrum immolátus est Christus.

Ipse enim verus est Agnus
qui ábstulit peccáta mundi.
Qui mortem nostram moriéndo destrúxit,
et vitam resurgéndo reparávit.

Quaprópter, profúsis paschálibus gáudiis,
totus in orbe terrárum mundus exsúltat.
Sed et supérnæ virtútes atque angélicæ potestátes
hymnum glóriæ tuæ cóncinunt, sine fine dicéntes:

Sanctus, Sanctus, Sanctus . . .

He appoints them to renew in his name
the sacrifice of our redemption
as they set before your family his paschal meal.
He calls them to lead your holy people in love,
nourish them by your word,
and strengthen them through the sacraments.
Father, they are to give their lives in your service
and for the salvation of your people
as they strive to grow in the likeness of Christ
and honor you by their courageous witness
    of faith and love.
We praise you, Lord, with all the angels and saints
in their song of joy:

Holy, holy, holy Lord, . . .

EASTER I   P21

THE PASCHAL MYSTERY

This preface is said during the Easter season.

In the Mass of the Easter Vigil: on this Easter night; on Easter Sunday and
during the octave: on this Easter day; on other days of the Easter season: in
this Easter season.

When Eucharistic Prayer I is used, the special forms of In union with the
whole Church and Father, accept this offering are said.

Father, all-powerful and ever-living God,
we do well always and everywhere to give you thanks
through Jesus Christ our Lord.
We praise you with greater joy than ever
on this Easter night (day) (in this Easter season),
when Christ became our paschal sacrifice.
He is the true Lamb who took away
the sins of the world.
By dying he destroyed our death;
by rising he restored our life.
And so, with all the choirs of angels in heaven
we proclaim your glory
and join in their unending
    hymn of praise:

Holy, holy, holy Lord, . . .

PASCHALIS II
DE VITA NOVA IN CHRISTO

42. Sequens præfatio dicitur tempore paschali.

Vere dignum et iustum est, æquum et salutáre:
Te quidem, Dómine, omni témpore confitéri,
sed in hoc potíssimum gloriósius prædicáre,
cum Pascha nostrum immolátus est Christus.
Per quem in ætérnam vitam fílii lucis oriúntur,
et fidélibus regni cæléstis átria reserántur.
Quia mors nostra est eius morte redémpta,
et in eius resurrectióne vita ómnium resurréxit.
Quaprópter, profúsis paschálibus gáudiis,
totus in orbe terrárum mundus exsúltat.
Sed et supérnæ virtútes
    atque angélicæ potestátes
hymnum glóriæ tuæ cóncinunt,
sine fine dicéntes:

Sanctus, Sanctus, Sanctus . . .

PASCHALIS III
DE CHRISTO VIVENTE ET SEMPER INTERPELLANTE PRO NOBIS

43. Sequens præfatio dicitur tempore paschali.

Vere dignum et iustum est, æquum et salutáre:
Te quidem, Dómine, omni témpore confitéri,
sed in hoc potíssimum gloriósius prædicáre,
cum Pascha nostrum immolátus est Christus.
Qui se pro nobis offérre non désinit,
nosque apud te perénni advocatióne deféndit;
qui immolátus iam non móritur,
sed semper vivit occísus.
Quaprópter, profúsis paschálibus gáudiis,
totus in orbe terrárum mundus exsúltat.
Sed et supérnæ virtútes atque angélicæ potestátes
hymnum glóriæ tuæ cóncinunt, sine fine dicéntes:

Sanctus, Sanctus, Sanctus . . .

PASCHALIS IV
DE RESTAURATIONE UNIVERSI PER MYSTERIUM PASCHALE

44. Sequens præfatio dicitur tempore paschali.

EASTER II   P22
NEW LIFE IN CHRIST

This preface is said during the Easter season.

Father, all-powerful and ever-living God,
we do well always and everywhere to give you thanks
through Jesus Christ our Lord.
We praise you with greater joy than ever
    in this Easter season,
when Christ became our paschal sacrifice.
He has made us children of the light,
rising to new and everlasting life.
He has opened the gates of heaven
to receive his faithful people.
His death is our ransom from death;
his resurrection is our rising to life.
The joy of the resurrection renews the whole world,
while the choirs of heaven sing for ever to your glory:

Holy, holy, holy Lord, . . .

EASTER III   P23
CHRIST LIVES AND INTERCEDES FOR US FOR EVER

This preface is said during the Easter season.

Father, all-powerful and ever-living God,
we do well always and everywhere to give you thanks
through Jesus Christ our Lord.
We praise you with greater joy than ever
    in this Easter season,
when Christ became our paschal sacrifice.
He is still our priest,
our advocate who always pleads our cause.
Christ is the victim who dies no more,
the Lamb, once slain, who lives for ever.
The joy of the resurrection renews the whole world,
while the choirs of heaven sing for ever to your glory:

Holy, holy, holy Lord, . . .

EASTER IV   P24
THE RESTORATION OF THE UNIVERSE THROUGH
THE PASCHAL MYSTERY

This preface is said during the Easter season.

Vere dignum et iustum est, æquum et salutáre:
Te quidem, Dómine, omni témpore confitéri,
sed in hoc potíssimum gloriósius prædicáre,
cum Pascha nostrum immolátus est Christus.

Quia, vetustáte destrúcta,
   renovántur univérsa deiécta,
et vitæ nobis in Christo reparátur intégritas.

Quaprópter, profúsis paschálibus gáudiis,
totus in orbe terrárum mundus exsúltat.

Sed et supérnæ virtútes atque angélicæ potestátes
hymnum glóriæ tuæ cóncinunt, sine fine dicéntes:

Sanctus, Sanctus, Sanctus . . .

PASCHALIS V

DE CHRISTO SACERDOTE ET VICTIMA

45.   Sequens præfatio dicitur tempore paschali.

Vere dignum et iustum est, æquum et salutáre:
Te quidem, Dómine, omni témpore confitéri,
sed in hoc potíssimum gloriósius prædicáre,
cum Pascha nostrum immolátus est Christus.

Qui, oblatióne córporis sui,
antíqua sacrifícia in crucis veritáte perfécit,
et, seípsum tibi pro nostra salúte comméndans,
idem sacérdos, altáre et agnus exhíbuit.

Quaprópter, profúsis paschálibus gáudiis,
totus in orbe terrárum mundus exsúltat.

Sed et supérnæ virtútes atque angélicæ potestátes
hymnum glóriæ tuæ cóncinunt,
sine fine dicéntes:

Sanctus, Sanctus, Sanctus . . .

I DE ASCENSIONE DOMINI

DE MYSTERIO ASCENSIONIS

46.   Sequens præfatio dicitur in die Ascensionis Domini; dici potest diebus post Ascensionem usque ad sabbatum ante Pentecosten, in Missis, quæ præfatione propria carent.

In die Ascensionis, quando adhibetur Canon Romanus, dicitur Communicántes proprium, ut infra.

Vere dignum et iustum est, æquum et salutáre,
nos tibi semper et ubíque grátias ágere:
Dómine, sancte Pater, omnípotens ætérne Deus:

Father, all-powerful and ever-living God,
we do well always and everywhere to give you thanks
through Jesus Christ our Lord.
We praise you with greater joy than ever in this Easter season,
when Christ became our paschal sacrifice.
In him a new age has dawned,
the long reign of sin is ended,
a broken world has been renewed,
and man is once again made whole.
The joy of the resurrection renews the whole world,
while the choirs of heaven sing for ever to your glory:

Holy, holy, holy Lord, . . .

EASTER V   P25

CHRIST IS PRIEST AND VICTIM

This preface is said during the Easter season.

Father, all-powerful and ever-living God,
we do well always and everywhere
to give you thanks
through Jesus Christ our Lord.
We praise you with greater joy than ever in this Easter season,
when Christ became our paschal sacrifice.
As he offered his body on the cross,
his perfect sacrifice fulfilled all others.
As he gave himself into your hands for our salvation,
he showed himself to be the priest,
the altar, and the lamb of sacrifice.
The joy of the resurrection renews the whole world,
while the choirs of heaven sing for ever to your glory:

Holy, holy, holy Lord, . . .

ASCENSION I   P26

THE MYSTERY OF THE ASCENSION

This preface is said on the Ascension, and it may also be said (or an Easter
preface) in all Masses which have no preface of their own, from the Ascension to the Saturday before Pentecost inclusive.

When Eucharistic Prayer I is used, the special form of In union with the
whole Church is said.

Father, all-powerful and ever-living God,
we do well always and everywhere
    to give you thanks.

Quia Dóminus Iesus, Rex glóriæ
peccáti triumphátor et mortis,
mirántibus Angelis, ascéndit (hódie) summa cælórum,
Mediátor Dei et hóminum,
　　Iudex mundi Dominúsque virtútum;
non ut a nostra humilitáte descéderet,
sed ut illuc confiderémus, sua membra, nos súbsequi
quo ipse, caput nostrum principiúmque, præcéssit.

Quaprópter, profúsis paschálibus gáudiis,
totus in orbe terrárum mundus exsúltat.
Sed et supérnæ virtútes atque angélicæ potestátes
hymnum glóriæ tuæ cóncinunt,
sine fine dicéntes:

Sanctus, Sanctus, Sanctus . . .

II DE ASCENSIONE DOMINI

DE MYSTERIO ASCENSIONIS

47.　Sequens præfatio dicitur in die Ascensionis Domini; dici potest diebus
post Ascensionem usque ad sabbatum ante Pentecosten, in Missis, quæ
præfatione propria carent.

In die Ascensionis, quando adhibetur Canon Romanus, dicitur Communicántes proprium, ut infra.

V ere dignum et iustum est, æquum et salutáre,
nos tibi semper et ubíque grátias ágere:
Dómine, sancte Pater, omnípotens ætérne Deus:
per Christum Dóminum nostrum.

Qui post resurrectiónem suam
ómnibus discípulis suis maniféstus appáruit,
et ipsis cernéntibus est elevátus in cælum,
ut nos divinitátis suæ tribúeret esse partícipes.

Quaprópter, profúsis paschálibus gáudiis,
totus in orbe terrárum mundus exsúltat.
Sed et supérnæ virtútes atque angélicæ potestátes
hymnum glóriæ tuæ cóncinunt, sine fine dicéntes:

Sanctus, Sanctus, Sanctus . . .

DOMINICA PENTECOSTES

DE MYSTERIO PENTECOSTES

V ere dignum et iustum est, æquum et salutáre,
nos tibi semper et ubíque grátias ágere:
Dómine, sancte Pater, omnípotens ætérne Deus:

(Today) the Lord Jesus, the king of glory,
the conqueror of sin and death,
ascended to heaven while the angels sang his praises.
Christ, the mediator between God and man,
judge of the world and Lord of all,
has passed beyond our sight,
not to abandon us but to be our hope.
Christ is the beginning, the head of the Church;
where he has gone, we hope to follow.
The joy of the resurrection and ascension
renews the whole world,
while the choirs of heaven sing
    for ever to your glory:

Holy, holy, holy Lord, . . .

ASCENSION II   P27

THE MYSTERY OF THE ASCENSION

This preface is said on the Ascension, and it may also be said (or an Easter preface) in all Masses which have no preface of their own, from the Ascension to the Saturday before Pentecost, inclusive.

When Eucharistic Prayer I is used, the special form of **In union with the whole Church** is said.

Father, all-powerful and ever-living God,
we do well always and everywhere
    to give you thanks
through Jesus Christ our Lord.
In his risen body he plainly showed himself
    to his disciples
and was taken up to heaven in their sight
to claim for us a share in his divine life.
And so, with all the choirs of angels
    in heaven
we proclaim your glory
and join in their unending hymn of praise:

Holy, holy, holy Lord, . . .

PENTECOST   P28

THE MYSTERY OF PENTECOST

Father, all-powerful and ever-living God,
we do well always and everywhere
    to give you thanks.

tu enim, sacraméntum paschále consúmmans,
quibus, per Unigéniti tui consórtium,
fílios adoptiónis esse tribuísti,
hódie Spíritum Sanctum es largítus;
qui, princípio nascéntis Ecclésiæ,
et cuntis géntibus sciéntiam índidit deitátis,
et linguárum diversitátem
    in uníus fídei confessióne sociávit.

Quaprópter, profúsis paschálibus gáudiis,
totus in orbe terrárum mundus exsúltat.
Sed et supérnæ virtútes atque angélicæ potestátes
hymnum glóriæ tuæ cóncinunt, sine fine dicéntes:

Sanctus, Sanctus, Sanctus . . .

I DE DOMINICIS «PER ANNUM»

DE MYSTERIO PASCHALI ET DE POPULO DEI

48.   Sequens præfatio dicitur in dominicis «per annum».

Vere dignum et iustum est, æquum et salutáre,
nos tibi semper et ubíque grátias ágere:
Dómine, sancte Pater, omnípotens ætérne Deus:
per Christum Dóminum nostrum.
Cuius hoc miríficum fuit opus
    per paschále mystérium,
ut de peccáto et mortis iugo ad hanc glóriam vocarémur,
qua nunc genus eléctum, regále sacerdótium,
gens sancta et acquisitiónis pópulus dicerémur,
et tuas annuntiarémus ubíque virtútes,
qui nos de ténebris ad tuum admirábile lumen vocásti.
Et ídeo cum Angelis et Archángelis,
cum Thronis et Dominatiónibus,
cumque omni milítia cæléstis exércitus,
hymnum glóriæ tuæ cánimus, sine fine dicéntes:

Sanctus, Sanctus, Sanctus . . .

II DE DOMINICIS «PER ANNUM»

DE MYSTERIO SALUTIS

49.   Sequens præfatio dicitur in dominicis «per annum».

Vere dignum et iustum est, æquum et salutáre,
nos tibi semper et ubíque grátias ágere:
Dómine, sancte Pater, omnípotens ætérne Deus:
per Christum Dóminum nostrum.

Today you sent the Holy Spirit
on those marked out to be your children
by sharing the life of your only Son,
and so you brought the paschal mystery
    to its completion.
Today we celebrate the great beginning of your Church
when the Holy Spirit made known to all peoples
    the one true God,
and created from the many languages of man
one voice to profess one faith.
The joy of the resurrection renews the whole world,
while the choirs of heaven sing for ever to your glory:

Holy, holy, holy Lord, . . .

SUNDAYS IN ORDINARY TIME I   P29
THE PASCHAL MYSTERY AND THE PEOPLE OF GOD
This preface is said on Sundays in ordinary time.

Father, all-powerful and ever-living God,
we do well always and everywhere
    to give you thanks
through Jesus Christ our Lord.
Through his cross and resurrection
he freed us from sin and death
and called us to the glory that has made us
a chosen race, a royal priesthood,
a holy nation, a people set apart.
Everywhere we proclaim your mighty works
for you have called us out of darkness
into your own wonderful light.
And so, with all the choirs of angels in heaven
we proclaim your glory
and join in their unending hymn of praise:

Holy, holy, holy Lord, . . .

SUNDAYS IN ORDINARY TIME II   P30
THE MYSTERY OF SALVATION
This preface is said on Sundays in ordinary time.

Father, all-powerful and ever-living God,
we do well always and everywhere
    to give you thanks
through Jesus Christ our Lord.

Qui, humánis miserátus erróribus,
de Vírgine nasci dignátus est.
Qui, crucem passus, a perpétua morte nos liberávit
et, a mórtuis resúrgens, vitam nobis donávit ætérnam.
Et ídeo cum Angelis et Archángelis,
cum Thronis et Dominatiónibus,
cumque omni milítia cæléstis exércitus,
hymnum glóriæ tuæ cánimus,
sine fine dicéntes:

Sanctus, Sanctus, Sanctus . . .

III DE DOMINICIS «PER ANNUM»

DE SALVATIONE HOMINIS PER HOMINEM

50. Sequens præfatio dicitur in dominicis «per annum».

Vere dignum et iustum est, æquum et salutáre,
nos tibi semper et ubíque grátias ágere:
Dómine, sancte Pater, omnípotens ætérne Deus:
Ad cuius imménsam glóriam pertinére cognóscimus
ut mortálibus tua deitáte succúrreres;
sed et nobis providéres de ipsa mortalitáte
    nostra remédium,
et pérditos quosque unde períerant, inde salváres,
per Christum Dóminum nostrum.
Per quem maiestátem tuam
    adórat exércitus Angelórum,
ante conspéctum tuum in æternitáte lætántium.
Cum quibus et nostras voces
    ut admítti iúbeas, deprecámur,
sócia exsultatióne dicéntes:

Sanctus, Sanctus, Sanctus . . .

IV DE DOMINICIS «PER ANNUM»

DE HISTORIA SALUTIS

51. Sequens præfatio dícitur in dominicis «per annum».

Vere dignum et iustum est, æquum et salutáre,
nos tibi semper et ubíque grátias ágere:
Dómine, sancte Pater, omnípotens ætérne Deus:
per Christum Dóminum nostrum.
Ipse enim nascéndo vetustátem hóminum renovávit,
patiéndo delévit nostra peccáta,

Out of love for sinful man,
he humbled himself to be born of the Virgin.
By suffering on the cross
he freed us from unending death,
and by rising from the dead
he gave us eternal life.
And so, with all the choirs of angels in heaven
we proclaim your glory
and join in their unending hymn of praise:
Holy, holy, holy Lord, . . .

SUNDAYS IN ORDINARY TIME III   P31

THE SALVATION OF MAN BY A MAN

This preface is said on Sundays in ordinary time.

Father, all-powerful and ever-living God,
we do well always and everywhere
    to give you thanks.
We see your infinite power
in your loving plan of salvation.
You came to our rescue by your power as God,
but you wanted us to be saved by one like us.
Man refused your friendship,
but man himself was to restore it
through Jesus Christ our Lord.
Through him the angels of heaven offer
    their prayer of adoration
as they rejoice in your presence for ever.
May our voices be one with theirs
in their triumphant hymn of praise:
Holy, holy, holy Lord, . . .

SUNDAYS IN ORDINARY TIME IV   P32

THE HISTORY OF SALVATION

This preface is said on Sundays in ordinary time.

Father, all-powerful and ever-living God,
we do well always and everywhere to give you thanks
through Jesus Christ our Lord.
By his birth we are reborn.
In his suffering we are freed from sin.
By his rising from the dead we rise to everlasting life.

ætérnæ vitæ áditum præstitit a mórtuis resurgéndo,
ad te Patrem ascendéndo cæléstes iánuas reserávit.
Et ídeo, cum Angelórum atque Sanctórum turba,
hymnum laudis tibi cánimus, sine fine dicéntes:

Sanctus, Sanctus, Sanctus . . .

V DE DOMINICIS «PER ANNUM»

DE CREATIONE

52. Sequens præfatio dicitur in dominicis «per annum».

Vere dignum et iustum est, æquum et salutáre,
nos tibi semper et ubíque grátias ágere:
Dómine, sancte Pater, omnípotens ætérne Deus:
Qui ómnia mundi eleménta fecísti,
et vices disposuísti témporum variári;
hóminem vero formásti ad imáginem tuam,
et rerum ei subiecísti univérsa mirácula,
ut vicário múnere dominarétur ómnibus quæ creásti,
et in óperum tuórum magnálibus
    iúgiter te laudáret,
per Christum Dóminum nostrum.
Unde et nos cum ómnibus Angelis te laudámus,
iucúnda celebratióne clamántes:

Sanctus, Sanctus, Sanctus . . .

VI DE DOMINICIS «PER ANNUM»

DE PIGNORE ÆTERNI PASCHATIS

53. Sequens præfatio dicitur in dominicis «per annum».

Vere dignum et iustum est, æquum et salutáre,
nos tibi semper et ubíque grátias ágere:
Dómine, sancte Pater, omnípotens ætérne Deus:
In quo vívimus, movémur et sumus,
atque in hoc córpore constitúti
non solum pietátis tuæ cotidiános
    experímur efféctus,
sed æternitátis étiam pígnora iam tenémus.
Primítias enim Spíritus habéntes,
per quem suscitásti Iesum a mórtuis,
paschále mystérium sperámus nobis
    esse perpétuum.

In his return to you in glory
we enter into your heavenly kingdom.
And so, we join the angels and the saints
as they sing their unending hymn of praise:

Holy, holy, holy Lord, . . .

SUNDAYS IN ORDINARY TIME V   P33

CREATION

This preface is said on Sundays in ordinary time.

Father, all-powerful and ever-living God,
we do well always and everywhere
     to give you thanks.
All things are of your making,
all times and seasons obey your laws,
but you chose to create man in your own image,
setting him over the whole world in all its wonder.
You made man the steward of creation,
to praise you day by day for the marvels of your
     wisdom and power,
through Jesus Christ our Lord.
We praise you, Lord, with all the angels
in their song of joy:

Holy, holy, holy Lord, . . .

SUNDAYS IN ORDINARY TIME VI   P34

THE PLEDGE OF AN ETERNAL EASTER

This preface is said on Sundays in ordinary time.

Father, all-powerful and ever-living God,
we do well always and everywhere
     to give you thanks.
In you we live and move
     and have our being.
Each day you show us a Father's love;
your Holy Spirit, dwelling within us,
gives us on earth the hope of unending joy.
Your gift of the Spirit,
who raised Jesus from the dead,
is the foretaste and promise
of the paschal feast of heaven.

Unde et nos cum ómnibus Angelis
   te laudámus,
iucúnda celebratióne clamántes:

Sanctus, Sanctus, Sanctus . . .

VII DE DOMINICIS «PER ANNUM»

DE SALUTE PER OBŒDIENTIAM CHRISTI

54.   Sequens præfatio dicitur in dominicis «per annum».

Vere dignum et iustum est, æquum et salutáre,
nos tibi semper et ubíque grátias ágere:
Dómine, sancte Pater, omnípotens ætérne Deus:
Quia sic mundum misericórditer dilexísti,
ut ipsum nobis mítteres Redemptórem,
quem absque peccáto
in nostra voluísti similitúdine conversári,
ut amáres in nobis quod diligébas in Fílio,
cuius obœdiéntia sumus ad tua dona reparáti,
quæ per inobœdiéntiam
   amiserámus peccándo.
Unde et nos, Dómine, cum Angelis et Sanctis univérsis
tibi confitémur, in exsultatióne dicéntes:

Sanctus, Sanctus, Sanctus . . .

VIII DE DOMINICIS «PER ANNUM»

DE ECCLESIA ADUNATA EX UNITATE TRINITATIS

55.   Sequens præfatio dicitur in dominicis «per annum».

Vere dignum et iustum est, æquum et salutáre,
nos tibi semper et ubíque grátias ágere:
Dómine, sancte Pater, omnípotens ætérne Deus:
Quia fílios, quos longe peccáti
   crimen abstúlerat,
per sánguinem Fílii tui
   Spiritúsque virtúte,
in unum ad te dénuo
   congregáre voluísti:
ut plebs, de unitáte Trinitátis adunáta,
in tuæ laudem sapiéntiæ multifórmis
Christi corpus templúmque Spíritus
   noscerétur Ecclésia.

With thankful praise,
in company with the angels,
we glorify the wonders of your power:

Holy, holy, holy Lord, . . .

SUNDAYS IN ORDINARY TIME VII P35

SALVATION THROUGH THE OBEDIENCE OF CHRIST

This preface is said on Sundays in ordinary time.

Father, all-powerful and ever-living God,
we do well always and everywhere
   to give you thanks.
So great was your love
that you gave us your Son as our redeemer.
You sent him as one like ourselves,
though free from sin,
that you might see and love in us
what you see and love in Christ.
Your gifts of grace, lost by disobedience,
are now restored by the obedience of your Son.
We praise you, Lord, with all the angels and saints
in their song of joy:

Holy, holy, holy Lord, . . .

SUNDAYS IN ORDINARY TIME VIII P36

THE CHURCH UNITED IN THE MYSTERY OF THE TRINITY

This preface is said on Sundays in ordinary time.

Father, all-powerful and ever-living God,
we do well always and everywhere
   to give you thanks.
When your children sinned
and wandered far from your friendship,
you reunited them with yourself
through the blood of your Son
and the power of the Holy Spirit.
You gather them into your Church,
to be one as you, Father, are one
with your Son and the Holy Spirit.
You call them to be your people,
to praise your wisdom in all your works.

Et ídeo,
    choris angélicis sociáti,
te laudámus
    in gáudio confiténtes:

Sanctus, Sanctus, Sanctus . . .

COMMUNIS I

DE UNIVERSALI RESTAURATIONE IN CHRISTO

69. Sequens præfatio dicitur in Missis, quæ præfatione propria carent, nec
sumere debent præfationem de tempore.

V ere dignum et iustum est, æquum et salutáre,
nos tibi semper et ubíque grátias ágere:
Dómine, sancte Pater, omnípotens ætérne Deus:
per Christum Dóminum nostrum.
In quo ómnia instauráre tibi complácuit,
et de plenitúdine eius nos omnes accípere tribuísti.
Cum enim in forma Dei esset,
    exinanívit semetípsum,
ac per sánguinem crucis suæ
    pacificávit univérsa;
unde exaltátus est super ómnia
et ómnibus obtemperántibus sibi
factus est causa salútis ætérnæ.
Et ídeo cum Angelis et Archángelis,
cum Thronis et Dominatiónibus,
cumque omni milítia cæléstis exércitus,
hymnum glóriæ tuæ cánimus, sine fine dicéntes:

Sanctus, Sanctus, Sanctus . . .

COMMUNIS II

DE SALUTE PER CHRISTUM

70. Sequens præfatio dicitur in Missis, quæ præfatione propria carent, nec
sumere debent præfationem de tempore.

V ere dignum et iustum est, æquum et salutáre,
nos tibi semper et ubíque grátias ágere:
Dómine, sancte Pater, omnípotens ætérne Deus:
Qui bonitáte hóminem condidísti,
ac iustítia damnátum misericórdia redemísti:
per Christum Dóminum nostrum.

You make them the body of Christ
and the dwelling-place of the Holy Spirit.
In our joy we sing to your glory
with all the choirs of angels:

Holy, holy, holy Lord, . . .

WEEKDAYS I   P37

ALL THINGS MADE ONE IN CHRIST

This preface is said in Masses which have no preface of their own, unless
they call for a seasonal preface.

Father, all-powerful and ever-living God,
we do well always and everywhere to give you thanks
through Jesus Christ our Lord.
In him you have renewed all things
and you have given us all a share in his riches.
Though his nature was divine,
he stripped himself of glory
and by shedding his blood on the cross
he brought his peace to the world.
Therefore he was exalted above all creation
and became the source of eternal life
to all who serve him.
And so, with all the choirs of angels
    in heaven
we proclaim your glory
and join in their unending hymn of praise:

Holy, holy, holy Lord, . . .

WEEKDAYS II   P38

SALVATION THROUGH CHRIST

This preface is said in Masses which have no preface of their own, unless
they call for a seasonal preface.

Father, all-powerful and ever-living God,
we do well always and everywhere
    to give you thanks.
In love you created man,
in justice you condemned him,
but in mercy you redeemed him,
through Jesus Christ our Lord.

Per quem maiestátem tuam laudant Angeli,
adórant Dominatiónes, tremunt Potestátes.
Cæli cælorúmque Virtútes, ac beáta Séraphim,
sócia exsultatióne concélebrant.
Cum quibus et nostras voces ut admítti iúbeas,
deprecámur, súpplici confessióne dicéntes:

Sanctus, Sanctus, Sanctus . . .

COMMUNIS III
LAUDES DEO PRO CREATIONE ET
REFORMATIONE HOMINIS

71. Sequens præfatio dicitur in Missis, quæ præfatione propria carent, nec sumere debent præfationem de tempore.

Vere dignum et iustum est, æquum et salutáre,
nos tibi semper et ubíque grátias ágere:
Dómine, sancte Pater, omnípotens ætérne Deus:
Qui per Fílium dilectiónis tuæ,
sicut cónditor géneris es humáni,
ita benigníssimus reformátor.
Unde mérito tibi cunctæ sérviunt creatúræ,
te redémpti rite colláudant univérsi,
et uno Sancti tui te corde benedícunt.
Quaprópter et nos cum ómnibus te Angelis celebrámus,
iucúnda semper confessióne dicéntes:

Sanctus, Sanctus, Sanctus . . .

COMMUNIS IV
DE LAUDE, DONO DEI

72. Sequens præfatio dicitur in Missis, quæ præfatione propria carent, nec sumere debent præfationem de tempore.

Vere dignum et iustum est, æquum et salutáre,
nos tibi semper et ubíque grátias ágere:
Dómine, sancte Pater, omnípotens ætérne Deus:
Quia, cum nostra laude non égeas,
tuum tamen est donum quod tibi grates rependámus,
nam te non augent nostra præcónia,
sed nobis profíciunt ad salútem,
per Christum Dóminum nostrum.
Et ídeo, choris angélicis sociáti,
te laudámus in gáudio confiténtes:

Sanctus, Sanctus, Sanctus . . .

Through him the angels
and all the choirs of heaven
worship in awe before your presence.
May our voices be one with theirs
as they sing with joy
the hymn of your glory:

Holy, holy, holy Lord, . . .

WEEKDAYS III   P39
THE PRAISE OF GOD IN CREATION AND
THROUGH THE CONVERSION OF MAN

This preface is said in Masses which have no preface of their own, unless
they call for a seasonal preface.

Father, all-powerful and ever-living God,
we do well always and everywhere to give you thanks.
Through your beloved Son
you created our human family.
Through him you restored us to your likeness.
Therefore it is your right
to receive the obedience of all creation,
the praise of the Church on earth,
the thanksgiving of your saints in heaven.
We too rejoice with the angels
as we proclaim your glory for ever:

Holy, holy, holy Lord, . . .

WEEKDAYS IV   P40
PRAISE OF GOD IS HIS GIFT

This preface is said in Masses which have no preface of their own, unless
they call for a seasonal preface.

Father, all-powerful and ever-living God,
we do well always and everywhere
to give you thanks.
You have no need of our praise,
yet our desire to thank you is itself your gift.
Our prayer of thanksgiving adds nothing to your greatness,
but makes us grow in your grace,
through Jesus Christ our Lord.
In our joy we sing to your glory
with all the choirs of angels:

Holy, holy, holy Lord, . . .

COMMUNIS V

PROCLAMATIO MYSTERII CHRISTI

73. Sequens præfatio dicitur in Missis, quæ præfatione propria carent, nec sumere debent præfationem de tempore.

V ere dignum et iustum est, æquum et salutáre,
nos tibi semper et ubíque grátias ágere:
Dómine, sancte Pater, omnípotens ætérne Deus:
per Christum Dóminum nostrum.
Cuius mortem in caritáte celebrámus,
resurrectiónem fide vívida confitémur,
advéntum in glória spe firmíssima præstolámur.
Et ídeo, cum Sanctis et Angelis univérsis,
te collaudámus, sine fine dicéntes:

Sanctus, Sanctus, Sanctus . . .

COMMUNIS VI

DE MYSTERIO SALUTIS IN CHRISTO

74. Sequens præfatio, e Prece eucharistica II deprompta, dicitur in Missis, quæ præfatione propria carent nec sumere debent præfationem de tempore.

V ere dignum et iustum est, æquum et salutáre,
nos tibi, sancte Pater, semper et ubíque grátias ágere
per Fílium dilectiónis tuæ Iesum Christum,
Verbum tuum per quod cuncta fecísti:
quem misísti nobis Salvatórem et Redemptórem,
incarnátum de Spíritu Sancto et ex Vírgine natum.
Qui voluntátem tuam adímplens
et pópulum tibi sanctum acquírens
exténdit manus cum paterétur,
ut mortem sólveret et resurrectiónem manifestáret.
Et ídeo cum Angelis et ómnibus Sanctis
glóriam tuam prædicámus, una voce dicéntes:

Sanctus, Sanctus, Sanctus . . .

DE SANCTISSIMA TRINITATE

DE MYSTERIO SANCTISSIMÆ TRINITATIS

V ere dignum et iustum est, æquum et salutáre,
nos tibi semper et ubíque grátias ágere:
Dómine, sancte Pater, omnípotens ætérne Deus:

WEEKDAYS V   P41

THE MYSTERY OF CHRIST IS PROCLAIMED

This preface is said in Masses which have no preface of their own, unless
they call for a seasonal preface.

Father, all-powerful and ever-living God,
we do well always and everywhere
    to give you thanks
through Jesus Christ our Lord.
With love we celebrate his death.
With living faith we proclaim his resurrection.
With unwavering hope we await his return in glory.
Now, with the saints and all the angels
we praise you for ever:

Holy, holy, holy Lord, . . .

WEEKDAYS VI   P42

SALVATION IN CHRIST

This preface, taken from Eucharistic Prayer II, is said in Masses which have
no preface of their own, unless they call for a seasonal preface.

Father, it is our duty and our salvation
always and everywhere to give you thanks
through your beloved Son, Jesus Christ.
He is the Word through whom you made the universe,
the Savior you sent to redeem us.
By the power of the Holy Spirit
he took flesh and was born of the Virgin Mary.
For our sake he opened his arms on the cross;
he put an end to death and revealed the resurrection.
In this he fulfilled your will and won for you a holy people.
And so we join the angels and the saints
in proclaiming your glory:

Holy, holy, holy Lord, . . .

HOLY TRINITY   P43

THE MYSTERY OF THE HOLY TRINITY

This preface is said in Masses of the Holy Trinity.

Father, all-powerful and ever-living God,
we do well always and everywhere
    to give you thanks.

Qui cum unigénito Fílio tuo et Spíritu Sancto
unus es Deus, unus es Dóminus:
non in uníus singularitáte persónæ,
sed in uníus Trinitáte substántiæ.
Quod enim de tua glória, reveXlánte te, crédimus,
hoc de Fílio tuo,
hoc de Spíritu Sancto,
sine discretióne sentímus.
Ut, in confessióne veræ sempiternǽque Deitátis,
et in persónis propríetas,
et in esséntia Únitas,
et in maiestáte adorétur æquálitas.
Quem laudant Angeli atque Archángeli,
Chérubim quoque ac Séraphim,
qui non cessant clamáre cotídie, una voce dicéntes:

Sanctus, Sanctus, Sanctus . . .

DE ANNUNTIATIONE DOMINI

DIE 25 MARTII

DE MYSTERIO INCARNATIONIS

Vere dignum et iustum est, æquum et salutáre,
nos tibi semper et ubíque grátias ágere:
Dómine, sancte Pater, omnípotens ætérne Deus:
per Christum Dóminum nostrum.
Quem inter hómines et propter hómines nascitúrum,
Spíritus Sancti obumbránte virtúte,
a cælésti núntio Virgo fidénter audívit
et immaculátis viscéribus amánter portávit,
ut et promissónis fíliis Israel perfíceret véritas,
et géntium exspectátio patéret
    ineffabíliter adimplénda.
Per quem maiestátem tuam
    adórat exércitus Angelórum,
ante conspéctum tuum in æternitáte lætántium.
Cum quibus et nostras voces ut admítti iúbeas, deprecámur,
sócia exsultatióne dicéntes:

Sanctus, Sanctus, Sanctus . . .

We joyfully proclaim our faith
in the mystery of your Godhead.
You have revealed your glory
as the glory also of your Son
and of the Holy Spirit:
three Persons equal in majesty,
undivided in splendor,
yet one Lord, one God,
ever to be adored
    in your everlasting glory.

And so, with all the choirs of angels in heaven
we proclaim your glory
and join in their unending
    hymn of praise:

Holy, holy, holy Lord, . . .

ANNUNCIATION   P44

MARCH 25

THE MYSTERY OF THE INCARNATION

Father, all-powerful and ever-living God,
we do well always and everywhere to give you thanks
through Jesus Christ our Lord.
He came to save mankind by becoming a man himself.
The Virgin Mary, receiving the angel's message in faith,
conceived by the power of the Spirit
and bore your Son in purest love.
In Christ, the eternal truth,
your promise to Israel came true.
In Christ, the hope of all peoples,
man's hope was realized beyond all expectation.
Through Christ the angels of heaven
offer their prayer of adoration
as they rejoice in your presence for ever.
May our voices be one with theirs
in their triumphant hymn of praise:

Holy, holy, holy Lord, . . .

DE SACRATISSIME CORDE IESU

DE IMMENSA CARITATE CHRISTI

Vere dignum et iustum est, æquum et salutáre,
nos tibi semper et ubíque grátias ágere:
Dómine, sancte Pater, omnípotens ætérne Deus:
per Christum Dóminum nostrum.
Qui, mira caritáte, exaltátus in cruce,
pro nobis trádidit semetípsum,
atque de transfíxo látere sánguinem fudit et aquam,
ex quo manárent Ecclésiæ sacraménta,
ut omnes, ad Cor apértum Salvatóris attrácti,
iúgiter haurírent e fóntibus salútis in gáudio.
Et ídeo, cum Sanctis et Angelis univérsis,
te collaudámus, sine fine dicéntes:

Sanctus, Sanctus, Sanctus . . .

DE EXALTATIONE SANCTÆ CRUCIS

DE VICTORIA CRUCIS GLORIOSAE

Vere dignum et iustum est, æquum et salutáre,
nos tibi semper et ubíque grátias ágere:
Dómine, sancte Pater, omnípotens ætérne Deus:
Qui salútem humáni géneris in ligno crucis constituísti,
ut unde mors oriebátur, inde vita resúrgeret;
et, qui in ligno vincébat, in ligno quoque vincerétur:
per Christum Dóminum nostrum.
Per quem maiestátem tuam laudant Angeli,
adórant Dominatiónes, tremunt Potestátes.
Cæli cælorúmque Virtútes, ac beáta Séraphim,
sócia exsultatióne concélebrant.
Cum quibus et nostras voces ut admítti iúbeas, deprecámur,
súpplici confessióne dicéntes:

Sanctus, Sanctus, Sanctus . . .

SACRED HEART   P45

THE BOUNDLESS LOVE OF CHRIST

This preface is said in Masses of the Sacred Heart.

Father, all-powerful and ever-living God,
we do well always and everywhere to give you thanks
through Jesus Christ our Lord.
Lifted high on the cross,
Christ gave his life for us,
so much did he love us.
From his wounded side flowed blood and water,
the fountain of sacramental life in the Church.
To his open heart the Savior invites all men,
to draw water in joy from the springs of salvation.
Now, with all the saints and angels,
we praise you for ever:

Holy, holy, holy Lord, . . .

TRIUMPH OF THE CROSS   P46

THE TRIUMPH OF THE GLORIOUS CROSS

This preface is said in Masses of the Holy Cross.

Father, all-powerful and ever-living God,
we do well always and everywhere to give you thanks.
You decreed that man should be saved
    through the wood of the cross.
The tree of man's defeat became
    his tree of victory;
where life was lost, there life has been restored
through Christ our Lord.
Through him the choirs of angels
and all the powers of heaven
praise and worship your glory.
May our voices blend with theirs
as we join in their unending hymn:

Holy, holy, holy Lord, . . .

I DE SS.MA EUCHARISTIA

DE SACRIFICIO ET DE SACRAMENTO CHRISTI

56. Sequens præfatio dicitur in Missa «In Cena Domini»; dici potest etiam in sollemnitate Ss.mi Corporis et Sanguinis Christi et in Missis votivis de Ss.ma Eucharistia.

Quando adhibetur Canon Romanus, in Missa «In Cena Domini» dicuntur Communicántes, Hanc ígitur et Qui prídie propria.

Vere dignum et iustum est, æquum et salutáre,
nos tibi semper et ubíque grátias ágere:
Dómine, sancte Pater, omnípotens ætérne Deus:
per Christum Dóminum nostrum.
Qui, verus æternúsque Sacérdos,
formam sacrifícii perénnis ínstituens,
hóstiam tibi se primus óbtulit salutárem,
et nos, in sui memóriam, præcépit offérre.
Cuius carnem pro nobis immolátam
dum súmimus, roborámur,
et fusum pro nobis sánguinem dum potámus, ablúimur.
Et ídeo cum Angelis et Archángelis,
cum Thronis et Dominatiónibus,
cumque omni milítia cæléstis exércitus,
hymnum glóriæ tuæ cánimus, sine fine dicéntes:
Sanctus, Sanctus, Sanctus . . .

II DE SS.MA EUCHARISTIA

DE FRUCTIBUS SANCTISSIMÆ EUCHARISTIÆ

57. Sequens præfatio dicitur in sollemnitate Ss.mi Corporis et Sanguinis Christi et in Missis votivis de Ss.ma Eucharistia.

Vere dignum et iustum est, æquum et salutáre,
nos tibi semper et ubíque grátias ágere:
Dómine, sancte Pater, omnípotens ætérne Deus:
per Christum Dóminum nostrum.
Qui cum Apóstolis suis
in novíssima cena convéscens,
salutíferam crucis memóriam
prosecutúrus in sǽcula,
Agnum sine mácula se tibi óbtulit,
perféctæ laudis munus accéptum.
Quo venerábili mystério fidéles tuos
aléndo sanctíficas,

HOLY EUCHARIST I   P47

THE SACRIFICE AND SACRAMENT OF CHRIST

This preface is said in the Mass of the Lord's Supper on Holy Thursday. It may be said on the solemnity of the Body and Blood of Christ and in votive Masses of the Holy Eucharist.

When the Roman canon is used in the Mass of the Lord's Supper on Holy Thursday, the special form of In union with the whole Church, Father accept this offering, and The day before he suffered are said.

F ather, all-powerful and ever-living God,
we do well always and everywhere to give you thanks
through Jesus Christ our Lord.
He is the true and eternal priest
who established this unending sacrifice.
He offered himself as a victim for our deliverance
and taught us to make this offering in his memory.
As we eat this body which he gave for us,
we grow in strength.
As we drink his blood which he poured out for us,
we are washed clean.
Now, with angels and archangels,
and the whole company of heaven,
we sing the unending hymn of your praise:

Holy, holy, holy Lord, . . .

HOLY EUCHARIST II   P48

THE EFFECTS OF THE HOLY EUCHARIST

This preface is said on the the solemnity of the Body and Blood of Christ and in votive Masses of the Holy Eucharist.

F ather, all-powerful and ever-living God,
we do well always and everywhere
   to give you thanks
through Jesus Christ our Lord.
At the last supper,
as he sat at table with his apostles,
he offered himself to you as the spotless lamb,
the acceptable gift that gives you perfect praise.
Christ has given us this memorial of his passion
to bring us its saving power until the end of time.

In this great sacrament you feed your people
and strengthen them in holiness,

ut humánum genus, quod cóntinet unus orbis,
una fides illúminet, cáritas una coniúngat.
Ad mensam ígitur accédimus tam mirábilis sacraménti,
ut, grátiæ tuæ suavitáte perfúsi,
ad cæléstis formæ imáginem transeámus.
Propter quod cæléstia tibi atque terréstria
cánticum novum cóncinunt adorándo,
et nos cum omni exercitu Angelórum
proclamámus, sine fine dicéntes:

Sanctus, Sanctus, Sanctus . . .

DE PRÆSENTATIONE DOMINI

DIE 2 FEBRUARII

DE MYSTERIO PRESENTATIONIS DOMINI

V ere dignum et iustum est, æquum et salutáre,
nos tibi semper et ubíque grátias ágere:
Dómine, sancte Pater, omnípotens ætérne Deus:
Quia coætérnus hódie
    in templo tuus Fílius præsentátus
glória Israel et lumen géntium
    a Spíritu declarátur.
Unde et nos,
    Salutári tuo in gáudiis occurréntes,
cum Angelis et Sanctis te laudámus,
    sine fine dicéntes:

Sanctus, Sanctus, Sanctus . . .

DE TRANSFIGURATIONE DOMINI

DIE 6 AUGUSTI

DE MYSTERIO TRANSFIGURATIONIS

V ere dignum et iustum est, æquum et salutáre,
nos tibi semper et ubíque grátias ágere:
Dómine, sancte Pater, omnípotens ætérne Deus:
per Christum Dóminum nostrum.
Qui coram eléctis téstibus suam glóriam revelávit,
et commúnem illam cum céteris córporis formam

so that the family of mankind
may come to walk in the light of one faith,
in one communion of love.
We come, then, to this wonderful sacrament
to be fed at your table
and grow into the likeness of the risen Christ.
Earth unites with heaven
to sing the new song of creation,
as we adore and praise you for ever:

Holy, holy, holy Lord, . . .

PRESENTATION OF THE LORD   P49

FEBRUARY 2

THE MYSTERY OF THE PRESENTATION OF THE LORD

Father, all-powerful and ever-living God,
we do well always and everywhere to give you thanks
through Jesus Christ our Lord.
Today your Son,
who shares your eternal splendor,
was presented in the temple,
and revealed by the Spirit
as the glory of Israel
and the light of all peoples.
Our hearts are joyful,
for we have seen your salvation,
and now with the angels and saints
we praise you for ever:

Holy, holy, holy Lord, . . .

TRANSFIGURATION   P50

AUGUST 6

THE MYSTERY OF THE TRANSFIGURATION

Father, all-powerful and ever-living God,
we do well always and everywhere
    to give you thanks
through Jesus Christ our Lord.
He revealed his glory to the disciples
to strengthen them for the scandal of the cross.

máximo splendóre perfúdit,
ut de córdibus discipulórum crucis scándalum tollerétur,
et in totíus Ecclésiæ córpore declaráret impléndum
quod eius mirabíliter præfúlsit in cápite.
Et ídeo cum cælórum Virtútibus
in terris te iúgiter celebrámus,
maiestáti tuæ sine fine clamántes:

Sanctus, Sanctus, Sanctus . . .

DE DOMINO NOSTRO IESU CHRISTO
UNIVERSORUM REGE

DE CHRISTO UNIVERSORUM REGE

Vere dignum et iustum est, æquum et salutáre,
nos tibi semper et ubíque grátias ágere:
Dómine, sancte Pater, omnípotens ætérne Deus:
Qui unigénitum Fílium tuum,
Dóminum nostrum Iesum Christum,
Sacerdótem ætérnum et universórum Regem,
óleo exsultatiónis unxísti:
ut, seípsum in ara crucis
hóstiam immaculátam et pacíficam ófferens,
redemptiónis humánæ sacraménta perágeret:
et, suo subiéctis império ómnibus creatúris,
ætérnum et universále regnum
imménsæ tuæ tráderet maiestáti:
regnum veritátis et vitæ
regnum sanctitátis et grátiæ;
regnum iustítiæ, amóris et pacis.
Et ídeo cum Angelis et Archángelis,
cum Thronis et Dominatiónibus,
cumque omni milítia cæléstis exércitus,
hymnum glóriæ tuæ cánimus, sine fine dicéntes:

Sanctus, Sanctus, Sanctus . . .

I DE DEDICATIONE ECCLESIÆ

IN ANNIVERSARIO DEDICATIONIS

A. In ipsa ecclesiæ dedicata

DE MYSTERIO TEMPLI DEI, QUOD EST ECCLESIA

His glory shone from a body like our own,
to show that the Church,
which is the body of Christ,
would one day share his glory.
In our unending joy we echo on earth
the song of the angels in heaven
as they praise your glory for ever:

Holy, holy, holy Lord, . . .

CHRIST THE KING   P51

CHRIST, THE KING OF THE UNIVERSE

Father, all-powerful and ever-living God,
we do well always and everywhere
   to give you thanks.
You anointed Jesus Christ, your only Son, with the oil
   of gladness,
as the eternal priest and universal king.
As priest he offered his life
   on the altar of the cross
and redeemed the human race
by this one perfect sacrifice of peace.
As king he claims dominion over all creation,
that he may present to you, his almighty Father,
an eternal and universal kingdom:
a kingdom of truth and life,
a kingdom of holiness and grace,
a kingdom of justice, love, and peace.
And so, with all the choirs of angels in heaven
we proclaim your glory
and join in their unending
   hymn of praise:

Holy, holy, holy Lord, . . .

DEDICATION OF A CHURCH I   P52

ANNIVERSARY OF THE DEDICATION

A. Celebration in the Dedicated Church

THE MYSTERY OF GOD'S TEMPLE, WHICH IS THE CHURCH

Vere dignum et iustum est, æquum et salutáre,
nos tibi semper et ubíque grátias ágere:
Dómine, sancte Pater, omnípotens ætérne Deus:
per Christum Dóminum nostrum.
Quia in domo visíbili quam nobis
    exstrúere concessísti,
ubi famíliæ in hoc loco ad te peregrinánti
    favére non désinis,
mystérium tuæ nobíscum communiónis
mire figúras et operáris:
hic enim tibi templum illud
    quod nos sumus ædíficas,
et Ecclésiam per orbem diffúsam
in domínici compágem córporis facis augéri,
in pacis visióne compléndam,
    cælésti civitáte Ierúsalem.
Et ídeo, cum multitúdine órdinum beatórum,
in templo glóriæ tuæ, te collaudámus,
benedícimus et magnificámus, dicéntes:

Sanctus, Sanctus, Sanctus . . .

II DE DEDICATIONE ECCLESIÆ

IN ANNIVERSARIO DEDICATIONIS

B. Extra ipsam ecclesiam dedicatam

DE MYSTERIO ECCLESIÆ, QUÆ EST SPONSA CHRISTI
TEMPLUMQUE SPIRITUS

Vere dignum et iustum est, æquum et salutáre,
nos tibi semper et ubíque grátias ágere:
Dómine, sancte Pater, omnípotens ætérne Deus:
Qui domum oratiónis muníficus
    inhabitáre dignáris,
ut, grátia tua perpétuis fovénte subsídiis,
templum Spíritus Sancti
    ipse nos perfícias,
acceptábilis vitæ splendóre corúscans.
Sed et visibílibus ædifíciis adumbrátam,
Christi sponsam Ecclésiam perénni
    operatióne sanctíficas,
ut, innumerábili prole mater exsúltans,
in glóriam tuam collocétur in cælis.

Father, all-powerful and ever-living God,
we do well always and everywhere
        to give you thanks.
We thank you now for this house of prayer
in which you bless your family
as we come to you on pilgrimage.
Here you reveal your presence
by sacramental signs,
and make us one with you
through the unseen bond of grace.
Here you build your temple of living stones,
and bring the Church to its full stature
as the body of Christ throughout the world,
to reach its perfection at last
in the heavenly city of Jerusalem,
which is the vision of your peace.
In communion with all the angels and saints
we bless and praise your greatness
in the temple of your glory:

Holy, holy, holy Lord, . . .

DEDICATION OF A CHURCH II   P53

ANNIVERSARY OF THE DEDICATION

B. Celebration in Other Churches

THE MYSTERY OF THE CHURCH, THE BRIDE OF CHRIST
AND THE TEMPLE OF THE SPIRIT

Father, all-powerful and ever-living God,
we do well always and everywhere
        to give you thanks.
Your house is a house of prayer,
and your presence makes it a place of blessing.
You give us grace upon grace
to build the temple of your Spirit,
creating its beauty from the holiness of our lives.
Your house of prayer
is also the promise of the Church in heaven.
Here your love is always at work,
preparing the Church on earth
for its heavenly glory as the sinless bride of Christ,
the joyful mother of a great company of saints.

Et ídeo, cum Sanctis et Angelis univérsis,
te collaudámus, sine fine dicéntes:

Sanctus, Sanctus, Sanctus . . .

I DE SPIRITU SANCTO

DE MISSIONE SPIRITUS A DOMINO IN ECCLESIAM

Vere dignum et iustum est, æquum et salutáre,
nos tibi semper et ubíque grátias ágere:
Dómine, sancte Pater, omnípotens ætérne Deus:
per Christum Dóminum nostrum.
Qui, ascéndens super omnes cælos
sedénsque ad déxteram tuam,
promíssum Spíritum Sanctum in fílios adoptiónis effúdit.
Quaprópter nunc et usque in sǽculum,
cum omni milítia Angelórum,
devóta tibi mente concínimus,
clamántes atque dicéntes:

Sanctus, Sanctus, Sanctus . . .

II DE SPIRITU SANCTO

DE ACTIONE SPIRITUS IN ECCLESIA

Vere dignum et iustum est, æquum et salutáre,
nos tibi semper et ubíque grátias ágere:
Dómine, sancte Pater, omnípotens ætérne Deus:
Qui síngulis quibúsque tempóribus aptánda dispénsas,
mirísque modis Ecclésiæ tuæ
　　gubernácula moderáris.
Virtúte enim Spíritus Sancti
ita eam adiuváre non désinis,
ut súbdito tibi semper afféctu
nec in tribulatióne supplicáre defíciat,
nec inter gáudia grátias reférre desístat,
per Christum Dóminum nostrum.
Et ídeo, choris angélicis sociáti,
te laudámus in gáudio confiténtes:

Sanctus, Sanctus, Sanctus . . .

Now, with the saints and all the angels
we praise you for ever:

Holy, holy, holy Lord, . . .

HOLY SPIRIT I P54

THE SPIRIT SENT BY THE LORD UPON HIS CHURCH

This preface is said in votive Masses of the Holy Spirit.

Father, all-powerful and ever-living God,
we do well always and everywhere to give you thanks
through Jesus Christ our Lord.
He ascended above all the heavens,
and from his throne at your right hand
poured into the hearts of your adopted children
the Holy Spirit of your promise.
With steadfast love
we sing your unending praise;
we join with the hosts of heaven
in their triumphant song:

Holy, holy, holy Lord, . . .

HOLY SPIRIT II P55

THE WORKING OF THE SPIRIT IN THE CHURCH

This preface is said in votive Masses of the Holy Spirit.

Father, all-powerful and ever-living God,
we do well always and everywhere
   to give you thanks.
You give your gifts of grace for every time and season
as you guide the Church
in the marvelous ways of your providence.
You give us your Holy Spirit
to help us always by his power,
so that with loving trust
we may turn to you in all our troubles,
and give you thanks in all our joys,
through Jesus Christ our Lord.
In our joy we sing to your glory
with all the choirs of angels:

Holy, holy, holy Lord, . . .

I DE BEATA MARIA VIRGINE

DE MATERNITATE B. MARIÆ V.

58. Sequens præfatio dicitur in Missis de B. Maria V., addita suo loco mentione celebrationis diei, prout in singulis Missis indicatur.

Vere dignum et iustum est, æquum et salutáre,
nos tibi semper et ubíque grátias ágere:
Dómine, sancte Pater, omnípotens ætérne Deus:
Et te in . . . beátæ Maríæ semper Vírginis collaudáre,
    benedícere et prædicáre.
Quæ et Unigénitum tuum Sancti Spíritus
    obumbratióne concépit,
et, virginitátis glória permanénte,
lumen ætérnum mundo effúdit,
Iesum Christum Dóminum nostrum.
Per quem maiestátem tuam laudant Angeli,
adórant Dominatiónes, tremunt Potestátes.
Cæli cælorúmque Virtútes, ac beáta Séraphim,
sócia exsultatióne concélebrant.
Cum quibus et nostras voces ut admítti iúbeas, deprecámur,
súpplici confessióne dicéntes:

Sanctus, Sanctus, Sanctus . . .

II DE BEATA MARIA VIRGINE

ECCLESIA, VERBIS MARIÆ, LAUDES DEO PERSOLVIT

59. Sequens præfatio dicitur in Missis de B. Maria V.

Vere dignum et iustum est, æquum et salutáre,
in ómnium Sanctórum provéctu te mirábilem confitéri,
et potíssimum, beátæ Vírginis Maríæ memóriam recoléntes,
cleméntiam tuam ipsíus grato magnificáre præcónio.
Vere namque in omnes terræ fines
    magna fecísti,
ac tuam in sǽcula prorogásti
    misericórdiæ largitátem,
cum ancíllæ tuæ humilitátem aspíciens,
per eam dedísti humánæ salútis auctórem,
Fílium tuum, Iesum Christum, Dóminum nostrum.
Per quem maiestátem tuam
    adórat exércitus Angelórum,
ante conspéctum tuum
    in æternitáte lætántium.

BLESSED VIRGIN MARY I   P56

MOTHERHOOD OF MARY

This preface is said in Masses of the Blessed Virgin Mary, with the mention
of the particular celebration, as indicated in the individual Masses.

Father, all-powerful and ever-living God,
we do well always and everywhere
    to give you thanks
(as we celebrate . . . of the Blessed Virgin Mary).
(as we honor the Blessed Virgin Mary).
Through the power of the Holy Spirit,
she became the virgin mother of
    your only Son,
our Lord Jesus Christ,
who is for ever the light of the world.
Through him the choirs of angels
and all the powers of heaven
praise and worship your glory.
May our voices blend with theirs
as we join in their unending hymn:

Holy, holy, holy Lord, . . .

BLESSED VIRGIN MARY II   P57

THE CHURCH ECHOES MARY'S SONG OF PRAISE

This preface is said in Masses of the Blessed Virgin Mary.

Father, all-powerful and ever-living God,
we do well always and everywhere to give you thanks,
and to praise you for your gifts
as we contemplate your saints in glory.
In celebrating the memory of the Blessed Virgin Mary,
it is our special joy to echo her song of thanksgiving.
What wonders you have worked throughout the world.
All generations have shared the greatness of your love.
When you looked on Mary your lowly servant,
you raised her to be the mother of Jesus Christ,
    your Son, our Lord,
the savior of all mankind.
Through him the angels of heaven
offer their prayer of adoration
as they rejoice in your presence for ever.

Cum quibus et nostras voces ut admítti iúbeas, deprecámur,
socia exultatióne dicéntes:

Sanctus, Sanctus, Sanctus . . .

DE CONCEPTIONE
IMMACULATA BEATÆ MARIÆ VIRGINIS

DIE 8 DECEMBRIS
DE MYSTERIO MARIÆ ET ECCLESIÆ

Vere dignum et iustum est, æquum et salutáre,
nos tibi semper et ubíque grátias ágere:
Dómine, sancte Pater, omnípotens ætérne Deus:
Qui beatíssimam Vírginem Maríam
ab omni originális culpæ labe præservásti,
ut in ea, grátiæ tuæ plenitúdine ditáta,
dignam Fílio tuo Genetrícem præparáres,
et Sponsæ eius Ecclésiæ
sine ruga vel mácula formósæ signáres exórdium.
Fílium enim erat puríssima Virgo datúra,
qui crímina nostra Agnus ínnocens aboléret;
et ipsam præ ómnibus tuo pópulo disponébas
advocátam grátiæ et sanctitátis exémplar.

Et ídeo, choris angélicis sociáti,
te laudámus in gáudio confiténtes:

Sanctus, Sanctus, Sanctus . . .

DE ASSUMPTIONE
BEATÆ MARIÆ VIRIGINIS

DIE 15 AUGUSTI
GLORIA MARIAE ASSUMPTÆ

Vere dignum et iustum est, æquum et salutáre,
nos tibi semper et ubíque grátias ágere:
Dómine, sancte Pater, omnípotens ætérne Deus:
per Christum Dóminum nostrum.
Quóniam in cælos hódie Virgo Deípara est assúmpta,
Ecclésiæ tuæ consummándæ inítium et imágo,
ac pópulo peregrinánti certæ spei
	et solácii documéntum;
corruptiónem enim sepúlcri eam
	vidére mérito noluísti,
quæ Fílium tuum, vitæ omnis auctórem,
ineffabíliter de se génuit incarnátum.

May our voices be one with theirs
in their triumphant hymn of praise:

Holy, holy, holy Lord, . . .

IMMACULATE CONCEPTION   P58

DECEMBER 8
THE MYSTERY OF MARY AND THE CHURCH

Father, all-powerful and ever-living God,
we do well always and everywhere to give you thanks.
You allowed no stain of Adam's sin
to touch the Virgin Mary.
Full of grace, she was to be a worthy mother of your Son,
your sign of favor to the Church at its beginning,
and the promise of its perfection as the bride of Christ,
    radiant in beauty.
Purest of virgins, she was to bring forth your Son,
the innocent lamb who takes away our sins.
You chose her from all women to be
    our advocate with you
and our pattern of holiness.
In our joy we sing to your glory
with all the choirs of angels:

Holy, holy, holy Lord, . . .

ASSUMPTION   P59

AUGUST 15
MARY ASSUMED INTO GLORY

Father, all-powerful and ever-living God,
we do well always and everywhere
    to give you thanks
through Jesus Christ our Lord.
Today the virgin Mother of God was taken up into heaven
to be the beginning and the pattern of the Church
    in its perfection,
and a sign of hope and comfort for your people
    on their pilgrim way.
You would not allow decay to touch her body,
for she had given birth to your Son, the Lord of all life,
in the glory of the incarnation.

Et ídeo, choris angélicis sociáti,
te laudámus in gáudio confiténtes:

Sanctus, Sanctus, Sanctus . . .

DE ANGELIS

DE GLORIA DEI PER ANGELOS

60.   Sequens præfatio dicitur in Missis de Ss. Angelis.

Vere dignum et iustum est, æquum et salutáre,
nos tibi semper et ubíque grátias ágere:
Dómine, sancte Pater, omnípotens ætérne Deus:
Et in Archángelis Angelísque tuis tua præcónia non tacére,
quia ad excelléntiam tuam recúrrit et glóriam
quod angélica creatúra tibi probábilis honorétur:
et, cum illa sit amplo decóre digníssima,
tu quam sis imménsus et super ómnia
     præferéndus osténderis,
per Christum Dóminum nostrum.
Per quem multitúdo Angelórum tuam
     célebrat maiestátem,
quibus adorántes in exsultatióne coniúngimur,
una cum eis laudis voce clamántes:

Sanctus, Sanctus, Sanctus . . .

DE IOANNE BAPTISTA

DE MISSIONE PRÆCURSORIS.

Vere dignum et iustum est, æquum et salutáre,
nos tibi semper et ubíque grátias ágere:
Dómine, sancte Pater, omnípotens ætérne Deus:
per Christum Dóminum nostrum.
In cuius Præcursóre beáto Ioánne
tuam magnificentiam
     collaudámus,
quem inter natos mulíerum honóre
     præcípuo consecrásti.
Qui cum nascendo
     multa gáudia præstitísset,
et nondum éditus exsultásset ad humánæ salútis advéntum,
ipse solus ómnium prophetárum
Ágnum redemptiónis osténdit.

In our joy we sing to your glory
with all the choirs of angels:

Holy, holy, holy Lord, . . .

ANGELS P60

THE GLORY OF GOD IN THE ANGELS

This preface is said in Masses of the angels.

Father, all-powerful and ever-living God,
we do well always and everywhere
    to give you thanks.
In praising your faithful angels and archangels,
we also praise your glory,
for in honoring them,
    we honor you, their creator.
Their splendor shows us your greatness,
which surpasses in goodness
    the whole of creation.
Through Christ our Lord
the great army of angels rejoices in your glory.
In adoration and joy
we make their hymn of praise our own:

Holy, holy, holy Lord, . . .

JOHN THE BAPTIST P61

THE MISSION OF JOHN THE BAPTIST

This preface is said in Masses of Saint John the Baptist.

Father, all-powerful and ever-living God,
we do well always and everywhere
    to give you thanks
through Jesus Christ our Lord.
We praise your greatness
as we honor the prophet
who prepared the way before your Son.
You set John the Baptist apart from other men,
marking him out with special favor.
His birth brought great rejoicing:
even in the womb he leapt for joy,
so near was man's salvation.
You chose John the Baptist from all the prophets
to show the world its redeemer, the lamb of sacrifice.

Sed et sanctificándis étiam aquæ fluéntis
ipsum baptísmatis lavit auctórem,
et méruit fuso sánguine suprémum
    illi testimónium exhibére.
Et ídeo, cum cælórum Virtútibus,
in terris te iúgiter prædicámus,
maiestáti tuæ sine fine clamántes:

Sanctus, Sanctus, Sanctus . . .

DE S. IOSEPH, SPONSO B. M. V.

DE MISSIONE S. IOSEPH

61. Sequens præfatio dicitur in Missis de S. Ioseph, addita suo loco
mentione celebrationis diei, prout in singulis Missis indicatur.

Vere dignum et iustum est, æquum et salutáre,
nos tibi semper et ubíque grátias ágere:
Dómine, sancte Pater, omnípotens ætérne Deus:
Et te in . . . beáti Ioseph
débitis magnificáre præcóniis, benedícere et prædicáre.
Qui et vir iustus, a te Deíparæ Vírgini Sponsus est datus,
et fidélis servus ac prudens,
super Famíliam tuam est constitútus,
ut Unigénitum tuum,
Sancti Spíritus obumbratióne concéptum,
patérna vice custodíret,
    Iesum Christum Dóminum nostrum.
Per quem maiestátem tuam laudant Angeli,
adórant Dominatiónes, tremunt Potestátes.
Cæli cælorúmque Virtútes, ac beáta Séraphim,
sócia exsultatióne concélebrant.
Cum quibus et nostras voces ut admítti iúbeas, deprecámur,
súpplici confessióne dicéntes:

Sanctus, Sanctus, Sanctus . . .

DE PETRE ET PAULE, APOSTOLORUM

DE DUPLICI MISSIONE PETRI ET PAULI IN ECCLESIA

Vere dignum et iustum est, æquum et salutáre,
nos tibi semper et ubíque grátias ágere:
Dómine, sancte Pater, omnípotens ætérne Deus:

He baptized Christ, the giver of baptism,
in waters made holy by the one who was baptized.
You found John worthy of a martyr's death,
his last and greatest act of witness to your Son.
In our unending joy we echo on earth
the song of the angels in heaven,
as they praise your glory for ever:

Holy, holy, holy Lord, . . .

JOSEPH, HUSBAND OF MARY   P62

THE MISSION OF SAINT JOSEPH

This preface is said in Masses of Saint Joseph.

Father, all-powerful and ever-living God,
we do well always and everywhere
    to give you thanks
as we honor Saint Joseph.
He is that just man,
that wise and loyal servant,
whom you placed at the head of your family.
With a husband's love he cherished Mary,
the virgin Mother of God.
With fatherly care he watched
    over Jesus Christ your Son,
conceived by the power of the Holy Spirit.
Through Christ the choirs of angels
and all the powers of heaven
praise and worship your glory.
May our voices blend with theirs
as we join in their unending hymn:

Holy, holy, holy Lord, . . .

PETER AND PAUL, APOSTLES   P63

THE TWOFOLD MISSION OF PETER
AND PAUL IN THE CHURCH

This preface is said in Masses of Saint Peter and Saint Paul.

Father, all-powerful and ever-living God,
we do well always and everywhere
    to give you thanks.

Quia nos beáti apóstoli Petrus et Paulus
tua dispositióne lætíficant:
hic princeps fídei confiténdæ,
ille intellegéndæ clarus assértor;
hic relíquiis Israel instítuens
    Ecclésiam primitívam,
ille magíster et doctor géntium
    vocandárum.
Sic divérso consílio unam Christi
    famíliam congregántes,
par mundo venerábile,
    una coróna sociávit.
Et ídeo cum Sanctis et Angelis univérsis
te collaudámus, sine fine dicéntes:

Sanctus, Sanctus, Sanctus . . .

I DE APOSTOLIS

DE APOSTOLIS PASTORIBUS POPULI DEI

62.   Sequens præfatio dicitur in Missis Apostolorum, præsertim sanctorum
Petri et Pauli.

Vere dignum et iustum est, æquum et salutáre,
nos tibi semper et ubíque grátias ágere:
Dómine, sancte Pater, omnípotens ætérne Deus:
Qui gregem tuum, Pastor ætérne, non déseris,
sed per beátos Apóstolos
    contínua protectióne custódis,
ut iísdem rectóribus gubernétur,
quos Fílii tui vicários eídem
    contulísti præésse pastóres.
Et ídeo cum Angelis et Archángelis,
cum Thronis et Dominatiónibus,
cumque omni milítia cæléstis exércitus,
hymnum glóriæ tuæ cánimus, sine fine dicéntes:

Sanctus, Sanctus, Sanctus . . .

II DE APOSTOLIS

DE APOSTOLICO FUNDAMENTO ET TESTIMONIO

63.   Sequens præfatio dicitur in Missis Apostolorum et Evangelistarum.

Vere dignum et iustum est, æquum et salutáre,
nos tibi semper et ubíque grátias ágere:

You fill our hearts with joy
as we honor your great apostles:
Peter, our leader in the faith,
and Paul, its fearless preacher.
Peter raised up the Church
from the faithful flock of Israel.
Paul brought your call to the nations,
and became the teacher of the world.
Each in his chosen way gathered into unity
the one family of Christ.
Both shared a martyr's death
and are praised throughout the world.
Now, with the apostles and all the angels and saints,
we praise you for ever:

Holy, holy, holy Lord, . . .

APOSTLES I   P64

THE APOSTLES ARE SHEPHERDS OF GOD'S PEOPLE

This preface is said in Masses of the Apostles, especially of Saints Peter and
Paul.

Father, all-powerful and ever-living God,
we do well always and everywhere to give you thanks.
You are the eternal Shepherd
who never leaves his flock untended.
Through the apostles
you watch over us and protect us always.
You made them shepherds of the flock
to share in the work of your Son,
and from their place in heaven they guide us still.
And so, with all the choirs of angels in heaven
we proclaim your glory
and join in their unending hymn of praise:

Holy, holy, holy Lord, . . .

APOSTLES II   P65

APOSTOLIC FOUNDATION AND WITNESS

This preface is said in Masses of the apostles and evangelists.

Father, all-powerful
    and ever-living God,

Dómine, sancte Pater, omnípotens ætérne Deus:
per Christum Dóminum nostrum.

Quóniam Ecclésiam tuam
in apostólicis tribuísti consístere fundaméntis,
ut signum sanctitátis tuæ in terris manéret ipsa perpétuum,
et cæléstia præbéret cunctis homínibus documénta.

Quaprópter nunc et usque in sǽculum
cum omni milítia Angelórum
devóta tibi mente concínimus, clamántes atque dicéntes:

Sanctus, Sanctus, Sanctus . . .

DE SANCTIS MARTYRIBUS

DE SIGNO ET EXEMPLO MARTYRII

66. Sequens præfatio dicitur in sollemnitatibus et festis Ss. Martyrum. Dici
potest in memoriis ipsorum.

Vere dignum et iustum est, æquum et salutáre,
nos tibi semper et ubíque grátias ágere:
Dómine, sancte Pater, omnípotens ætérne Deus:
Quóniam beáti mártyris N.
    pro confessióne nóminis tui,
ad imitatiónem Christi,
sanguis effúsus tua mirabília maniféstat,
quibus pérficis in fragilitáte virtútem,
et vires infírmas ad testimónium róboras,
per Christum Dóminum nostrum.
Et ídeo, cum cælórum Virtútibus,
in terris te iúgiter celebrámus,
maiestáti tuæ sine fine clamántes:

Sanctus, Sanctus, Sanctus . . .

DE SANCTIS PASTORIBUS

DE PRÆSENTIA SANCTORUM PASTORUM IN ECCLESIA

67. Sequens præfatio dicitur in sollemnitatibus et festis Ss. Pastorum. Dici
potest in memoriis ipsorum.

Vere dignum et iustum est, æquum et salutáre,
nos tibi semper et ubíque grátias ágere:
Dómine, sancte Pater, omnípotens ætérne Deus:
per Christum Dóminum nostrum.
Quia sic tríbuis Ecclésiam tuam
    sancti N. festivitáte gaudére,

we do well always and everywhere
    to give you thanks.
You founded your Church on the apostles
to stand firm for ever
as the sign on earth of your infinite holiness
and as the living gospel for all men to hear.
With steadfast love
we sing your unending praise:
we join with the hosts of heaven in their triumphant song:

Holy, holy, holy Lord, . . .

MARTYRS   P66

THE SIGN AND EXAMPLE OF MARTYRDOM

This preface is said on the solemnities and feasts of martyrs. It may also be said on the memorials of martyrs.

Father, all-powerful and ever-living God,
we do well always and everywhere
    to give you thanks.
Your holy martyr N. followed the example of Christ
and gave his (her) life for the glory of your name.
His (her) death reveals your power
shining through our human weakness.
You choose the weak and make them strong
in bearing witness to you,
through Jesus Christ our Lord.
In our unending joy we echo on earth
the song of the angels in heaven
as they praise your glory for ever:

Holy, holy, holy Lord, . . .

PASTORS   P67

THE PRESENCE OF SHEPHERDS IN THE CHURCH

This preface is said on the solemnities and feasts of pastors. It may also be said on the memorials of pastors.

Father, all-powerful
    and ever-living God,
we do well always and everywhere
    to give you thanks.
You give the Church this feast
    in honor of Saint N.;

ut eam exémplo piæ conversatiónis corróbores,
verbo prædicatiónis erúdias,
gratáque tibi supplicatióne tueáris.
Et ídeo, cum Angelórum atque Sanctórum turba,
hymnum laudis tibi cánimus, sine fine dicéntes:

Sanctus, Sanctus, Sanctus . . .

DE SANCTIS VIRGINIBUS ET RELIGIOSIS

DE SIGNO VITÆ DEO CONSECRATÆ

68.   Sequens præfatio dicitur in sollemnitatibus et festis Ss. Virginum et Ss.
Religiosorum. Dici potest in memoriis ipsorum.

Vere dignum et iustum est, æquum et salutáre,
nos tibi semper et ubíque grátias ágere:
Dómine, sancte Pater, omnípotens ætérne Deus:
In Sanctis enim, qui Christo se dedicavérunt
propter regnum cælórum,
tuam decet providéntiam celebráre mirábilem,
qua humánam substántiam
et ad primæ oríginis révocas sanctitátem,
et ad experiénda dona,
quæ in novo sǽculo sunt habénda, perdúcis.
Et ídeo, cum Sanctis et Angelis univérsis,
te collaudámus, sine fine dicéntes:

Sanctus, Sanctus, Sanctus . . .

I DE SANCTIS

DE GLORIA SANCTORUM

64.   Sequens præfatio dicitur in Missis «de Omnibus Sanctis», de Sanctis
Patronis et Titularibus ecclesiæ, et in sollemnitatibus et festis Sanctorum,
nisi præfatio magis propria sit dicenda. Dici potest in memoriis Sanctorum.

Vere dignum et iustum est, æquum et salutáre,
nos tibi semper et ubíque grátias ágere:
Dómine, sancte Pater, omnípotens ætérne Deus:
Qui in Sanctórum concílio celebráris,
et eórum coronándo mérita tua
     dona corónas.
Qui nobis eórum conversatióne largíris exémplum,
et communióne consórtium,
     et intercessióne subsídium;
ut, tantis téstibus confirmáti,
ad propósitum certámen currámus invícti

you inspire us by his holy life,
instruct us by his preaching,
and give us your protection in answer to his prayers.
We join the angels and the saints
as they sing their unending hymn of praise:

Holy, holy, holy Lord, . . .

VIRGINS AND RELIGIOUS   P68

THE SIGN OF A LIFE CONSECRATED TO GOD

This preface is said on the solemnities and feasts of virgins and religious.
It may also be said on the memorials of virgins and religious.

Father, all-powerful and ever-living God,
we do well always and everywhere
   to give you thanks.
Today we honor your saints
who consecrated their lives to Christ
for the sake of the kingdom of heaven.
What love you show us
as you recall mankind to its innocence,
and invite us to taste on earth
the gifts of the world to come!
Now, with the saints and all the angels
we praise you for ever:

Holy, holy, holy Lord, . . .

HOLY MEN AND WOMEN I   P69

THE GLORY OF THE SAINTS

This preface is said in Masses of all saints, patrons, and titulars of churches,
and on the solemnities and feasts of saints which have no preface of their
own. It may also be said on the memorials of saints.

Father, all-powerful and ever-living God,
we do well always and everywhere
   to give you thanks.

You are glorified in your saints,
for their glory is the crowning of your gifts.
In their lives on earth
you gave us an example.
In our communion with them,
you give us their friendship.
In their prayer for the Church
you give us strength and protection.

et immarcescíbilem cum eis
    corónam glóriæ consequámur,
per Christum Dóminum nostrum.
Et ídeo cum Angelis et Archángelis,
cumque multíplici congregatióne Sanctórum,
hymnum laudis tibi cánimus, sine fine dicéntes:

Sanctus, Sanctus, Sanctus . . .

II DE SANCTIS

DE ACTIONE SANCTORUM

65. Sequens præfatio dicitur in Missis «de Omnibus Sanctis», de Sanctis
Patronis et Titularibus ecclesiæ, et in sollemnitatibus et festis Sanctorum,
nisi præfatio magis propria sit dicenda. Dici potest in memoriis Sanctorum.

V ere dignum et iustum est, æquum et salutáre,
nos tibi semper et ubíque grátias ágere:
Dómine, sancte Pater, omnípotens ætérne Deus:
per Christum Dóminum nostrum.
Tu enim Sanctórum tuórum confessióne mirábili
Ecclésiam tuam nova semper virtúte fecúndas,
nobísque certíssima præbes tuæ dilectiónis indícia.
Sed étiam, ad mystéria salútis implénda,
et ipsórum insígni incitámur exémplo
et pia intercessióne perpétuo commendámur.
Unde et nos, Dómine, cum Angelis et Sanctis univérsis
tibi confitémur, in exsultatióne dicéntes:

Sanctus, Sanctus, Sanctus . . .

DE OMNIS SANCTORUM

Die 1 novembris

DE GLORIA MATRIS NOSTRÆ IERUSALEM.

V ere dignum et iustum est, æquum et salutáre,
nos tibi semper et ubíque grátias ágere:
Dómine, sancte Pater, omnípotens ætérne Deus:
Nobis enim hódie civitátem tuam
    tríbuis celebráre,
quæ mater nostra est,
        cælestísque Ierúsalem,
ubi fratrum nostrórum iam te in ætérnum coróna colláudat.
Ad quam peregríni, per fidem accedéntes,
    alácriter festinámus,

This great company of witnesses spurs us on to victory,
to share their prize of everlasting glory,
through Jesus Christ our Lord.

With angels and archangels
and the whole company of saints
we sing our unending hymn of praise:

Holy, holy, holy Lord, . . .

HOLY MEN AND WOMEN II   P70

THE ACTIVITY OF THE SAINTS

This preface is said in Masses of all saints, patrons, and titulars of churches,
and on the solemnities and feasts of saints which have no preface of their
own. It may also be said on the memorials of saints.

Father, all-powerful and ever-living God,
we do well always and everywhere
   to give you thanks.

You renew the Church in every age
by raising up men and women outstanding in holiness,
living witnesses of your unchanging love.
They inspire us by their heroic lives,
and help us by their constant prayers
to be the living sign of your saving power.
We praise you, Lord, with all the angels and saints
in their song of joy:

Holy, holy, holy Lord, . . .

ALL SAINTS   P71

NOVEMBER 1

JERUSALEM, OUR MOTHER

Father, all-powerful and ever-living God,
we do well always and everywhere
   to give you thanks.
Today we keep the festival of your holy city,
the heavenly Jerusalem, our mother.
Around your throne
the saints, our brothers and sisters, sing your praise for ever.
Their glory fills us with joy,
and their communion with us in your Church
gives us inspiration and strength

congaudéntes de Ecclésiæ
sublímium glorificatióne membrórum,
qua simul fragilitáti nostræ adiuménta et exémpla concédis.
Et ídeo, cum ipsórum Angelorúmque frequéntia,
una te magnificámus, laudis voce clamántes:

Sanctus, Sanctus, Sanctus . . .

DE MATRIMONIO I

DE DIGNITATE FOEDERIS NUPTIARUM.

V ere dignum et iustum est, æquum et salutáre,
nos tibi semper et ubíque grátias ágere:
Dómine, sancte Pater, omnípotens ætérne Deus:
Qui fœdera nuptiárum blando concórdiæ iugo
et insolúbili pacis vínculo nexuísti,
ut multiplicándis adoptiónum fíliis
sanctórum connubiórum fecúnditas pudíca servíret.

Tua enim, Dómine, providéntia,
tuáque grátia ineffabílibus
    modis utrúmque dispénsas,
ut, quod generátio ad mundi prodúxit ornátum,
regenerátio ad Ecclésiæ perdúcat augméntum:
per Christum Dóminum nostrum.

Per quem, cum Angelis
    et ómnibus Sanctis,
hymnum laudis tibi cánimus,
    sine fine dicéntes:

Sanctus, Sanctus, Sanctus . . .

DE MATRIMONIO II

DE MAGNO SACRAMENTO MATRIMONII

V ere dignum et iustum est, æquum et salutáre,
nos tibi semper et ubíque grátias ágere:
Dómine, sancte Pater, omnípotens ætérne Deus:
per Christum Dóminum nostrum.
Quia novum exuísti cum tuo pópulo testaméntum,
ut, quem mortis et resurrectiónis redemísses mystério,
divínæ in Christo fáceres natúræ consórtem
eiúsque in cælis glóriæ coherédem.

as we hasten on our pilgrimage of faith,
eager to meet them.
With their great company and all the angels
we praise your glory
as we cry out with one voice:

Holy, holy, holy Lord, ...

MARRIAGE I P72

THE DIGNITY OF THE MARRIAGE BOND

Father, all-powerful and ever-living God,
we do well always and everywhere to give you thanks.
By this sacrament your grace unites man and woman
in an unbreakable bond of love and peace.
You have designed the chaste love of husband and wife
for the increase both of the human family
and of your own family born in baptism.
You are the loving Father of the world of nature;
you are the loving Father of the new creation of grace.
In Christian marriage you bring together
    the two orders of creation:
nature's gift of children enriches the world
and your grace enriches also your Church.
Through Christ the choirs of angels and all the saints
praise and worship your glory.
May our voices blend with theirs
as we join in their unending hymn:

Holy, holy, holy Lord, ...

MARRIAGE II P73

THE GREAT SACRAMENT OF MARRIAGE

Father, all-powerful and ever-living God,
we do well always and everywhere to give you thanks
through Jesus Christ our Lord.
Through him you entered into a new covenant with
    your people.
You restored man to grace
in the saving mystery of redemption.
You gave him a share in the divine life
through his union with Christ.
You made him an heir of Christ's eternal glory.

Cuius piíssimam grátiæ largitáte
in viri mulierísque significásti connúbio,
ut ad ineffábile tui amóris consílium
nos revocáret quod ágitur sacraméntum.
Et ídeo cum Angelis
    et ómnibus Sanctis,
te laudámus, sine fine dicéntes:

Sanctus, Sanctus, Sanctus . . .

DE MATRIMONIO III

DE MATRIMONIO UT SIGNUM DIVINÆ CARITATIS

V ere dignum et iustum est, æquum et salutáre,
nos tibi semper et ubíque grátias ágere:
Dómine, sancte Pater, omnípotens ætérne Deus:
Qui hóminem pietátis tuæ dono creátum
ad tantam voluísti dignitátem extólli,
ut in viri mulierísque consórtio
veram relínqueres tui amóris imáginem;
quem enim ex caritáte creásti,
eum ad caritátis legem vocáre non désinis,
ut ætérnæ tuæ caritátis partícipem esse concédas.
Cuius connúbii sancti mystérium
dum tuæ dilectiónis signum exsístit,
amórem sacrat humánum:
per Christum Dóminum nostrum.
Per quem, cum Angelis et ómnibus Sanctis
hymnum laudis tibi cánimus, sine fine dicéntes:

Sanctus, Sanctus, Sanctus . . .

DE PROFESSIONE RELIGIOSA

DE VITA RELIGIOSA UT SERVITIUM DEI PER CHRISTI IMITATIONEM

V ere dignum et iustum est, æquum et salutáre,
nos tibi semper et ubíque grátias ágere:
Dómine, sancte Pater, omnípotens ætérne Deus:
per Christum Dóminum nostrum.
Qui, de radíce Vírginis flos illibátus egréssus,
mundos corde dixit beátos
suáque conversatióne dócuit castitátis fastígium.

This outpouring of love in the new covenant of grace
is symbolized in the marriage covenant
that seals the love of husband and wife
and reflects your divine plan of love.
And so, with the angels and all the saints in heaven
we proclaim your glory
and join in their unending hymn of praise:

Holy, holy, holy Lord, . . .

MARRIAGE III   P74

MARRIAGE, A SIGN OF GOD'S LOVE

Father, all-powerful and ever-living God,
we do well always and everywhere
    to give you thanks.
You created man in love to share your divine life.
We see his high destiny in the love of husband and wife,
which bears the imprint of your own divine love.
Love is man's origin,
love is his constant calling,
love is his fulfillment in heaven.
The love of man and woman
is made holy in the sacrament of marriage,
and becomes the mirror of your everlasting love.
Through Christ the choirs of angels and all the saints
praise and worship your glory.
May our voices blend with theirs
as we join in their unending hymn:

Holy, holy, holy Lord, . . .

RELIGIOUS PROFESSION   P75

THE RELIGIOUS LIFE,
SERVING GOD BY IMITATING CHRIST

Father, all-powerful and ever-living God,
we do well always and everywhere
    to give you thanks
through Jesus Christ our Lord.
He came, the son of a virgin mother,
named those blessed who were pure of heart,
and taught by his whole life the perfection of chastity.

Qui tuis semper beneplácitis optávit hærére,
et, usque ad mortem pro nobis factus obœdiens,
hóstiam se tibi vóluit perféctæ suavitátis offérre.

Qui ómnia propter te relinquéntes in terris
ad servítium tuæ maiestátis dicávit impénsius
et cælórum confirmávit inventúros esse thesáurum.

Et ídeo cum Angelórum atque Sanctórum turba,
hymnum laudis tibi cánimus, sine fine dicéntes:

Sanctus, Sanctus, Sanctus . . .

DE UNITATE CHRISTIANORUM

DE UNITATE CORPORIS CHRISTI, QUOD EST ECCLESIA

Vere dignum et iustum est, æquum et salutáre,
nos tibi semper et ubíque grátias ágere:
Dómine, sancte Pater, omnípotens ætérne Deus:
per Christum Dóminum nostrum.
Per ipsum enim nos adduxísti
　　ad agnitiónem tuæ veritátis,
ut uníus fídei et baptísmi vínculo
　　Corpus eius efficerémur;
per ipsum in cunctis géntibus
largítus es Spíritum Sanctum tuum,
qui, in diversitáte donorum
　　mirábilis operátor
et unitátis efféctor,
fílios adoptiónis inhábitat
totámque replet et regit Ecclésiam.
Et ídeo, choris angélicis sociáti,
te laudámus in gáudio confiténtes:

Sanctus, Sanctus, Sanctus . . .

I DE DEFUNCTIS

DE SPE RESURRECTIONIS IN CHRISTO

75. Sequens præfatio dicitur in Missis defunctorum.

Vere dignum et iustum est, æquum et salutáre,
nos tibi semper et ubíque grátias ágere:
Dómine, sancte Pater, omnípotens ætérne Deus:
per Christum Dóminum nostrum.

He chose always to fulfill your holy will,
and became obedient even to dying for us,
offering himself to you a perfect oblation.
He consecrated more closely to your service
those who leave all things for your sake,
and promised that they would find a heavenly treasure.
And so, we join the angels and the saints
as they sing their unending hymn of praise:

Holy, holy, holy Lord, . . .

CHRISTIAN UNITY   P76

THE UNITY OF CHRIST'S BODY, WHICH IS THE CHURCH

Father, all-powerful and ever-living God,
we do well always and everywhere to give you thanks
through Jesus Christ our Lord.
Through Christ you bring us
    to the knowledge of your truth,
that we may be united by one faith and one baptism
to become his body.
Through Christ you have given the Holy Spirit
    to all peoples.
How wonderful the works of the Spirit,
revealed in so many gifts!
Yet how marvelous is the unity
the Spirit creates from the diversity,
as he dwells in the hearts of your children,
filling the whole Church with his presence
and guiding it with his wisdom!
In our joy we sing to your glory
with all the choirs of angels:

Holy, holy, holy Lord, . . .

CHRISTIAN DEATH I   P77

THE HOPE OF RISING IN CHRIST

This preface is said in Masses for the dead.

Father, all-powerful and ever-living God,
we do well always and everywhere
    to give you thanks
through Jesus Christ our Lord.

In quo nobis spes beátæ resurrectiónis effúlsit,
ut, quos contrístat certa moriéndi condício,
eósdem consolétur futúræ immortalitátis promíssio.
Tuis enim fidélibus, Dómine, vita mutátur, non tóllitur,
et, dissolúta terréstris huius incolátus domo,
ætérna in cælis habitátio comparátur.

Et ídeo cum Angelis et Archángelis,
cum Thronis et Dominatiónibus,
cumque omni milítia cæléstis exércitus,
hymnum glóriæ tuæ cánimus,
sine fine dicéntes:

Sanctus, Sanctus, Sanctus . . .

II DE DEFUNCTIS

CHRISTUS MORTUUS EST PRO VITA NOSTRA

76. Sequens præfatio dicitur in Missis defunctorum.

V̇ere dignum et iustum est, æquum et salutáre,
nos tibi semper et ubíque grátias ágere:
Dómine, sancte Pater, omnípotens ætérne Deus:
per Christum Dóminum nostrum.
Ipse enim mortem unus accépit,
ne omnes nos morerémur;
immo unus mori dignátus est,
ut omnes tibi perpétuo viverémus.

Et ídeo, choris angélicis sociáti,
te laudámus in gáudio confiténtes:

Sanctus, Sanctus, Sanctus . . .

III DE DEFUNCTIS

CHRISTUS, SALUS ET VITA

77. Sequens præfatio dicitur in Missis defunctorum.

V̇ere dignum et iustum est, æquum et salutáre,
nos tibi semper et ubíque grátias ágere:
Dómine, sancte Pater, omnípotens ætérne Deus:
per Christum Dóminum nostrum.
Qui est salus mundi, vita hóminum,
    resurréctio mortuórum.

Per quem maiestátem tuam adórat exércitus Angelórum,
ante conspéctum tuum in æternitáte lætántium.

In him, who rose from the dead,
our hope of resurrection dawned.
The sadness of death gives way
to the bright promise of immortality.

Lord, for your faithful people life is changed, not ended.
When the body of our earthly dwelling lies in death
we gain an everlasting dwelling place in heaven.

And so, with all the choirs of angels in heaven
we proclaim your glory
and join in their unending hymn of praise:

Holy, holy, holy Lord, . . .

CHRISTIAN DEATH II   P78

CHRIST'S DEATH, OUR LIFE

This preface is said in Masses for the dead.

Father, all-powerful and ever-living God,
we do well always and everywhere
    to give you thanks
through Jesus Christ our Lord.
He chose to die
that he might free all men from dying.
He gave his life
that we might live to you alone for ever.
In our joy we sing to your glory
with all the choirs of angels:

Holy, holy, holy Lord, . . .

CHRISTIAN DEATH III   P79

CHRIST, SALVATION AND LIFE

This preface is said in Masses for the dead.

Father, all-powerful and ever-living God,
we do well always and everywhere to give you thanks
through Jesus Christ our Lord.
In him the world is saved, man is reborn,
and the dead rise again to life.
Through Christ the angels of heaven
offer their prayer of adoration
as they rejoice in your presence for ever.

Cum quibus et nostras voces
  ut admítti iúbeas, deprecámur,
sócia exsultatióne dicéntes:

Sanctus, Sanctus, Sanctus . . .

IV DE DEFUNCTIS

DE VITA TERRENA AD GLORIAM CÆLESTEM

78.   Sequens præfatio dicitur in Missis defunctorum.

Vere dignum et iustum est, æquum et salutare,
nos tibi semper et ubíque grátias ágere:
Dómine, sancte Pater, omnípotensætérne Deus:
Cuius império náscimur, cuius arbítro régimur,
cuius præcépto in terra, de qua sumpti sumus,
peccáti lege absólvimur.
Et, qui per mortem Fílii tui redémpti sumus,
ad ipsíus resurrectiónis glóriam
tuo nutu excitámur.
Et ídeo, cum Angelórum atque Sanctórum turba,
hymnum laudis tibi cánimus, sine fine dicéntes:

Sanctus, Sanctus, Sanctus . . .

V DE DEFUNCTIS

DE RESURRECTIONE NOSTRA PER VICTORIAM CHRISTI

79.   Sequens præfatio dicitur in Missis defunctorum.

Vere dignum et iustum est, æquum et salutáre,
nos tibi semper et ubíque grátias ágere:
Dómine, sancte Pater, omnípotens ætérne Deus:
Quia, etsi nostri est mériti quod perímus,
tuæ tamen est pietátis et grátiæ
quod, pro peccáto morte consúmpti,
per Christi victóriam redémpti,
cum ipso revocámur ad vitam.
Et ídeo, cum cælórum Virtútibus,
in terris te iúgiter celebrámus,
maiestáti tuæ sine fine clamántes:

Sanctus, Sanctus, Sanctus . . .

May our voices be one with theirs
in their triumphant hymn of praise:

Holy, holy, holy Lord, . . .

CHRISTIAN DEATH IV   P80
FROM EARTHLY LIFE TO HEAVEN'S GLORY

This preface is said in Masses for the dead.

Father, all-powerful and ever-living God,
we do well always and everywhere
    to give you thanks.
By your power you bring us to birth.
By your providence you rule our lives.
By your command you free us at last from sin
as we return to the dust from which we came.
Through the saving death of your Son
we rise at your word to the glory of the resurrection.
Now we join the angels and the saints
as they sing their unending hymn of praise:

Holy, holy, holy Lord, . . .

CHRISTIAN DEATH V   P81
OUR RESURRECTION THROUGH CHRIST'S VICTORY

This preface is said in Masses for the dead.

Father, all-powerful and ever-living God,
we do well always and everywhere to give you thanks
through Jesus Christ our Lord.
Death is the just reward for our sins,
yet, when at last we die,
your loving kindness calls us back to life
in company with Christ,
whose victory is our redemption.
Our hearts are joyful,
for we have seen your salvation,
and now with the angels and saints we praise you for ever:

Holy, holy, holy Lord, . . .

[In the dioceses of the United States]

INDEPENDENCE DAY AND   P82
OTHER CIVIC OBSERVANCES I

Father,
all-powerful and ever-living God,
we do well to sing your praise for ever,
and to give you thanks in all we do
through Jesus Christ our Lord.
He spoke to men a message of peace
and taught us to live as brothers.
His message took form in the vision of our fathers
as they fashioned a nation
where men might live as one.
This message lives on in our midst
as a task for men today
and a promise for tomorrow.
We thank you, Father, for your blessings in the past
and for all that, with your help, we must yet achieve.
And so, with hearts full of love,
we join the angels today and every day of our lives,
to sing your glory in a hymn of endless praise:

Holy, holy, holy Lord, . . .

INDEPENDENCE DAY AND   P83
OTHER CIVIC OBSERVANCES II

Father, all-powerful and ever-living God,
we praise your oneness and truth.
We praise you as the God of creation,
as the Father of Jesus, the Savior of mankind,
in whose image we seek to live.
He loved the children of the lands he walked
and enriched them with his witness of justice and truth.
He lived and died that we might be reborn in the Spirit
and filled with love of all men.
And so, with hearts full of love,
we join the angels, today and every day of our lives,
to sing your glory in a hymn of endless praise:

Holy, holy, holy Lord, . . .

THANKSGIVING DAY   P84

Father, we do well to join all creation,
in heaven and on earth,
in praising you, our mighty God,
through Jesus Christ our Lord.
You made man to your own image
and set him over all creation.
Once you chose a people
and gave them a destiny
and, when you brought them
    out of bondage to freedom,
they carried with them the promise
that all men would be blessed
and all men could be free.
What the prophets pledged
was fulfilled in Jesus Christ,
your Son and our saving Lord.
It has come to pass in every generation
for all men who have believed that Jesus
by his death and resurrection
gave them a new freedom in his Spirit.
It happened to our fathers,
who came to this land as if out of the desert
into a place of promise and hope.
It happens to us still, in our time,
as you lead all men through your Church
to the blessed vision of peace.
And so, with hearts full of love,
we join the angels, today and every day of our lives,
to sing your glory in a hymn of endless praise:

Holy, holy, holy Lord, . . .

PREX EUCHARISTICA I

(SEU CANON ROMANUS)

80. Sacerdos, manibus extensis, dicit:

T e ígitur, clementíssime Pater,
per Iesum Christum, Fílium tuum,
    Dóminum nostrum,
súpplices rogámus ac pétimus,

iungit manus et dicit:

uti accépta hábeas

signat semel super panem et calicem simul, dicens:

et benedícas ✠ hæc dona, hæc múnera,
hæc sancta sacrifícia illibáta,

extensis manibus prosequitur:

in primis, quæ tibi offérimus
pro Ecclésia tua sancta cathólica:
quam pacificáre, custodíre, adunáre
et régere dignéris toto orbe terrárum:
una cum fámulo tuo Papa nostro N.
et Antístite nostro N.*
et ómnibus orthodóxis atque cathólicæ
et apostólicæ fídei cultóribus.

81. COMMEMORATIO PRO VIVIS

M eménto, Dómine, famulórum
    famularúmque tuárum N. et N.

Iungit manus et orat aliquantulum pro quibus orare intendit.

Deinde, manibus extensis, prosequitur:

et ómnium circumstántium,
quorum tibi fides cógnita est et nota devótio,
pro quibus tibi offérimus:

---

* Hic fieri potest mentio de Episcopis Coadiutoribus vel Auxiliariis ut in
   Institutione Generali Missalis Romani (=IGMR), 109, notatur.

EUCHARISTIC PRAYER I

(ROMAN CANON)   **kneel**

In the first eucharistic prayer, the words in brackets may be omitted. The priest, with hands extended, says:

We come to you, Father,

with praise and thanksgiving,
through Jesus Christ your Son.

He joins his hands and, making the sign of the cross once over both bread and chalice, says:

Through him we ask you to accept and bless ✠
these gifts we offer you in sacrifice.

With hands extended, he continues:

We offer them for your holy catholic Church,
watch over it, Lord, and guide it;
grant it peace and unity throughout the world.
We offer them for N. our Pope,
for N. our bishop,[10]
and for all who hold and teach
     the catholic faith
that comes to us from the apostles.

COMMEMORATION OF THE LIVING

Remember, Lord, your people,
especially those for whom we now pray, N. and N.

He prays for them briefly with hands joined.

Then, with hands extended, he continues:

Remember all of us gathered here
     before you.
You know how firmly we believe in you

---

10. When several are to be named, a general form is used: **for** N. **our bishop and his assistant bishops**, as in GIRM, 172.

vel qui tibi ófferunt hoc sacrifícium laudis,
pro se suísque ómnibus:
pro redemptióne animárum suárum,
pro spe salútis et incolumitátis suæ:
tibíque reddunt vota sua
ætérno Deo, vivo et vero.

82. Infra Actionem

PC
or
C2

Communicántes,
et memóriam venerántes,
in primis gloriósæ semper Vírginis Maríæ,
Genetrícis Dei et Dómini nostri Iesu Christi:
† sed et beáti Ioseph, eiúsdem Vírginis Sponsi,
et beatórum Apostolórum ac Mártyrum tuórum,
Petri et Pauli, Andréæ,

> [Iacóbi, Ioánnis,
> Thomæ, Iacóbi, Philíppi,
> Bartholomǽi, Matthǽi,
> Simónis et Thaddǽi:
> Lini, Cleti, Cleméntis, Xysti,
> Cornélii, Cypriáni,
> Lauréntii, Chrysógoni,
> Ioánnis et Pauli,
> Cosmæ et Damiáni]

et ómnium Sanctórum tuórum;
quorum méritis precibúsque concédas,
ut in ómnibus protectiónis tuæ muniámur auxílio.

> [Per Christum Dóminum nostrum. Amen.]

COMMUNICANTES PROPRIA

In Nativitate Domini et per octavam

83. Communicántes,
et (noctem sacratíssimam) diem sacratíssimum celebrántes,
(qua) quo beátæ Maríæ intemeráta virgínitas
huic mundo édidit Salvatórem:

and dedicate ourselves to you.
We offer you this sacrifice of praise
for ourselves and those who are dear to us.
We pray to you, our living
      and true God,
for our well-being and redemption.

In union with the whole Church
      we honor Mary,
the ever-virgin mother of Jesus Christ
      our Lord and God.
† We honor Joseph, her husband,
the apostles and martyrs
Peter and Paul, Andrew,

      [James, John, Thomas,
      James, Philip,
      Bartholomew, Matthew, Simon and Jude;
      we honor Linus, Cletus, Clement, Sixtus,
      Cornelius, Cyprian, Lawrence, Chrysogonus,
      John and Paul, Cosmas and Damian]

and all the saints.
May their merits
      and prayers
gain us your constant help
      and protection.

      [Through Christ our Lord. Amen.]

SPECIAL FORMS of In union with the whole Church
Christmas and during the Christmas Octave
In union with the whole Church
we celebrate that day (night)
when Mary without loss of her virginity
gave the world its savior.

sed et memóriam venerántes,
in primis eiúsdem gloriósæ semper Vírginis Maríæ,
Genetrícis eiúsdem Dei et Dómini nostri Iesu Christi: †

In Epiphania Domini

84.Communicántes,
et diem sacratíssimum celebrántes,
quo Unigénitus tuus,
in tua tecum glória coætérnus,
in veritáte carnis nostræ visibíliter corporális appáruit:
sed et memóriam venerántes,
in primis gloriósæ semper Vírginis Maríæ,
Genetrícis eiúsdem Dei et Dómini nostri Iesu Christi: †

Feria Quinta Hebdomadæ Sanctæ

Communicántes,
et diem sacratíssimum celebrántes
quo Dóminus noster Jesus Christus
pro nobis est tráditus,
sed et memóriam venerántes,
in primis gloriósæ semper Vírginis Maríæ,
Genetrícis eiúsdem Dei et Dómini nostri Iesu Christi: †

A Missa Vigiliæ paschalis
usque ad dominicam II Paschæ

85.Communicántes,
et (noctem sacratíssimam) diem sacratíssimum celebrántes
Resurrectiónis Dómini nostri Iesu Christi secúndum carnem:
sed et memóriam venerántes,
in primis gloriósæ semper Vírginis Maríæ,
Genetrícis eiúsdem Dei et Dómini nostri Iesu Christi: †

In Ascensione Domini

86.Communicántes,
et diem sacratíssimum celebrántes,
quo Dóminus noster,
unigénitus Fílius tuus,
unítam sibi fragilitátis nostræ substántiam
in glóriæ tuæ déxtera collocávit:
sed et memóriam venerántes,
in primis gloriósæ semper Vírginis Maríæ,
Genetrícis eiúsdem Dei et Dómini nostri Iesu Christi: †

We honor Mary,
the ever-virgin mother of
    Jesus Christ our Lord and God. †

Epiphany

In union with the whole Church
we celebrate that day
when your only Son,
sharing your eternal glory,
showed himself in a human body.
We honor Mary,
the ever-virgin mother of
    Jesus Christ our Lord and God.†

Holy Thursday

In union with the whole Church
we celebrate that day
when Jesus Christ, our Lord,
was betrayed for us.
We honor Mary,
the ever-virgin mother of
    Jesus Christ our Lord and God.†

From the Easter Vigil to
the Second Sunday of Easter Inclusive

In union with the whole Church
we celebrate that day (night)
when Jesus Christ, our Lord,
rose from the dead in his human body.
We honor Mary,
the ever-virgin mother of Jesus Christ our Lord and God.†

Ascension

In union with the whole Church
we celebrate that day
when your only Son, our Lord,
took his place with you
and raised our frail human nature
    to glory.
We honor Mary,
the ever-virgin mother of
    Jesus Christ our Lord and God.†

In dominica Pentecostes

87.Communicántes,
et diem sacratíssimum Pentecóstes celebrántes,
quo Spíritus Sanctus
Apóstolis in ígneis linguis appáruit:
sed et memóriam venerántes,
in primis gloriósæ semper Vírginis Maríæ,
Genetricis Dei et Dómini nostri Iesu Christi: †

---

88.   Manibus extensis, prosequitur:

Hanc ígitur oblatiónem servitútis nostræ,
sed et cunctæ famíliæ tuæ,
quǽsumus, Dómine, ut placátus accípias:
diésque nostros in tua pace dispónas,
atque ab ætérna damnatióne nos éripi
et in electórum tuórum iúbeas grege numerári.

Iungit manus.

[Per Christum Dóminum nostrum. Amen.]

HANC IGITUR PROPIA
Feria Quinta Hebdomadæ Sanctæ

Hanc ígitur oblatiónem servitútis nostræ,
sed et cunctæ famíliæ tuæ,
quam tibi offérimus ob diem,
in qua Dóminus noster Iesus Christus
trádidit discipulis suis
quǽsumus, Dómine, ut placátus accípias:
diésque nostros in tua pace dispónas,
atque ab ætérna damnatióne nos éripi
et in electórum tuórum iúbeas grege numerári.

Iungit manus.

[Per Christum Dóminum nostrum. Amen.]

A Missa Vigiliæ paschalis usque ad dominicam II Paschæ

89.Hanc ígitur oblatiónem servitútis nostræ,
sed et cunctæ famíliæ tuæ,
quam tibi offérimus
pro his quoque, quos regeneráre dignátus es ex aqua
     et Spíritu Sancto,

Pentecost

In union with the whole Church
we celebrate the day of Pentecost
when the Holy Spirit appeared to the apostles
in the form of countless tongues.
We honor Mary,
the ever-virgin mother of
    Jesus Christ our Lord and God.✝

With hands extended, he continues:

Father, accept this offering
from your whole family.
Grant us your peace in this life,
save us from final damnation,
and count us among those
    you have chosen.

He joins his hands.

    [Through Christ our Lord. Amen.]

SPECIAL FORMS of Father, accept this offering
Holy Thursday

Father, accept this offering
from your whole family
in memory of the day when Jesus Christ, our Lord,
gave the mysteries of his body and blood
for his disciples to celebrate.
Grant us your peace in this life,
save us from final damnation,
and count us among those
    you have chosen.

He joins his hands.

    [Through Christ our Lord. Amen.]

From the Easter Vigil to Second Sunday of Easter Inclusive

Father, accept this offering
from your whole family
and from those born
    into the new life
of water and the Holy Spirit,

tríbuens eis remissiónem ómnium peccatórum,
quǽsumus, Dómine, ut placátus accípias:
diésque nostros in tua pace dispónas,
atque ab ætérna damnatióne nos éripi
et in electórum tuórum iúbeas grege numerári.

Iungit manus.

[Per Christum Dóminum nostrum. Amen.]

---

90.   Tenens manus expansas, super oblata, dicit:

Quam oblatiónem tu, Deus,
    in ómnibus, quǽsumus,
benedíctam, adscríptam, ratam,
rationábilem, acceptabilémque fácere dignéris:
ut nobis Corpus et Sanguis fiat dilectíssimi Fílii tui,
Dómini nostri Iesu Christi.

Iungit manus.

[Per Christum Dóminum nostrum. Amen.]

91.   In formulis quæ sequuntur, verba Dómini proferantur distincte et
aperte, prouti natura eorundem verborum requirit.

Qui, prídie quam paterétur,

accipit panem, eumque parum elevatum super altare tenens, prosequitur:

accépit panem in sanctas ac venerábiles manus suas,

elevat oculos,

et elevátis óculis in cælum
ad te Deum Patrem suum omnipoténtem,
tibi grátias agens benedíxit,
fregit,
dedítque discípulis suis, dicens:

parum se inclinat

with all their sins forgiven.
Grant us your peace in this life,
save us from final damnation,
and count us among those
   you have chosen.

He joins his hands.

[Through Christ our Lord. Amen.]

With hands outstretched over the offerings, he says:

B less and approve our offering;
make it acceptable to you,
an offering in spirit and in truth.
Let it become for us
the body and blood of Jesus Christ,
your only Son, our Lord.

He joins his hands.

[Through Christ our Lord. Amen.]

The words of the Lord in the following formulas should be spoken clearly
and distinctly, as their meaning demands.

T he day before he suffered[11]

He takes the bread and, raising it a little above the altar, continues:

he took bread in his sacred hands

He looks upward.

and looking up to heaven,
to you, his almighty Father,
he gave you thanks and praise.
He broke the bread,
gave it to his disciples, and said:

He bows slightly.

---

11. HOLY THURSDAY

The day before he suffered
to save us and all men,
that is today,

ACCÍPITE ET MANDUCÁTE EX HOC OMNES:
HOC EST ENIM CORPUS MEUM,
QUOD PRO VOBIS TRADÉTUR.

Hostiam consecratam ostendit populo, reponit super patenam, et
genuflexus adorat.

92. Postea prosequitur:

Símili modo, postquam cenátum est,

accipit calicem, eumque parum elevatum super altare tenens, prosequitur:

accípiens et hunc præclárum cálicem
in sanctas ac venerábiles manus suas,
item tibi grátias agens benedíxit,
dedítque discípulis suis, dicens:

parum se inclinat:

ACCÍPITE ET BÍBITE EX EO OMNES:
HIC EST ENIM CALIX SÁNGUINIS MEI
NOVI ET ÆTÉRNI TESTAMÉNTI,
QUI PRO VOBIS ET PRO MULTIS EFFUNDÉTUR
IN REMISSIÓNEM PECCATÓRUM.
HOC FÁCITE IN MEAM COMMEMORATIÓNEM.

Calicem ostendit populo, depónit super corporale, et genuflexus adorat.

93. Deinde dicit:

Mystérium fídei.

Et populus prosequitur, acclamans:

Mortem tuam annuntiámus, Dómine,
et tuam resurrectiónem confitémur,
      donec vénias.

TAKE THIS, ALL OF YOU, AND EAT IT:
THIS IS MY BODY WHICH WILL BE GIVEN UP FOR YOU.

He shows the consecrated host to the people, places it on the paten, and genuflects in adoration.

Then he continues:

When supper was ended,

He takes the chalice and, raising it a little above the altar, continues:

he took the cup.
Again he gave you thanks and praise,
gave the cup to his disciples, and said:

He bows slightly.

TAKE THIS, ALL OF YOU, AND DRINK FROM IT:
THIS IS THE CUP OF MY BLOOD,
THE BLOOD OF THE NEW AND EVERLASTING COVENANT.
IT WILL BE SHED FOR YOU AND FOR ALL
SO THAT SINS MAY BE FORGIVEN.
DO THIS IN MEMORY OF ME.

He shows the chalice to the people, places it on the corporal, and genuflects in adoration.

Then he sings or says:

Let us proclaim the mystery of faith:

People with celebrant and concelebrants:

Christ has died,
Christ is risen,
Christ will come again.

or:

Dying you destroyed our death,
rising you restored our life.
Lord Jesus, come in glory.

Vel:

**Quotiescúmque manducámus panem hunc
et cálicem bíbimus,
mortem tuam annuntiámus, Dómine, donec vénias.**

Vel:

**Salvátor mundi, salva nos,
qui per crucem et resurrectiónem tuam
liberásti nos.**

94.   Postea, extensis manibus, sacerdos dicit:

Unde et mémores, Dómine,
nos servi tui,
sed et plebs tua sancta,
eiúsdem Christi, Fílii tui, Dómini nostri,
tam beátæ passiónis,
necnon et ab ínferis resurrectiónis,
sed et in cælos gloriósæ ascensiónis:
offérimus præcláræ maiestáti tuæ
de tuis donis ac datis
hóstiam puram,
hóstiam sanctam,
hóstiam immaculátam,
Panem sanctum vitæ ætérnæ
et Cálicem salútis perpétuæ.

95. Supra quæ propítio ac seréno vultu
respícere dignéris:
et accepta habére,
sícuti accépta habére dignátus es
múnera púeri tui iusti Abel,
et sacrifícium Patriárchæ nostri Abrahæ,
et quod tibi óbtulit
      summus sacérdos tuus Melchísedech,
sanctum sacrifícium, immaculátam hóstiam.

or:

When we eat this bread and drink this cup,
we proclaim your death, Lord Jesus,
until you come in glory.

or:

Lord, by your cross and resurrection
you have set us free.
You are the Savior of the world.

Then, with hands extended, the priest says:

Father, we celebrate the memory of Christ,
   your Son.
We, your people and
   your ministers,
recall his passion,
his resurrection from the dead,
and his ascension into glory;
and from the many gifts
   you have given us
we offer to you, God of
   glory and majesty,
this holy and perfect sacrifice:
the bread of life
and the cup of eternal salvation.

Look with favor on these offerings
and accept them as once
   you accepted
the gifts of your servant Abel,
the sacrifice of Abraham,
   our father in faith,
and the bread and wine
   offered by your priest Melchisedech.

96. Inclinatus, iunctis manibus, prosequitur:

Súpplices te rogámus, omnípotens Deus:
iube hæc perférri per manus sancti Angeli tui
in sublíme altáre tuum,
in conspéctu divínæ maiestátis tuæ;
ut, quotquot ex hac altáris participatióne
sacrosánctum Fílii tui Corpus
      et Sánguinem sumpsérimus,

erigit se atque seipsum signat, dicens:

omni benedictióne cælésti et grátia repleámur.

Iungit manus.

   [Per Christum Dóminum nostrum. Amen.]

97. COMMEMORATIO PRO DEFUNCTIS

Manibus extensis, dicit:

Meménto étiam, Dómine, famulórum
      famularúmque tuárum N. et N.,
qui nos præcessérunt cum signo fídei,
et dórmiunt in somno pacis.

Iungit manus et orat aliquantulum pro iis defunctis, pro quibus orare
intendit.

Deinde, extensis manibus, prosequitur:

Ipsis, Dómine, et ómnibus in Christo quiescéntibus,
locum refrigérii, lucis et pacis,
ut indúlgeas, deprecámur.

Iungit manus.

   [Per Christum Dóminum nostrum. Amen.]

98. Manu dextera percutit sibi pectus, dicens:

Nobis quoque peccatóribus fámulis tuis,

et extensis manibus prosequitur:

de multitúdine miseratiónum
      tuárum sperántibus,
partem áliquam et societátem donáre dignéris

Bowing, with hands joined, he continues:

Almighty God,
we pray that your angel may take
    this sacrifice
to your altar in heaven.
Then, as we receive from this altar
the sacred body
    and blood of your Son,

He stands up straight and makes the sign of the cross, saying:

let us be filled with every grace and blessing.

He joins his hands.

[Through Christ our Lord. Amen.]

COMMEMORATION OF THE DEAD

With hands extended, he says:

Remember, Lord, those who have died
and have gone before us marked
    with the sign of faith,
especially those for whom we now pray, N. and N.

The priest prays for them briefly with joined hands. Then, with hands extended, he continues:

May these, and all who sleep in Christ,
find in your presence
light, happiness, and peace.

He joins his hands.

[Through Christ our Lord. Amen.]

With hands extended, he continues:

For ourselves, too, we ask
some share in the fellowship
    of your apostles and martyrs,
with John the Baptist,
    Stephen, Matthias, Barnabas,

I

cum tuis sanctis Apóstolis et Martýribus:
cum Ioánne, Stéphano,
Matthía, Bárnaba,

  [Ignátio, Alexándro,
   Marcellíno, Petro,
   Felicitáte, Perpétua,
   Agatha, Lúcia,
   Agnéte, Cæcília, Anastásia]

et ómnibus Sanctis tuis:
intra quorum nos consórtium,
non æstimátor mériti, sed véniæ,
quǽsumus, largítor admítte.

  Iungit manus.

Per Christum Dóminum nostrum.

  99. Et prosequitur:

Per quem hæc ómnia, Dómine,
semper bona creas, sanctíficas,
vivíficas, benedícis, et præstas nobis.

  100. Accipit patenam cum hostia et calicem, et utrumque elevans, dicit:

Per ipsum,
et cum ipso,
et in ipso,
est tibi Deo Patri omnipoténti,
in unitáte Spíritus Sancti,
omnis honor et glória
per ómnia sæcula sæculórum.

  Populus acclamat: **Amen.**

  Deinde sequitur ritus communionis, p. 266.

[Ignatius, Alexander, Marcellinus, Peter,
Felicity, Perpetua, Agatha, Lucy,
Agnes, Cecilia, Anastasia]

and all the saints.

The priest strikes his breast with the right hand, saying:

Though we are sinners,
we trust in your mercy and love.

With his hands extended as before, he continues:

Do not consider what we truly deserve,
but grant us your forgiveness.

He joins his hands.

Through Christ our Lord.

He continues:

Through him you give us all these gifts.
You fill them with life and goodness,
you bless them and make them holy.

He takes the chalice and the paten with the host and, lifting them up, sings or says:

Through him,
with him,
in him,
in the unity of the Holy Spirit,
all glory and honor is yours,
almighty Father,
for ever and ever.

The people respond: **Amen.**

The communion rite follows, p. 267.

PREX EUCHARISTICA II

101.

V. Dóminus vobíscum.
R. **Et cum spíritu tuo.**

V. Sursum corda.
R. **Habémus ad Dóminum.**

V. Grátias agámus Dómino Deo nostro.
R. **Dignum et iustum est.**

V̇ere dignum et iustum est,
    æquum et salutáre,
nos tibi, sancte Pater, semper et ubíque
    grátias ágere
per Fílium dilectiónis tuæ Iesum Christum,
Verbum tuum per quod cuncta fecísti:
quem misísti nobis Salvatórem et Redemptórem,
incarnátum de Spíritu Sancto
    et ex Vírgine natum.

Qui voluntátem tuam adímplens
et pópulum tibi sanctum acquírens
exténdit manus cum paterétur,
ut mortem sólveret
    et resurrectiónem manifestáret.

Et ídeo cum Angelis et ómnibus Sanctis
glóriam tuam prædicámus,
    una voce dicéntes:

Sanctus, Sanctus,
    Sanctus Dóminus Deus Sábaoth.
Pleni sunt cæli et terra glória tua.
Hosánna in excélsis.
Benedíctus qui venit in nómine Dómini.
Hosánna in excélsis.

EUCHARISTIC PRAYER II

This may be replaced by another preface.   **stand**

Priest: The Lord be with you.
People: **And also with you.**

Priest: Lift up your hearts.
People: **We lift them up to the Lord.**

Priest: Let us give thanks to the Lord our God.
People: **It is right to give him thanks and praise.**

Father,
it is our duty and our salvation,
always and everywhere
to give you thanks
through your beloved Son, Jesus Christ.

He is the Word through whom you made the universe,
the Savior you sent to redeem us.
By the power of the Holy Spirit
he took flesh and was born of the Virgin Mary.

For our sake he opened his arms on the cross;
he put an end to death
and revealed the resurrection.
In this he fulfilled your will
and won for you a holy people.

And so we join the angels and the saints
in proclaiming your glory
    as we say:

Holy, holy, holy Lord,
    God of power and might,
heaven and earth are full of your glory.
    Hosanna in the highest.
Blessed is he who comes in the name of the Lord.
    Hosanna in the highest.

II

102. Sacerdos, manibus extensis, dicit:

V ere Sanctus es, Dómine,
fons omnis sanctitátis.

103. Iungit manus, easque expansas super oblata tenens, dicit:

Hæc ergo dona, quǽsumus,
Spíritus tui rore sanctífica,

iungit manus
et signat semel super panem et calicem simul, dicens:

ut nobis Corpus ✠ et Sanguis fiant
Dómini nostri Iesu Christi.

Iungit manus.

104. In formulis quæ sequuntur, verba Domini proferantur distincte et
aperte, prouti natura eorundem verborum requirit.

Q ui cum Passióni voluntárie
        traderétur,

accipit panem, eumque parum elevatum super altare tenens, prosequitur:

accépit panem et grátias agens
        fregit,
dedítque discípulis suis, dicens:

parum se inclinat

ACCÍPITE ET MANDUCÁTE EX HOC OMNES:

HOC EST ENIM CORPUS MEUM,

QUOD PRO VOBIS TRADÉTUR.

Hostiam consecratam ostendit populo, reponit super patenam, et
genuflexus adorat.

105. Postea prosequitur:

S ímili modo, postquam cenátum est,

accipit cálicem, eumque parum elevatum super altare tenens, prosequitur:

kneel

The priest, with hands extended, says:

Lord, you are holy indeed,
the fountain of all holiness.

He joins his hands and holding them outstretched over the offerings, says:

Let your Spirit come upon these gifts
    to make them holy,
so that they may become for us

He joins his hands and, making the sign of the cross once over both bread and chalice, says:

the body ✠ and blood of our Lord,
    Jesus Christ.

He joins his hands.

The words of the Lord in the following formulas should be spoken clearly and distinctly, as their meaning demands.

Before he was given up to death,
a death he freely accepted,

He takes the bread and, raising it a little above the altar, continues:

he took bread and gave you thanks.
He broke the bread,
gave it to his disciples, and said:

He bows slightly.

TAKE THIS, ALL OF YOU, AND EAT IT:
THIS IS MY BODY WHICH WILL BE GIVEN UP FOR YOU.

II

He shows the consecrated host to the people, places it on the paten, and genuflects in adoration.

Then he continues:

When supper was ended, he took the cup.

He takes the chalice and, raising it a little above the altar, continues:

accípiens et cálicem,
íterum grátias agens dedit discípulis suis, dicens:

parum se inclinat

ACCÍPITE ET BÍBITE EX EO OMNES:

HIC EST ENIM CALIX SÁNGUINIS MEI

NOVI ET ÆTÉRNI TESTAMÉNTI,

QUI PRO VOBIS ET PRO MULTIS EFFUNDÉTUR

IN REMISSIÓNEM PECCATÓRUM.

HOC FÁCITE IN MEAM COMMEMORATIÓNEM.

Calicem ostendit populo, deponit super corporale, et genuflexus
adorat.
106. Deinde dicit:

Mystérium fídei:

Et populus prosequitur, acclamans:

Mortem tuam annuntiámus, Dómine,
et tuam resurrectiónem confitémur,
    donec vénias.

Vel:

Quotiescúmque manducámus panem hunc
et cálicem bíbimus,
mortem tuam annuntiámus, Dómine, donec vénias.

Vel:

Salvátor mundi, salva nos,
qui per crucem et resurrectiónem tuam
    liberásti nos.

Again he gave you thanks and praise,
gave the cup to his disciples, and said:

He bows slightly.

TAKE THIS, ALL OF YOU, AND DRINK FROM IT:

THIS IS THE CUP OF MY BLOOD,

THE BLOOD OF THE NEW AND EVERLASTING COVENANT.

IT WILL BE SHED FOR YOU AND FOR ALL

SO THAT SINS MAY BE FORGIVEN.

DO THIS IN MEMORY OF ME.

He shows the chalice to the people, places it on the corporal, and genuflects in adoration.

Then he sings or says:

Let us proclaim the mystery of faith:

People with celebrant and concelebrants:

**Christ has died,
Christ is risen,
Christ will come again.**

or:

**Dying you destroyed our death,
rising you restored our life.
Lord Jesus, come in glory.**

or:

**When we eat this bread and drink this cup,
we proclaim your death, Lord Jesus,
until you come in glory.**

or:

**Lord, by your cross and resurrection
you have set us free.
You are the Savior of the world.**

II

107. Deinde sacerdos, extensis manibus, dicit:

CC

Mémores ígitur mortis et resurrectiónis eius,
tibi, Dómine, panem vitæ
et cálicem salútis offérimus,
grátias agéntes quia nos dignos habuísti
astáre coram te et tibi ministráre.

Et súpplices deprecámur
ut Córporis et Sánguinis Christi partícipes
a Spíritu Sancto congregémur in unum.

PC
or
C1

Recordáre, Dómine,
    Ecclésiæ tuæ toto orbe diffúsæ,
ut eam in caritáte perfícias
una cum Papa nostro N. et Epíscopo nostro N.*
et univérso clero.

In Missis pro defunctis addi potest:

PC
or
C1

Meménto fámuli tui (fámulæ tuæ) N.,
quem (quam) (hódie)
    ad te ex hoc mundo vocásti.
Concéde, ut, qui (quæ) complantátus (complantáta)
    fuit similitúdini mortis Fílii tui,
simul fiat et resurrectiónis ipsíus.

PC
or
C2

Meménto étiam fratrum nostrórum,
qui in spe resurrectiónis dormiérunt,
omniúmque in tua miseratióne defunctórum,
et eos in lumen vultus tui admítte.
Omnium nostrum,
    quǽsumus, miserére,
ut cum beáta Dei Genetríce
    Vírgine María,

---

* Hic fieri potest mentio de Episcopis Coadiutoribus vel Auxiliariis, ut in IGMR 109, notatur.

Then, with hands extended, the priest says:

In memory of his death and resurrection,
we offer you, Father, this life-giving bread,
this saving cup.
We thank you for counting us worthy
to stand in your presence and serve you.
May all of us who share in the body
    and blood of Christ
be brought together in unity by the Holy Spirit.

Lord, remember your Church
    throughout the world;
make us grow in love,
together with N. our Pope,
N. our bishop,[12] and all the clergy.

In Masses for the dead the following may be added:

Remember N., whom
    you have called from this life.
In baptism he (she) died with Christ:
may he (she) also share
    his resurrection.

Remember our brothers and sisters
who have gone to their rest
in the hope of rising again;
bring them and all the departed
into the light of your presence.
Have mercy on us all;
make us worthy to share eternal life
with Mary, the virgin mother of God,

II

12. When several are to be named, a general form is used: for N. our
    bishop and his assistant bishops as in GIRM, 172.

beatis Apóstolis et ómnibus Sanctis,
qui tibi a sǽculo placuérunt,
ætérnæ vitæ mereámur esse consórtes,
et te laudémus et glorificémus

   iungit manus

per Fílium tuum Iesum Christum.

108. *Accipit patenam cum hostia et calicem, et utrumque elevans, dicit:*

Per ipsum,
et cum ipso,
et in ipso,
est tibi Deo Patri omnipoténti,
in unitáte Spíritus Sancti,
omnis honor et glória
per ómnia sǽcula sæculórum.

PC
or **CC**

   Populus acclamat: **Amen.**

   Deinde sequitur ritus communionis, p. 266.

with the apostles, and with all the saints
who have done your will throughout the ages.
May we praise you in union with them,
and give you glory

He joins his hands.

through your Son, Jesus Christ.

He takes the chalice and the paten with the host and, lifting them up, sings or says:

Through him,
with him,
in him,
in the unity of the Holy Spirit,
all glory and honor is yours,
almighty Father,
for ever and ever.

The people respond: **Amen.**

The communion rite follows, p. 267.

II

PREX EUCHARISTICA III

109. Sacerdos, manibus extensis, dicit:

PC

Vere Sanctus es, Dómine,
et mérito te laudat omnis a te cóndita creatúra,
quia per Fílium tuum,
Dóminum nostrum Iesum Christum,
Spíritus Sancti operánte virtúte,
vivíficas et sanctíficas univérsa,
et pópulum tibi congregáre non désinis,
ut a solis ortu usque ad occásum
oblátio munda offerátur nómini tuo.

110. Iungit manus, easque expansas super oblata tenens, dicit:

CC

Súpplices ergo te, Dómine, deprecámur,
ut hæc múnera, quæ tibi sacránda detúlimus,
eódem Spíritu sanctificáre dignéris,

iungit manus
et signat semel super panem et calicem simul, dicens:

ut Corpus et ✠ Sanguis fiant
Fílii tui Dómini nostri Iesu Christi,

iungit manus

cuius mandáto hæc mystéria celebrámus.

111. In formulis quæ sequuntur, verba Domini proferantur distincte et
aperte, prouti natura eorundem verborum requirit:

Ipse enim in qua nocte tradebátur

accipit panem eumque parum elevatum super altare tenens, prosequitur:

accépit panem
et tibi grátias agens benedíxit,
fregit, dedítque discípulis suis, dicens:

parum se inclinat

EUCHARISTIC PRAYER III

kneel

The priest, with hands extended, says:

Father, you are holy indeed,
and all creation rightly gives you praise.
All life, all holiness comes from you
through your Son, Jesus Christ our Lord,
by the working of the Holy Spirit.
From age to age you gather a people to yourself,
so that from east to west
a perfect offering may be made
to the glory of your name.

He joins his hands and, holding them outstretched over the offerings, says:

And so, Father, we bring you these gifts.
We ask you to make them holy
by the power of your Spirit,

He joins his hands and, making the sign of the cross once over both bread and chalice, says:

that they may become the body ✠ and blood
of your Son, our Lord Jesus Christ,
at whose command we celebrate this eucharist.

He joins his hands.

The words of the Lord in the following formulas should be spoken clearly and distinctly, as their meaning demands.

On the night he was betrayed,

He takes the bread and, raising it a little above the altar, continues:

III

He took bread and gave you thanks and praise.
He broke the bread, gave it to his disciples,
     and said:

He bows slightly.

ACCÍPITE ET MANDUCÁTE EX HOC OMNES:
HOC EST ENIM CORPUS MEUM,
QUOD PRO VOBIS TRADÉTUR.

Hostiam consecratam ostendit populo, deponit super patenam, et genuflexus adorat.

112. Postea prosequitur:

Símili modo, postquam cenátum est,

accipit calicem, eumque parum elevatum super altare tenens, prosequitur:

accípiens cálicem,
et tibi grátias agens benedíxit,
dedítque discípulis suis, dicens:

parum se inclinat

ACCÍPITE ET BÍBITE EX EO OMNES:
HIC EST ENIM CALIX SÁNGUINIS MEI
NOVI ET ÆTÉRNI TESTAMÉNTI,
QUI PRO VOBIS ET PRO MULTIS EFFUNDÉTUR
IN REMISSIÓNEM PECCATÓRUM.
HOC FÁCITE IN MEAM COMMEMORATIÓNEM.

Calicem ostendit populo, deponit super corporale, et genuflexus adorat.

113. Deinde dicit:

Mystérium fídei:

Et populus prosequitur, acclamans:

Mortem tuam annuntiámus, Dómine,
et tuam resurrectiónem confitémur,
    donec vénias.

Vel:

Take this, all of you, and eat it:
this is my body which will be given up for you.

He shows the consecrated host to the people, places it on the paten, and genuflects in adoration.

Then he continues:

When supper was ended, he took the cup.

He takes the chalice and, raising it a little above the altar, continues:

Again he gave you thanks and praise,
gave the cup to his disciples,
    and said:

He bows slightly.

Take this, all of you, and drink from it:
this is the cup of my blood,
the blood of the new and everlasting covenant.
It will be shed for you and for all
so that sins may be forgiven.
Do this in memory of me.

He shows the chalice to the people, places it on the corporal, and genuflects in adoration.

Then he sings or says:

Let us proclaim the mystery of faith:

People with celebrant and concelebrants:

Christ has died,
Christ is risen,
Christ will come again.

or:

Dying you destroyed our death,
rising you restored our life.
Lord Jesus, come in glory.

or:

III

**Quotiescúmque manducámus panem hunc
et cálicem bíbimus,
mortem tuam annuntiámus, Dómine, donec vénias.**

Vel:

**Salvátor mundi, salva nos,
qui per crucem et resurrectiónem tuam
    liberásti nos.**

114. Deinde sacerdos, extensis manibus, dicit:

Mémores ígitur, Dómine,
eiúsdem Fílii tui salutíferæ passiónis
necnon mirábilis resurrectiónis
et ascensiónis in cælum,
sed et præstolántes álterum eius advéntum,
offérimus tibi, grátias referéntes,
hoc sacrifícium vivum et sanctum.

Réspice, quǽsumus, in oblatiónem Ecclésiæ tuæ
et, agnóscens Hóstiam,
cuius voluísti immolatióne placári,
concéde, ut qui Córpore et Sánguine Fílii tui refícimur,
Spíritu eius Sancto repléti,
unum corpus et unus spíritus inveniámur in Christo.

Ipse nos tibi perfíciat munus ætérnum,
ut cum eléctis tuis hereditátem
    cónsequi valeámus,
in primis cum beatíssima Vírgine, Dei Genetríce María,
cum beátis Apóstolis tuis et gloriósis Martýribus
(cum Sancto N.: Sancto diei vel patrono)
et ómnibus Sanctis, quorum intercessióne
perpétuo apud te confídimus adiuvári.

Hæc Hóstia nostræ reconciliatiónis profíciat,
quǽsumus, Dómine,
ad totíus mundi pacem atque salútem.

**When we eat this bread and drink this cup,
we proclaim your death, Lord Jesus,
until you come in glory.**

or:

**Lord, by your cross and resurrection
you have set us free.
You are the Savior of the world.**

Then, with hands extended, the priest says:

Father, calling to mind the death your Son
    endured for our salvation,
his glorious resurrection
and ascension into heaven,
and ready to greet him when he comes again,
we offer you in thanksgiving
    this holy and living sacrifice.

Look with favor on your Church's offering,
and see the Victim whose death has reconciled us
    to yourself.
Grant that we, who are nourished by his body
    and blood,
may be filled with his Holy Spirit,
and become one body, one spirit in Christ.

May he make us an everlasting gift to you
and enable us to share
    in the inheritance of your saints,
with Mary, the virgin mother of God;
with the apostles, the martyrs,
(Saint N. —the saint of the day or the patron saint)
    and all your saints,
on whose constant intercession we rely for help.

Lord, may this sacrifice,
which has made our peace with you,
advance the peace and salvation of all the world.

III

Ecclésiam tuam, peregrinántem in terra,
in fide et caritáte firmáre dignéris
cum fámulo tuo Papa nostro N.
    et Epíscopo nostro N.,*
cum episcopáli órdine et univérso clero
et omni pópulo acquisitiónis tuæ.
Votis huius famíliæ, quam tibi astáre voluísti,
adésto propítius.
Omnes fílios tuos ubíque dispérsos
tibi, clemens Pater, miserátus coniúnge.

†Fratres nostros defúnctos
et omnes qui, tibi placéntes, ex hoc sǽculo transiérunt,
in regnum tuum benígnus admítte,
ubi fore sperámus,
ut simul glória tua perénniter satiémur,

iungit manus

per Christum Dóminum nostrum,
per quem mundo
    bona cuncta largíris. †

115. Accipit patenam cum hostia et calicem, et utrumque elevans, dicit:

Per ipsum,
et cum ipso,
et in ipso,
est tibi Deo Patri omnipoténti,
in unitáte Spíritus Sancti,
omnis honor et glória
per ómnia sǽcula sæculórum.

Populus acclamat: **Amen.**

Deinde sequitur ritus communionis, p. 266.

_____

* Hic fieri potest mentio de Episcopis Coadiutoribus vel Auxiliariis, ut in
  IGMR 109, notatur.

Strengthen in faith and love your pilgrim Church
    on earth;
your servant, Pope N., our bishop N.,[13]
and all the bishops,
with the clergy and the entire people your Son has
    gained for you.
Father, hear the prayers of the family
you have gathered here before you.
In mercy and love unite all your children wherever
    they may be.*

Welcome into your kingdom our departed brothers
    and sisters,
and all who have left this world
    in your friendship.

He joins his hands.

We hope to enjoy for ever the vision of your glory,
through Christ our Lord,
    from whom all good things come.

He takes the chalice and the paten with the host and, lifting them up, sings
or says:

Through him,
with him,
in him,
in the unity of the Holy Spirit,
all glory and honor is yours,
almighty Father,
for ever and ever.

The people respond: **Amen.**

The communion rite follows, p. 267

III

---

13. When several are to be named, a general form is used: for N. our
    bishop and his assistant bishops, as in GIRM, 172.

  * In Masses for the dead, see next page.

116. Quando hæc prex eucharistica in Missis pro defunctis adhibetur, dici
potest:

†**M**eménto fámuli tui (fámulæ tuæ) N.,
quem (quam) (hodie)
     ad te ex hoc mundo vocásti.

Concéde, ut, qui (quæ) complantátus (complantáta)
fuit similitúdini mortis Fílii tui,
simul fiat et resurrectiónis ipsíus,
quando mórtuos suscitábit in carne de terra
et corpus humilitátis nostræ
configurábit córpori claritátis suæ.
Sed et fratres nostros defúnctos,
et omnes qui, tibi placéntes, ex hoc sæculo transiérunt,
in regnum tuum benígnus admítte,
ubi fore sperámus,
ut simul glória tua perénniter satiémur,
quando omnem lácrimam abstérges ab óculis nostris,
quia te, sícuti es, Deum nostrum vidéntes,
tibi símiles érimus cuncta per sæcula,
et te sine fine laudábimus,

     iungit manus

per Christum Dóminum nostrum,
per quem mundo bona cuncta largíris. †

     Accipit patenam cum hostia et calicem, et utrumque elevans, dicit:

Per ipsum,
et cum ipso,
et in ipso,
est tibi Deo Patri omnipoténti,
in unitáte Spíritus Sancti,
omnis honor et glória
per ómnia sæcula sæculórum.

     Populus acclamat: **Amen.**

     Deinde sequitur ritus communionis, p. 266.

*When this eucharistic prayer is used in Masses for the dead, the following may be said:

Remember N.
In baptism he (she) died with Christ:
may he (she) also share his resurrection,
when Christ will raise our mortal bodies
and make them like his own in glory.

Welcome into your kingdom our departed
     brothers and sisters,
and all who have left this world
     in your friendship.
There we hope to share in your glory
when every tear will be wiped away.
On that day we shall see you, our God,
     as you are.

He joins his hands.

We shall become like you
and praise you for ever through Christ our Lord,
from whom all good things come.

He takes the chalice and paten with the host and, lifting them up, says:

Through him,
with him,
in him,
in the unity of the Holy Spirit,
all glory and honor is yours,
almighty Father,
for ever and ever.

III

The people respond: **Amen.**

The communion rite follows, p. 267.

PREX EUCHARISTICA IV

117.

V. Dóminus vobíscum.
R. **Et cum spíritu tuo.**

V. Sursum corda.
R. **Habémus ad Dóminum.**

V. Grátias agámus Dómino Deo nostro.
R. **Dignum et iustum est.**

Vere dignum est tibi grátias ágere,
vere iustum est te glorificáre, Pater sancte,
quia unus es Deus vivus et verus,
qui es ante sǽcula et pérmanes in ætérnum,
inaccessíbilem lucem inhábitans;
sed et qui unus bonus
     atque fons vitæ cuncta fecísti,
ut creatúras tuas benedictiónibus adimpléres
multásque lætificáres tui lúminis claritáte.
Et ídeo coram te innúmeræ astant turbæ
angelórum,
qui die ac nocte sérviunt tibi
et, vultus tui glóriam contemplántes,
te incessánter gloríficant.
Cum quibus et nos et, per nostram vocem,
omnis quæ sub cælo est creatúra
nomen tuum in exsultatióne confitémur, canéntes:

Sanctus, Sanctus,
     Sanctus Dóminus Deus Sábaoth.
Pleni sunt cæli et terra glória tua.
Hosánna in excélsis.
Benedíctus qui venit in nómine Dómini.
Hosánna in excélsis.

EUCHARISTIC PRAYER IV

stand

Priest: The Lord be with you.
People: **And also with you.**

Priest: Lift up your hearts.
People: **We lift them up to the Lord.**

Priest: Let us give thanks to the Lord our God.
People: **It is right to give him thanks and praise.**

Father in heaven,
it is right that we should give you thanks
    and glory:
you are the one God, living and true.
Through all eternity you live
    in unapproachable light.
Source of life and goodness,
    you have created all things,
to fill your creatures with every blessing
and lead all men to the joyful vision of your light.
Countless hosts of angels stand before you
    to do your will;
they look upon your splendor
and praise you, night and day.
United with them,
and in the name of every creature under heaven,
we too praise your glory as we say:

Holy, holy, holy Lord,
    God of power and might,
heaven and earth are full of your glory.
    Hosanna in the highest.
Blessed is he who comes in the name of the Lord.
    Hosanna in the highest.

IV

118. Sacerdos, manibus extensis, dicit:

PC

Confitémur tibi, Pater sancte,
quia magnus es et ómnia ópera tua
in sapiéntia et caritáte fecísti.
Hóminem ad tuam imáginem condidísti,
eíque commisísti mundi curam univérsi,
ut, tibi soli Creatóri sérviens,
creatúris ómnibus imperáret.
Et cum amicítiam tuam, non obœ́diens, amisísset,
non eum dereliquísti in mortis império.
Omnibus enim misericórditer subvenísti,
ut te quæréntes invenírent.
Sed et fœ́dera plúries homínibus obtulísti
eósque per prophétas erudísti
　　　in exspectatióne salútis.
Et sic, Pater sancte, mundum dilexísti,
ut, compléta plenitúdine témporum,
Unigénitum tuum nobis mítteres Salvatórem.
Qui, incarnátus de Spíritu Sancto
et natus ex María Vírgine,
in nostra condiciónis forma est conversátus
per ómnia absque peccáto;
salútem evangelizávit paupéribus,
redemptiónem captívis,
mæstis corde lætítiam.
Ut tuam vero dispensatiónem impléret,
in mortem trádidit semetípsum
ac, resúrgens a mórtuis,
mortem destrúxit vitámque renovávit.
Et, ut non ámplius nobismetípsis viverémus,
sed sibi qui pro nobis mórtuus est atque surréxit,
a te, Pater, misit Spíritum Sanctum
primítias credéntibus,
qui, opus suum in mundo perfíciens,
omnem sanctificatiónem compléret.

The priest, with hands extended, says: **kneel**

Father, we acknowledge your greatness:
all your actions show
	your wisdom and love.
You formed man in your own likeness
and set him over the whole world
to serve you, his creator,
and to rule over all creatures.
Even when he disobeyed you and lost your friendship
you did not abandon him to the power of death,
but helped all men to seek and find you.
Again and again you offered a covenant to man,
and through the prophets taught him to hope
	for salvation.
Father, you so loved the world
that in the fullness of time you sent
	your only Son to be our Savior.
He was conceived through the power of the Holy Spirit,
and born of the Virgin Mary,
a man like us in all things but sin.
To the poor he proclaimed
	the good news of salvation,
to prisoners, freedom,
and to those in sorrow, joy.
In fulfillment of your will
he gave himself up to death;
but by rising from the dead,
he destroyed death and restored life.
And that we might live no longer for ourselves
	but for him,
he sent the Holy Spirit from you, Father,
as his first gift to those who believe,
to complete his work on earth
and bring us the fullness of grace.

IV

119. Iungit manus, easque expansas super oblata tenens, dicit:

Quǽsumus ígitur, Dómine,
ut idem Spíritus Sanctus
hæc múnera sanctificáre dignétur,

iungit manus et signat semel super panem et calicem simul, dicens:

ut Corpus et ✠ Sanguis fiant
Dómini nostri Iesu Christi

iungit manus

ad hoc magnum mystérium celebrándum,
quod ipse nobis relíquit in fœdus ætérnum.

120. In formulis quæ sequuntur, verba Domini proferantur distincte et
aperte, prouti natura eorundem verborum requirit.

Ipse enim, cum hora venísset
ut glorificarétur a te,
    Pater sancte,
ac dilexísset suos qui erant in mundo,
in finem diléxit eos:
et cenántibus illis

accipit panem, eumque parum elevatum super altare tenens, prosequitur:

accépit panem, benedíxit ac fregit,
dedítque discípulis suis, dicens:

parum se inclinat

ACCÍPITE ET MANDUCÁTE EX HOC OMNES:

HOC EST ENIM CORPUS MEUM,

QUOD PRO VOBIS TRADÉTUR.

Hostiam consecratam ostendit populo, deponit super patenam, et
genuflexus adorat.

121. Postea prosequitur:

Símili modo

accipit calicem, eumque parum elevatum super altare tenens, prosequitur:

He joins his hands and, holding them outstretched over the offering, says:

Father, may this Holy Spirit sanctify
    these offerings.

He joins his hands and, making the sign of the cross once over both bread and chalice, says:

Let them become the body ✠ and blood
of Jesus Christ our Lord

He joins his hands.

as we celebrate the great mystery
which he left us as an everlasting covenant.

The words of the Lord in the following formulas should be spoken clearly and distinctly, as their meaning demands.

He always loved those who were his own
    in the world.
When the time came for him to be glorified by you,
his heavenly Father,
he showed the depth of his love.

While they were at supper,

He takes the bread and, raising it a little above the altar, continues:

he took bread, said the blessing, broke the bread,
and gave it to his disciples, saying:

He bows slightly.

TAKE THIS, ALL OF YOU, AND EAT IT:

THIS IS MY BODY WHICH WILL BE GIVEN UP FOR YOU.

IV

He shows the consecrated host to the people, places it on the paten, and genuflects in adoration.

Then he continues:

In the same way, he took the cup, filled with wine.

He takes the chalice and, raising it a little above the altar, continues:

accípiens cálicem, ex genímine vitis replétum,
grátias egit, dedítque discípulis suis, dicens:

parum se inclinat

ACCÍPITE ET BÍBITE EX EO OMNES:
HIC EST ENIM CALIX SÁNGUINIS MEI
NOVI ET ÆTÉRNI TESTAMÉNTI,
QUI PRO VOBIS ET PRO MULTIS EFFUNDÉTUR
IN REMISSIÓNEM PECCATÓRUM.
HOC FÁCITE IN MEAM COMMEMORATIÓNEM.

Calicem ostendit populo, deponit super corporale, et genuflexus
adorat.

122. Deinde dicit:

Mystérium fídei:

Et populus prosequitur, acclamans:

Mortem tuam annuntiámus, Dómine,
et tuam resurrectiónem confitémur,
    donec vénias.

Vel:

Quotiescúmque manducámus panem hunc
et cálicem bíbimus,
mortem tuam annuntiámus, Dómine, donec vénias.

Vel:

Salvátor mundi, salva nos,
qui per crucem et resurrectiónem tuam
    liberásti nos.

123. Deinde sacerdos, extensis manibus, dicit:

He gave you thanks,
>   and giving the cup to his disciples, said:

He bows slightly.

TAKE THIS, ALL OF YOU, AND DRINK FROM IT:
THIS IS THE CUP OF MY BLOOD,
THE BLOOD OF THE NEW AND EVERLASTING COVENANT.
IT WILL BE SHED FOR YOU AND FOR ALL
SO THAT SINS MAY BE FORGIVEN.
DO THIS IN MEMORY OF ME.

He shows the chalice to the people, places it on the corporal, and genuflects in adoration.

Then he sings or says:

Let us proclaim the mystery of faith:

People with celebrant and concelebrants:

**Christ has died,
Christ is risen,
Christ will come again.**

or:

**Dying you destroyed our death,
rising you restored our life.
Lord Jesus, come in glory.**

or:

**When we eat this bread and drink this cup,
we proclaim your death, Lord Jesus,
until you come in glory.**

or:

**Lord, by your cross and resurrection
you have set us free.
You are the Savior of the world.**

Then, with hands extended, the priest says:

IV

Unde et nos, Dómine, redemptiónis   CC
    nostræ memoriále nunc celebrántes,
mortem Christi
eiúsque descénsum ad ínferos recólimus,
eius resurrectiónem
et ascensiónem ad tuam déxteram profitémur,
et, exspectántes ipsíus advéntum in glória,
offérimus tibi eius Corpus et Sánguinem,
sacrifícium tibi acceptábile et toti mundo salutáre.

Réspice, Dómine, in Hóstiam,
quam Ecclésiæ tuæ ipse parásti,
et concéde benígnus ómnibus
qui ex hoc uno pane participábunt et cálice,
ut, in unum corpus a Sancto Spíritu congregáti,
in Christo hóstia viva perficiántur,
ad laudem glóriæ tuæ.

Nunc ergo, Dómine, ómnium recordáre,   PC
pro quibus tibi hanc oblatiónem offérimus: or
in primis fámuli tui, Papæ nostri N.,   C1
Epíscopi nostri N.,* et Episcopórum órdinis univérsi,
sed et totíus cleri, et offeréntium,
et circumstántium,
et cuncti pópuli tui,
et ómnium, qui te quærunt corde sincéro.

Meménto étiam illórum,
qui obiérunt in pace Christi tui,
et ómnium defunctórum,
quorum fidem tu solus cognovísti.

---

*   Hic fieri potest mentio de Episcopis Coadiutoribus vel Auxiliariis, ut in
    IGMR 109, notatur.

Father, we now celebrate this memorial
  of our redemption.
We recall Christ's death, his descent among the dead,
his resurrection, and his ascension to your right hand;
and, looking forward to his coming in glory,
we offer you his body and blood,
the acceptable sacrifice
which brings salvation
  to the whole world.

Lord, look upon this sacrifice which you have given
  to your Church;
and by your Holy Spirit, gather all who share
  this one bread and one cup
into the one body of Christ,
  a living sacrifice of praise.

Lord, remember those for whom we offer
  this sacrifice,
especially N. our Pope,
N. our bishop,[14] and bishops
  and clergy everywhere.
Remember those who take part in this offering,
those here present and all your people,
and all who seek you with a sincere heart.

Remember those who have died
  in the peace of Christ
and all the dead whose faith is known
  to you alone.

IV

---

14. When several are to be named, a general form is used: for N. our
bishop and his assistant bishops, as in GIRM, 172.

Nobis ómnibus, fíliis tuis,
clemens Pater, concéde,
ut cæléstem hereditátem cónsequi valeámus
cum beáta Vírgine, Dei Genetríce, María,
cum Apóstolis et Sanctis tuis
in regno tuo, ubi cum univérsa creatúra,
a corruptióne peccáti et mortis liberáta,
te glorificémus per Christum Dóminum nostrum,

iungit manus,

per quem mundo bona cuncta largíris.

124. Accipit patenam cum hostia et calicem, et utrumque elevans, dicit:

P er ipsum,
et cum ipso,
et in ipso,
est tibi Deo Patri omnipoténti,
in unitáte Spíritus Sancti,
omnis honor et glória
per ómnia sǽcula sæculórum.

Populus acclamat:　　　　　**Amen.**

Deinde sequitur ritus communionis, p. 266.

Father, in your mercy grant also to us, your children,
to enter into our heavenly inheritance
in the company of the Virgin Mary, the Mother of God,
and your apostles and saints.
Then, in your kingdom, freed
      from the corruption of sin and death,
we shall sing your glory with every creature through
      Christ our Lord,

He joins his hands.

through whom you give us everything that is good.

He takes the chalice and the paten with the host and, lifting them up, sings
or says:

Through him,
with him,
in him,
in the unity of the Holy Spirit,
all glory and honor is yours,
almighty Father,
for ever and ever.

The people respond: **Amen.**

The communion rite follows, p. 267.

RITUS COMMUNIONIS

PATER NOSTER

125. Calice et patena depositis, sacerdos, iunctis manibus, dicit:

Præcéptis salutáribus móniti,
et divína institutióne formáti,
audémus dícere:

Vel:

Et nunc oratiónem,
quam Christus Dóminus nos dócuit,
omnes simul dicámus:

Vel:

Precem nostram pergámus,
advéntum regni Dei quæréndo:

Extendit manus et, una cum populo, pergit:

Pater noster, qui es in cælis:
sanctificétur nomen tuum;
advéniat regnum tuum;
fiat volúntas tua, sicut in cælo, et in terra.
Panem nostrum cotidiánum da nobis hódie;
et dimítte nobis débita nostra,
sicut et nos dimíttimus debitóribus nostris;
et ne nos indúcas in tentatiónem;
sed líbera nos a malo.

126. Manibus extensis, sacerdos solus prosequitur, dicens:

COMMUNION RITE

stand

LORD'S PRAYER

The priest sets down the chalice and paten and, with hands joined, sings or says:

A. Let us pray with confidence to the Father
in the words our Savior gave us:

or:

B. Jesus taught us to call God our Father,
and so we have the courage to say:

or:

C. Let us ask our Father to forgive our sins and to
bring us to forgive those who sin against us.

or:

D. Let us pray for the coming of the kingdom
as Jesus taught us.

He extends his hands and continues, with the people:

Our Father, who art in heaven,
hallowed be thy name;
thy kingdom come;
thy will be done on earth as it is in heaven.
Give us this day our daily bread;
and forgive us our trespasses
as we forgive those who trespass against us;
and lead us not into temptation,
but deliver us from evil.

With hands extended, the priest continues alone:

Líbera nos, quǽsumus, Dómine, ab ómnibus malis,
da propítius pacem in diébus nostris,
ut, ope misericórdiæ tuæ adiúti,
et a peccáto simus semper líberi
et ab omni perturbatióne secúri:
exspectántes beátam spem
et advéntum Salvatóris nostri Iesu Christi.

Iungit manus.

DOXOLOGIA

Populus orationem concludit, acclamans:

Quia tuum est regnum, et potéstas, et glória in sǽcula.

RITUS PACIS

127. Deinde sacerdos, manibus extensis, clara voce dicit:

Dómine Iesu Christe, qui dixísti Apóstolis tuis:
Pacem relínquo vobis, pacem meam do vobis:
ne respícias peccáta nostra,
sed fidem Ecclésiæ tuæ;
eámque secúndum voluntátem tuam
pacificáre et coadunáre dignéris.

Iungit manus.

Qui vivis et regnas in sǽcula sæculorum.

Populus respondet: **Amen.**

128. Sacerdos, ad populum conversus, extendens et iungens manus, subdit:

Pax Dómini sit semper vobíscum.

Populus respondet: **Et cum spíritu tuo.**

129. Deinde, pro opportunitate, diaconus, vel sacerdos, subiungit:

Offérte vobis pacem.

Et omnes, iuxta locorum consuetudines, pacem et caritatem sibi invicem
significant; sacerdos pacem dat diacono vel ministro.

Deliver us, Lord, from every evil,
and grant us peace in our day.
In your mercy keep us free from sin
and protect us from all anxiety
as we wait in joyful hope
for the coming of our Savior,
    Jesus Christ.

He joins his hands.

DOXOLOGY

The people end the prayer with the acclamation:

**For the kingdom, the power, and the glory are
yours, now and for ever.**

SIGN OF PEACE

Then the priest, with hands extended, says aloud:

Lord Jesus Christ, you said to your apostles:
I leave you peace, my peace I give you.
Look not on our sins, but on the faith
    of your Church,
and grant us the peace and unity
    of your kingdom

He joins his hands.

where you live for ever and ever.

The people answer: **Amen.**

The priest, extending and joining his hands, adds:

The peace of the Lord be with you always.

The people answer: **And also with you.**

Then the deacon (or the priest) may add:

Let us offer each other the sign of peace.

*All make an appropiate sign of peace, according to local custom.
The priest gives the sign of peace to the deacon or the minister.*

FRACTIO PANIS

130. Deinde accipit hostiam eamque super patenam frangit, et particulam immittit in calicem, dicens secreto:

Hæc commíxtio Córporis et Sánguinis Dómini nostri Iesu Christi fiat accipiéntibus nobis in vitam ætérnam.

131. Interim cantatur vel dicitur:

Agnus Dei, qui tollis peccáta mundi:
   miserére nobis.

Agnus Dei, qui tollis peccáta mundi:
   miserére nobis.

Agnus Dei, qui tollis peccáta mundi:
   dona nobis pacem.

Quod etiam pluries repeti potest, si fractio panis protrahitur. Ultima tamen vice dicitur: dona nobis pacem.

PREPARATIO PRIVATA SACERDOTIS

132. Sacerdos deinde, manibus iunctis, dicit secreto:

Dómine Iesu Christe, Fili Dei vivi, qui ex voluntáte Patris, cooperánte Spíritu Sancto, per mortem tuam mundum vivificásti: líbera me per hoc sacrosánctum Corpus et Sánguinem tuum ab ómnibus iniquitátibus meis et univérsis malis: et fac me tuis semper inhærére mandátis, et a te numquam separári permíttas.

Vel:

Percéptio Córporis et Sánguinis tui, Dómine Iesu Christe, non mihi provéniat in iudícium et condemnatiónem: sed pro tua pietáte prosit mihi ad tutaméntum mentis et córporis, et ad medélam percipiéndam.

BREAKING OF THE BREAD   **kneel**

Then the following is sung or said:

Lamb of God, you take away the sins of the world:
    have mercy on us.

Lamb of God, you take away the sins of the world:
    have mercy on us.

Lamb of God, you take away the sins of the world:
    grant us peace.

This may be repeated until the breaking of the bread is finished, but the last phrase is always Grant us peace.

Meanwhile, he takes the host and breaks it over the paten. He places a small piece in the chalice, saying inaudibly:

May this mingling of the body and blood
    of our Lord Jesus Christ
bring eternal life to us who receive it.

PRIVATE PREPARATION OF THE PRIEST[15]

Then the priest joins his hands and says inaudibly:

Lord Jesus Christ, Son of the living God, by the will of the Father and the work of the Holy Spirit your death brought life to the world. By your holy body and blood free me from all my sins and from every evil. Keep me faithful to your teaching, and never let me be parted from you.

or:

Lord Jesus Christ, with faith in your love and mercy I eat your body and drink your blood. Let it not bring me condemnation, but health in mind and body.

---

15. GIRM, 56f.

COMMUNIO

133. Sacerdos genuflectit, accipit hostiam, eamque aliquantulum elevatam super patenam tenens, ad populum versus, clara voce dicit:

Ecce Agnus Dei,
   ecce qui tollit peccáta mundi.
Beáti qui ad cenam Agni vocáti sunt.

Et una cum populo semel subdit:

Dómine, non sum dignus ut intres
   sub tectum meum:
sed tantum dic verbo, et sanábitur ánima mea.

134. Et sacerdos, ad altare versus, secreto dicit:

Corpus Christi custódiat me in vitam ætérnam.

Et reverenter sumit Corpus Christi. Deinde accipit calicem et secreto dicit:

Sanguis Christi custódiat me in vitam ætérnam.

Et reverenter sumit Sanguinem Christi.

135. Postea accipit patenam vel pyxidem, accedit ad communicandos, et hostiam parum elevatam unicuique eorum ostendit, dicens:

Corpus Christi.

Communicandus respondet: Amen.

Et communicatur.

Eo modo agit et diaconus, si sacram Communionem distribuit.

136. Si adsint sub utraque specie communicandi, servetur ritus suo loco descriptus.

COMMUNION

The priest genuflects. Taking the host, he raises it slightly over the paten and, facing the people, says aloud:

**This is the Lamb of God
who takes away the sins of the world.
Happy are those who are called to his supper.**

He adds, once only, with the people:

**Lord, I am not worthy to receive you,
but only say the word and I shall be healed.**

Facing the altar, the priest says quietly:

May the body of Christ bring me to everlasting life.

He reverently consumes the body of Christ. Then he takes the chalice and says inaudibly:

May the blood of Christ bring me to everlasting life.

He reverently drinks the blood of Christ.

After this he takes the paten or other vessel and goes to the communicants. He takes a host for each one, raises it a little, and shows it, saying:

The body of Christ.

The communicant answers: **Amen.**

and receives communion.

When a deacon gives communion, he does the same.

The sign of communion is more complete when given under both kinds, since the sign of the eucharistic meal appears more clearly. The intention of Christ that the new and eternal covenant be ratified in his blood is better expressed, as is the relation of the eucharistic banquet to the heavenly banquet.[16]

If any are receiving in both kinds, the rite described elsewhere is followed. When he presents the chalice, the priest or deacon says:

The blood of Christ.

The communicant answers: **Amen.**   and drinks it.

The deacon and other ministers may receive communion from the chalice.[17]

---

16. GIRM, 240.
17. GIRM, 242.

ANTIPHONA AD COMMUNIONEM

137. Dum sacerdos sumit Corpus Christi, incipit cantus ad Communionem.

138. Distributione Communionis expleta, sacerdos vel diaconus vel acolythus purificat patenam super calicem et ipsum calicem.

Dum purificationem peragit, sacerdos dicit secreto:

Quod ore súmpsimus, Dómine,
pura mente capiámus,
et de múnere temporáli
    fiat nobis remédium sempitérnum.

SACRUM SILENTIUM

139. Tunc sacerdos ad sedem redire potest. Pro opportunitate sacrum silentium, per aliquod temporis spatium, servari, vel psalmus aut canticum laudis proferri potest.

ORATIO POST COMMUNIONEM

140. Deinde, stans ad sedem vel ad altare, sacerdos dicit:

Orémus.

Et omnes una cum sacerdote per aliquod temporis spatium in silentio orant, nisi silentium iam praecesserit. Deinde sacerdos, manibus extensis, dicit orationem post Communionem. Populus in fine acclamat:

Amen.

COMMUNION SONG

While the priest receives the body of Christ, the communion song is begun.

The vessels are cleansed by the priest or deacon or acolyte after the communion or after Mass, if possible at the side table.[18]

Meanwhile he says inaudibly:

Lord, may I receive these gifts in purity of heart.
May they bring me healing and strength,
   now and for ever.

PERIOD OF SILENCE OR SONG OF PRAISE

Then the priest may return to the chair. A period of silence may now be observed, or a psalm or song of praise may be sung.

PRAYER AFTER COMMUNION

Then, standing at the chair or at the altar, the priest sings or says:

Let us pray.

Priest and people pray in silence for a while, unless a period of silence has already been observed. Then the priest extends his hands and sings or says the prayer after communion, at the end of which the people respond:

Amen.

---

18. GIRM, 238.

RITUS CONCLUSIONIS

141. Sequuntur, si habendæ sint, breves annuntiationes ad populum.

SALUTATIONE

142. Deinde fit dimissio. Sacerdos, versus ad populum, extendens manus, dicit:

Dóminus vobíscum.

Populus respondet: **Et cum spíritu tuo.**

BENEDICTIO

A.

Sacerdos benedicit populum, dicens:

**Benedícat vos omnípotens Deus,
Pater, et Fílius, ✠ et Spíritus Sanctus.**

Populus respondet: **Amen.**

Quibusdam diebus vel occasionibus, huic formulæ benedictionis præmittitur, iuxta rubricas, alia formula benedictionis sollemnior, vel oratio super populum.

B. Benedictio solemnis

Diaconus vel ipse sacerdos:

Inclináte vos ad benedictiónem.

Deinde, sacerdos, manibus super populum extensis, dicit benedictionem, omnibus respondentibus

Amen.

Sacerdos benedicit populum, dicens:

**Benedícat vos omnípotens Deus,
Pater, et Fílius, ✠ et Spíritus Sanctus.**

Populus respondet: **Amen.**

C. Oratio super populo

Diaconus vel ipse sacerdos:

Inclináte vos ad benedictiónem.

CONCLUDING RITE

If there are any brief announcements, they are made at this time.

GREETING

The rite of dismissal takes place. Facing the people, the priest extends his hands and sings or says:

The Lord be with you.

The people answer: **And also with you**.

BLESSING

A. Simple form

The priest blesses the people with these words:

May almighty God bless you, the Father, and the Son, ✠ and the Holy Spirit.

The people answer: **Amen.**

On certain days or occasions another more solemn form of blessing or prayer over the people may be used as the rubrics direct.

B. Solemn blessing

Deacon:

Bow your heads and pray for God's blessing.

The priest always concludes the solemn blessing, adding:

May almighty God bless you, the Father, and the Son, ✠ and the Holy Spirit.

The people answer: **Amen.**

C. Prayer over the people

Deacon:

Bow your heads and pray for God's blessing.

Deinde, sacerdos, manibus super populum extensis, dicit benedictionem, omnibus respondentibus : **Amen.**

Sacerdos benedicit populum, dicens:

Benedícat vos omnípotens Deus,
Pater, et Fílius, ✠ et Spíritus Sanctus.

Populus respondet: **Amen.**

DIMISSIO

143. Deinde diaconus, vel ipse sacerdos, manibus iunctis, ad populum versus dicit:

Ite, missa est.

Populus respondet: **Deo grátias.**

144. Deinde sacerdos altare osculo de more veneratur, ut initio. Facta denique debita reverentia cum ministris, recedit.

145. Si qua actio liturgica immediate sequatur, ritus dimissionis omittuntur.

After the prayer over the people, the priest always adds:

May almighty God bless you,
the Father, and the Son, ✠ and the Holy Spirit.

The people answer: **Amen.**

DISMISSAL

The dismissal sends each member of the congregation to do good works, praising and blessing the Lord.[19]

The deacon (or the priest), with hands joined, sings or says:

A. **Go in the peace of Christ.**

B. **The Mass is ended, go in peace.**

C. **Go in peace to love and serve the Lord.**

The people answer: **Thanks be to God.**

The priest kisses the altar as at the beginning. Then he makes the customary reverence with the ministers and leaves.

If any liturgical service follows immediately, the rite of dismissal is omitted.

19.Cf. GIRM, 57.

ORATIONES POST MISSAM

PLACEAT

Pláceat tibi, sancta Trínitas, obséquium servitútis meæ: et præsta; ut sacrifícium, quod óculis tuæ maiestátis indígnus óbtuli, tibi sit acceptábile, mihíque et ómnibus, pro quibus illud óbtuli, sit, te miseránte, propitiábile. Per Christum Dóminum nostrum. Amen.

ORATIO S. THOMÆ DE AQUINO

Grátias tibi ago,
Dómine, sancte Pater, omnípotens ætérne Deus,
qui me peccatórem, indígnum fámulum tuum,
nullis meis méritis,
   sed sola dignatióne misericórdiæ tuæ
satiáre dignátus es pretióso
   Córpore et Sánguine Fílii tui,
Dómini nostri Iesu Christi.
Et precor, ut hæc sancta commúnio
non sit mihi reátus ad pœnam,
sed intercéssio salutáris ad véniam.
Sit mihi armatúra fídei,
   et scutum bonæ voluntátis.
Sit vitiórum meórum evacuátio,
concupiscéntiæ et libídinis exterminátio,
caritátis et patiéntiæ,

PRAYERS AFTER MASS

PRAYER TO THE BLESSED TRINITY
(FOR PRIESTS)

May the tribute of my humble ministry be pleasing to you, Holy Trinity. Grant that the sacrifice which I—unworthy as I am—have offered in the presence of your majesty, may be acceptable to you. Through your mercy may it bring forgiveness to me and to all for whom I have offered it: through Christ our Lord. Amen.

PRAYER OF ST. THOMAS AQUINAS

Lord, Father, all-powerful and ever-living God,
I thank you, for even though I am a sinner,
your unprofitable servant,
not because of my worth
but in the kindness of your mercy,
you have fed me with the precious body and blood
   of your Son,
our Lord Jesus Christ.
I pray that this holy communion
may bring me not condemnation and punishment,
but forgiveness and salvation.
May it be a helmet of faith
and a shield of good will.
May it purify me from evil ways
and put an end to my evil passions.
May it bring me charity and patience,

humilitátis et obœdiéntiæ,
omniúmque virtútum augmentátio:
contra insídias inimicórum ómnium,
tam visibílium quam invisibílium,
   firma defénsio:
mótuum meórum,
   tam carnálium quam spiritálium,
perfécta quietátio:
in te uno ac vero Deo firma adhaésio,
atque finis mei felix consummátio.
Et precor te, ut ad illud ineffábile convívium
me peccatórem perdúcere dignéris,
ubi tu, cum Fílio tuo et Spíritu Sancto,
Sanctis tuis es lux vera,
   satíetas plena,
gáudium sempitérnum,
   iucúnditas consummáta et felícitas perfécta.
Per Christum Dóminum nostrum. Amen.

ORATIO S. BONAVENTURÆ

Transfíge, dulcíssime Dómine Iesu,
medúllas et víscera ánimæ meæ
suavíssimo ac salubérrimo amóris tui vúlnere,
vera serenáque et apostólica sanctíssima caritáte,
ut lángueat et liquefíat ánima mea
solo semper amóre et desidério tui;
te concupíscat et defíciat in átria tua,
cúpiat dissólvi et esse tecum.
Da ut ánima mea te esúriat, panem Angelórum,
refectiónem animárum sanctárum;
panem nostrum cotidiánum, supersubstantiálem,
habéntem omnem dulcédinem et sapórem,
et omne delectaméntum suavitátis.
Te, in quem desíderant Angeli prospícere,

humility and obedience,
and growth in the power to do good.
May it be my strong defense
against all my enemies, visible and invisible,
and the perfect calming of all my evil impulses,
bodily and spiritual.
May it unite me more closely to you,
    the one true God,
and lead me safely through death
to everlasting happiness with you.
And I pray that you will lead me, a sinner,
to the banquet where you,
    with your Son and Holy Spirit,
are true and perfect light,
total fulfillment, everlasting joy,
gladness without end,
and perfect happiness to your saints.
Grant this through Christ our Lord. Amen.

PRAYER OF ST. BONAVENTURE

Pierce, O most sweet Lord Jesus,
my inmost soul with the most joyous
    and healthful wound of your love,
with true, serene, and most holy apostolic charity,
that my soul may ever languish and melt
with love and longing for you,
that it may yearn for you and faint for your courts,
and long to be dissolved and to be with you.
Grant that my soul may hunger after you,
the bread of angels, the refreshment of holy souls,
our daily and supersubstantial bread,
having all sweetness and savor
    and every delight of taste;
let my heart ever hunger after and feed upon you,

semper esúriat et cómedat cor meum,
et dulcédine sapóris tui repleántur
víscera ánimæ meæ;
te semper sítiat fontem vitæ,
fontem sapiéntiæ et sciéntiæ,
fontem ætérni lúminis, torréntem voluptátis,
ubertátem domus Dei.
Te semper ámbiat, te quærat, te invéniat,
ad te tendat, ad te pervéniat,
te meditétur, te loquátur,
et ómnia operétur in laudem et glóriam nóminis tui,
cum humilitáte et discretióne,
cum dilectióne et delectatióne,
cum facilitáte et afféctu,
cum perseverántia usque in finem;
ut tu sis solus semper spes mea, tota fidúcia mea,
divítiæ meæ, delectátio mea, iucúnditas mea,
gáudium meum, quies et tranquíllitas mea,
pax mea,
suávitas mea, odor meus, dulcédo mea, cibus meus,
reféctio mea, refúgium meum, auxílium meum,
sapiéntia mea, pórtio mea,
posséssio mea, thesáurus meus,
in quo fixa et firma et immobíliter
semper sit radicáta
    mens mea et cor meum. Amen.

ASPIRATIONES AD S. REDEMPTOREM

Anima Christi, sanctífica me.
Corpus Christi, salva me.
Sanguis Christi, inébria me.
Aqua láteris Christi, lava me.
Pássio Christi, confórta me.
O bone Iesu, exáudi me.
Intra tua vúlnera abscónde me.

upon whom the angels desire to look,
and may my inmost soul be filled
with the sweetness of your savor;
may it ever thirst after you, the fountain of life,
the fountain of wisdom and knowledge,
the fountain of eternal light, the torrent of pleasure,
the richness of the house of God;
may it ever compass you, seek you, find you,
run to you, attain you,
meditate upon you, speak of you,
and do all things to the praise
    and glory of your name,
with humility and discretion,
with love and delight, with ease and affection,
and with perseverance unto the end;
may you alone be ever my hope,
my entire assurance,
my riches, my delight, my pleasure,
my joy, my rest and tranquillity, my peace,
my sweetness, my fragrance, my sweet savor,
my food, my refreshment, my refuge, my help,
my wisdom, my portion,
my possession and my treasure,
in whom may my mind and my heart are fixed
and firm and rooted immovably henceforth
    and for ever. Amen.

PRAYER TO OUR REDEEMER

Soul of Christ, sanctify me.
Body of Christ, heal me.
Blood of Christ, drench me.
Water from the side of Christ, wash me.
Passion of Christ, strengthen me.
Good Jesus, hear me.
In your wounds shelter me.

Ne permíttas me separári a te.
Ab hoste malígno defénde me.
In hora mortis meæ voca me.
Et iube me veníre ad te,
ut cum Sanctis tuis laudem te
in sǽcula sæculórum. Amen.

OBLATIO SUI

Súscipe, Dómine, univérsam meam libertátem.
Accipe memóriam,
   intelléctum atque voluntátem omnem.
Quidquid hábeo vel possídeo, mihi largítus es:
id tibi totum restítuo,
   ac tuæ prorsus voluntáti trado gubernándum.
Amórem tui solum cum grátia tua mihi dones,
et dives sum satis, nec áliud quidquam ultra posco.

AD IESUM CHRISTUM CRUCIFIXUM

En ego, o bone et dulcíssime Iesu,
ante conspéctum tuum génibus me provólvo,
ac máximo ánimi ardóre te oro atque obtéstor,
ut meum in cor vívidos
   fídei, spei et caritátis sensus,
atque veram peccatórum meórum pæniténtiam,
eáque emendándi firmíssimam voluntátem
   velis imprímere;
dum magno ánimi afféctu et dolóre
tua quinque vúlnera mecum ipse consídero
   ac mente contémplor,
illud præ óculis habens,
quod iam in ore ponébat tuo David prophéta de te,
   o bone Iesu:
"Fodérunt manus meas et pedes meos:
dinumeravérunt ómnia ossa mea." (Ps 21:17)

From turning away keep me.
From the evil one protect me.
At the hour of my death call me.
Into your presence lead me,
to praise you with all your saints
for ever and ever. Amen.

SELF-DEDICATION TO JESUS CHRIST

Lord Jesus Christ, take all my freedom,
my memory, my understanding, and my will.
All that I have and cherish you have given me.
I surrender it all to be guided by your will.
Your grace and your love
are wealth enough for me.
Give me these, Lord Jesus,
and I ask for nothing more.

PRAYER TO JESUS CHRIST CRUCIFIED

My good and dear Jesus,
I kneel before you,
asking you most earnestly
to engrave upon my heart
    a deep and lively faith, hope, and charity,
with true repentance for my sins,
and a firm resolve to make amends.
As I reflect upon your five wounds,
and dwell upon them
    with deep compassion and grief,
I recall, good Jesus,
the words the prophet David spoke
long ago concerning you:
"They have pierced my hands and my feet,
they have counted all my bones!"
(Ps 21:17)

ORATIO UNIVERSALIS

(sub nomine Clementis Pp. XI vulgata)

Credo, Dómine, sed credam fírmius;
spero, sed sperem secúrius;
amo, sed amem ardéntius;
dóleo, sed dóleam veheméntius.

Adóro te ut primum princípium;
desídero ut finem últimum;
laudo ut benefactórem perpétuum;
ínvoco ut defensórem propítium.

Tua me sapiéntia dírige,
iustítia cóntine,
cleméntia soláre,
poténtia prótege.

Offero tibi, Dómine, cogitánda, ut sint ad te;
dicénda, ut sint de te;
faciénda, ut sint secúndum te;
ferénda, ut sint propter te.

Volo quidquid vis,
volo quia vis,
volo quómodo vis,
volo quámdiu vis.

Oro, Dómine: intelléctum illúmines,
voluntátem inflámmes,
cor emúndes,
ánimam sanctífices.

Défleam prætéritas iniquitátes,
repéllam futúras tentatiónes,
córrigam vitiósas propensiónes,
éxcolam idóneas virtútes.

Tríbue mihi, bone Deus,
amórem tui, ódium mei,
zelum próximi,
contémptum mundi.

THE UNIVERSAL PRAYER

(attributed to pope Clement XI)

Lord, I believe in you: increase my faith.
I trust in you: strengthen my trust.
I love you: let me love you more and more.
I am sorry for my sins: deepen my sorrow.

I worship you as my first beginning,
I long for you as my last end,
I praise you as my constant helper,
and call on you as my loving protector.

Guide me by your wisdom,
correct me with your justice,
comfort me with your mercy,
protect me with your power.

I offer you, Lord, my thoughts: to be fixed on you;
my words: to have you for their theme;
my actions: to reflect my love for you;
my sufferings: to be endured for your greater glory.

I want to do what you ask of me:
in the way you ask,
for as long as you ask,
because you ask it.

Lord, enlighten my understanding,
strengthen my will,
purify my heart,
and make me holy.

Help me to repent of my past sins
and to resist temptation in the future.
Help me to rise above my human weakness
and to grow stronger as a Christian.

Let me love you, my Lord and my God,
and see myself as I really am:
a pilgrim in this world,
a Christian called to respect and love

Stúdeam superióribus obœdíre,
inferióribus subveníre,
amícis consúlere,
inimícis párcere.

Vincam voluptátem austeritáte,
avarítiam largitáte,
iracúndiam lenitáte,
tepiditátem fervóre.

Redde me prudéntem in consíliis,
constántem in perículis,
patiéntem in advérsis,
húmilem in prósperis.

Fac, Dómine, ut sim in oratióne atténtus,
in épulis sóbrius,
in múnere sédulus,
in propósito firmus.

Curem habére innocéntiam interiórem,
modéstiam exteriórem,
conversatiónem exemplárem,
vitam regulárem.

Assídue invígilem natúræ domándæ,
grátiæ fovéndæ,
legi servándæ,
salúti promeréndæ.

Discam a te quam ténue quod terrénum,
quam grande quod divínum,
quam breve quod temporáneum,
quam durábile quod ætérnum.

Da, ut mortem prævéniam,
iudícium pertímeam,
inférnum effúgiam,
paradísum obtíneam.

Per Christum Dóminum nostrum. Amen.

all whose lives I touch,
those in authority over me
or those under my authority,
my friends and my enemies.
Help me to conquer anger by gentleness,
greed by generosity, apathy by fervor.
Help me to forget myself
and reach out toward others.
Make me prudent in planning,
courageous in taking risks.
Make me patient in suffering,
unassuming in prosperity.
Keep me, Lord, attentive in prayer,
temperate in food and drink,
diligent in my work,
firm in my good intentions.
Let my conscience be clear,
my conduct without fault,
my speech blameless,
my life well-ordered.
Put me on guard against my human weaknesses.
Let me cherish your love for me,
keep your law,
and come at last to your salvation.
Teach me to realize that this world is passing,
that my true future is the happiness of heaven,
that life on earth is short,
and the life to come eternal.
Help me to prepare for death
with a proper fear of judgment,
but a greater trust in your goodness.
Lead me safely through death
    to the endless joy of heaven.
Grant this through Christ our Lord. Amen.

ORATIO AD BEATAM MARIAM VIRGINEM

O María, Virgo et Mater sanctíssima,
ecce suscépi dilectíssimum Fílium tuum,
quem immaculáto útero tuo concepísti, genuísti,
lactásti atque suavíssimis ampléxibus strinxisti.
Ecce, cuius aspéctu lætabáris
et ómnibus delíciis replebáris,
illum ipsum tibi humíliter
     et amánter repræsénto et óffero,
tuis brácchiis constringéndum, tuo corde amándum,
sanctissimǽque Trinitáti
     in suprémum latríæ cultum,
pro tui ipsíus honóre et glória et pro meis
     totiúsque mundi necessitátibus, offeréndum.
Rogo ergo te, piíssima Mater, ímpetra mihi véniam
     ómnium peccatórum meórum,
uberémque grátiam ipsi deínceps
     fidélius serviéndi,
ac dénique grátiam finálem, ut eum tecum laudáre
     possim per ómnia sǽcula sæculórum. Amen.

ORATIO AD S. IOSEPH

Vírginum custos et pater, sancte Ioseph,
cujus fidéli custódiæ ipsa Innocéntia,
Christus Iesus et Virgo vírginum María
     commíssa fuit;
te per hoc utrúmque caríssimum
pignus Iesum et Maríam óbsecro et obtéstor,
ut me, ab omni immundítia præservátum,
mente incontamináta,
puro corde et casto córpore
     Iesu et Maríæ
semper fácias castíssime famulári. Amen.

PRAYER TO THE VIRGIN MARY

Mary, holy virgin mother,
I have received your Son, Jesus Christ.
With love you became his mother,
gave birth to him, nursed him,
and helped him grow to manhood.
With love I return him to you,
to hold once more,
to love with all your heart,
and to offer to the Holy Trinity
as our supreme act of worship
for your honor and for the good
of all your pilgrim brothers and sisters.

Mother, ask God to forgive my sins
and to help me serve him more faithfully.
Keep me true to Christ until death,
and let me come to praise him with you
for ever and ever. Amen.

PRAYER TO ST. JOSEPH

St. Joseph, father and guardian of virgins,
to whose faithful keeping Christ Jesus,
    innocence itself,
and Mary, the virgin of virgins, were entrusted,
I pray and beseech you by that twofold
and most precious charge, by Jesus and Mary,
to save me from all uncleanness,
to keep my mind untainted,
my heart pure, and my body chaste;
and to help me always to serve
Jesus and Mary in perfect chastity. Amen.

CANTICUM TRIUM PUERORUM

Dan 3:57-88 et 56

Ant.   Trium puerórum * cantémus hymnum, quem cantábant sancti in camíno ignis, benedicéntes Dóminum. (T. P. Alleluia).

1. Benedícite, ómnia ópera Dómini, Dómino, *
   laudáte et superexaltáte eum in sǽcula.

2. Benedícite, cæli, Dómino, *
   benedícite, ángeli Dómini, Dómino.

3. Benedícite, aquæ omnes
      quæ super cælos sunt Dómino, *
   benedícat omnis virtus Dómino.

4. Benedícite, sol et luna, Dómino, *
   benedícite, stellæ cæli, Dómino.

5. Benedícite, omnis imber et ros, Dómino, *
   benedícite, omnes venti, Dómino.

6. Benedícite, ignis et æstus, Dómino, *
   benedícite, frigus et æstus, Dómino.

7. Benedícite, rores et pruína, Dómino, *
   benedícite, gelu et frigus, Dómino.

8. Benedícite, glácies et nives, Dómino, *
   benedícite, noctes et dies, Dómino.

9. Benedícite, lux et ténebræ, Dómino, *
   benedícite, fúlgura et nubes, Dómino.

10. Benedícat terra Dóminum, *
    laudet et superexáltet eum in sǽcula.

11. Benedícite, montes et colles, Dómino, *
    benedícite, univérsa germinántia in terra,
    Dómino.

12. Benedícite, mária et flúmina, Dómino, *
    benedícite, fontes, Dómino.

CANTICLE OF THE THREE CHILDREN

Ant.   Let us sing the hymn of the three children, *
which these holy ones sang of old in the fiery furnace, giving praise to the Lord (Easter Time Alleluia).

1. Bless the Lord, all you works of the Lord;
   praise and exalt him above all for ever.

2. Heavens, bless the Lord;
   angels of the Lord, bless the Lord.

3. All you waters that are above the heavens,
      bless the Lord,
   let all the powers bless the Lord.

4. Sun and moon, bless the Lord;
   stars of heaven, bless the Lord.

5. Every shower and dew, bless the Lord;
   all you winds, bless the Lord.

6. Fire and heat, bless the Lord;
   cold and heat, bless the Lord.

7. Dews and hoar frosts, bless the Lord;
   frost and cold, bless the Lord.

8. Ice and snow, bless the Lord;
   nights and days, bless the Lord.

9. Light and darkness, bless the Lord;
   lightnings and clouds, bless the Lord.

10. Let the earth bless the Lord;
    let it praise and exalt him above all for ever.

11. Mountains and hills, bless the Lord;
    everything growing from the earth, bless the
    Lord.

12. Seas and rivers, bless the Lord;
    fountains, bless the Lord.

13. Benedícite, cete et ómnia quæ movéntur
    in aquis, Dómino, *
  benedícite, omnes vólucres cæli, Dómino.

14. Benedícite, omnes béstiæ et pécora, Dómino, *
  benedícite, fílii hóminum, Dómino.

15. Bénedic, Israel, Dómino, *
  laudáte et superexaltáte eum in sǽcula.

16. Benedícite, sacerdotes Dómini, Dómino, *
  benedícite, servi Dómini, Dómino.

17. Benedícite, spíritus et ánimæ iustórum, Dómino, *
  benedícite, sancti et húmiles corde, Dómino.

18. Benedícite, Ananía, Azaría, Mísael, Dómino, *
  laudáte et superexaltáte eum in sǽcula.

19. Benedicámus Patrem et Fílium
    cum Sancto Spíritu; *
  laudémus et superexaltémus eum in sǽcula.

20. Benedíctus es in firmaménto cæli *
  et laudábilis et gloriósus in sǽcula.

Hic non dícitur **Gloria Patri** . . . neque **Amen**.

Psalmus 150

1. Laudáte Dóminum in sanctuário eius, *
  laudáte eum in firmaménto virtútis eius.

2. Laudáte eum in magnálibus eius, *
  laudáte eum secúndum multitúdinem
    magnitúdinis eius.

3. Laudáte eum in sono tubæ, *
  laudáte eum in psaltério et cíthara.

4. Laudáte eum in týmpano et choro, *
  laudáte eum in chordis et órgano.

5. Laudáte eum
    in cýmbalis benesonántibus, *

13. Whales and all that move in the waters,
      bless the Lord;
    all you fowls of the air, bless the Lord.
14. All you beasts and cattle, bless the Lord;
    sons of men, bless the Lord.
15. Israel, bless the Lord;
    praise and exalt him above all for ever.
16. Priests of the Lord, bless the Lord;
    servants of the Lord, bless the Lord.
17. Spirits and souls of the just, bless the Lord;
    holy men of humble heart, bless the Lord.
18. Ananias, Azarias and Misael, bless the Lord;
    praise and exalt him above all for ever.
19. Let us bless the Father and the Son,
      with the Holy Spirit;
    let us praise and exalt him above all for ever.
20. Blessed are you, Lord, in the firmament of heaven;
    and worthy of praise, and glorious
      above all for ever.

Neither the **Glory Be** nor **Amen** is said.

Psalm 150

1. Praise the Lord in his holy place,
   praise him in his mighty heavens.
2. Praise him for his powerful deeds,
   praise his surpassing greatness.

3. O praise him with sound of trumpet,
   praise him with lute and harp.
4. Praise him with timbrel and dance,
   praise him with strings and pipes.
5. O praise him with resounding cymbals,
   praise him with clashing of cymbals.

laudáte eum in cýmbalis iubilatiónis: *
    omne quod spirat, laudet Dóminum.

Gloria Patri...

Ant. Trium puerórum * cantémus hymnum, quem
cantábant sancti in camíno ignis, benedicéntes Dóminum (T. P. Alleluia).

Kýrie, eléison. Christe, eléison. Kýrie, eléison.
Pater noster . . .

V. Et ne nos indúcas in tentatiónem.

R. **Sed líbera nos a malo.**

V. Confiteántur tibi, Dómine, ómnia ópera tua.

R. **Et Sancti tui benedícant tibi.**

V. Exsultábunt sancti in glória.

R. **Lætabúntur in cubílibus suis.**

V. Non nobis, Dómine, non nobis.

R. **Sed nómini tuo da glóriam.**

V. Dómine exáudi orátionem meam.

R. **Et clámor meus ad te véniat.**

Sacerdotes addunt:

V. Dóminus vobíscum.

R. **Et cum spíritu tuo.**

Orémus.

Deus, qui tribus púeris mitigásti flammas ígnium:
concéde propítius; ut nos fámulos tuos non exúrat
flamma vitiórum.

Actiónes nostras, quǽsumus, Dómine, aspirándo
prǽveni et adiuvándo proséquere: ut cuncta nostra
orátio et operátio a te semper incípiat, et per te cœpta
finiátur.

Da nobis, quǽsumus, Dómine, vitiórum nostrórum flammas extínguere: qui beáto Lauréntio tribuísti tormentórum suórum incéndia superáre. Per
Christum, Dóminum nostrum. R. **Amen.**

Let everything that lives and breathes
    give praise to the Lord.

Glory Be.

Ant. Let us sing the hymn of the three children, which these holy ones sang of old in the fiery furnace, giving praise to the Lord (Easter Time Alleluia).

Lord, have mercy. Christ, have mercy. Lord, have mercy. Our Father.

V. And lead us not into temptation,

R. But deliver us from evil.

V. Let all your works praise you, Lord.

R. And let your saints bless you.

V. Your saints shall rejoice in glory.

R. They shall rejoice in their resting place.

V. Not unto us, Lord, not unto us,

R. But unto your name give glory.

V. O Lord, hear my prayer.

R. And let my cry come unto you.

Priests add:

V. The Lord be with you.

R. And also with you.

Let us pray.

God, who allayed the flames of fire for three children, grant in your mercy that the flame of vice may not consume us your servants.

Direct, we beseech you, Lord, our actions by your inspirations and further them by your assistance, so that every word and work of ours may begin always from you and by you be likewise ended.

Quench in us, we beseech you, Lord, the flame of vice, even as you enabled blessed Lawrence to overcome his fire of sufferings. Through Christ our Lord.
R. Amen.

PSALMUS 2

Ant.   Regnum eius* regnum sempitérnum est, et omnes reges sérvient ei et obœdient (T. P. Allelúia).

1. Quare fremuérunt gentes, *
   et pópuli meditáti sunt inánia?

2. Astitérunt reges terræ,
   et príncipes convenérunt in unum *
   advérsus Dóminum et advérsus christum eius:

3. "Dirumpámus víncula eórum *
   et proiciámus a nobis iugum ipsórum!"

4. Qui hábitat in cælis irridébit eos, *
   Dóminus subsannábit eos.

5. Tunc loquétur ad eos in ira sua *
   et in furóre suo conturbábit eos:

6. "Ego autem constítui regem meum *
   super Sion, montem sanctum meum!"

7. Prædicábo decrétum eius.
   Dóminus dixit ad me:
   "Fílius meus es tu; * ego hódie génui te.

8. "Póstula a me, et dabo tibi gentes
      hereditátem tuam *
   et possessiónem tuam términos terræ.

9. Reges eos in virga férrea *
   et tamquam vas fíguli confrínges eos".

10. Et nunc reges intellégite, *
    erudímini, qui iudicátis terram.

PSALM 2

This messianic psalm should inspire us with courage to persevere in spite of the attacks of the devil against the kingdom of God on earth. It also reminds us that our hope comes from our being children of God.

Ant. His kingdom is a kingdom of all ages, and all kings shall serve and obey him (Easter Time Alleluia).

1. Why this tumult among nations, *
   among peoples this useless murmuring?

2. They arise, the kings of the earth; *
   princes plot against the Lord
        and his Anointed.

3. "Come, let us break their fetters; *
   come, let us cast off their yoke."

4. He who sits in the heavens laughs *;
   the Lord is laughing them to scorn.

5. Then he will speak in his anger, *
   his rage will strike them with terror.

6. "It is I who have set up my king on Zion, *
   my holy mountain."

7. I will announce the decree of the Lord:
   The Lord said to me: "You are my Son. *
   It is I who have begotten you this day.

8. "Ask and I shall bequeath to you
        the nations,
   put the ends of the earth in your possession.

9. "With a rod of iron you will break them *
   shatter them like a potter's jar."

10. Now, O kings, understand; *
    take warning, rulers of the earth;

11. Servíte Dómino in timóre *
   et exsultáte ei cum tremóre.
12. Apprehéndite disciplínam, ne quando irascátur,
   et pereátis de via, * cum exárserit in brevi ira eius.
   Beáti omnes, * qui confídunt in eo.
13. Glória Patri...

Ant.　Regnum eius * regnum sempitérnum est, et
omnes reges sérvient ei et obœdient (T. P. Allelúia).

V. Dómine, exáudi oratiónem meam.

R. Et clamor meus ad te véniat.

Sacerdos addunt:

V. Dóminus vobíscum.

R. Et cum spíritu tuo.

Orémus.

Omnípotens sempitérne Deus, qui in dilécto Fílio
tuo, universórum Rege, ómnia instauráre voluísti:
concéde propítius; ut cunctæ famíliæ géntium, peccáti vúlnere disgregátæ, eius suavíssimo subdántur
império: Qui tecum vivit et regnat in unitáte Spíritus
Sancti Deus: per ómnia sæcula sæculórum.

R. Amen.

ORATIO AD S. MICHAEL ARCHANGELUM

Sancte Míchael Archángele,
defénde nos in proélio,
contra nequítiam et insídias diáboli
esto præsídium.
Imperet illi Deus, súpplices deprecámur:
tuque, princeps milítiæ cæléstis,
sátanam aliósque spíritus malígnos,
qui ad perditiónem animárum pervagántur in
mundo, divína virtúte,
in inférnum detrúde. Amen.

11. Serve the Lord *
    with awe and trembling.

12. Pay him your homage, lest he be angry and you
    perish, * for suddenly his anger will blaze.
    Blessed are they * who put their trust in God.

13. Glory Be.

Ant.   His kingdom is a kingdom of all ages, and all
kings shall serve and obey him (Easter Time Alleluia).

V. O Lord, hear my prayer.

R. **And let my cry come unto you.**
   Priests add:

V. The Lord be with you.

R. **And also with you.**

Let us pray.

Almighty and eternal God, you have renewed all
creation in your beloved Son, the king of the whole
universe. May all the people of the earth, now torn
apart by the wound of sin, become subject to the
gentle rule of your only-begotten Son: Who lives and
reigns with you and the Holy Spirit, one God, for
ever and ever. R. **Amen**.

PRAYER TO ST. MICHAEL THE ARCHANGEL

Saint Michael the Archangel,
defend us in battle;
be our defense against the wickedness
and snares of the devil.
May God rebuke him, we humbly pray.
And do you, O prince of the heavenly host,
by the power of God
thrust into hell Satan and all the evil spirits
who prowl about the world
    for the ruin of souls. Amen.

LITANY OF HUMILITY

Cardinal Merry del Val, who composed this litany,
often recited it after the celebration of the holy Mass.

O Jesus! meek and humble of heart,   **Hear me.**

From the desire of being esteemed, **Deliver me, Jesus.**

From the desire of being loved, . . .

From the desire of being extolled, . . .

From the desire of being honored, . . .

From the desire of being praised, . . .

From the desire of being preferred to others, . . .

From the desire of being consulted, . . .

From the desire of being approved, . . .

From the fear of being humiliated, . . .

From the fear of being despised, . . .

From the fear of suffering rebukes, . . .

From the fear of being calumniated, . . .

From the fear of being forgotten, . . .

From the fear of being ridiculed, . . .

From the fear of being wronged, . . .

From the fear of being suspected, . . .

That others may be loved more
    than I,   **Jesus, grant me
                        the grace to desire it.**

That others may be esteemed more than I, . . .

That in the opinion of the world
    others may increase and I may decrease, . . .

That others may be chosen and I set aside, . . .

That others may be praised and I unnoticed, . . .

That others may be preferred to me in everything, . . .

That others become holier than I, provided that
    I may become as holy as I should, . . .

COMMUNION OUTSIDE MASS

SHORT RITE

The place where Communion outside Mass is ordinarily given is a church or an oratory in which the Eucharist is regularly celebrated or reserved, or a church, an oratory, or another place where the local community regularly gathers for the liturgical assembly on Sundays or other days. Communion may be given in other places, however, including private homes, when it is a question of the sick, prisoners, or others who cannot leave a place without danger or serious difficulty.[1]

Among the possible forms, this form of service is used when the longer, more elaborate form is unsuitable.

GREETING

V. The Lord be with you.

R. **And also with you.**

PENITENTIAL RITE

V. My brothers and sisters, to prepare ourselves for this celebration, let us call to mind our sins.

A pause for silent reflection follows. All say:

**I confess to almighty God,
and to you, my brothers and sisters,
that I have sinned through my own fault**

1: *Holy Communion and Worship of the Eucharist Outside the Mass*, ICEL, 1974.

They strike their breast:

**in my thoughts and in my words,
in what I have done,
and in what I have failed to do;
and I ask blessed Mary, ever virgin,
all the angels and saints,
and you, my brothers and sisters,
to pray for me to the Lord our God.**

The priest says the absolution:

May almighty God have mercy on us,
forgive us our sins,
and bring us to everlasting life.

The people answer: **Amen.**

READING OF THE SCRIPTURE

The minister should read a short scriptural text:

A reading of the holy gospel according to John. 6:51
Jesus says: "I am the living bread, which has come
down from heaven. Anyone who eats this bread will
live for ever; and the bread that I shall give is my
flesh, for the life of the world."

V. The Gospel of the Lord.

R. **Praise to you, Lord Jesus Christ.**

LORD'S PRAYER AND HOLY COMMUNION

The minister takes the ciborium or pyx containing the body of
the Lord, places it on the altar, and genuflects. He then introduces the Lord's Prayer in these or similar words:

Let us pray with confidence to the Father
in the words our Savior gave us:

He continues with the people:

Our Father, . . .

The minister genuflects. Taking the host, he raises it slightly over the vessel or pyx and, facing the people, says:

V. **This is the Lamb of God**
   who takes away the sins of the world.
   Happy are those who are called to his supper.

The communicants say once:

R. **Lord, I am not worthy to receive you,**
   but only say the word and I shall be healed.

The minister takes a host for each one and says:

V. **The body of Christ.**

R. **Amen.**

After Communion, the minister puts any particles left on the plate into the pyx, and he may wash his hands. He returns any remaining hosts to the tabernacle ,and genuflects.

A period of silence may now be observed, or a psalm or song of praise may be sung.

Meanwhile, not forming part of the rite, one may pray inaudibly:

How holy this feast
in which Christ is our food:
His passion is recalled,
grace fills our hearts,
and we receive a pledge of the glory
   to come (Easter Time Alleluia).

The minister then says the concluding prayer:

Let us pray.
Lord Jesus Christ,
you gave us the Eucharist
as the memorial of your suffering and death.
May our worship of this sacrament of your
   body and blood
help us to experience the salvation you won for us

and the peace of the kingdom
where you live with the Father and the Holy Spirit,
one God, for ever and ever.

R. **Amen**.

During Easter Time the following prayer is preferred:

Let us pray.
Lord,
you have nourished us
    with your Easter sacraments.
Fill us with your Spirit
and make us one in peace and love.
We ask this through Christ our Lord.

R. **Amen**.

CONCLUDING RITE AND BLESSING

If the minister is a priest or deacon, he extends his hands and, facing the people, says:

V. The Lord be with you.

R. **And also with you.**

He blesses the people with these words:

V. May almighty God bless you, the Father,

and the Son, ✠ and the Holy Spirit.

R. **Amen.**

V. Go in the peace of Christ.

R. **Thanks be to God.**

COMMUNION OF THE SICK OR ELDERLY

When a minister of the Church brings Communion, the sick or elderly person shares in the eucharistic meal of the community. This holy Communion manifests the support and concern of the community for its members who are not able to be present. Holy Communion is a bond to the community for its members who are not able to be present. Holy Communion is a bond to the community, as it is a union with Christ. When the Eucharist is brought to the home, the family should prepare a table with a cloth and a lighted candle. All members of the household may receive Communion with the sick person, according to the usual norms. The following texts are among many that may be chosen from the *Rite of Communion of the Sick*.[2]

ITEMS THAT MAY BE NEEDED

A briefcase to carry the following items:

White stole (for the priest or deacon)
Holy water sprinkler
Ritual, or card with prayers
Crucifix
Purificator

One should check with the priest as to what is needed; in some cases (e.g., Communion in a hospital), the requirements differ. The priest usually does not wear a surplice during the trip but does wear a narrow white stole under his suit coat.

GREETING

All make the Sign of the Cross. The minister of Communion speaks the following or a similar greeting:

V. **Peace be with this house and with all who live here.**

All respond:

R. **And also with you.**

2. *Ibidem.*

SPRINKLING WITH HOLY WATER

The Blessed Sacrament is placed on the table. The sick person and all present may be sprinkled with holy water. Before this sprinkling, the minister of Communion says:

Let this water call to mind our baptism into Christ, who by his death and resurrection has redeemed us.

PENITENTIAL RITE

The minister invites all to join in the penitential rite:

My brothers and sisters, let us turn with confidence to the Lord and ask forgiveness for all our sins.

After a brief silence, the penitential rite continues:

I confess to almighty God,
and to you, my brothers and sisters,
that I have sinned through my own fault

They strike their breast:

in my thoughts and in my words,
in what I have done,
and in what I have failed to do;
and I ask blessed Mary, ever virgin,
all the angels and saints,
and you, my brothers and sisters,
to pray for me to the Lord our God.

or

V. Lord Jesus, you healed the sick:
    Lord, have mercy.

R. Lord, have mercy.

V. Lord Jesus, you forgave sinners:
    Christ, have mercy.

R. Christ, have mercy.

V. Lord Jesus, you give us yourself to heal us
    and to bring us strength:
    Lord, have mercy.

R. Lord, have mercy.

Then the minister concludes the penitential rite:

May almighty God have mercy on us,
forgive us our sins,
and bring us to everlasting life.

R. **Amen.**

READING OF THE SCRIPTURE

Then a selection from the Scriptures is read. An appropriate reading should be selected and prepared by the family or the minister of Communion. The following Scriptures are appropriate but are not intended to limit the choice of a reading.

A reading of the holy gospel according to John   **6:51**
Jesus says: "I am the living bread which has come down from heaven. Anyone who eats this bread will live for ever; and the bread that I shall give is my flesh, for the life of the world."

V. The Gospel of the Lord.

R. **Praise to you, Lord Jesus Christ.**

or   **John 15: 5**

or   **1 John 4:16**

LORD'S PRAYER AND COMMUNION

Following a time of silence, all join in prayers of intercession. Then, in preparation for holy Communion, all recite the Lord's Prayer.

Now let us pray to God as our Lord Jesus Christ taught us.

Our Father, . . .

After this, the minister shows the eucharistic bread to those present, saying:

This is the Lamb of God
who takes away the sins of the world.
Happy are those who are called to his supper.

All who are to receive Communion respond:

Lord, I am not worthy to receive you,
but only say the word and I shall be healed.

The minister gives Communion saying, "The body of Christ," "The blood of Christ," as appropriate. The sick person answers "**Amen.**" All who wish to do so receive Communion in the usual way. After a time of silence, the minister says the following or another prayer:

All-powerful and ever-living God,
may the body and blood of Christ your Son
be for our brother (sister) N.
a lasting remedy for body and soul.
We ask this through Christ our Lord.
R. Amen.

VIATICUM

Viaticum is the sacrament of the dying. When the minister has brought holy Communion, the rite may begin with the renewal of the dying person's profession of faith (p. 549).

Viaticum is then celebrated in the same manner as Communion of the Sick (p. 309), except that after giving Communion, the minister says:

May the Lord Jesus Christ protect you
and lead you to eternal life.
R. Amen.

The concluding prayer follows:

God of peace,
you offer eternal healing to those who believe in you;
you have refreshed your servant N.
with food and drink from heaven:
lead him (her) safely into the kingdom of light.
We ask this through Christ our Lord.
R. Amen.

EUCHARISTIC ADORATION

"The Catholic Church has always offered and still offers to the sacrament of the Eucharist the cult of adoration, not only during Mass, but also outside of it, reserving the consecrated hosts with the utmost care, exposing them to the solemn veneration of the faithful, and carrying them in procession."[1]

"The tabernacle was first intended for the reservation of the Eucharist in a worthy place so that it could be brought to the sick and those absent, outside of Mass. As faith in the real presence of Christ in his Eucharist deepened, the Church became conscious of the meaning of silent adoration of the Lord present under the Eucharistic species.

"It is for this reason that the tabernacle should be located in an especially worthy place in the church and should be constructed in such a way that it emphasizes and manifests the truth of the real presence of Christ in the Blessed Sacrament. It is highly fitting that Christ should have wanted to remain present to his Church in this unique way. . . . He wanted to give us his sacramental presence; . . . he wanted us to have the memorial of the love with which *he loved us 'to the end'*. . . ."[2]

"The Church and the world have a great need for Eucharistic worship. Jesus awaits us in this sacrament of love. Let us not refuse the time to go to meet him in adoration, in contemplation full of faith, and open to making amends for the serious offenses and crimes of the world. Let our adoration never cease."[3]

1. Paul VI, *Mysterium Fidei* 56.
2. Cf. *Catechism of the Catholic Church* (=CCC), 1379-1380, Libreria Editrice Vaticana, 1994.
3. John Paul II, *Dominicæ Cenæ*, 3.

RITE OF EXPOSITION AND BENEDICTION

Toward the beginning of the thirteenth century, great emphasis was being placed on the truth of the Real Presence of Christ in the Blessed Sacrament. Although Catholics had always believed that Jesus is actually present in the Eucharist, the fact was now being stressed to counteract some false ideas that were prevalent at the time. To correct mistaken notions and even superstition in regard to the doctrine, the Church fostered a renewal in the faith and devotion toward the Real Presence. In 1246, the feast of Corpus Christ, honoring the Body of Our Lord was established. Also in this period, St. Thomas Aquinas, the Angelic Doctor, composed his beautiful hymns praising the Holy Eucharist. (Anthony Teolis, "Mary at Benediction," *Homiletic and Pastoral Review*, vol. XCVII, no. 2 p. 54).

EXPOSITION

After the people have assembled, a song may be sung while the minister comes to the altar. If the holy Eucharist is not reserved at the altar where the exposition is to take place, the minister puts on a humeral veil and brings the sacrament from the place of reservation; he is accompanied by servers or by the faithful with lighted candles.

The ciborium or monstrance should be placed upon the table of the altar, which is covered with a cloth. After exposition, if the monstrance is used, the minister incenses the sacrament. If the adoration is to be lengthy, he may then withdraw.

ADORATION

During the exposition there should be prayers, songs, and readings to direct the attention of the faithful to the worship of Christ the Lord.

To encourage a prayerful spirit, there should be readings from Scripture with a homily or brief exhortation to develop a better understanding of the eucharistic mystery. It is desirable also for the people to respond to the word of God by singing and to spend some periods of time in religious silence.

Part of the Liturgy of the Hours, especially the principal hours, may be celebrated before the Blessed Sacrament when there is a lengthy period of exposition. This liturgy extends the praise and thanksgiving offered to God in the eucharistic celebration to the several hours of the day; it directs the prayers of the Church to Christ and through him to the Father in the name of the whole world. One of the following hymns may be sung.

O Saving Victim opening wide
The gates of heav'n to man below!
Our foes press on from every side;
Thine aid supply, Thy strength bestow.

To Thy great name be endless praise
Immortal Godhead, One in Three;
Oh, grant us endless length of days,
In our true native land with Thee. Amen.

O salutáris Hóstia
Quæ cæli pandis óstium.
Bella premunt hostília;
Da robur fer auxílium.

Uni trinóque Dómino
Sit sempitérna glória:
Qui vitam sine término,
Nobis donet in pátria. Amen.

---

or: *Adoro Te Devote* (p. 320: in English, p. 321)

BENEDICTION

Eucharistic hymn and incensation

Toward the end, the priest or deacon goes to the altar, genuflects, and kneels. As a hymn or other eucharistic song is sung, the minister, while kneeling, incenses the sacrament, if the exposition has taken place with the monstrance. A hymn such as the following may be sung.

Pange, lingua, gloriósi
córporis mystérium,
sanguinisque pretiósi,
quem in mundi prétium
fructus ventris generósi
Rex effúdit géntium.

Nobis datus, nobis natus
ex intácta Vírgine,
et in mundo conversátus,
sparso verbi sémine,
sui moras incolátus
miro clausit órdine.

In suprémae nocte cenae
recúmbens cum frátribus,
observáta lege plene
cibis in legálibus,
cibum turbae duodénae
se dat suis mánibus.

Verbum caro panem verum
verbo carnem éfficit
fitque sanguis Christi merum,
et, si sensus déficit,
ad firmándum cor sincérum
sola fides súfficit.

Tantum ergo sacraméntum
venerémur cernui,
et antíquum documéntum
novo cedat rítui;
praestet fides suppleméntum
sensuum deféctui.

Genitóri Genitóque
laus et iubilátio,
salus, honor, virtus quoque
sit et benedictio;
procedénti ab utróque
compar sit laudátio. Amen.

Sing, my tongue, the Savior's glory,
Of his flesh the mystery sing,
Of the blood, all price exceeding,
Shed by our immortal King;
Destined for the world's redemption,
From a noble womb to spring.

Of a pure and spotless Virgin
Born for us on earth below,
He, as man with man conversing,
Stayed, the seeds of truth to sow;
Then he closed in solemn order
Wondrously his life of woe.

On the night of that last supper,
Seated with his chosen band,
He, the paschal victim eating,
First fulfills the law's command;
Then as food to all his brethren,
Gives himself with his own hand.

Word made flesh, the bread of nature
By his word to flesh he turns;
Wine into his blood he changes:
What though sense no change discerns?
Only be the heart in earnest,
Faith her lesson quickly learns.

Down in adoration falling,
Lo, the sacred Host we hail;
Lo, o'er ancient forms departing
Newer rites of grace prevail;
Faith for all defects supplying
Where the feeble senses fail.

To the everlasting Father,
And the Son who reigns on high,
With the Holy Spirit proceeding
Forth from each eternally
Be salvation, honor, blessing,
Might, and endless majesty. Amen.

V. Panem de cælo præstitísti eis (T. P. Allelúia).

R. **Omne delectaméntum in se habéntem (T. P. Allelúia).**

Orémus.

Deus, qui nobis sub sacraménto mirábili, passiónis tuæ memóriam reliquísti: tríbue, quǽsumus, ita nos córporis et Sánguinis tui sacra mystéria venerári, ut redemptiónis tuæ fructum in nobis iúgiter sentiámus: Qui vivis et regnas in sǽcula sæculórum.

V. You have given them bread from heaven (Easter Time Alleluia).

R. **Having all sweetness within it (Easter Time Alleluia).**

Let us pray.

Lord Jesus Christ, | you gave us the Eucharist | as the memorial of your suffering and death. | May our worship of this sacrament of your body and blood | help us to experience the salvation you won for us | and the peace of the kingdom | where you live with the Father and the Holy Spirit, | one God, for ever and ever.

R. **Amen.**

R. **Amen.**

Then the priest or deacon makes the Sign of the Cross over the people with the monstrance or ciborium, in silence. The Divine Praises may be said:

Blessed be God.
Blessed be his holy name.
Blessed be Jesus Christ, true God and true man.
Blessed be the name of Jesus.
Blessed be his most Sacred Heart.
Blessed be his most Precious Blood.
Blessed be Jesus in the most holy Sacrament of the Altar.
Blessed be the Holy Spirit, the Paraclete.

Blessed be the great Mother of God, Mary most holy.
Blessed be her holy and Immaculate Conception.
Blessed be her glorious Assumption.
Blessed be the name of Mary, virgin and mother.
Blessed be St. Joseph, her most chaste spouse.
Blessed be God in his angels and in his saints. Amen.

At this moment, the pious custom of reciting the Prayer of
Reparation to the Eucharistic Heart of Jesus may be observed.

May the Heart of Jesus in the most Blessed Sacrament be praised, adored, and loved with grateful affection at every moment in all the tabernacles of the
world, now and until the end of time. Amen.

After that, the priest or deacon who gave the blessing, or another priest or deacon, replaces the Blessed Sacrament in the
tabernacle and genuflects. Meanwhile, the people may sing:

O Sacrament most holy,
O Sacrament divine,
All praise and all thanksgiving
Be every moment Thine,
Be every moment Thine.
    or:

Holy God, we praise thy name!
Lord of all, we bow before thee;
All on earth thy scepter claim,
All in heav'n above adore thee;
Infinite thy vast domain,
Everlasting is thy reign.
    or:

Laudáte Dóminum omnes gentes;
Laudáte eum omnes pópuli.
Quóniam confirmáta est super nos misericórdia eius;
Et véritas Dómini manet in ætérnum. Glória Patri . . .

Following an ancient tradition, the Salve service (p. 471), particularly on Saturdays, may be added here.

ADORO TE DEVOTE

Adóro te devóte, latens Déitas,
Quæ sub his figúris vere látitas:
Tibi se cor meum totum súbiicit,
Quia te contémplans totum déficit.

Visus, tactus, gustus in te fállitur,
Sed audítu solo tuto créditur.
Credo, quidquid dixit Dei Fílius:
Nil hoc verbo Veritátis vérius.

In cruce latébat sola Déitas,
At hic latet simul et humánitas;
Ambo tamen credens atque cónfitens,
Peto quod petívit latro paénitens.

Plagas, sicut Thomas, non intúeor;
Deum tamen meum te confíteor.
Fac me tibi semper magis crédere,
In te spem habére, te dilígere.

O memoriále mortis Dómini!
Panis vivus, vitam præstans hómini!
Præsta meæ menti de te vívere.
Et te illi semper dulce sápere.

Pie pellicáne, Iesu Dómine,
Me immúndum munda tuo sánguine.
Cuius una stilla salvum fácere
Totum mundum quit ab omni scélere.

Iesu, quem velátum nunc aspício,
Oro fiat illud quod tam sítio;
Ut te reveláta cernens fácie,
Visu sim beátus tuæ glóriæ. Amen.

I DEVOUTLY ADORE YOU

That the body and blood of Christ are truly present
in the Blessed Sacrament is something that cannot
be apprehended by the senses, but can be known
by faith only; faith that relies on divine authority.

I devoutly adore you, O hidden God,
truly hidden beneath these appearances.
My whole heart submits to you
and in contemplating you
    it surrenders itself completely.

Sight, touch, taste are all deceived
    in their judgment of you,
but hearing suffices firmly to believe.
I believe all that the Son of God has spoken:
there is nothing truer than this word of Truth.

On the Cross only the Divinity was hidden,
but here the Humanity is also hidden.
I believe and confess both
and I ask for what the repentant thief asked.

I do not see the wounds as Thomas did,
but I confess that you are my God.
Make me believe more and more in you,
hope in you, and love you.

O Memorial of our Lord's death!
Living bread that gives life to man,
grant my soul to live on you
and always to savor your sweetness.

Lord Jesus, good Pelican,
wash me clean with your blood,
one drop of which can free
the entire world of all its sins.

Jesus, whom now I see hidden,
I ask you to fulfill what I so desire:
that on seeing you face to face,
I may be happy in seeing your glory. Amen.

VISIT TO THE BLESSED SACRAMENT

Some Christians have the custom of entering a church, sometime during the day, in order to make a visit to Christ present in the Blessed Sacrament. They spend a few moments of intimacy with the Lord, as they recite prayers and express personal petitions. A short time before the Blessed Sacrament will help us to recall the presence of God in our daily routine.

"Jesus has remained in the Sacred Host for us so as to stay by our side, to sustain us, to guide us. And love can be repaid with love only.

"How could we not turn to the Blessed Sacrament each day, even if it is only for a few minutes, to bring him our greetings and our love as children and as brothers?"[4]

Recite three times:

V. Adorémus in æter-num Sanctíssimum Sacramentum.

R. Adorémus in æter-num Sanctíssimum Sacramentum.

V. Let us for ever adore the most Holy Sacra-ment.

R. Let us for ever adore the most Holy Sacra-ment.

Pater Noster. . . .
Ave Maria. . . .
Gloria Patri. . . .

Our Father.
Hail Mary.
Glory Be.

Spiritual Communion

I wish, my Lord, to receive you with the purity, humility, and devotion with which your most holy Mother received you, with the spirit and fervor of the saints.

---

4. Josemaría Escrivá, *Furrow, 686;* Scepter Publishers: Princeton, N. J., 1986.

GUIDE FOR A GOOD CONFESSION

"To those who have been far away from the sacrament of Reconciliation and forgiving love, I make this appeal: Come back to this source of grace; do not be afraid! Christ himself is waiting for you. He will heal you, and you will be at peace with God!"[1]

The basic requirement for a good Confession is to have the intention of returning to God like the *Prodigal son* and of acknowledging our sins with true sorrow before his representative, the priest.

Examination of Conscience

Examine your conscience. Recall your sins. Calmly ask yourself what you have done with full knowledge and full consent against God's Commandments.

THE FIRST COMMANDMENT

- Have I performed my duties toward God reluctantly or grudgingly?
- Did I neglect my prayer life? Did I recite my usual prayers?
- Did I receive holy Communion in the state of mortal sin or without the necessary preparation?
- Did I violate the one-hour Eucharistic fast?
- Did I fail to mention some grave sin in my previous confessions?

---

1. Homily of pope John Paul II on September 13, 1987, at Westover Hills, San Antonio, Texas.

- Did I seriously believe in something superstitious or engage in a superstitious practice (palm-reading or fortune telling for instance)?
- Did I seriously doubt a matter of Faith?
- Did I put my faith in danger—without a good reason—by reading a book, pamphlet, or magazine that contains material contrary to Catholic faith or morals?
- Did I endanger my faith by joining or attending meetings of organizations opposed to the Catholic faith (non-catholic services, the Communist Party, Freemasonry, "new age" cults, or other religions)? Did I take part in one of its activities?
- Have I committed the sin of sacrilege (profanation of a sacred person, place or thing)?

THE SECOND COMMANDMENT

- Did I fail to try my best to fulfill the promises and resolutions that I made to God?
- Did I take the name of God in vain? Did I make use of God's name mockingly, jokingly, angrily, or in any other irreverent manner?
- Did I make use of the Blessed Virgin Mary's name or another saint's name mockingly, jokingly, angrily, or in any other irreverent manner?
- Have I been a sponsor in Baptism or participate actively in other ceremonies outside the Catholic Church?
- Did I tell a lie under oath?
- Did I break (private or public) vows?

The Third Commandment

- Did I miss Mass on a Sunday or a holy day of obligation?
- Did I fail to dress appropiately for Mass?
- Have I, without sufficient reason, arrived at Mass so late that I failed to fulfill the Sunday or holy Day of obligation?
- Did I allow myself to be distracted during Mass, by not paying attention, looking around out of curiosity, etc.?
- Did I cause another to be distracted?
- Have I performed any work or business activity that would inhibit the worship due to God, the joy proper to the Lord's Day, or the appropriate relaxation of mind and body, on a Sunday or a holy day of obligation?
- Did I fail to generously help the Church in her necessities to the extent that I am able?
- Did I fail to fast or abstain on a day prescribed by the Church?

The Fourth Commandment
(For Parents)

- Have I neglected to teach my children their prayers, send them to church, or give them a Christian education?
- Have I given them bad example?
- Have I neglected to watch over my children, to monitor their companions, the books they read, the movies and TV shows they watch?
- Have I failed to see to it that my child made the First Confession and First Communion?

- Have I failed to see to it that my children have received the sacrament of Confirmation?

(FOR CHILDREN)

- Was I disobedient toward my parents?
- Did I neglect to help my parents when my help was needed?
- Did I treat my parents with little affection or respect?
- Did I react proudly when I was corrected by my parents?
- Did I have a disordered desire for independence?
- Did I do my chores?

THE FIFTH COMMANDMENT

- Did I easily get angry or lose my temper?
- Was I envious or jealous of others?
- Did I injure or take the life of anyone? Was I ever reckless in driving?
- Was I an occasion of sin for others by way of conversation, the telling of jokes religiously, racially, or sexually offensive, my way of dressing, inviting somebody to attend certain shows, lending harmful books or magazines, helping someone to steal, etc.? Did I try to repair the scandal done?
- How many persons did I lead to sin? What sin or sins were involved?
- Did I neglect my health? Did I attempt to take my life?
- Have I mutilated myself or another?
- Did I get drunk or use prohibited drugs?

- Did I eat or drink more than a sufficient amount, allowing myself to get carried away by gluttony?
- Did I participate in any form of physical violence?
- Did I consent to or actively take part in direct sterilization (tubal ligation, vasectomy, etc.)? Do I realize that this will have a permanent effect on my married life and that I will have to answer to God for its consequences?
- Did I consent to, advise, or actively take part in an abortion? Was I aware that the Church punishes with automatic excommunication *(latæ sententiæ)* those who *procure and achieve* abortion? Do I realize that this is a very grave crime?
- Did I cause harm to anyone with my words or actions?
- Did I desire revenge or harbor enmity, hatred, or ill-feelings when someone offended me?
- Did I ask pardon whenever I offended anyone?
- Did I insult or offensively tease others?
- Did I quarrel with one of my brothers or sisters?

THE SIXTH AND NINTH COMMANDMENTS

- Did I willfully entertain impure thoughts?
- Did I consent to evil desires against the virtue of purity, even though I may not have carried them out? Were there any circumstances that aggravated the sin: affinity (relationship by marriage), consanguinity (blood relationship), either the married state or the consecration to God of a person involved?

- Did I engage in impure conversations? Did I start them?

- Did I look for fun in forms of entertainment that placed me in proximate occasions of sin, such as certain dances, movies, shows, or books with immoral contents? Did I frequent houses of ill-repute or keep bad company?

- Did I realize that I might already have been committing a sin by placing myself in a proximate occasion of sin, such as sharing a room with a person I find sexually attractive, or being alone with such a person in circumstances that could lead to sin?

- Did I fail to take care of those details of modesty and decency that are the safeguards of purity?

- Did I fail, before going to a show or reading a book, to find out its moral implications, so as not to put myself in immediate danger of sinning and in order to avoid distorting my conscience?

- Did I willfully look at an indecent picture or cast an immodest look upon myself or another? Did I willfully desire to commit such a sin?

- Did I lead others to sins of impurity or immodesty? What sins?

- Did I commit an impure act? By myself, through masturbation (which is objectively a mortal sin)? With someone else? How many times? With someone of the same or opposite sex? Was there any circumstance of relationship (such as affinity) that could have given the sin special gravity? Did this illicit relationship result in pregnancy? Did I do anything to prevent or end that pregnancy?

- Do I have friendships that are habitual occasions of sexual sins? Am I prepared to end them?

- In courtship, is true love my fundamental reason for wanting to be with the other person? Do I live the constant and cheerful sacrifice of not putting the person I love in danger of sinning? Do I degrade human love by confusing it with selfishness or mere pleasure?

- Did I engage in acts such as "petting," "necking," passionate kisses, or prolonged embraces?

(FOR MARRIED PEOPLE)

- Did I, without serious reason, deprive my spouse of the marital right? Did I claim my own rights in a way which showed no concern for my spouse's state of mind or health? Did I betray conjugal fidelity in desire or in deed?

- Did I take "the pill" or use any other artificial birth control device before or after new life had already been conceived?

- Did I without grave reason, with the intention of avoiding conception, make use of marriage on only those days when offspring would not likely be engendered?

- Did I suggest to another person the use of birth-control pills or another artificial method of preventing pregnancy (like condoms)?

- Did I have a hand in contributing to the *contraceptive mentality* by my advice, jokes, or attitudes?

(On abortion, contraception, sterilization, etc., see also THE FIFTH COMMANDMENT).

THE SEVENTH AND TENTH COMMANDMENTS

- Did I steal? How much money? Or how much was the object worth? Did I give it back, or at least have the intention of doing so?

- Have I done or caused damage to another person's property? To what extent?
- Did I harm anyone by deception, fraud, or coercion in business contracts or transactions?
- Did I unnecessarily spend beyond my means? Do I spend too much money because of vanity, or caprice?
- Do I give alms according to my capacity?
- Was I envious of my neighbor's goods?
- Did I neglect to pay my debts?
- Did I knowingly accept stolen goods?
- Did I desire to steal?
- Did I give in to laziness or love of comfort rather than diligently work or study?
- Was I greedy? Do I have an excessively materialistic view of life?

THE EIGHTH COMMANDMENT

- Did I tell lies? Did I repair any damage that may have resulted as a consequence of this?
- Have I unjustly or rashly accused others?
- Did I sin by detraction, that is, by telling the faults of another person without necessity?
- Did I sin by calumny, that is, by telling derogatory lies about another person?
- Did I engage in gossip, backbiting, or taletelling?
- Did I reveal a secret without due cause?

Shorter Examination of Conscience

- When was my last good Confession? Did I receive Communion or other sacraments while in the state of mortal sin? Did I intentionally fail to confess some mortal sin in my previous Confession?

- Did I willfully and seriously doubt my faith, or put myself in danger of losing it by reading literature hostile to Catholic teachings or by getting involved with non-Catholic sects? Did I engage in superstitious activities: palm reading, fortune telling?

- Did I take the name of God in vain? Did I curse or take a false oath? Did I use bad language?

- Did I miss Mass on a Sunday or a holy day of obligation through my own fault, without any serious reason? Did I fast and abstain on the prescribed days?

- Did I disobey my parents or lawful superiors in important matters?

- Was I selfish in how I treated others, especially my spouse, my brothers and sisters, my relatives, or my friends? Did I hatefully, quarrel with anyone, or desire revenge? Did I refuse to forgive? Did I cause physical injury or even death? Did I get drunk? Did I take illicit drugs? Did I consent to, advise, or actively take part in an abortion?

- Did I willfully look at indecent pictures or watch immoral movies? Did I read immoral books or magazines? Did I engage in impure jokes or conversations? Did I willfully entertain impure thoughts or feelings? Did I commit impure acts, alone or with others? Did I take contraceptive or abortifacient pills, or use other artificial means in order to prevent conception?

- Did I steal or damage another's property? How much? Have I made reparation for the damages done? Have I been honest in my business relations?

- Did I tell lies? Did I sin by slander? By detraction—telling unknown grave faults of others without necessity? Did I judge others rashly in serious matters? Have I tried to make restitution for any damage of reputation that I have caused?

If you remember other serious sins besides those indicated here, include them also in your Confession.

Before Confession

Be truly sorry for your sins.

The essential act of Penance, on the part of the penitent, is *contrition*, a clear and decisive rejection of the sin committed, together with a resolution not to commit it again, out of the love one has for God (which is reborn with repentance). Understood in this way, *contrition* is, therefore, the beginning and the heart of *conversion*, of that evangelical *metanoia* which brings the person back to God like the Prodigal Son returning to his father, and which has in the sacrament of Penance its visible sign, and which perfects attrition (imperfect contrition—born of the consideration of sin's ugliness or the fear of eternal damnation and other penalties threatening the sinner).[2]

The *resolution to avoid committing these sins in the future* (amendment) is a sure sign that your sorrow is genuine and authentic.

This does not mean that one has to promise never to fall again into sin. A resolution to try to avoid the

near occasions of sin suffices for true repentance.
God's grace in cooperation with the intention to rec-
tify your life will give you the strength to resist and
overcome temptation in the future.

Act of Contrition

> O my God, I am heartily sorry for having of-
> fended you, and I detest all my sins, because
> I dread the loss of heaven and the pains of
> hell; but most of all because they offend you,
> my God, who are all good and deserving of
> all my love. I firmly resolve, with the help of
> your grace, to confess my sins, to do penance,
> and to amend my life. Amen.

or :

> My God,
> I am sorry for my sins with all my heart.
> In choosing to do wrong
> and failing to do good,
> I have sinned against you
> whom I should love above all things.
> I firmly intend with your help,
> to do penance,
> to sin no more,
> and to avoid whatever leads me to sin.
> Our Savior Jesus Christ
> suffered and died for us.
> In his name, my God, have mercy.

or :

I confess (p. 59).

You are now ready to go to Confession. The rite is presented on p. 335.

During Confession

- You can begin your confession by making the Sign of the Cross and greeting the priest: "**Bless me, Father, for I have sinned**."

- The priest gives you a blessing. One response you might give is these words St. Peter said to Christ: "**Lord, you know all things; you know that I love you**" (Jn 21:17). One then continues with the time since one's last confession: "**My last good confession was ... (approximately how many weeks, months or years).**"

- *Say the sins that you remember.* Start with the one that is most difficult to say; after this it will be easier to mention the rest. If you received general absolution, tell this to the priest and mention the sins forgiven then.

- If you do not know how to confess, or you feel uneasy or ashamed, simply ask the priest to assist you. Be assured that he will help you to make a good confession. Simply answer his questions without hiding anything out of shame or fear. Place your trust in God: he is your merciful Father and wants to forgive you.

- If you do not remember any serious sins, be sure to confess at least some of your venial sins, adding at the end: "**I am sorry for these and all the sins of my past life, especially for ...**" (mention in general any past sin for which you are particularly sorry; for example, all my sins against charity).

- The priest will assign you some penance and give you some advice to help you to be a better Christian.

- Listen to the words of absolution attentively. At the end answer: **"Amen."** Be willing to do the penance as soon as possible. This *penance* will diminish the temporal punishment due to sins already forgiven.

After Confession

- *Give thanks* to God for having forgiven you once again.

- Promptly and devoutly *fulfill the penance* given by the priest. Although you may receive holy Communion even before performing your penance, it is advisable to do it as soon as possible.

- If you *recall some serious sin* that you forgot to tell, rest assured that it has been forgiven with the others, but be sure to include it in your next Confession.

Rite of Confession

After the customary greetings, the penitent crosses himself:

In the name of the Father, and of the Son, and of the Holy Spirit. Amen.

The priest urges the penitent to have confidence in God. The priest may say:

May the Lord be in your heart
and help you to confess your sins with true sorrow.

Either the priest or the penitent may read or say by heart some words taken from the holy Scripture about the mercy of God and repentance, e.g.:

"Lord, you know all things; you know that I love you (John 21:17)."

The penitent accuses himself of his sins. The priest gives opportune advice, imposes the penance on him, and invites the penitent to manifest his contrition. The penitent may say:

**Lord Jesus, Son of God,
have mercy on me, a sinner.**

The priest gives him the absolution:

God, the Father of mercies, | through the death and resurrection of his Son | has reconciled the world to himself | and sent the Holy Spirit among us | for the forgiveness of sins; | through the ministry of the Church, | may God give you pardon and peace, | and I absolve you from your sins | in the name of the Father, and of the Son, ✠ | and of the Holy Spirit.

The penitent answers: **Amen**

The priest dismisses the penitent with this or any of the alternative formulae:

May the Passion of our Lord Jesus Christ, | the intercession of the Blessed Virgin Mary and of all the saints, | whatever good you do and suffering you endure | heal your sins, help you to grow in holiness, | and reward you with eternal life. | Go in peace.

The penitent should fulfill the penance imposed.

DEVOTIONS TO
THE BLESSED TRINITY

"The mystery of the Most Holy Trinity is the central mystery of Christian faith and life. It is the mystery of God in himself. It is therefore the source of all the other mysteries of faith, the light that enlightens them. It is the most fundamental and essential teaching in the 'hierarchy of the truths of faith.' The whole history of salvation is identical with the history of the way and the means by which the one true God, Father, Son, and Holy Spirit, reveals himself to men 'and reconciles and unites with himself those who turn away from sin.'"[1]

"Christians are baptized 'in the name of the Father and of the Son and of the Holy Spirit.' Before receiving the sacrament they respond to a three-part question when asked to confess the Father, the Son, and the Spirit: 'I do.' 'The faith of all Christians rests on the Trinity.'"[2]

TE DEUM

This hymn of praise can be traced back to the first centuries of Christendom. During the Middle Ages it was ascribed to Saints Ambrose and Augustine. It has also been attributed to bishop Nicetas of Remesiana. Since the sixth century, it has been recited as part of the Divine Office.

---

1. *Catechism of the Catholic Church* (=CCC), 234, Libreria Editrice Vaticana, 1994.

2. CCC, 232.

TE DEUM

1. Te Deum laudámus: *
   te Dóminum confitémur.

2. Te ætérnum Patrem, *
   omnis terra venerátur.

3. Tibi omnes ángeli, *
   tibi cæli et univérsæ potestátes:

4. Tibi chérubim et séraphim *
   incessábili voce proclámant:

5. Sanctus, * Sanctus, * Sanctus *
   Dóminus Deus Sábaoth.

6. Pleni sunt cæli et terra*
   maiestátis glóriæ tuæ.

7. Te gloriósus *
   Apostolórum chorus:

8. Te prophetárum *
   laudábilis númerus:

9. Te mártyrum candidátus*
   laudat exércitus.

10. Te per orbem terrárum*
    sancta confitétur Ecclésia,

11. Patrem *
    imménsæ maiestátis;

12. Venerándum tuum verum *
    et únicum Fílium;

13. Sanctum quoque *
    Paráclitum Spíritum.

14. Tu rex glóriæ, *
    Christe.

15. Tu Patris *
    sempitérnus es Fílius.

16. Tu, ad liberándum susceptúrus hóminem, *
    non horruísti Vírginis úterum.

TE DEUM

1. We praise you, O God,
   we acknowledge you to be the Lord.
2. You, the Father everlasting,
   all the earth does worship.
3. To you all the angels,
   to you the heavens, and all the powers,
4. To you the cherubim and seraphim
   cry out without ceasing:
5. Holy, holy, holy,
   Lord God of hosts.
6. Full are the heavens
   and the earth of the majesty of your glory.
7. You, the glorious
   choir of the apostles,
8. You, the admirable
   company of the prophets,
9. You, the whiterobed army
   of martyrs do praise.
10. You, the holy Church
    throughout the world confess:
11. The Father
    of incomprehensible majesty;
12. Your adorable, true,
    and only Son,
13. And the Holy Spirit
    the Paraclete.
14. You, O Christ,
    are the King of glory.
15. You are the everlasting
    Son of the Father.
16. Having taken upon yourself to deliver man,
    you did not disdain the Virgin's womb.

17. Tu, devícto mortis acúleo, *
    aperuísti credéntibus
       regna cælórum.
18. Tu ad déxteram Dei sedes *
    in glória Patris.
19. Iudex credéris *
    esse ventúrus.
20. Te ergo quǽsumus, tuis fámulis súbveni, *
    quos pretióso sánguine redemísti.

21. Ætérna fac cum sanctis tuis *
    in glória numerári.
22. Salvum fac pópulum tuum, Dómine, *
    et bénedic hereditáti tuæ.
23. Et rege eos, *
    et extólle illos usque in ætérnum.
24. Per síngulos dies *
    benedícimus te;
25. et laudámus nomen tuum in sǽculum, *
    et in sǽculum sǽculi.
26. Dignáre, Dómine, die isto *
    sine peccáto nos custodíre.
27. Miserére nostri, Dómine, *
    miserére nostri.
28. Fiat misericórdia tua, Dómine, super nos, *
    quemádmodum sperávimus in te.
29. In te, Dómine, sperávi: *
    non confúndar in ætérnum.
V. Benedíctus es, Dómine, Deus patrum nostrórum.
R. **Et laudábilis, et gloriósus et superexaltátus in**
    saécula.
V. Benedicámus Patrem, et Fílium cum Sancto
    Spíritu.

17. Having overcome the sting of death,
    you have opened to believers
        the kingdom of heaven.

18. You sit at the right hand of God,
    in the glory of the Father.

19. You, we believe,
    are the Judge to come.

20. We beseech you, therefore, to help your servants
    whom you have redeemed
        with your precious blood.

21. Make them to be numbered with your saints
    in glory everlasting.

22. O Lord, save your people, and bless your
    inheritance.

23. And govern them,
    and exalt them for ever.

24. Day by day
    we bless you.

25. And we praise your name for ever;
    yes, for ever and ever.

26. Vouchsafe, O Lord, this day,
    to keep us without sin.

27. Have mercy on us, O Lord;
    have mercy on us.

28. Let your mercy, O Lord, be upon us;
    as we have trusted in you.

29. In you, O Lord, have I trusted:
    let me not be confounded for ever.

V. Blessed are you, O Lord, the God of our fathers.

R. **And worthy to be praised, and glorified for
ever.**

V. Let us bless the Father, and the Son, with the
Holy Spirit.

R. **Laudémus, et superexaltémus eum in saécula.**

V. Benedíctus es, Dómine, in firmaménto cæli.

R. **Et laudábilis, et gloriósus, et superexaltátus in saécula.**

V. Bénedic, ánima mea, Dómino.

R. **Et noli oblivísci omnes retributiónes eius.**

V. Dómine, exáudi oratiónem meam.

R. **Et clámor meus ad te véniat.**

Sacerdotes addunt:

V. Dóminus vobíscum.

R. **Et cum spíritu tuo.**

Orémus.

Deus, cuius misericórdiæ non est númerus, et bonitátis infinítus est thesáurus: piíssimæ Maiestáti tuæ pro collátis donis grátias ágimus, tuam semper cleméntiam exorántes; ut, qui peténtibus postuláta concédis, eósdem non déserens, ad praémia futúra dispónas.

Deus, qui corda fidélium Sancti Spíritus illustratióne docuísti: da nobis in eódem Spíritu recta sápere; et de eius semper consolatióne gaudére.

Deus, qui néminem in te sperántem nímium afflígi permíttis, sed pium précibus præstas audítum: pro postulatiónibus nostris, votísque suscéptis grátias ágimus, te piíssime deprecántes; ut a cunctis semper muniámur advérsis. Per Christum Dóminum nostrum.

R. **Amen.**

R. **Let us praise and exalt him for ever.**

V. Blessed are you, O Lord, in the firmament of heaven.

R. **And worthy of praise, and glorious, and exalted above all for ever.**

V. Bless the Lord, O my soul.

R. **And forget not all his benefits.**

V. O Lord, hear my prayer.

R. **And let my cry come to you.**

Priests add:

V. The Lord be with you.

R. **And also with you.**

Let us pray.

O God, of your mercies there is no number, and of your goodness the treasure is infinite; we render thanks to your most gracious majesty for the gifts you have bestowed upon us, evermore imploring your clemency that as you grant the petitions of them that ask you, you may never forsake them, but may prepare them for the rewards to come.

O God, who have taught the hearts of the faithful by the light of the Holy Spirit, grant us, by the same Spirit, to relish what is right, and evermore to rejoice in his consolation.

O God, who suffer none that hope in you to be afflicted overmuch, but listens graciously to their prayers, we render you thanks, because you have received our supplications and vows; and we most humbly beseech you that we may evermore be protected from all adversities. Through Christ our Lord.

R. **Amen.**

QUICÚMQUE

Ant.   Glória tibi, Trínitas * æquális, una Déitas, et ante ómnia sǽcula, et nunc, et in perpétuum (T. P. Allelúia).

1. Quicúmque vult salvus esse, *
    ante ómnia opus est, ut téneat cathólicam fidem:

2. Quam nisi quisque íntegram
        inviolatámque serváverit, *
    absque dúbio in ætérnum períbit.

3. Fides autem cathólica hæc est: *
    ut unum Deum in Trinitáte,
        et Trinitátem in unitáte venerémur.

4. Neque confundéntes persónas, *
    neque substántiam separántes.

5. Alia est enim persóna Patris ália Fílii, *
    ália Spíritus Sancti:

6. Sed Patris, et Fílii, et Spíritus Sancti
        una est divínitas, *
    æquális glória, coætérna maiéstas.

7. Qualis Pater, talis Fílius, *
    talis Spíritus Sanctus.

ATHANASIAN CREED (QUICÚMQUE)

Taking its name from St. Athanasius (+373), even though it is no longer attributed to him, this prayer enumerates the essential doctrines of Christianity, especially the mysteries of the Holy Trinity. St. Teresa of Avila recounts a meditation on this creed as follows: "Once, when I was reciting the *Quicúmque vult*, I was shown so clearly how it was possible for there to be One God alone and Three Persons, that it caused me both amazement and much comfort. It was of the greatest help in teaching me to know more of the greatness of God and of his marvels."

Ant.   Glory be to you, equal Trinity, one Godhead, before all time, now and for ever (Easter Time Alleluia).

1. Whoever wishes to be saved must,
   above all, keep the Catholic faith.

2. For unless a person keeps this faith
        whole and entire,
   he will undoubtedly be lost for ever.

3. This is what the Catholic faith teaches:
   we worship one God in the Trinity
        and the Trinity in unity.

4. We distinguish among the Persons,
   but we do not divide the substance.

5. For the Father is a distinct Person; the Son is
        a distinct Person;
   and the Holy Spirit is a distinct Person.

6. Still, the Father and the Son and the Holy Spirit
        have one divinity,
   equal glory, and coeternal majesty.

7. What the Father is, the Son is,
   and the Holy Spirit is.

1. St. Teresa of Avila, *Life*, 25, 39, London: Sheed and Ward, 1946.

8. Increátus Pater, increátus Fílius, *
   increátus Spíritus Sanctus.

9. Imménsus Pater, imménsus Fílius, *
   imménsus Spíritus Sanctus.

10. Ætérnus Pater, ætérnus Fílius, *
    ætérnus Spíritus Sanctus.

11. Et tamen non tres ætérni, *
    sed unus ætérnus.

12. Sicut non tres increáti,
    nec tres imménsi, *
    sed unus increátus,
    et unus imménsus.

13. Simíliter omnípotens Pater,
    omnípotens Fílius, *
    omnípotens Spíritus Sanctus.

14. Et tamen non tres omnipoténtes, *
    sed unus omnípotens.

15. Ita Deus Pater, Deus Fílius, *
    Deus Spíritus Sanctus.

16. Et tamen non tres dii, *
    sed unus est Deus.

17. Ita Dóminus Pater, Dóminus Fílius, *
    Dóminus Spíritus Sanctus.

18. Et tamen non tres Dómini, *
    sed unus est Dóminus.

19. Quia, sicut singillátim unamquámque
    persónam Deum ac Dóminum
    confitéri christiána veritáte compéllimur: *
    ita tres Deos aut Dóminos
    dícere cathólica religióne prohibémur.

20. Pater a nullo est factus: *
    nec creátus, nec génitus.

8. The Father is uncreated, the Son is uncreated,
   and the Holy Spirit is uncreated.

9. The Father is boundless, the Son is boundless,
   and the Holy Spirit is boundless.

10. The Father is eternal, the Son is eternal,
    and the Holy Spirit is eternal.

11. Nevertheless, there are not three eternal beings,
    but one eternal being.

12. Thus there are not three uncreated beings,
        nor three boundless beings,
    but one uncreated being
        and one boundless being.

13. Likewise, the Father is omnipotent,
        the Son is omnipotent,
    and the Holy Spirit is omnipotent.

14. Yet there are not three omnipotent beings,
    but one omnipotent being.

15. Thus the Father is God, the Son is God,
    and the Holy Spirit is God.

16. But there are not three gods,
    but one God.

17. The Father is Lord, the Son is Lord,
    and the Holy Spirit is Lord.

18. There are not three Lords,
    but one Lord.

19. For according to Christian truth,
        we must profess that each of the Persons
            individually is God;
    and according to Christian religion, we are
        forbidden to say that
            there are three gods or three lords.

20. The Father is not made by anyone,
    nor created by anyone, nor generated by anyone.

21. Fílius a Patre solo est: *
    non factus, nec creátus, sed génitus.

22. Spíritus Sanctus a Patre et Fílio: *
    non factus, nec creátus,
            nec génitus, sed procédens.

23. Unus ergo Pater, non tres Patres:
            unus Fílius, non tres Fílii: *
    unus Spíritus Sanctus, non tres Spíritus Sancti.

24. Et in hac Trinitáte nihil prius aut postérius,
            nihil maius aut minus: *
    sed totæ tres persónæ coætérnæ
            sibi sunt et coæquáles.

25. Ita ut per ómnia, sicut iam supra dictum est, *
    et únitas in Trinitáte,
            et Trínitas in unitáte veneránda sit.

26. Qui vult ergo salvus esse, *
    ita de Trinitáte séntiat.

27. Sed necessárium est ad ætérnam salútem, *
    ut incarnatiónem quoque Dómini
            nostri Iesu Christi fidéliter credat.

28. Est ergo fides recta ut credámus et confiteámur, *
    quia Dóminus noster Iesus Christus,
            Dei Fílius, Deus et homo est.

29. Deus est ex substántia Patris
            ante sǽcula génitus: *
    et homo est ex substántia matris in sǽculo natus.

30. Perféctus Deus, perféctus homo: *
    ex ánima rationáli et humána carne subsístens.

31. Æquális Patri secúndum divinitátem; *
    minor Patre secúndum humanitátem.

32. Qui, licet Deus sit et homo, *
    non duo tamen, sed unus est Christus.

21. The Son is not made nor created,
    but is generated by the Father alone.

22. The Holy Spirit is not made
        nor created nor generated,
    but proceeds from the Father and the Son.

23. There is, then, one Father, not three fathers;
        one Son, not three sons;
    one Holy Spirit, not three holy spirits.

24. In this Trinity, there is nothing greater,
        nothing less than anything else:
    But all three Persons are coeternal
        and coequal with one another.

25. So that, as we have said,
    we worship complete unity in the Trinity
        and the Trinity in unity.

26. This, then, is what one who wishes to be saved
    must believe about the Trinity.

27. It is also necessary for eternal salvation
    that one believe steadfastly
        in the incarnation of our Lord Jesus Christ.

28. The true faith is: we believe and profess that our
    Lord Jesus Christ, the Son of God,
        is both God and man.

29. As God, he was begotten
        of the substance of the Father before time;
    as man, he was born in time
        of the substance of his Mother.

30. He is perfect God; and he is perfect man,
    with a rational soul and human flesh.

31. He is equal to the Father in his divinity,
    but he is inferior to the Father in his humanity.

32. Although he is God and man,
    he is not two, but one Christ.

33. Unus autem non conversióne divinitátis
       in carnem,*
    sed assumptióne humanitátis in Deum.

34. Unus omníno, non confusióne substántiæ, *
    sed unitáte persónæ.

35. Nam sicut ánima rationális
       et caro unus est homo: *
    ita Deus et homo unus est Christus.

36. Qui passus est pro salúte nostra:
       descéndit ad ínferos: *
    tértia die resurréxit a mórtuis.

37. Ascéndit ad cælos,
       sedet ad déxteram Dei Patris omnipoténtis: *
    inde ventúrus est iudicáre vivos et mórtuos.

38. Ad cuius advéntum omnes hómines
       resúrgere habent cum corpóribus suis: *
    et reddituri sunt de factis própriis rationém.

39. Et qui bona egérunt,
       ibunt in vitam ætérnam: *
    qui vero mala,
       in ignem ætérnum.

40. Hæc est fides cathólica, *
    quam nisi quisque fidéliter firmitérque
       credíderit, salvus esse non póterit.

Glória Patri . . .

Ant.   Glória tibi, Trínitas æquális, una Déitas, et
ante ómnia sǽcula, et nunc, et in perpétuum (T. P.
Allelúia).

V. Dómine, exáudi oratiónem meam.

R. **Et clamor meus ad te véniat.**

Sacerdotes addunt:

33. And he is one, not because his divinity
       was changed into flesh,
   but because his humanity was assumed to God.

34. He is one, not at all because of a mingling of
     substances, but because he is one person.

35. As a rational soul
       and flesh are one man:
   so God and man are one Christ.

36. He died for our salvation,
       descended to hell,
   arose from the dead on the third day,

37. Ascended into heaven, sits
       at the right hand of God the Father almighty,
   and from there he shall come
       to judge the living and the dead.

38. At his coming, all are to arise
       with their own bodies;
   and they are to give an account of their lives.

39. Those who have done good deeds
       will go into eternal life;
   those who have done evil
       will go into everlasting fire.

40. This is the Catholic faith.
   Everyone must believe it, firmly and steadfastly;
       otherwise, one cannot be saved.

Glory Be.

Ant.   Glory be to you, equal Trinity, one Godhead, before all time, now and for ever (Easter Time Alleluia).

V. O Lord, hear my prayer.

R. **And let my cry come unto you.**

Priests add:

V. Dóminus vobíscum

R. **Et cum spíritu tuo.**

Orémus.

Omnípotens sempitérne Deus, qui dedísti fámulis tuis, in confessióne veræ fídei, ætérnæ Trinitátis glóriam agnóscere, et in poténtia maiestátis adoráre unitátem: quaésumus; ut eiúsdem fídei firmitáte, ab ómnibus semper muniámur advérsis. Per Dóminum nostrum Iesum Christum Fílium tuum; qui tecum vivit et regnat in unitáte Spíritus Sancti, Deus, per ómnia saécula sæculórum.

R. **Amen.**

ANGÉLICUM TRISAGIUM

In nómine Patris et Fílii et Spíritus Sancti. Amen.

V. Dómine, lábia mea apéries.

R. **Et os meum annuntiábit laudem tuam.**

V. Deus, in adiutórium meum inténde.

R. **Dómine, ad adiuvándum me festína.**

V. Glória Patri,…

R. **Sicut erat…**

V. The Lord be with you.

R. **And also with you.**

Let us pray.

Almighty, ever-living God, who have permitted us, your servants, in our profession of the true faith, to acknowledge the glory of the eternal Trinity, and in the power of that majesty to adore the Unity, grant that, by steadfastness in this same faith, we may be ever guarded against all adversity. We ask this through our Lord Jesus Christ, your Son, who lives and reigns with you and the Holy Spirit, one God, for ever and ever.

R. **Amen.**

ANGELIC TRISAGION

The Holy Trinity is the central mystery of our faith. The feast of the Holy Trinity, which is celebrated on the Sunday after Pentecost, was established for the whole Western Church in 1134 by pope John XII. The Angelic Trisagion is said for the three days prior to Trinity Sunday.

In the name of the Father, and of the Son, and of the Holy Spirit. Amen.

V. Lord, open my lips.

R. **And my mouth shall declare your praise.**

V. O God, come to my assistance.

R. **O Lord, make haste to help me.**

V. Glory be . . .

R. **As it was . . .**

DECADES

All say the invocation, **Holy is God (Sanctus Deus)**; afterwards, the Lord's Prayer is said as usual, with the priest (or whoever presides) answered by the people. Then, nine times whoever presides says the prayer **To You, O Blessed Trinity**

Sanctus Deus, Sanctus fortis, Sanctus immortális, miserére nobis.

Pater Noster.

V. Tibi laus, tibi glória, tibi gratiárum áctio in saécula sempitérna, O Beáta Trínitas.

R. **Sanctus, Sanctus, Sanctus Dóminus Deus exercítuum. Pleni sunt cæli et terra glória tua.**

V. Glória Patri,...

R. **Sicut erat...**

Ant.　　Te Deum Patrem ingénitum, te Fílium uni-génitum, te Spíritum Sanctum Paráclitum, sanctam et indivíduam Trinitátem, toto corde et ore confitémur, laudámus, atque benedícimus: Tibi glória in saécula.

V. Benedicámus Patrem, et Fílium cum Sancto Spíritu.

R. **Laudémus et superexaltémus eum in saécula.**

Oremus.

Omnípotens sempitérne Deus, qui dedísti fámulis tuis in confessióne veræ fídei, ætérnæ Trinitátis glóriam agnóscere, et in poténtia maiestátis adoráre Unitátem: quaésumus, ut eiúsdem fídei firmitáte, ab ómnibus semper muniámur advérsis. Per Christum Dóminum nostrum.

R. **Amen.**

Líbera nos, salva nos, vivífica nos, o Beáta Trínitas!

(Tibi Laus). Each time, the people answer with the prayer **Holy, Holy, . . .** After the last repetition, the Glory Be is said.

Holy is God! Holy and strong! Holy Immortal One, have mercy on us.

Our Father.

V. To you, O Blessed Trinity, be praise and honor and thanksgiving, for ever and ever!

R. Holy, holy, holy Lord, God of hosts. Heaven and earth are filled with your glory.

V. Glory be . . .

R. As it was . . .

The second and third decades are said in the same way, beginning with the words: **Holy is God (Sanctus Deus) . . .**

Ant.   God the Father unbegotten, only-begotten Son, and Holy Spirit, the Comforter: holy and undivided Trinity, with all our hearts we acknowledge you: Glory to you for ever.

V. Let us bless the Father, and the Son with the Holy Spirit.

R. Be praised and exalted above all things for ever.

Let us pray.

Almighty, ever-living God, who have permitted us, your servants, in our profession of the true faith, to acknowledge the glory of the eternal Trinity, and in the power of that majesty to adore the Unity, grant that, by steadfastness in this same faith, we may be ever guarded against all adversity. Through Christ our Lord.

R. Amen.

After this, all say:

Set us free, save us, vivify us, O Blessed Trinity!

DEVOTIONS TO
OUR LORD JESUS CHRIST

"Jesus Christ, having entered the sanctuary of heaven once an for all, intercedes constantly for us as the mediator who assures us of the permanent out-pouring of the Holy Spirit." There is no other way to the Father but through Christ.[1]

FIRST FRIDAY DEVOTION

"The prayer of the Church venerates and honors the *Heart of Jesus* . . . which, out of love for men, he allowed to be pierced by our sins."[2]

Devotion to the Sacred Heart of Jesus is of great antiquity in the Church. It was St. Margaret Mary Alacoque, however, who made this devotion widespread. In 1675, within the octave of the feast of Corpus Christi, our Lord appeared to her and said: "Behold this heart which, notwithstanding the burning love for men with which it is consumed and exhausted, meets with no other return from most Christians than sacrilege, contempt, indifference and ingratitude, even in the sacrament of my love [the Eucharist]. But what pierces my heart most deeply is that I am subjected to these insults by persons especially consecrated to my service."[3]

To those who show him love and who make reparation for sins, however, our Lord made a great pledge: "I promise you in the unfathomable mercy of my heart that my omnipotent love will procure

---

1. Cf. *Catechism of the Catholic Church* (=CCC), 667, 2664, 2665.
2. Cf. CCC, 2669.
3. St. Margaret M. Alacoque, *Autobiography* (=MMAA).

the grace of final penitence for all those who receive communion on nine successive first Fridays of the month; they will not die in my disfavor, or without having received the sacraments, since my divine heart will be their sure refuge in the last moments of their life."[4]

The great promise of the Sacred Heart is most consoling: the grace of final perseverance and the joy of having Jesus' heart as our sure refuge and infinite ocean of mercy in our last hour.

To gain this grace, we must:

• Receive holy Communion on nine consecutive first Fridays.
• Have the intention of honoring the Sacred Heart of Jesus and of reaching final perseverance.
• Offer each holy Communion as an act of atonement for offenses against the Blessed Sacrament.

Introductory Prayer

Almighty and everlasting God, look upon the heart of your well-beloved Son and upon the praise and satisfaction which he offers to you in the name of all sinners; and grant them pardon when they seek your mercy. We ask this in the name of Jesus Christ, your Son, who lives and reigns with you for ever and ever.
R. **Amen.**

Reading   Jn 19:31-37

Since it was the day of Preparation, in order to prevent the bodies from remaining on the cross on the Sabbath (for that Sabbath was a high day), the Jews asked Pilate that their legs might be broken, and that they might be taken away. So the soldiers

---

4. Ibidem.

came and broke the legs of the first, and of the
other who had been crucified with him; but when
they came to Jesus and saw that he was already
dead, they did not break his legs. But one of the
soldiers pierced his side with a spear, and at once
there came out blood and water.
He who saw it has borne witness—his testimony is
true, and he knows that he tells the truth—that you
also may believe. For these things took place that
the scripture might be fulfilled, "Not a bone of him
shall be broken." And again another scripture says,
"They shall look on him whom they have pierced."

Considerations[5]

1. Love is revealed to us in the Incarnation, the redemptive journey which Jesus Christ made on our
earth, culminating in the supreme sacrifice of the
cross. And on the cross it showed itself through a
new sign: "One of the soldiers pierced his side with a
spear, and at once there came out blood and water."
This water and blood of Jesus speak to us of a self-
sacrifice brought to the last extreme: "It is finished"—everything is achieved, for the sake of
love. . . .
The fullness of God is revealed and given to us in
Christ, in the love of Christ, in Christ's heart. For it is
the heart of him in whom "the whole fullness of de-
ity dwells bodily." Were one to lose sight of this
great plan of God—the overflow of love in the world
through the Incarnation, the Redemption and Pentecost—he could not understand the refinement with
which our Lord deals with us.

---

5. Blessed Josemaría Escrivá, *"Finding Peace in the Heart of Christ,"* 162-170,
   Princeton, N.J.: Scepter Publishers,1974. Footnotes used by the author
   in the original homily are omitted.

2. Let us realize all the richness hidden in the words "the Sacred Heart of Jesus." When we speak of a person's heart, we refer not just to his sentiments, but to the whole person in his loving dealings with others. In order to help us understand divine things, Scripture uses the expression "heart" in its full human meaning, as the summary and source, expression and ultimate basis, of one's thoughts, words and actions. One is worth what one's heart is worth. . . .

So, when we talk about the heart of Jesus, we stress the certainty of God's love and the truth of his commitment to us. When we recommend devotion to the Sacred Heart, we are recommending that we should give our whole selves to Jesus, to the whole Jesus— our souls, our feelings and thoughts, our words and actions, our joys.

That is what true devotion to the heart of Jesus means. It is knowing God and ourselves. It is looking at Jesus and turning to him, letting him encourage and teach and guide us. The only difficulty that could beset this devotion would be our own failure to understand the reality of an incarnate God.

3. Jesus on the cross, with his heart overflowing with love for us, is such an eloquent commentary on the value of people and things that words only get in the way. Men, their happiness and their lives, are so important that the very Son of God gave himself to redeem and cleanse and raise them up. "Who will not love this heart so wounded?" a contemplative asks in this connection. "Who will not return love for love? Who will not embrace a heart so pure? We, who are made of flesh, will repay love with love. We will embrace our wounded One, whose hands and feet ungodly men have nailed; we will cling to his side and to his heart. Let us pray that we be worthy

of linking our heart with his love and of wounding it with a lance, for it is still hard and impenitent. . . ."

But note that God does not say: "In exchange for your own heart, I will give you a will of pure spirit." No, he gives us a heart, a human heart, like Christ's. I don't have one heart for loving God and another for loving people. I love Christ and the Father and the Holy Spirit and our Lady with the same heart with which I love my parents and my friends. I shall never tire of repeating this. We must be very human, for otherwise we cannot be divine. . . .

If we don't learn from Jesus, we will never love. If, like some people, we were to think that to keep a clean heart, a heart worthy of God, means "not mixing it up, not contaminating it" with human affection, we would become insensitive to other people's pain and sorrow. We would be capable of only an "official charity," something dry and soulless. But ours would not be the true charity of Jesus Christ, which involves affection and human warmth. In saying this, I am not supporting the mistaken theories—pitiful excuses—that misdirect hearts away from God and lead them into occasions of sin and perdition. . . .

4. But I have still a further consideration to put before you. We have to fight vigorously to do good, precisely because it is difficult for us to resolve seriously to be just, and there is a long way to go before human relations are inspired by love and not hatred or indifference. We should also be aware that, even if we achieve a reasonable distribution of wealth and a harmonious organization of society, there will still be the suffering of illness, of misunderstanding, of loneliness, of the death of loved ones, of the experience of our own limitations.

Faced with the weight of all this, a Christian can find only one genuine answer, a definitive answer: Christ on the cross, a God who suffers and dies, a God who gives us his heart opened by a lance for the love of us all. Our Lord abominates injustice and condemns those who commit it. But he respects the freedom of each individual. He permits injustice to happen because, as a result of original sin, it is part and parcel of the human condition. Yet his heart is full of love for men. Our suffering, our sadness, our anguish, our hunger and thirst for justice . . . he took all these tortures on himself by means of the cross. . . .

Suffering is part of God's plans. This is the truth, however difficult it may be for us to understand it. It was difficult for Jesus Christ the man to undergo his passion: "Father, if you are willing, remove this cup from me; nevertheless, not my will, but yours, be done." In this tension of pleading and acceptance of the Father's will, Jesus goes calmly to his death, pardoning those who crucify him.

This supernatural acceptance of suffering was, precisely, the greatest of all conquests. By dying on the cross, Jesus overcame death. God brings life from death. The attitude of a child of God is not one of resignation to a possibly tragic fate; it is the sense of achievement of someone who has a foretaste of victory. In the name of this victorious love of Christ, we Christians should go out into the world to be sowers of peace and joy through everything we say and do. We have to fight—a fight of peace—against evil, against injustice, against sin. Thus do we serve notice that the present condition of mankind is not definitive. *Only* the love of God, shown in the heart of Christ, will attain our glorious spiritual triumph.

ACT OF CONSECRATION
TO THE SACRED HEART OF JESUS

St. Margaret Mary Alacoque

To the Sacred Heart of our Lord, Jesus Christ, I give myself and I consecrate my person and my life, my actions, pains, and sufferings, so that I may be unwilling to make use of any part of my being other than to honor, love, and glorify the Sacred Heart.

This is my unchanging purpose, namely, to be all his and to do all things for the love of him, at the same time renouncing with all my heart whatever is displeasing to him. I therefore take you, O Sacred Heart, to be the only object of my love, the guardian of my life, my assurance of salvation, the remedy of my weakness and inconstancy, the atonement for all the faults of my life, and my sure refuge at the hour of death.

Be then, O Heart of goodness, my justification before God the Father, and turn away from me the strokes of his righteous anger. O Heart of love, I put all my confidence in you, for I fear everything from my own wickedness and frailty, but I hope for all things from your goodness and bounty.

Remove from me all that can displease you or resist your holy will; let your pure love imprint your image so deeply upon my heart that I shall never be able to forget you or to be separated from you.

May I obtain from your loving kindness the grace of having my name written in your heart, for in you I desire to place all my happiness and glory, living and dying in bondage to you.

Concluding Prayer

Father,
we honor the heart of your Son,
broken by our cruelty,
yet symbol of love's triumph,
pledge of all that we are called to be.
Teach us to see Christ in the lives we touch
and to offer him living worship
by love-filled service to our brothers and sisters.

We ask this through Christ our Lord.

LITANY OF THE SACRED HEART OF JESUS

According to tradition, this litany, approved in 1899 for public recitation, originated at Marseilles, where devotion to the Sacred Heart became very popular during the early eighteenth century.

Lord, have mercy.	**Lord, have mercy.**
Christ, have mercy.	**Christ, have mercy.**
Lord, have mercy.	**Lord, have mercy.**
God our Father in heaven	**Have mercy on us.**

God the Son, Redeemer
  of the world, . . .

God the Holy Spirit, . . .

Holy Trinity, one God, . . .

Heart of Jesus, Son of the eternal Father, . . .

Heart of Jesus, formed by the Holy Spirit
  in the womb of the Virgin Mother, . . .

Heart of Jesus, one with the eternal Word, . . .

Heart of Jesus, infinite in majesty, . . .

Heart of Jesus, holy temple of God, . . .

Heart of Jesus, tabernacle of the Most High, . . .

Heart of Jesus, house of God and gate of heaven, . . .

Heart of Jesus, aflame with love for us, . . .

Heart of Jesus, source of justice and love, . . .

Heart of Jesus, full of goodness and love, . . .

Heart of Jesus, wellspring of all virtue, . . .

Heart of Jesus, worthy of all praise, . . .

Heart of Jesus, king and center of all hearts, . . .

Heart of Jesus, treasure house of wisdom
  and knowledge, . . .

Heart of Jesus, in whom there dwells
  the fullness of God, . . .

Heart of Jesus, in whom the Father
is well pleased, ...

Heart of Jesus, from whose fullness
we have all received.   **Have mercy on us.**

Heart of Jesus, desire of the eternal hills, · · ·

Heart of Jesus, patient and full of mercy, · · ·

Heart of Jesus, generous to all who turn to you, · · ·

Heart of Jesus, fountain of life and holiness, · · ·

Heart of Jesus, atonement for our sins, · · ·

Heart of Jesus, overwhelmed with insults, · · ·

Heart of Jesus, broken for our sins, · · ·

Heart of Jesus, obedient even to death, · · ·

Heart of Jesus, pierced by a lance, · · ·

Heart of Jesus, source of all consolation, · · ·

Heart of Jesus, our life and resurrection, · · ·

Heart of Jesus, our peace and reconciliation, · · ·

Heart of Jesus, victim for our sins, · · ·

Heart of Jesus, salvation of all who trust in you, · · ·

Heart of Jesus, hope of all who die in you, · · ·

Heart of Jesus, delight of all the saints, · · ·

Lamb of God, you take away
the sins of the world.   **Have mercy on us.**

Lamb of God, you take away
the sins of the world.   **Have mercy on us.**

Lamb of God, you take away
the sins of the world.   **Have mercy on us.**

V. Jesus, gentle and humble of heart,

R. **Touch our hearts and make them like your own.**

Let us pray.

Father, we rejoice in the gifts of love | we have received from the heart of Jesus, your Son. | Open our hearts to share his life | and continue to bless us with his love. | We ask this in the name of Jesus the Lord. R. **Amen.**

STATIONS OF THE CROSS [6]

The Christian loves to follow the Way of the Cross in the Savior's footsteps. The Stations, from the Prætorium to Golgotha and the tomb, trace the passion and death of Christ, who by his holy cross has redeemed the world. To understand the mystery of Redemption and the *salvific meaning of suffering*, one ought to meditate upon the sufferings of our Lord, which he took upon himself to save us from sin. God is always with those who suffer. His omnipotence is manifested precisely in the fact that he freely accepted suffering. He could have chosen not to do so. He could have chosen to demonstrate his omnipotence even at the moment of the Crucifixion.[7]

In the name of the Father, and of the Son, and of the Holy Spirit. Amen.

My Lord and my God,
under the loving eyes of our Mother,
we are making ready to accompany You
along this path of sorrow,
which was the price paid for our redemption.
We wish to suffer all that You suffered,
to offer You our poor, contrite hearts,
because You are innocent, and yet
You are going to die for us,
who are the only really guilty ones.
My mother, Virgin of sorrows,
help us to relive those bitter hours,
which your Son wished to spend on earth,
so that we, who were made from a handful of clay,
may finally live
in libertatem gloriæ filiorum Dei,
in the freedom and glory of the children of God.

6. Blessed Josemaria Escrivá, *The Way of the Cross*, Princeton, NJ: Scepter Publishers, 1976. Text reprinted here as "Stations of the Cross."

7. Cf. John Paul II, Apostolic Exhortation *The Meaning of Suffering* 14, Rome: Libreria Editrice Vaticane, 1984.

FIRST STATION

JESUS IS CONDEMNED TO DEATH

V. We adore you, O Christ, and we bless you.

R. **Because, by your holy cross, you have redeemed the world.**

It is after ten in the morning. The trial is moving to its close. There has been no conclusive evidence. The judge knows that his enemies have handed Jesus over to him out of envy, and he tries an absurd move: a choice between Barabbas, a criminal accused of robbery and murder, and Jesus, who says he is Christ. The people choose Barrabas, and Pilate exclaims: *What am I to do, then, with Jesus?* (Mt 27:22).

They all reply: *Crucify him!* The judge insists: *Why, what evil has he done?* Once again they respond, shouting: *Crucify him! Crucify him!*

Pilate is frightened by the growing uproar. So he sends for water and washes his hands in the sight of the people, saying as he does so: *I am innocent of the blood of this just man; it is your affair* (Mt 27:24).

And having had Jesus scourged, he hands him over to them to be crucified. Their frenzied and possessed throats fall silent, as if God had already been vanquished.

* Jesus is all alone. Far off now are the days when the words of the Man-God brought light and hope to men's hearts, those long processions of sick people whom he healed, the triumphant acclaim of Jerusalem when the Lord arrived, riding on a gentle donkey. If only men had wanted to give a different outlet for God's love! If only you and I had recognized the day of the Lord!

---

* You may wish to kneel here.

SECOND STATION

JESUS TAKES UP HIS CROSS

V. We adore you, O Christ, and we bless you.

R. **Because, by your holy cross, you have redeemed the world.**

Outside the city, to the northwest of Jerusalem, there is a little hill: Golgotha is its name in Aramaic; *locus Calvariæ*, in Latin: the place of skulls, or Calvary.

Offering no resistance, Jesus gives himself up to the execution of the sentence. He is to be spared nothing, and upon his shoulders falls the weight of the ignominious cross. But, through love, the cross is to become the throne from which he reigns.

The people of Jerusalem and those from abroad who have come for the Passover push their way through the city streets, to catch a passing glimpse of Jesus of Nazareth, the King of the Jews. There is a tumult of voices, and, now and then, short silences—perhaps when Jesus fixes his eyes on someone:

If anyone wishes to come after me, let him take up his cross daily and follow me (Mt 16:24).

How lovingly Jesus embraces the wood which is to bring him to death!

* Is it not true that as soon as you cease to be afraid of the cross, of what people call the cross, when you set your will to accept the will of God, then you find happiness, and all your worries, all your sufferings, physical or moral, pass away?

Truly the cross of Jesus is gentle and lovable. There, sorrows cease to count; there is only the joy of knowing that we are co-redeemers with him.

THIRD STATION

JESUS FALLS THE FIRST TIME

V. We adore you, O Christ, and we bless you.

R. **Because, by your holy cross, you have redeemed the world.**

The heavy cross cuts and tears into our Lord's shoulders.

The crowd has swollen into a multitude, and the legionaries can scarcely contain the angry, surging mob which, like a river that has burst its banks, flows through the streets and alleyways of Jerusalem.

The worn-out body of Jesus staggers now beneath the huge cross. His most loving heart can barely summon up another breath of life for his poor wounded limbs.

To his right and left, our Lord sees the multitude moving around like sheep without a shepherd. He could call them one by one by their names—by our names. There they are, those who were fed at the multiplication of the loaves and fishes, those who were cured of their ailments, those he taught by the lakeside, on the mountain and in the porticoes of the Temple.

A sharp pain pierces the soul of Jesus; our Lord falls to the ground, exhausted.

* You and I can say nothing: now we know why the cross of Jesus weighs so much. We weep over our wretched failings and also for the terrible ingratitude of the human heart. From the depths of our soul there comes an act of real contrition, which lifts us up from the prostration of sin. Jesus has fallen that we might get up: once and for all.

FOURTH STATION

JESUS MEETS HIS BLESSED MOTHER

V. We adore you, O Christ, and we bless you.

R. **Because, by your holy cross, you have redeemed the world.**

No sooner has Jesus risen from his first fall than he meets his Blessed Mother, standing by the wayside where he is passing.

With immense love Mary looks at Jesus, and Jesus at his mother. Their eyes meet, and each heart pours into the other its own deep sorrow. Mary's soul is steeped in bitter grief, the grief of Jesus Christ.

O all you that pass by the way, look and see, was there ever a sorrow to compare with my sorrow! (Lm 1:12).

But no one notices, no one pays attention; only Jesus.

Simeon's prophecy has been fulfilled: *Thine own soul a sword shall pierce* (Lk 2:35).

In the dark loneliness of the Passion, our Lady offers her son a comforting balm of tenderness, of union, of faithfulness; a "yes" to the divine will.

* Hand in hand with Mary, you and I also want to console Jesus, by accepting always and in everything the will of his Father, of our Father.

Only thus will we taste the sweetness of Christ's cross and come to embrace it with all the strength of Love, carrying it in triumph along the ways of the earth.

FIFTH STATION

SIMON OF CYRENE HELPS JESUS
TO CARRY THE CROSS

V. We adore you, O Christ, and we bless you.

R. **Because, by your holy cross, you have redeemed the world.**

Jesus is exhausted. His footsteps become more and more unsteady, and the soldiers are in a hurry to be finished. So when they are going out of the city through the Judgment Gate, they take hold of a man who is coming in from a farm, a man called Simon of Cyrene, the father of Alexander and Rufus, and they force him to carry the cross of Jesus (cf. Mk 15:21).

In the whole context of the Passion, this help does not add up to very much. But, for Jesus, a smile, a word, a gesture or a little bit of love is enough for him to pour out his grace bountifully on the soul of his friend. Years later, Simon's sons, Christians by then, will be known and held in high esteem among their brothers in the faith. And it all started with this unexpected meeting with the cross.

I went to those who were not looking for me; I was found by those that sought me not (Is 65:1).

* At times the cross appears without our looking for it: It is Christ who is seeking *us* out. And if by chance, before this unexpected cross which, perhaps, is therefore more difficult to understand, your heart were to show repugnance . . . don't give it consolations. And, filled with a noble compassion, when it asks for them, say to it slowly, as one speaking in confidence: "Heart: heart on the cross! Heart on the cross!"

SIXTH STATION

VERONICA WIPES THE FACE OF JESUS

V. We adore you, O Christ, and we bless you.

R. **Because, by your holy cross, you have redeemed the world.**

There is no beauty in him, nor comeliness: and we have seen him and there was no sightliness, that we should be attracted to him. Despised and the most abject of men, a man of sorrows and acquainted with infirmity; and his look was, as it were, hidden and despised. Whereupon we esteemed him not (Is 53:2-3).

It is the Son of God who is passing by, a madman ... madly in love!

A woman, Veronica by name, makes her way through the crowd, with a white linen cloth folded in her hands, and with this she reverently wipes the face of Jesus. Our Lord leaves the impression of his holy Face on the three parts of the veil.

The beloved face of Jesus, which had smiled upon children and was transfigured with glory on Mount Tabor, is now, as it were, concealed by suffering. But this suffering is our purification; the sweat and the blood which disfigure and tarnish his features, serve to cleanse us.

* Lord, help me to decide to tear off, through penance, this pitiful mask that I have fashioned with my wretched doings. ... Then, and only then, by following the path of contemplation and atonement, will my life begin to copy faithfully the features of your life. I will find myself becoming more and more like you.

We will be other Christs, Christ himself, *ipse Christus*.

SEVENTH STATION

JESUS FALLS A SECOND TIME

V. We adore you, O Christ, and we bless you.

R. **Because, by your holy cross, you have redeemed the world.**

Outside the walls of the city, the body of Jesus again gives way through weakness, and he falls a second time, amid the shouts of the crowd and the rough handling of the soldiers.

Infirmity of body and bitterness of soul have caused Jesus to fall again. All the sins of men—mine too—weigh down on his Sacred Humanity.

He has borne our infirmities and carried our sorrows, and we have taken him for a leper, and as one struck by God and afflicted. But he was wounded for our iniquities and bruised for our sins. On him fell the punishment that brought us salvation, and by his wounds we have been healed (Is 53:4-5).

Jesus stumbles, but his fall lifts us up; his death brings us back to life.

To our falling again and again into evil, Jesus responds with his determination to redeem us, with an abundance of forgiveness. And, so that no one may despair, again he wearily raises himself, embracing the cross.

*May our stumbles and defeats separate us from him no more. Just as a feeble child throws himself contritely into the strong arms of his father, you and I will hold tightly to the yoke of Jesus. Only a contrition and humility like this can transform our human weakness into the fortitude of God.

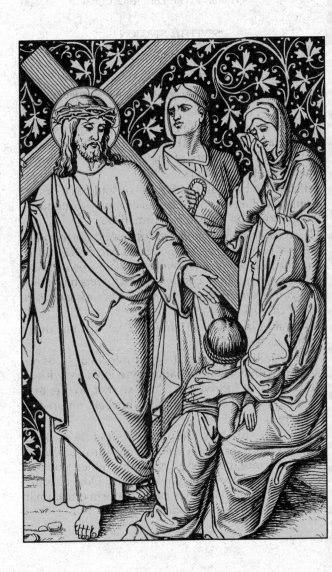

EIGHTH STATION

JESUS CONSOLES
THE WOMEN OF JERUSALEM

V. We adore you, O Christ, and we bless you.

R. **Because, by your holy cross, you have redeemed the world.**

Among the people watching our Lord as he passes by are a number of women who, unable to restrain their compassion, break into tears, perhaps recalling those glorious days spent with Jesus, when everyone exclaimed in amazement: *Bene omnia fecit* (Mk 7:37). He has done all things well.

But our Lord wishes to channel their weeping towards a more supernatural motive. He invites them to weep for sins, which are the cause of the Passion and which will draw down the rigor of divine justice:

Daughters of Jerusalem, weep not for me, but for yourselves and for your children. . . . For if they do these things to the green wood, what shall be done to the dry? (Lk 23:28, 31).

* Your sins, my sins, the sins of all men, rise up. All the evil we have done and the good that we have neglected to do. The desolate panorama of the countless crimes and iniquities which we would have committed, if he, Jesus, had not strengthened us with the light of his most loving glance.

How little a life is for making atonement!

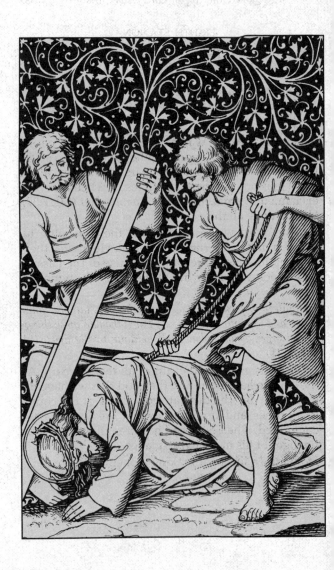

NINTH STATION

JESUS FALLS THE THIRD TIME

V. We adore you, O Christ, and we bless you.

R. **Because, by your holy cross, you have redeemed the world.**

Our Lord falls for the third time, on the slope leading up to Calvary, with only forty or fifty paces between him and the summit. Jesus can no longer stay on his feet: his strength has failed him, and he lies on the ground in utter exhaustion.

He offered himself up because it was his will; abused and ill-treated, he opened not his mouth, as a sheep led to the slaughter, dumb as a lamb before its shearers (Is 53:7).

Everyone against him . . . the people of the city and those from abroad, and the Pharisees and the soldiers and the chief priests. . . . All of them executioners. His mother—my mother—weeps.

Jesus fulfills the will of his Father! Poor; naked. Generous: what is there left for him to surrender? *Dilexit me, et tradidit semetipsum pro me* (Gal 2:20), he loved me and delivered himself up unto death for me.

* My God! May I hate sin and unite myself to you, taking the holy cross into my arms, so that I, in my turn, may fulfill your most lovable will, . . . stripped of every earthly attachment, with no other goal but your glory, . . . generously, not keeping anything back, offering myself with you in a perfect holocaust.

TENTH STATION

JESUS IS STRIPPED OF HIS GARMENTS

V. We adore you, O Christ, and we bless you.

R. **Because, by your holy cross, you have redeemed the world.**

When our Lord arrives at Calvary, he is given some wine to drink mixed with gall, as a narcotic to lessen in some way the pain of the crucifixion. But Jesus, after tasting it to show his gratitude for that kind service, he has not wanted to drink (cf. Mt 27:34). He gives himself up to death with the full freedom of love.

Then the soldiers strip Christ of his garments.

From the soles of his feet to the top of his head, there is nothing healthy in him: wounds and bruises and swelling sores. They are not bound up, nor dressed, nor anointed with oil (Is 1:6).

The executioners take his garments and divide them into four parts. But the cloak is without seam, so they say:

It would be better not to tear it, but let us cast lots for it to see whose it shall be (Jn 19:24).

Thus, Scripture is again fulfilled: *They divided my garments among them, and upon my vesture they cast lots* (Ps 21:19).

* Despoiled, stripped, left in the most absolute poverty, our Lord is left with nothing, save the wood of the cross.

For us to reach God, Christ is the way; but Christ is on the cross, and to climb up to the cross we must have our heart free, not tied to earthly things.

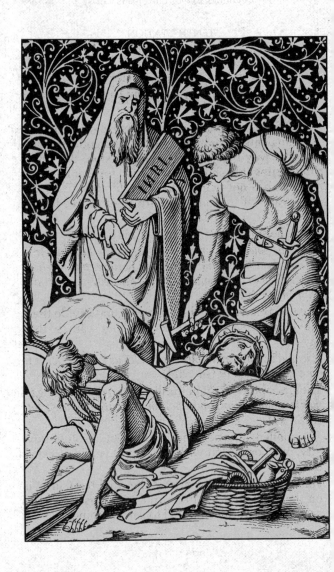

ELEVENTH STATION

JESUS IS NAILED TO THE CROSS

V. We adore you, O Christ, and we bless you.

R. **Because, by your holy cross, you have redeemed the world.**

Now they are crucifying our Lord, and with him two thieves, one on his right and one on his left. Meanwhile, Jesus says:

Father, forgive them, for they do not know what they are doing (Lk 23:34).

It is Love that has brought Jesus to Calvary. And, on the cross, all his gestures, all his words are of love, a love both calm and strong.

With a gesture befitting an eternal priest without father or mother, without lineage (cf. Hb 7:3), he opens his arms to the whole human race.

With the hammerblows with which Jesus is being nailed, there resound the prophetic words of holy Scripture: *They have pierced my hands and feet. I can count all my bones, they stare and gloat over me* (Ps 21:17-18).

My people, what have I done to thee, or in what have I saddened thee? Answer me! (Mi 6:3).

* And we, our souls rent with sorrow, say to Jesus in all sincerity: I am yours, and I give my whole self to you; gladly I accept being nailed myself to your cross, ready to be in the crossroads of this world a soul dedicated to you, to your glory, to the work of Redemption, the co-redemption of the whole human race.

TWELFTH STATION
JESUS DIES ON THE CROSS

V. We adore you, O Christ, and we bless you.

R. **Because, by your holy cross, you have redeemed the world.**

On the uppermost part of the cross, the reason for the sentence is written: *Jesus of Nazareth, King of the Jews* (Jn 19:19). And all who pass by insult him and jeer at him. *If he is the king of Israel, let him come down here and now from the cross* (Mt 27:42).

One of the thieves comes to his defense: *This man has done no evil . . .* (Lk 23:41). Then, turning to Jesus, he makes a humble request, full of faith: *Lord, remember me when thou comest into thy kingdom* (Lk 23:42).

Truly, I say to thee: This day thou shalt be with me in Paradise (Lk 23:43).

At the foot of the cross stands his mother, Mary, with other holy women. Jesus looks at her; then he looks at the disciple whom he loves, and he says to his mother: *Woman, behold thy son.* Then he says to the disciple: *Behold thy mother* (Jn 19:26-27).

The sun's light is extinguished, and the earth is left in darkness. It is close to three o'clock, when Jesus cries out: *Eli, Eli, lamma sabacthani? That is: My God, my God, why hast thou forsaken me?* (Mt 27:46).

Then, knowing that all things are about to be accomplished, that the scriptures may be fulfilled, he says: *I am thirsty* (Jn 19:28).

The soldiers soak a sponge in vinegar and, placing it on a reed of hyssop, put it to his mouth. Jesus sips the vinegar, and exclaims: *It is accomplished!*

The veil of the temple is rent, and the earth trembles, when the Lord cries out in a loud voice: *Father, into thy hands I commend my spirit.* And he expires.

* Love sacrifice; it is a fountain of interior life. Love the cross, which is an altar of sacrifice. Love pain, until you drink, as Christ did, the very dregs of the chalice.

THIRTEENTH STATION

JESUS IS LAID IN THE ARMS OF HIS BLESSED MOTHER

V. We adore you, O Christ, and we bless you.

R. **Because, by your holy cross, you have redeemed the world.**

Mary stands by the cross, engulfed in grief. And John is beside her. But it is getting late, and the Jews press for our Lord to be removed from there.

Having obtained from Pilate the permission required by Roman law for the burial of condemned prisoners, there comes to Calvary *a councillor named Joseph, a good and upright man, a native of Arimathea. He has not consented to their counsel and their doings, but is himself one of those waiting for the kingdom of God* (Lk 23:50-51). With him, too, comes Nicodemus, *the same man who earlier visited Jesus by night; he brings with him a mixture of myrrh and aloes about a hundred pounds in weight* (Jn 19:39).

These men are not known publicly as disciples of the Master. They were not present at the great miracles, nor did they accompany him on his triumphal entry into Jerusalem. But now, when things have turned bad, when the others have fled, they are not afraid to stand up for their Lord.

Between the two of them they take down the body of Jesus and place it in the arms of his most holy mother. Mary's grief is renewed.

* *Where has thy Beloved gone, o fairest of women? Where has he whom thou lovest gone, and we will seek him with thee?* (Cant 5:17).

The Blessed Virgin is our mother, and we do not wish to—we cannot—leave her alone.

FOURTEENTH STATION

JESUS IS LAID IN THE TOMB

V. We adore you, O Christ, and we bless you.

R. Because, by your holy cross, you have redeemed the world.

Very near Calvary, in an orchard, Joseph of Arimathea had had a new tomb made, cut out of the rock. Since it is the eve of the solemn Pasch of the Jews, Jesus is laid there. Then Joseph, *rolling a great stone, closes the grave door and goes away* (Mt 27:60).

Jesus came into the world with nothing. So, too, with nothing—not even the place where he rests—he has left us.

The mother of our Lord—my mother—and the women who have followed the Master from Galilee, after taking careful note of everything, also take their leave. Night falls.

Now it is all over. The work of our redemption has been accomplished. We are now children of God, because Jesus has died for us and his death has ransomed us. *Empti enim estis pretio magno!* (1 Col 6:20). You and I have been bought at a great price.

* We must bring into our life, to make them our own, the life and death of Christ. We must die through mortification and penance, so that Christ may live in us through love. And then follow in the footsteps of Christ, with a zeal to co-redeem all mankind.

We must give our life for others. That is the only way to live the life of Jesus Christ and to become one and the same thing with him.

ACCEPTANCE OF DEATH

We, too, O God, will descend into the grave whenever it shall please you, as it shall please you, and wheresoever it shall please you. Let your just decrees be fulfilled; let our sinful bodies return to their parent dust, but, in your great mercy, receive our immortal souls, and when our bodies have risen again, place them likewise in your kingdom, that we may love and bless you for ever and ever.

R. Amen.

or:

Dear God and Father of mine, Lord of life and death, with an immutable decree you have established that, as a just chastisement for our sins, all of us have to die. Look at me here bent low before you. From the bottom of my heart, I abhor my past faults, for which I have merited death a thousand times, a death that I now accept as atonement for my sins and as proof of my submission to your lovable will. O Lord, happily will I die at the moment, in the place, and in the way that you want. And until that day I will take advantage of the days of life that remain in order to fight against my defects and grow in your love, to break the bonds that tie my heart to creatures, and to prepare my soul to appear in your presence; and from this moment on I abandon myself without reserve into the arms of your fatherly providence.

Prayer for a Happy Death

O my Creator and Father, I beg of you the most important of all your graces: that of final perseverance and a holy death. Despite the fact that I have greatly misused the life you have given me, grant me the grace to live it well from this moment on and to end it in your holy love.

Let me die as the holy patriarchs died, leaving this valley of tears without sadness, to go and enjoy eternal rest in my true homeland.

Let me die as did glorious St. Joseph, accompanied by Jesus and Mary, pronouncing those sweetest of names, which I hope to extol for all eternity.

Let me die as did the Immaculate Virgin, in the purest of love and with the desire of uniting myself to the only object of my love.

Let me die as did Jesus on the cross, fully identified with the will of the Father and made into a holocaust for the sake of love.

Jesus, having accepted death for me, grant me the grace of dying in an act of perfect love for you.

Holy Mary, Mother of God, pray for me now and at the hour of my death.

St. Joseph, my father and lord, win for me the favor of dying as one of the just.

Prayer for the Moment of Death

O Lord, my God, from this moment on I accept with a good will, as something coming from your hand, whatever kind of death you want to send me, with all its anguish, pain, and sorrow.

V. Jesus, Mary, and Joseph,

R. I give you my heart and my soul.

V. Jesus, Mary, and Joseph,

R. Assist me in my last agony.

V. Jesus, Mary, and Joseph,

R. May I sleep and take my rest in peace with you.

ORATIO S. AUGUSTINI

Dómine Iesu, nóverim me, nóverim te,
Nec áliquid cúpiam nisi te.
Oderim me et amem te.
Omnia agam propter te.
Humíliem me, exáltem te.
Nihil cógitem nisi te.
Mortíficem me et vivam in te.
Quæcúmque evéniant accipiam a te.
Pérsequar me, sequar te,
Sempérque optem sequi te.
Fúgiam me, confúgiam ad te,
Ut mérear deféndi a te.
Tímeam mihi, tímeam te,
Et sim inter eléctos a te.
Diffídam mihi, fidam in te.
Obœdíre velim propter te.
Ad nihil affíciar nisi ad te,
Et pauper sim propter te.
Aspice me, ut dilígam te.
Voca me, ut vídeam te,
Et in ætérnum fruar te.
Amen.

PRAYER OF ST. AUGUSTINE

Lord Jesus, let me know myself and know you,
And desire nothing, save only you.
Let me hate myself and love you.
Let me do everything for the sake of you.
Let me humble myself and exalt you.
Let me think of nothing except you.
Let me die to myself and live in you.
Let me accept whatever happens as from you.
Let me banish self and follow you,
And ever desire to follow you.
Let me fly from myself and take refuge in you,
That I may deserve to be defended by you.
Let me fear for myself, let me fear you,
And let me be among those who are chosen by you.
Let me distrust myself and put my trust in you.
Let me be willing to obey for the sake of you.
Let me cling to nothing, save only to you,
And let me be poor because of you.
Look upon me, that I may love you.
Call me, that I may see you,
And for ever enjoy you.
Amen.

SONNET TO OUR LORD ON THE CROSS

ANOMYMOUS

I am not moved to love you, O my God,
That I might hope in promised heaven to dwell;
Nor am I moved by fear of pain in hell
To turn from sin and follow where you trod.
You move me, Lord, broken beneath the rod,
Or stretched out on the cross, as nails compel
Your hand to twitch. It moves me that we sell,
To mockery and death, your precious blood.
It is, O Christ, your love which moves me so,
That my love rests not on a promised prize;
Nor holy fear on threat of endless woe;
It is not milk and honey, but the flow
Of blood from blessed wounds before my eyes,
That waters my buried soul and makes it grow.

PRAYER OF ST. ANDREW (O BONA CRUX)

The apostle Andrew was martyred. He died nailed to a cross. His desire to be identified with Christ was so great that, when he was being led toward the place of his martyrdom and saw his own cross in the distance, he cried:

O bona crux, quæ decórem et pulchritúdinem de membris Dómini suscepísti: diu desideráta, sollícite amáta, sine intermissióne quæsíta et aliquándo cupiénti ánimo preparáta: áccipe me ab homínibus, et redde me magístro meo. Súscipe discípulum Christi, ac per te me recípiat, qui per te móriens me redémit. Amen.

O good Cross, made beautiful by the body of the Lord: long have I desired you, ardently have I loved you, unceasingly have I sought you out; and now you are ready for my eager soul. Receive me from among men and restore me to my Master, so that he—who, by means of you, in dying redeemed me—may receive me. Amen.

DEVOTIONS TO
THE HOLY SPIRIT

"The traditional form of petition to the Holy Spirit is to invoke the Father through Christ our Lord to give us the Consoler Spirit. Jesus insists on this petition to be made in his name at the very moment when he promised the gift of the Spirit of Truth. But the simplest and most direct prayer is also traditional, 'Come, Holy Spirit,' and every liturgical tradition has developed it in antiphons and hymns."[1]

TEN-DAY DEVOTION TO THE HOLY SPIRIT

The day before you begin the Ten-Day Devotion, which is the eve of the glorious Ascension of our divine Redeemer, you must prepare yourself by making a firm resolution to live an interior life and, once you have begun, never again abandon it. Do not ask yourself how much this is going to cost you; look at only how much it is worth. This has always been the case: What is worth a lot costs a lot. And what is the effort we put into knowing ourselves, when we compare it with the great benefits that we derive from it?[2]

FIRST DAY

Introductory Prayer[3]

Come, O Holy Spirit! Enlighten my understanding in order that I may know your commands; strengthen

---

1. *Catechism of the Catholic Church* (=CCC), 2671, Libreria Editrice Vaticana, 1994; cf. Luke 11:13; John 14:17, 15:26, 16:13.
2. F. J. del Valle, *About the Holy Spirit*, Dublin: Four Court Press, 1981.
3. Cf. Postulation for the Cause of Beatification and Canonization of Msgr. Josemaría Escrivá: *Historical Registry of the Founder [of Opus Dei]*, 20172, p. 145.

my heart against the snares of the enemy; enkindle
my will. I have heard your voice, and I do not want to
harden my heart and resist, saying, "Later . . . tomorrow." *Nunc coepi!* Right now! Lest there be no tomorrow for me.

O Spirit of truth and of wisdom, Spirit of understanding and of counsel, Spirit of joy and of peace! I
want what you want, because you want it, as you
want it, when you want it.

Consideration[4]

*Pentecost: the day when the Holy Spirit
came down upon the Lord's disciples*

Having just read in the Acts of the Apostles about
Pentecost, the day when the Holy Spirit came down
upon the Lord's disciples, we are conscious of being
present at the great display of God's power with
which the Church's life began to spread among all
nations. The victory Christ achieved through his
obedience, his offering of himself on the cross, and
his resurrection—his triumph over death and sin—
is revealed here in all its divine splendor.

The disciples, witnesses of the glory of the risen
Christ, were filled with the strength of the Holy
Spirit. Their minds and hearts were opened to a new
light. They had followed Christ and accepted his
teachings with faith, but they were not always able
to fathom the full meaning of his words. The Spirit
of truth, who was to teach them all things,[5] had not
yet come. They knew that Jesus alone could give
them words of eternal life, and they were ready to

---

4. The homily "The Great Unknown," in *Christ Is Passing By*, by Blessed
   Josemaría Escrivá, is reprinted here and divided into ten "Consider-
   ations."
5. Cf. John 16:12-13.

follow him and to give their lives for him. But they were weak, and, in the time of trial, they fled and left him alone.

On Pentecost, all that is a thing of the past. The Holy Spirit, who is the Spirit of strength, has made them firm, strong, daring. The word of the apostles resounds forcefully through the streets of Jerusalem.

The men and women who have come to the city from all parts of the world listen with amazement. "Parthians and Medes and Elamites, and inhabitants of Mesopotamia, Judea, and Cappadocia, Pontus and Asia, Phrygia and Pamphylia, Egypt and the parts of Libya about Cyrene, and visitors from Rome, Jews as well as proselytes, Cretans and Arabs, we have heard them speaking in our own languages of the wonderful works of God."[6] These wonders, which take place before their own eyes, lead them to listen to the preaching of the apostles. The Holy Spirit himself, who is acting through our Lord's disciples, moves the hearts of their listeners and leads them to the faith.

St. Luke tells us that after St. Peter had spoken and proclaimed Christ's resurrection, many of those present came up to him and asked: "Brethren, what shall we do?" The apostle answered: "Repent and be baptized, every one of you, in the name of Jesus Christ, for the forgiveness of your sins; and you will receive the gift of the Holy Spirit." And, on that day, the sacred text tells us, about three thousand were added to the Church.[7]

The solemn coming of the Holy Spirit on Pentecost was not an isolated event. There is hardly a page in

6. Acts 2:9-11.
7. Cf. Acts 2:37-41.

the Acts of the Apostles where we fail to read about him and the action by which he guides, directs and enlivens the life and work of the early Christian community. It is he who inspires St. Peter's preaching, who strengthens the faith of the disciples, who confirms with his presence the calling of the Gentiles, who sends Saul and Barnabas to the distant lands where they will open new paths for the teachings of Jesus.[8] In a word, his presence and doctrine are everywhere.

Concluding Prayer

Holy and divine Spirit! Through the intercession of the Blessed Virgin Mary, your spouse, bring the fullness of your gifts into our hearts. Comforted and strengthened by you, may we live according to your will and may we die praising your infinite mercy. Through Christ our Lord. Amen.

SECOND DAY

Introductory Prayer

Come, O Holy Spirit! Enlighten my understanding in order that I may know your commands; strengthen my heart against the snares of the enemy; enkindle my will. I have heard your voice, and I do not want to harden my heart and resist, saying, "Later . . . tomorrow." *Nunc coepi!* Right now! Lest there be no tomorrow for me.

O Spirit of truth and of wisdom, Spirit of understanding and of counsel, Spirit of joy and of peace! I want what you want, because you want it, as you want it, when you want it.

8. Cf. Acts 4:8, 4:31, 10:44-47, 13:2-4.

Consideration

The Holy Spirit: present in the Church for all time

The profound reality which we see in the texts of holy Scripture is not a remembrance from the past, from some golden age of the Church which has since been buried in history. Despite the weaknesses and the sins of every one of us, it is the reality of today's Church and the Church of all time. "I will ask the Father," our Lord told his disciples, "and he will give you another Counselor to dwell with you for ever."[9] Jesus has kept his promise. He has risen from the dead, and, in union with the eternal Father, he sends us the Holy Spirit to sanctify us and to give us life.

The strength and the power of God light up the face of the earth. The Holy Spirit is present in the Church of Christ for all time, so that it may be, always and in everything, a sign raised up before all nations, announcing to all people the goodness and the love of God. In spite of our great limitations, we can look up to heaven with confidence and joy: God loves us and frees us from our sins. The presence and the action of the Holy Spirit in the Church are a foretaste of eternal happiness, of the joy and peace for which we are destined by God.

Like the men and women who came up to Peter on Pentecost, we too have been baptized. In Baptism, our Father God has taken possession of our lives, has made us share in the life of Christ, and has given us the Holy Spirit. Holy Scripture tells us that God has saved us "through the baptism of regeneration and renewal by the Holy Spirit; whom he has

---

9. Cf. Isaiah 11:12.

abundantly poured out upon us through Jesus
Christ our Savior, in order that, justified by his
grace, we may be heirs in hope to life everlasting."[10]
The experience of our weakness and of our failings,
the painful realization of the smallness and mean-
ness of some who call themselves Christians, the apparent failure or aimlessness of some works of
apostolate—all these things, which bring home to us
the reality of sin and human limitation, can still be a
trial of our faith. Temptation and doubt can lead us
to ask: where are the strength and the power of
God? When that happens, we have to react by prac-
ticing the virtue of hope with greater purity and
forcefulness and striving to be more faithful.

Concluding Prayer

Holy and divine Spirit! Through the intercession of
the Blessed Virgin Mary, your spouse, bring the fullness of your gifts into our hearts. Comforted and
strengthened by you, may we live according to your
will and may we die praising your infinite mercy.
Through Christ our Lord. Amen.

THIRD DAY

Introductory Prayer

Come, O Holy Spirit! Enlighten my understanding in
order that I may know your commands; strengthen
my heart against the snares of the enemy; enkindle
my will. I have heard your voice, and I do not want to
harden my heart and resist, saying, "Later . . . tomorrow." *Nunc coepi!* Right now! Lest there be no tomorrow for me.

---

10. Titus 3:5-7.

O Spirit of truth and of wisdom, Spirit of under-standing and of counsel, Spirit of joy and of peace! I want what you want, because you want it, as you want it, when you want it.

Consideration

The Church: the body of Christ,
enlivened by the Holy Spirit

Let me tell you about an event of my own personal life, that happened many years ago. One day I was with a friend of mine, a man who had a good heart but who did not have faith. Pointing toward a globe, he said, "Look, from North to South, from East to West." "What do you want me to look at?" I asked. His answer was: "The failure of Christ. For twenty centuries people have been trying to bring his doctrine to men's lives, and look at the result." I was filled with sadness. It is painful to realize that many people still don't know our Lord, and that, among those who do know him, many live as though they did not. But that feeling lasted only a moment. It was shortly overcome by love and thankfulness, because Jesus has wanted every man to cooperate freely in the work of redemption. *He has not failed.* His doctrine and life have been effective in the world at all times. The redemption carried out by him is sufficient, and more than sufficient.

God does not want slaves, but children. *He respects our freedom.* The work of salvation is still going on, and each one of us has a part in it. It is Christ's will, St. Paul tells us in impressive words, that we should fulfill—in our flesh, in our life—that which is lacking in his Passion, "for the good of his body, which is the Church."[11]

---

11. Cf. Colossians 1:24: *pro corpore eius, quod est Ecclesia.*

It is worthwhile to put our lives on the line, to give ourselves completely, so as to answer to the love and the confidence that God has placed in us. It is worthwhile, above all, to decide to take our Christian life seriously. When we recite the Creed, we state that we believe in God the Father Almighty, in his Son Jesus Christ, who died and rose again, and in the Holy Spirit, the Lord and giver of life. We affirm that the Church—one, holy, catholic, and apostolic—is the body of Christ, enlivened by the Holy Spirit. We rejoice in the forgiveness of sins and in the hope of our own resurrection. But do those words penetrate to the depths of our own heart? Or do they remain only on our lips? The divine message of victory, the joy and the peace of Pentecost, should be the unshakable foundation for every Christian's way of thinking and acting and living.

Concluding Prayer

Holy and divine Spirit! Through the intercession of the Blessed Virgin Mary, your spouse, bring the fullness of your gifts into our hearts. Comforted and strengthened by you, may we live according to your will and may we die praising your infinite mercy. Through Christ our Lord. Amen.

FOURTH DAY

Introductory Prayer

Come, O Holy Spirit! Enlighten my understanding in order that I may know your commands; strengthen my heart against the snares of the enemy; enkindle my will. I have heard your voice, and I do not want to harden my heart and resist, saying, "Later . . . tomorrow." *Nunc coepi!* Right now! Lest there be no tomorrow for me.

O Spirit of truth and of wisdom, Spirit of understanding and of counsel, Spirit of joy and of peace! I
want what you want, because you want it, as you
want it, when you want it.

Consideration

Our faith in the Holy Spirit: necessarily complete

The arm of the Lord has not been shortened."[12] God
is no less powerful today than he was in other times;
his love for us is no less true. Our faith teaches us
that all creation, the movement of the earth and the
other heavenly bodies, the good actions of creatures
and all the good that has been achieved in history—
in short, everything—comes from God and is directed toward him.

The action of the Holy Spirit can pass unnoticed, because God does not reveal to us his plans, and because man's sin clouds over the divine gifts. But
faith reminds us that God is always acting. He has
created us and maintains us in existence, and he
leads all creation by his grace toward the glorious
freedom of the children of God.[13]

For this reason, Christian tradition has summarized
the attitude that we should adopt toward the Holy
Spirit in just one idea: docility. This means that we
should be aware of the work of the Holy Spirit all
around us and that in our own selves we should recognize the gifts he distributes, the movements and institutions he inspires, the affections and decisions he
provokes in our hearts. The Holy Spirit carries out in
the world the works of God. He is, as we read in a liturgical hymn, the giver of grace, the light of our
hearts, the soul's guest, our rest in work, our consolation in sorrow. Without his help there is nothing inno-

---

12. Isaiah 59:1: *Non est abbreviata manus Domini.*
13. Cf. Romans 8:21.

cent or valuable in man, because he is the one who cleanses the soiled, heals what is sick, sets on fire what is cold, straightens what is bent, and guides men toward the safe harbor of salvation and eternal joy.[14]

But our faith in the Holy Spirit must be complete— not a merely vague belief in his presence in the world, but a grateful acceptance of the signs and realities into which he has poured forth his power in a special way. When the Spirit of truth comes, our Lord tells us, "He will glorify me, for he will take of what is mine and declare it to you."[15] The Holy Spirit is the Spirit sent by Christ to carry out in us the work of holiness that our Lord merited for us on earth.

And so there cannot be faith in the Holy Spirit if there is not faith in Christ, in his sacraments, in his Church. One cannot act in accordance with his Christian faith, cannot truly believe in the Holy Spirit, without loving the Church and trusting it. A man cannot be a coherent Christian if he limits himself to pointing out the deficiencies and limitations of some who represent the Church—if he judges her from the outside, as though he were not her son. Consider, moreover, the extraordinary importance and abundance of the Paraclete when the priest renews the sacrifice of Calvary by celebrating Mass on our altars.

Concluding Prayer

Holy and divine Spirit! Through the intercession of the Blessed Virgin Mary, your spouse, bring the fullness of your gifts into our hearts. Comforted and strengthened by you, may we live according to your will and may we die praising your infinite mercy. Through Christ our Lord. Amen.

14. Sequence *Veni Sancte Spiritus*, Mass of Pentecost Sunday.
15. John 16:14.

FIFTH DAY

Introductory Prayer

Come, O Holy Spirit! Enlighten my understanding in order that I may know your commands; strengthen my heart against the snares of the enemy; enkindle my will. I have heard your voice, and I do not want to harden my heart and resist, saying, "Later . . . tomorrow." *Nunc coepi!* Right now! Lest there be no tomorrow for me.

O Spirit of truth and of wisdom, Spirit of understanding and of counsel, Spirit of joy and of peace! I want what you want, because you want it, as you want it, when you want it.

Consideration

The Holy Spirit: present among us

We Christians carry the great treasures of grace in vessels of clay.[16] God has entrusted his gifts to the weakness and fragility of human freedom. We can be certain of the help of God's power, but our lust, our love of comfort, and our pride sometimes cause us to reject his grace and to fall into sin. For more than twenty-five years, when I have recited the Creed and asserted my faith in the divine origin of the Church as "one, holy, catholic, and apostolic," I have frequently added, "in spite of everything." When I mention this custom of mine and someone asks me what I mean, I answer, "I mean your sins and mine."

All this is true, but it does not authorize us in any way to judge the Church in a human manner, without theological faith. We cannot consider only the greater or lesser merits of certain churchmen or other

16. Cf. 2 Corinthians 4:7.

Christians. To do this would be to limit ourselves to the surface of things. *What is most important in the Church is not how we humans react, but how God acts.* This is what the Church is: Christ present in our midst, God coming toward us in order to save us, calling us with his revelation, sanctifying us with his grace, maintaining us with his constant help, in the great and small battles of our daily life.

We might come to mistrust other people, and we should each mistrust ourselves (and end each day with a *mea culpa*, an act of contrition that is profound and sincere). But we have no right to doubt God. And to doubt the Church, its divine origin and its effectiveness for our salvation through its doctrine and its sacraments, would be the same as doubting God himself, the same as not fully believing in the reality of the coming of the Holy Spirit.

"Before Christ was crucified," writes St. John Chrysostom, "there was no reconciliation. And while there was no reconciliation, the Holy Spirit was not sent. . . . The absence of the Holy Spirit was a sign of the anger of God. Now that you see him sent in fullness, do not doubt the reconciliation. But what if people should ask, 'Where is the Holy Spirit now? We can talk of his presence when the miracles took place, when the dead were raised and the lepers were healed. But how are we to know that he is truly present now?' Do not be concerned. I will show you that the Holy Spirit is present among us now as well.

"If the Holy Spirit were not present, we would not be able to say, 'Jesus is the Lord,' for no one can invoke Jesus as the Lord unless it is in the Holy Spirit (1 Cor 12:3). If the Holy Spirit were not present, we would not be able to pray with confidence. For when we pray, we say, 'Our Father, who art in heaven' (Mt 6:9). If the Holy Spirit were not present, we could not call God our Father. How do we know this? Because the apostle teaches us: 'And, because you are his children, God has sent the Spirit of his Son into our hearts, crying, "Abba! Father!"' (Gal 4:6).

"When you call on God the Father, remember that it is the Spirit who, with his motion in your soul, has given you this prayer. If the Holy Spirit were not present, there would be no word of wisdom or knowledge in the Church; for it is written, 'The word of wisdom is given through the Spirit' (1 Cor 12:8). . . . If the Holy Spirit were not present, the Church would not exist. But if the Church exists, there is no doubt of the presence of the Holy Spirit."[17]

Beyond all human deficiencies and limitations, the Church is the sign and, in a certain sense, though not in the strict sense in which the Church has defined the nature of the seven sacraments of the new law, the universal sacrament of the presence of God in the world. To be a Christian is to be reborn of God and sent to announce the news of salvation. If we had a strong faith, a living faith, if we were bold in making Christ known to others, we would see with our own eyes miracles such as those that took place in the time of the apostles.

Today, too, the blind who have lost the ability to look up to heaven and contemplate the wonderful works of God recover their sight. The lame and the crippled who have been bound by their passions,

17. St. John Chrysostom, *Sermones panegyrici in solemnitates D.N. Iesu Christi*, homily I, *De Sancta Pentecoste, n.* 3-4 in J. P. Migne (ed.), *Patrologia Graeca* (=PG), 50, 457, París, 1857-1866.

and whose hearts have forgotten love recover their freedom. The deaf who did not want to know God are given back their hearing. The dumb whose tongues were bound because they did not want to acknowledge their defeats begin to talk. And the dead in whom sin had destroyed life come to life again. We see once more that "the word of God is living and active, sharper than any two-edged sword."[18] And, just as the first Christians did, we rejoice when we contemplate the power of the Holy Spirit and see the results of his action on the minds and wills of his creatures.

Concluding Prayer

Holy and divine Spirit! Through the intercession of the Blessed Virgin Mary, your spouse, bring the fullness of your gifts into our hearts. Comforted and strengthened by you, may we live according to your will and may we die praising your infinite mercy. Through Christ our Lord. Amen.

SIXTH DAY

Introductory Prayer

Come, O Holy Spirit! Enlighten my understanding in order that I may know your commands; strengthen my heart against the snares of the enemy; enkindle my will. I have heard your voice, and I do not want to harden my heart and resist, saying, "Later . . . tomorrow." *Nunc coepi!* Right now! Lest there be no tomorrow for me.

O Spirit of truth and of wisdom, Spirit of understanding and of counsel, Spirit of joy and of peace! I want what you want, because you want it, as you want it, when you want it.

18. Hebrews 4:12.

Consideration

*The action of the Holy Spirit:
teaching how to correspond to it*

I see all the circumstances of life—those of every individual person's existence, as well as, in some way, those of the great crossroads of history—as so many calls that God makes to men, to bring them face to face with truth, and as occasions that are offered to us Christians, so that we may announce, with our deeds and with our words strengthened by grace, the Spirit to whom we belong.[19]

Every generation of Christians needs to redeem, to sanctify its own time. In order to do this, we must understand and share the desires of other men—as equals—in order to make known to them, with a *gift of tongues*, how they are to correspond to the action of the Holy Spirit, to that permanent outflow of rich treasures that comes from our Lord's heart. We Christians are called upon to announce, in our own time, to this world to which we belong and in which we live, the message—old and at the same time new—of the Gospel.

It is not true that everyone today, in general, is closed or indifferent to what our Christian faith teaches about man's being and destiny. It is not true that men in our time are turned toward only the things of this earth and have forgotten to look up to heaven. There is no lack of narrow ideologies, it is true, or of persons who maintain them. But in our time we find both great desires and base attitudes, heroism and cowardice, zeal and disenchantment: those who dream of a new world, more just and

19. Cf. Luke 9:55.

more human, and others who—discouraged, perhaps, by the failure of their youthful idealism—hide themselves in the selfishness of seeking only their own security or remaining immersed in their errors. To all these men and women, wherever they may be, in their more exalted moments or in their crises and defeats, we have to bring the solemn and unequivocal message of St. Peter in the days that followed Pentecost: Jesus is the cornerstone, the Redeemer, the hope of our lives. "For there is no other name under heaven given to men by which we must be saved."[20]

Concluding Prayer

Holy and divine Spirit! Through the intercession of the Blessed Virgin Mary, your spouse, bring the fullness of your gifts into our hearts. Comforted and strengthened by you, may we live according to your will and may we die praising your infinite mercy. Through Christ our Lord. Amen.

SEVENTH DAY

Introductory Prayer

Come, O Holy Spirit! Enlighten my understanding in order that I may know your commands; strengthen my heart against the snares of the enemy; enkindle my will. I have heard your voice, and I do not want to harden my heart and resist, saying, "Later . . . tomorrow." *Nunc coepi!* Right now! Lest there be no tomorrow for me.

O Spirit of truth and of wisdom, Spirit of understanding and of counsel, Spirit of joy and of peace! I want what you want, because you want it, as you want it, when you want it.

---

20. Acts 4:12.

Consideration

The gift of wisdom: making us know
God and rejoice in his presence

I would say that, among the gifts of the Holy Spirit,
there is one that we all need in a special way: the gift
of wisdom. It makes us know God and rejoice in his
presence, thereby placing us in a perspective from
which we can judge accurately the situations and
events of this life. Had we been consistent with our
faith when we looked around us and contemplated
the world and its history, we would have been unable to avoid feeling in our own hearts the same sentiments that filled the heart of our Lord: "Seeing the
crowds, he was moved with compassion for them,
because they were bewildered and dejected, like
sheep without a shepherd."[21]

Not that the Christian should neglect to see all that
is good in humanity, to appreciate its healthy joys,
or to participate in its enthusiasm and ideals. On the
contrary, a true Christian will vibrate in unison with
all the good he finds in the world. And he will live
in the midst of it with a special concern, because of
knowing, better than anyone, the depth and the
richness of the human spirit.

A Christian's faith does not diminish his spirit or
limit the noble impulses of his soul—rather, it makes
them grow with the realization of their true and authentic meaning. We do not exist in order to pursue
just any happiness. We have been called to penetrate
the intimacy of God's own life, to know and love
God the Father, God the Son, and God the Holy
Spirit, and to love also—in that same love of the one
God in three divine Persons—the angels and all men.

21. Matthew 9:36.

This is the great boldness of the Christian faith: to proclaim the value and dignity of human nature and to affirm that we have been created to achieve the dignity of children of God, through the grace that raises us up to a supernatural level. An incredible boldness it would be, were it not founded on the promise of salvation given us by God the Father, confirmed by the blood of Christ, and reaffirmed and made possible by the constant action of the Holy Spirit.

We must live by faith. We must grow in faith, up to the point where it will be possible to describe any one of us in the terms used by one of the great Doctors of the Eastern Church to describe Christians in general: "In the same way that a transparent body, upon receiving a ray of light, becomes resplendent and shines out, so the souls that are borne and illuminated by the Holy Spirit become themselves spiritual and carry to others the light of grace. From the Holy Spirit comes knowledge of future events, understanding of mysteries, comprehension of hidden truths, giving of gifts, heavenly citizenship, conversation with the angels. From him comes never-ending joy, perseverance in God, likeness to God, and the most sublime state that can be conceived, that of becoming God-like."[22]

Together with humility, the realization of the greatness of man's dignity—and of the overwhelming fact that, by grace, we are made children of God—forms a single attitude. It is not our own forces that save us and give us life; it is the grace of God. This is a truth which can never be forgotten. If it were, the *divinization* of our life would be perverted and would become presumption, pride. And this would lead, sooner or later, to a breakdown of spiritual life,

22. St. Basil, *De Spiritu Sancto*, 9, 23 (PG 32, 110).

when the soul came face to face with its own weakness and wretchedness.

"And shall I dare to say, 'I am holy'?" asks St. Augustine. "If I mean by 'holy' that I bring holiness and that I need no one to make me holy, I would be a liar and full of pride. But if by 'holy' I understand that one is made holy as we read in Leviticus, 'You will be holy, because I, God, am holy,' then the whole body of Christ, down to the last person living at the ends of the earth, may dare to say, together with its head and under him, 'I am holy.'"[23]

Love the Third Person of the most Blessed Trinity. Listen in the intimacy of your being to the divine motions of encouragement or reproach you receive from him. Walk through the world in the light that is poured out in your soul. And the God of hope will fill you with all peace, so that this hope may grow in you more and more each day, by the power of the Holy Spirit.[24]

Concluding Prayer

Holy and divine Spirit! Through the intercession of the Blessed Virgin Mary, your spouse, bring the fullness of your gifts into our hearts. Comforted and strengthened by you, may we live according to your will and may we die praising your infinite mercy. Through Christ our Lord. Amen.

EIGHTH DAY

Introductory Prayer

Come, O Holy Spirit! Enlighten my understanding in order that I may know your commands; strengthen my heart against the snares of the enemy; enkindle

---

23. St. Augustine, *Enarrationes in psalmos*, 85, 4 (PL 37, 1084).
24. Cf. Romans 15:13.

my will. I have heard your voice, and I do not want to harden my heart and resist, saying, "Later . . . tomorrow." *Nunc coepi!* Right now! Lest there be no tomorrow for me.

O Spirit of truth and of wisdom, Spirit of understanding and of counsel, Spirit of joy and of peace! I want what you want, because you want it, as you want it, when you want it.

Consideration

The Holy Spirit: living according to him

To live according to the Holy Spirit means to live by faith and hope and charity—to allow God to take possession of our lives and to change our hearts, to make us resemble him more and more. A mature and profound Christian life cannot be improvised, because it is the result of the growth of God's grace in us. In the Acts of the Apostles we find the early Christian community described in a single sentence that is brief but full of meaning: "And they continued steadfastly in the teaching of the apostles and in the communion of the breaking of the bread and in prayers."[25]

This is how the early Christians lived, and this is how we, too, should live: meditating upon the doctrine of our faith until it becomes a part of us; receiving our Lord in the Eucharist; meeting him in the personal dialogue of our prayer, not trying to hide behind an impersonal kind of conduct, but coming face to face with him. These means should become the very substance of our attitude. If they are lacking, we shall have, perhaps, the ability to think in an erudite manner, an activity that is more or less in-

---

25. Acts 2:42.

tense, some practices and devotions. But we shall not have an authentically Christian way of life, because we are all, equally, called to sanctity. There are no second-class Christians, obliged to practice only a "simplified version" of the Gospel. We have all received the same Baptism, and although there is a great variety of spiritual gifts and human situations, there is only one Spirit who distributes God's gifts—only one faith, only one hope, only one love.[26]

And so we can apply to ourselves the question asked by the apostle: "Do you not know that you are the temple of God, and that the Spirit of God dwells in you?"[27] And we can understand it as an invitation to deal with God in a more personal and direct manner. For some, unfortunately, the Paraclete is the Great Stranger, the Great Unknown. He is merely a name that is mentioned, but not Someone, not one of the three Persons (in the one God) with whom we can talk and with whose life we can live.

We have to deal with him simply and trustingly, as we are taught by the Church in its liturgy. Then we will come to know our Lord better, and at the same time we will realize more fully the great favor that has been granted us when we became Christians. We will see all the greatness and truth of the *divinization* to which I referred earlier, which is a sharing in God's own life.

Concluding Prayer

Holy and divine Spirit! Through the intercession of the Blessed Virgin Mary, your spouse, bring the fullness of your gifts into our hearts. Comforted and strengthened by you, may we live according to your

26. Cf. 1 Corinthians 12:4-6, 13:1-13.
27. 1 Corinthians 3:16.

will and may we die praising your infinite mercy. Through Christ our Lord. Amen.

NINTH DAY

Introductory Prayer

Come, O Holy Spirit! Enlighten my understanding in order that I may know your commands; strengthen my heart against the snares of the enemy; enkindle my will. I have heard your voice, and I do not want to harden my heart and resist, saying, "Later . . . tomorrow." *Nunc coepi!* Right now! Lest there be no tomorrow for me.

O Spirit of truth and of wisdom, Spirit of understanding and of counsel, Spirit of joy and of peace! I want what you want, because you want it, as you want it, when you want it.

Consideration

> *Docility, life of prayer, and union*
> *with the cross: fundamental points*

"The Holy Spirit is not an artist who draws the divine substance in us, as though he were alien to it. It is not in this way that he leads us to a resemblance with God—but rather, being God and proceeding from God, he himself marks the hearts of those who receive him, as a seal upon wax. In this way, by the communication of his own life and resemblance, he restores nature according to the beauty of the divine model, and returns to us our resemblance to God."[28]

Let us see how this truth applies to our daily lives. Let us describe, at least in general, the way of life

---

28. St. Cyril of Alexandria, *Thesaurus de sancta et consubstantiali Trinitate*, 34 (PG 75, 609).

that will bring us to deal in a familiar manner with the Holy Spirit, and, together with him, the Father and the Son.

We can fix our attention on three fundamental points: docility, a life of prayer, and union with the cross.

First of all, docility, because it is the Holy Spirit who, with his inspirations, gives a supernatural tone to our thoughts, desires, and actions. It is he who leads us to receive Christ's teaching and to assimilate it in a profound way. It is he who gives us the light by which we perceive our personal calling and the strength to carry out all that God expects of us. If we are docile to the Holy Spirit, the image of Christ will be formed more and more fully in us, and we will be brought closer every day to God the Father. "For whoever are led by the Spirit of God, they are the children of God."[29]

If we let ourselves be guided by this life-giving principle, the Holy Spirit in us, our spiritual vitality will grow. We will place ourselves in the hands of our Father God, with the same spontaneity and confidence with which children abandon themselves to their fathers' care. Our Lord has said: "Unless you become like little children, you will not enter the kingdom of heaven."[30] This is the old and well-known "way of childhood," which is not sentimentality or lack of human maturity. It is a supernatural maturity, which makes us realize more deeply the wonders of God's love, while leading us to acknowledge our own smallness and identify our will fully with the will of God.

---

29. Romans 8:14.
30. Matthew 18:3.

In the second place, a life of prayer, because the giving of one's self, the obedience and meekness of a Christian, are born of love and lead to love. And love leads to a personal relationship, to conversation and friendship. Christian life requires a constant dialogue with God, one in three Persons, and it is to this intimacy that the Holy Spirit leads us. "For who among men knows the things of a man save the spirit of the man which is in him? Even so, the things of God no one knows but the Spirit of God."[31] If we have a constant relationship with the Holy Spirit, we ourselves will become spiritual, we will realize that we are Christ's brothers and children of God, and we will not hesitate to call upon our Father at any time.[32]

Let us acquire the habit of conversation with the Holy Spirit, who is the one who will make us holy. Let us trust in him and ask his help and feel his closeness to us. In this way our poor hearts will grow; we will have a greater desire to love God and to love all creatures for God's sake. And our lives will reproduce that final vision of the Apocalypse: the Spirit and the Spouse, the Holy Spirit and the Church—and every Christian—calling on Jesus Christ to come and be with us for ever.[33]

And, finally, union with the cross, because in the life of Christ, the Resurrection and Pentecost were preceded by Calvary. This is the order that must be followed in the life of any Christian. We are, as St. Paul tells us, "heirs indeed of God and joint heirs with

---

31. 1 Corinthians 2:11.
32. Cf. Galatians 4:6; Romans 8:15.
33. Cf. Revelation 22:17.

Christ, provided, however, we suffer with him, that we may also be glorified with him."[34] The Holy Spirit comes to us as a result of the cross—as a result of our total abandonment to the will of God, of our seeking only his glory and renouncing ourselves completely.

Only when we are faithful to grace and determined to place the cross in the centers of our souls, denying ourselves for the love of God, detaching ourselves in a real way from all selfishness and false human security, only then—when we live by faith in a real way—will we receive the fullness of the great fire, the great light, the great comfort of the Holy Spirit.

It is then, too, that souls begin to experience the peace and freedom that Christ has won for us,[35] and that are given to us with the grace of the Holy Spirit. The fruit of the Spirit is: charity, joy, peace, patience, kindness, goodness, long-suffering, mildness, faith, modesty, continency, chastity;[36] and "where the Spirit of the Lord is, there is freedom."[37]

Concluding Prayer

Holy and divine Spirit! Through the intercession of the Blessed Virgin Mary, your spouse, bring the fullness of your gifts into our hearts. Comforted and strengthened by you, may we live according to your will and may we die praising your infinite mercy. Through Christ our Lord. Amen.

---

34. Romans 8:17.
35. Cf. Galatians 4:31.
36. Cf. Galatians 5:22-23.
37. 2 Corinthians 3:17.

TENTH DAY

Introductory Prayer

Come, O Holy Spirit! Enlighten my understanding in order that I may know your commands; strengthen my heart against the snares of the enemy; enkindle my will. I have heard your voice, and I do not want to harden my heart and resist, saying, "Later . . . tomorrow." *Nunc coepi!* Right now! Lest there be no tomorrow for me.

O Spirit of truth and of wisdom, Spirit of understanding and of counsel, Spirit of joy and of peace! I want what you want, because you want it, as you want it, when you want it.

Consideration

Beginning: and beginning again

In the midst of the limitations that accompany our present life, in which sin is still present in us to some extent at least, we Christians perceive with a particular clearness all the wealth of our divine filiation, when we realize that we are fully free because we are doing our Father's work, when our joy becomes constant because no one can take our hope away. It is then that we can admire at the same time all the great and beautiful things of this earth, can appreciate the richness and goodness of creation, and can love with all the strength and purity for which the human heart was made. It is then that sorrow for sin does not degenerate into a bitter gesture of despair or pride, because sorrow and knowledge of human weakness lead us to identify ourselves again with Christ's work of redemption and feel more deeply our solidarity with others.

It is then, finally, that we Christians experience in our own life the sure strength of the Holy Spirit, in such a way that our own failures do not drag us down. Rather, they are an invitation to begin again and to continue being faithful witnesses of Christ in all the moments of our life—in spite of our own personal weaknesses, which, in such a case, are normally no more than small failings that hardly perturb the soul. And even if they are grave sins, the sacrament of Penance, received with true sorrow, enables us to recover our peace with God and to become again a good witness of his mercy.

Such is the brief summary, which can barely be expressed in human language, of the richness of our faith and of our Christian life, if we let ourselves be guided by the Holy Spirit. That is why I can end these words in only one way: by voicing a prayer, contained in one of the liturgical hymns for the feast of Pentecost, which is like an echo of the unceasing petition of the whole Church: "Come, creating Spirit, to the minds of those who belong to you, and fill, with grace from above, the hearts that you have created. . . . Grant that through you we may know the Father and become acquainted with the Son; may we believe in you, the Spirit who proceeds from the Father and Son, for ever. Amen."[38]

Concluding Prayer

Holy and divine Spirit! Through the intercession of the Blessed Virgin Mary, your spouse, bring the fullness of your gifts into our hearts. Comforted and strengthened by you, may we live according to your will and may we die praising your infinite mercy. Through Christ our Lord. Amen.

---

38. Hymn *Veni, Creator*, Divine Office of Pentecost Sunday, cf. pp 428ff., overleaf..

VENI CREATOR

Veni, Creátor Spíritus,
mentes tuórum vísita,
imple supérna grátia,
quæ tu creásti, péctora.
Qui díceris Paráclitus,
donum Dei altíssimi,
fons vivus, ignis, cáritas
et spiritális únctio.
Tu septifórmis múnere,
dextræ Dei tu dígitus,
tu rite promíssum Patris
sermóne ditans gúttura.
Accénde lumen sénsibus,
infúnde amórem córdibus,
infírma nostri córporis
virtúte firmans pérpeti.
Hostem repéllas lóngius
pacémque dones prótinus;
ductóre sic te praévio
vitémus omne nóxium.
Per te sciámus da Patrem
noscámus atque Fílium,
te utriúsque Spíritum
credámus omni témpore.
Deo Patris sit glória,
Et Fílio, qui a mórtuis
surréxit, ac Paráclito
in sæculórum saécula. Amen.

V. Emítte Spíritum tuum et creabúntur.
R. Et renovábis fáciem terræ.
Orémus.

Deus, qui corda fidélium Sancti Spíritus illustratióne
docuísti; da nobis in eódem Spíritu recta sápere; et
de eius semper consolatióne gaudére. Per Christum
Dóminum nostrum. **R. Amen.**

COME, HOLY SPIRIT

Come, Holy Spirit, Creator, come
From thy bright heavenly throne!
Come, take possession of our souls,
And make them all thine own!
Thou who art called the Paraclete,
Best gift of God above,
The living spring, the living fire,
Sweet unction, and true love!
Thou who art sevenfold in thy grace,
Finger of God's right hand,
His promise, teaching little ones
To speak and understand!
O guide our minds with thy blest light,
With love our hearts inflame,
And with thy strength which ne'er decays
Confirm our mortal frame.
Far from us drive our hellish foe,
True peace unto us bring,
And through all perils guide us safe
Beneath thy sacred wing.
Through thee may we the Father know,
Through thee, the eternal Son,
And thee, the Spirit of them both,
Thrice-blessed Three in one.
All glory to the Father be,
And to the risen Son;
The same to thee, O Paraclete,
While endless ages run. Amen.

V. Send forth thy Spirit, and they shall be created.

R. **And thou shalt renew the face of the earth**.

Let us pray.

O God, who hast taught the hearts of the faithful
by the light of the Holy Spirit, grant that by the gift of
the same Spirit we may be always truly wise and ever
rejoice in his consolation. Through Christ our Lord.

R. **Amen**.

PRAYER FOR PURITY OF BODY AND MIND

Lord, set aflame my heart and my entire being with
the fire of the Holy Spirit, that I may serve you with
chaste body and pure mind. Through Christ our
Lord. Amen.

DEVOTIONS TO
THE BLESSED VIRGIN MARY

"'All generations will call me blessed': 'The Church's devotion to the Blessed Virgin is intrinsic to Christian worship.' The Church rightly honors 'the Blessed Virgin with special devotion. From the most ancient times the Blessed Virgin has been honored with the title of "Mother of God," to whose protection the faithful fly in all their dangers and needs.... This very special devotion ... differs essentially from the adoration which is given to the incarnate Word and equally to the Father and the Holy Spirit, and greatly fosters this adoration.' The liturgical feasts dedicated to the Mother of God and Marian prayer, such as the Rosary, an 'epitome of the whole Gospel,' express this devotion to the Virgin Mary."[1]

THE HOLY ROSARY

The Rosary is a very old way of praying. "Medieval piety in the West developed the prayer of the Rosary as a popular substitute for the Liturgy of the Hours." It is a meditation on the life of our Lord and the Virgin Mary. "Christian prayer tries above all to meditate on the mysteries of Christ, as in ... the Rosary." "Meditation engages thought, imagination, emotion, and desire. This mobilization of faculties is necessary in order to deepen our convictions of faith, prompt the conversion of our heart, and strengthen our will to follow Christ." Meditation upon these mysteries leads us to con-

---

1. *Catechism of the Catholic Church* (=CCC), 971, Libreria Editrice Vaticana, 1994; Paul VI, *Marialis Cultus*, 42, 56; *Lumen Gentium*(=LG), 66.

templation: "This form of prayerful reflection is of great value, but Christian prayer should go further: to the knowledge of the love of the Lord Jesus, to union with him." [2]

The Rosary is divided into three parts; each part, into five mysteries. For each mystery one Our Father and ten Hail Marys (a "decade") are said. In many Christian families, there is a pious custom of reciting daily a third part of the Rosary.

Make the Sign of the cross:

In the name of the Father, and of the Son, and of the Holy Spirit. Amen.

Pray the Apostles' Creed:

I believe in God, the Father almighty,
    creator of heaven and earth.
I believe in Jesus Christ, his only Son, our Lord.
    He was conceived by the power of the Holy Spirit
        and born of the Virgin Mary.
    He suffered under Pontius Pilate,
        was crucified, died, and was buried.
    He descended into hell.
    On the third day he rose again.
    He ascended into heaven,
        and is seated at the right hand of the Father.
    He will come again to judge the living
        and the dead.
I believe in the Holy Spirit,
    the holy Catholic Church,
    the communion of saints,
    the forgiveness of sins,
    the resurrection of the body,
    and the life everlasting. Amen.

---

2. CCC 2678, 2708.

Then, for an increase in the virtues of faith, hope and charity:

Our Father.
Three Hail Marys.
Glory Be.

Now, begin the mysteries of the day. Start each decade by meditating on the mystery. On the large bead say the **Our Father**. On the ten small beads, say ten **Hail Marys**. Then pray the **Glory Be**.

Each decade is a contemplation of the life of our Lord, witnessed by Mary—one aspect of the paschal mystery. At the end of every decade, one of the following prayers may be said:

O my Jesus, forgive us our sins, save us from the fire of hell, draw all souls to heaven, especially those who are in most need of your mercy.

or:

Mary, mother of grace, mother of mercy, shield me from the enemy and receive me at the hour of my death. Amen.

At the end of the Rosary you may say the **Hail Holy Queen** (p. 471) followed by the prayer O God, whose only-begotten Son, . . . (p. 438); or the *Sub tuum Præsidium* (We Fly to Your Patronage) followed by the **Litany of the Blessed Virgin Mary**.

You may pray for **the intentions of the holy Father:**

Our Father. Hail Mary. Glory Be.

Mysteries of the Rosary

Joyful

SUNDAYS OF ADVENT; MONDAYS AND THURSDAYS

1. The Annunciation (Lk 1:30-33)
2. The Visitation (Lk 1:50-53)
3. The Nativity (Lk 2:10-11)
4. The Presentation (Lk 2:29-32)
5. The Finding of Jesus in the Temple (Lk 2:48-52)

Sorrowful

SUNDAYS OF LENT TUESDAYS AND FRIDAYS

1. The Agony in the Garden (Mt 26:38-39)
2. The Scourging at the Pillar (Jn 19:1)
3. The Crowning with Thorns (Mk 15:16-17)
4. The Carrying of the Cross (Jn 19:17)
5. The Crucifixion (Jn 19:28-30)

Glorious

SUNDAYS FROM CHRISTMAS UNTIL LENT
AND FROM EASTER UNTIL ADVENT;
WEDNESDAYS AND SATURDAYS

1. The Resurrection (Mk 16:6-8)
2. The Ascension (Acts 1:10-11)
3. The Descent of the Holy Spirit (Acts 2:1-4)
4. The Assumption (Song of Songs 2:3-6)
5. The Coronation of the Bl. Virgin (Lk 1:51-54)

WE FLY TO YOUR PATRONAGE

Sub tuum præsídium confúgimus, sancta Dei Génetrix; nostras deprecatiónes ne despícias in necessitátibus nostris sed a perículis cunctis líbera nos semper, Virgo gloriósa et benedícta.

We fly to your patronage, O holy Mother of God. Despise not our petitions in our necessities, but deliver us from all dangers, O ever-glorious and blessed Virgin.

LITANY OF THE BLESSED VIRGIN MARY

The litany is a way of praying found among many peoples. It is a prayer made to be repeated; one phrase coming over and over again, so that the person praying is caught up in the prayer itself. Often litanies are chanted.

The Litany of the Blessed Virgin Mary (called the Litany of Loreto, also) took shape over several centuries. It is rooted in images that we find in the Scriptures. It may be said after praying the Rosary.

Kýrie, eléison.
Kýrie, eléison.
Christe, eléison.
Christe, eléison.
Kýrie, eléison.
Kýrie, eléison.
Christe, audi nos.
Christe, audi nos.
Christe, exáudi nos.
Christe, exáudi nos.

Pater de cælis Deus,
Miserére nobis.
Fili, Redémptor
mundi Deus,
Miserére nobis.
Spíritus Sancte Deus,
Miserére nobis.
Sancta Trínitas,
unus Deus,
Miserére nobis.

Lord, have mercy on us.
Christ, have mercy on us.
Lord, have mercy on us.
Christ, hear us.
Christ, graciously hear us.

God the Father of heaven,
Have mercy on us.
God the Son,
Redeemer of the world,
Have mercy on us.
God the Holy Spirit,
Have mercy on us.
Holy Trinity,
one God,
Have mercy on us.

Sancta María,	Holy Mary,
ora pro nobis	**pray for us.**
Sancta Dei Génetrix,	Holy Mother of God,
Sancta Virgo vírginum,	Holy Virgin of virgins,
Mater Christi,	Mother of Christ,
Mater Ecclésiæ,	Mother of the Church,
Mater divínæ grátiæ,	Mother of divine grace,
Mater puríssima,	Mother most pure,
Mater castíssima,	Mother most chaste,
Mater invioláta,	Mother inviolate,
Mater intemeráta,	Mother undefiled,
(Mater immaculáta,)	[Mother immaculate,]
Mater amábilis,	Mother most amiable,
Mater admirábilis,	Mother most admirable,
Mater boni consílii,	Mother of good counsel,
Mater Creatóris,	Mother of our Creator,
Mater Salvatóris,	Mother of our Savior,
Virgo prudentíssima,	Virgin most prudent,
Virgo veneránda,	Virgin most venerable,
Virgo prædicánda,	Virgin most renowned,
Virgo potens,	Virgin most powerful,
Virgo clemens,	Virgin most merciful,
Virgo fidélis,	Virgin most faithful,
Spéculum iustítiæ,	Mirror of justice,
Sedes sapiéntiæ,	Seat of wisdom,
Causa nostræ lætítiæ,	Cause of our joy,
Vas spirituále,	Spiritual vessel,
Vas honorábile,	Vessel of honor,
Vas insígne devotiónis,	Singular vessel of devotion,
Rosa mýstica,	Mystical rose,

Turris Davídica,	Tower of David,
Turris ebúrnea,	Tower of ivory,
Domus áurea,	House of gold,
Fœderis arca,	Ark of the covenant,
Iánua cœli,	Gate of heaven,
Stella matutína,	Morning star,
Salus infirmórum,	Health of the sick,
Refúgium peccatórum,	Refuge of sinners,
Consolátrix afflictórum,	Comforter of the afflicted,
Auxílium Christianórum,	Help of Christians,
Regína Angelórum,	Queen of angels,
Regína Patriarchárum,	Queen of patriarchs,
Regína Prophetárum,	Queen of prophets,
Regína Apostolórum,	Queen of apostles,
Regína Mártyrum,	Queen of martyrs,
Regína Confessórum,	Queen of confessors,
Regína Vírginum,	Queen of virgins,
Regína Sanctórum ómnium,	Queen of all saints,
Regína sine labe origináli concépta,	Queen conceived without original sin,
Regína in cælum assúmpta,	Queen assumed into heaven,
Regína Sacratíssimi Rosárii,	Queen of the most holy Rosary,
Regina familiæ,	Queen of the family,
Regína pacis,	Queen of peace,

V. Agnus Dei, qui tollis peccáta mundi,

V. Lamb of God, who take away the sins of the world,

R. **Parce nobis, Dómine.**

R. **Spare us, O Lord.**

V. Agnus Dei, qui tollis peccáta mundi,

R. **Exáudi nos, Dómine.**

V. Agnus Dei, qui tollis peccáta mundi,

R. **Miserére nobis.**

V. Ora pro nobis, Sancta Dei Génetrix,

R. **Ut digni efficiámur promissiónibus Christi.**

V. Lamb of God, who take away the sins of the world,

R. **Graciously hear us, O Lord.**

V. Lamb of God, who take away the sins of the world,

R. **Have mercy on us.**

V. Pray for us, O holy Mother of God,

R. **That we may be made worthy of the promises of Christ.**

Let us pray.

O God, whose only-begotten Son, by his life, death, and resurrection, has purchased for us the rewards of everlasting life; grant, we beseech you, that, we, who meditate on these mysteries of the most holy Rosary of the Blessed Virgin Mary, we may imitate what they contain, and obtain what they promise. Through Christ our Lord. R. **Amen.**

A pious custom suggests the addition of the following intercessional prayers after the litany:

For the needs of the Church and of the nation:
Our Father. Hail Mary. Glory Be.

For the (arch)bishop of this diocese and his intentions:
Our Father. Hail Mary. Glory Be.

For the holy souls in purgatory:
Our Father. Hail Mary. May they rest in peace.

R. **Amen.**

MEDITATIONS ON
THE MYSTERIES OF THE ROSARY [3]

3. Blessed Josemaría Escrivá, *Holy Rosary*, Princeton: N.J. Scepter Publications, 1972.

JOYFUL MYSTERIES

FIRST JOYFUL MYSTERY

THE ANNUNCIATION

Don't forget, my friend, that we are children. The Lady of the sweet name, Mary, is absorbed in prayer. You, in that house, can be whatever you wish: a friend, a servant, an onlooker, a neighbor. . . . For the moment I don't dare to be anything. I hide behind you, and, full of awe, I watch what's happening.

The Archangel delivers his message. . . . *Quomodo fiet istud, quoniam virum non cognosco?* "But how can this come about, since I am a virgin?" (Lk 1:34). Our mother's voice reminds me—by contrast—of all the impurities of men, . . . mine too.

And then how I hate those low, mean things of the earth. . . . What resolutions!

Fiat mihi secundum verbum tuum. "Let it be done to me according to your word" (Lk 1:38). At the enchantment of this virginal phrase, the Word became flesh.

The first decade is about to end. . . . I still have time to tell God, before anyone else does, "Jesus, I love you."

SECOND JOYFUL MYSTERY

THE VISITATION

By now, my little friend, you have no doubt learned to manage on your own. Joyfully keep Joseph and Mary company . . . and you will hear the traditions of the House of David.

You will hear about Elizabeth and Zechariah, you will be moved by Joseph's pure love, and your heart will pound whenever they mention the Child who will be born in Bethlehem.

We walk in haste towards the mountains to a town of the tribe of Judah (Lk 1:39).

We arrive. It is the house where John the Baptist is to be born. Elizabeth gratefully hails the mother of her Redeemer: "Blessed are you among women, and blessed is the fruit of your womb. Why should I be honored with a visit from the mother of my Lord?" (Lk 1:42-43).

The unborn Baptist quivers . . . (Lk 1:41). Mary's humility pours forth in the *Magnificat*. . . . And you and I, who are proud—who were proud—promise to be humble.

THIRD JOYFUL MYSTERY

THE NATIVITY

Caesar Augustus has issued a decree for a census to be taken of the whole world. For this purpose, everyone must go to the city of his ancestors. And, since Joseph belongs to the house and line of David, he goes with the Virgin Mary from Nazareth to the town of David, called Bethlehem, in Judea (Lk 2:1-5).

And in Bethlehem is born our God: Jesus Christ! There is no room in the inn; he is born in a stable. And his mother wraps him in swaddling clothes and lays him in a manger (Lk 2:7).

Cold. Poverty. . . . I am Joseph's little servant. How good Joseph is! He treats me like a son. He even forgives me if I take the Child in my arms and spend hour after hour saying sweet and loving things to him.

And I kiss him—you kiss him, too!—and I rock him in my arms, and I sing to him and call him King, Love, my God, my Only-one, my All. . . ! How beautiful is the Child . . . and how short the decade!

FOURTH JOYFUL MYSTERY

THE PRESENTATION

When the time has come for the mother's purification, in accordance with the Law of Moses, the Child must be taken to Jerusalem to be presented to the Lord (Lk 2:22).

And this time it will be you, my friend, who carries the cage with the doves (Lk 2:24).

Just think: She—Mary Immaculate!—submits to the Law as if she were defiled.

Through this example, foolish child, won't you learn to fulfill the holy law of God regardless of any personal sacrifice?

Purification! You and I certainly do need purification.

Atonement and, more than atonement, love. Love as a searing iron to cauterize our soul's uncleanness, and as a fire to kindle with divine flames the wretchedness of our hearts.

An upright and devout man has come to the Temple, led by the Holy Spirit (it has been revealed to him that he would not die until he had set eyes on the Christ). He takes the Messiah into his arms and says: "Now, my Lord, you can let your servant go from this world in peace, just as you promised, because my eyes have seen the Savior" (Lk 2:25-30).

FIFTH JOYFUL MYSTERY

THE FINDING OF THE CHILD JESUS
IN THE TEMPLE

Where is Jesus? The Child, my Lady! Where is he?
Mary is crying. In vain you and I have run from
group to group, from caravan to caravan: no one has
seen him. Joseph, after fruitless attempts to keep
from crying, cries too. . . . And you. . . . And I.

Being a rough little fellow, I cry my eyes out and
wail to heaven and earth, . . . to make up for the
times when I lost him through my own fault and did
not cry.

Jesus: may I never lose you again. . . . Then you and I
are united in misfortune and grief, as we were
united in sin. And, from the depths of our being
come sighs of heartfelt sorrow and burning phrases,
which the pen cannot and should not record.

And, as we are consoled by the joy of finding Jesus—
three days he was gone!—debating with the teachers
of Israel (Lk 2:46), you and I will be left deeply im-
pressed by the duty to leave our home and family to
serve our heavenly Father.

SORROWFUL MYSTERIES

FIRST SORROWFUL MYSTERY

THE AGONY IN THE GARDEN

"Pray that you may not enter into temptation." And Peter fell asleep. And the other apostles. And you, little friend, fell asleep . . . and I too was another sleepy-headed Peter.

Jesus, alone and sad, suffers and soaks the earth with his blood.

Kneeling on the hard ground, he perseveres in prayer. . . . He weeps for you . . . and for me. The weight of the sins of men overwhelms him.

Pater, si vis, transfer calicem istum a me: "Father, if you are willing, remove this cup from me. . . . Yet not my will, but yours be done" (Lk 22:42).

An angel from heaven comforts him. Jesus is in agony. He continues *prolixius*, praying more intensely. . . . He comes over to us and finds us asleep: "Rise," he says again, "and pray that you may not enter into temptation" (Lk 22:46).

Judas the traitor: a kiss. Peter's sword gleams in the night. Jesus speaks: "Have you come out as against a robber, with swords and clubs to capture me?" (Mk 14:48).

We are cowards: we follow him from afar—but awake and praying. Prayer. . . . Prayer. . . .

SECOND SORROWFUL MYSTERY

THE SCOURGING AT THE PILLAR

Pilate speaks: "It is your custom that I release one prisoner to you at the Passover. Whom shall I set free: Barabbas—a thief jailed with others for murder—or Jesus?" (Mt 27:17). The crowd, spurred on by their rulers, cry: "Put this man to death and release Barabbas" (Lk 23:18).

Pilate speaks again: "What shall I do, then, with Jesus who is called Christ?" (Mt 27:22). *Crucifige eum:* "Crucify him!" (Mk 15:14).

Pilate, for the third time, says to them: "Why, what evil has he done? I have found in him no crime deserving death" (Lk 23:22).

The clamor of the mob grows louder: "Crucify him; Crucify him!" (Mk 15:14).

And Pilate, wanting to please the crowd, releases Barabbas to them and orders Jesus to be scourged.

Bound to the pillar. Covered with wounds.

The blows of the lash sound upon his torn flesh, upon his undefiled flesh, which suffers for your sinful flesh. More blows. More fury. Still more. . . . It is a last extreme of human cruelty.

Finally, exhausted, they untie Jesus. And the body of Christ yields to pain and falls limp, broken and half dead.

You and I cannot speak. Words are not needed. Look at him, look at him . . . slowly. After this . . . can you ever fear penance?

THIRD SORROWFUL MYSTERY

THE CROWNING WITH THORNS

Our King's eagerness for suffering has been fully satisfied! They lead my Lord to the courtyard of the palace, and there call together the whole troop (Mk 15:16). The brutal soldiers strip his most pure body. They drape a dirty purple rag about Jesus. They place a reed, as a scepter, in his right hand.

The crown of thorns, driven in by blows, makes him a mock king. . . . *Ave, Rex Iudæorum:* "Hail, King of the Jews!" (Mk 15:18). And with their blows they wound his head. And they strike him . . . and spit on him.

Crowned with thorns and clothed in rags of purple, Jesus is shown to the Jewish crowd. *Ecce Homo:* "Here is the man!" And again the chief priests and their attendants raise the cry, saying, "Crucify him! Crucify him!" (Jn 19:5-6).

You and I . . . haven't we crowned him anew with thorns and struck him and spat on him?

Never again, Jesus, never again. . . . And a firm and practical resolution marks the end of these ten Hail Marys.

FOURTH SORROWFUL MYSTERY

THE CARRYING OF THE CROSS

Carrying his cross, Jesus goes out of the city to the place of the skulls—called Golgotha in Hebrew (Jn 19:17). And they lay hold of a certain Simon from Cyrene, who is coming in from the country; and they make him take the cross and carry it behind Jesus (Lk 23:26).

The prophecy of Isaiah (53:12) is being fulfilled—*cum sceleratis reputatus est* ("he was counted among the wicked")—for two others are being led out with him to be put to death (Lk 23:32).

If anyone would follow me. . . . Little friend, we are sad, living the Passion of our Lord Jesus. See how lovingly he embraces the cross. Learn from him. Jesus carries the cross for you: You . . . carry it for Jesus.

But don't drag the cross. . . .Carry it squarely on your shoulder, because your cross, if you carry it so, will not be just any cross. . . . It will be the holy cross. Don't carry your cross with resignation: resignation is not a generous word. Love the cross. When you really love it, your cross will be . . . a Cross without a cross.

And, surely, you will find Mary on the way, just as Jesus did.

FIFTH SORROWFUL MYSTERY

THE CRUCIFIXION AND DEATH
OF OUR LORD

For Jesus of Nazareth, King of the Jews, the throne of triumph is ready. You and I do not see him writhe on being nailed. Suffering all that can be suffered, he spreads his arms in the gesture of an Eternal Priest. . . .

The soldiers take his holy garments and divide them into four parts. In order not to tear the tunic, they cast lots to decide whose it shall be. And so, once more, the words of Scripture are fulfilled: "They parted my garments among them, and for my clothes they cast lots" (Jn 19:23-24).

Now he is on high. . . . And close to her Son, at the foot of the cross, stand Mary . . . and Mary, the wife of Cleophas, and Mary Magdalene. And John, the disciple Jesus loved. *Ecce Mater tua:* "Behold your mother": he gives us his mother to be ours.

Earlier, they had offered him wine mixed with vinegar, and, when he had tasted it, he would not drink it (Mt 27:34).

Now, he thirsts . . . for love, for souls.

Consummatum est: "It is accomplished" (Jn 19:30).

Foolish child, look: All this . . . He has suffered it all for you. . . . And for me. Can you keep from crying?

GLORIOUS MYSTERIES

FIRST GLORIOUS MYSTERY

THE RESURRECTION

When the Sabbath was over, Mary of Magdala and Mary, the mother of James, and Salome, bought spices with which to anoint the dead body of Jesus. It is very early on the following day; just as the sun is rising, they come to the tomb (Mk 16:1-2). And upon entering it they are dismayed, for they cannot find the body of our Lord. A youth, clothed in white, says to them: "Do not be afraid. I know that you seek Jesus of Nazareth. *Non est hic, surrexit enim sicut dixit:* He is not here; for he has risen, as he said" (Mt 28:5).

He has risen! Jesus has risen: he is not in the tomb. Life has overcome death.

He appears to his most holy mother. He appears to Mary Magdalene, who is carried away by love. And to Peter and the rest of the apostles. And to you and me, who are his disciples and more in love than Mary Magdalene. The things we say to him! May we never die through sin; may our spiritual resurrection be eternal. And, before the decade is over, you kiss the wounds in his feet, . . . and I, more daring—because I am more a child—place my lips upon his open side.

SECOND GLORIOUS MYSTERY

THE ASCENSION

Now the Master is teaching his disciples: he has opened their minds to understand the Scriptures, and he appoints them witnesses of his life and his miracles, of his passion and death, and of the glory of his resurrection (Lk 24:45 and 48).

Then he brings them out as far as the outskirts of Bethany and blesses them. And as he does so, he withdraws from them and is carried up to heaven (Lk 24:51) until a cloud takes him out of sight (Acts 1:9).

Jesus has gone to the Father. Two angels in white approach us and say, "Men of Galilee, why do you stand looking up to heaven?" (Acts 1:11).

Peter and the others go back to Jerusalem *cum gaudio magno:* "with great joy" (Lk 24:52). It is fitting that the sacred humanity of Christ should receive the homage, praise, and adoration of all the hierarchies of the angels and of all the legions of the blessed in heaven.

But you and I feel like orphans: we are sad, and we go to Mary for consolation.

THIRD GLORIOUS MYSTERY

THE DESCENT OF THE HOLY SPIRIT

our Lord had said: "I shall ask the Father, and he will give you another Advocate, another Consoler, to be with you for ever" (Jn 14:16). The disciples are gathered together in one room, when suddenly they hear what sounds like a powerful wind from heaven, the noise of which fills the entire house where they are assembled. At the same time something appears that seems like tongues of fire; these separate and come to rest on the head of each of them (Acts 2:1-3).

The apostles are so filled with the Holy Spirit that they seem to be drunk (Acts 2:13).

Then Peter stands up with the Eleven and addresses the people in a loud voice. We, people from a hundred nations, hear him. Each of us hears him in his own language—you and I in ours. He speaks to us of Christ Jesus and of the Holy Spirit and of the Father.

Peter is neither stoned nor thrown into prison. Of those who have heard him, three thousand are converted and baptized.

You and I, after helping the apostles administer Baptism, bless God the Father for his Son Jesus, and we, too, feel drunk with the Holy Spirit.

FOURTH GLORIOUS MYSTERY

THE ASSUMPTION

Assumpta est Maria in cælum: gaudent angeli. God has taken Mary, body and soul, to heaven; and the angels rejoice!

So sings the Church. And so, with that same cry of joy, we begin our contemplation in this decade of the Holy Rosary.

The Mother of God has fallen asleep. Around her bed are the twelve apostles (Matthias in the place of Judas).

And we also, through a grace respected by all, are at her side.

But Jesus wants to have his mother, body and soul, in heaven. And the heavenly court, arrayed in all its splendor, greets our Lady. You and I—children, after all—take the train of Mary's magnificent blue cloak, and thus we are able to watch the marvelous scene.

The most blessed Trinity receives and showers honors on the Daughter, Mother and Spouse of God. . . . And so great is the Lady's majesty that the angels exclaim: Who is she?

FIFTH GLORIOUS MYSTERY

THE CORONATION OF THE BLESSED VIRGIN

You are completely fair, and without blemish. You are a garden enclosed, my sister, my Bride, an enclosed garden, a sealed fountain. *"Veni, coronaberis":* "Come, you shall be crowned" (Song of Songs 4:7, 12, 8).

If you and I had been able, we too would have made her Queen and Lady of all creation.

"A great sign appeared in heaven: a woman with a crown of twelve stars upon her head, adorned with the sun and the moon at her feet" (Rev 12:1). Mary, Virgin without stain, has made up for the fall of Eve; she has crushed the head of hell's serpent with her immaculate heel. Daughter of God, Mother of God, Spouse of God.

The Father, the Son, and the Holy Spirit crown her as the rightful Empress of the Universe.

And the angels pay her homage as her subjects . . . and the patriarchs and prophets and apostles . . . and the martyrs and confessors and virgins and all the saints . . . and all sinners, including you and me.

SALVE REGINA

Salve, Regína, mater misericórdiæ;
vita, dulcédo, et spes nostra, salve.
Ad te clamámus, éxsules fílii Evæ.
Ad te suspirámus, geméntes et flentes
in hac lacrimárum valle.
Eia ergo, advocáta nostra,
illos tuos misericórdes óculos
ad nos convérte.
Et Iesum, benedíctum fructum ventris tui,
nobis post hoc exsílium osténde.
O clemens, O pia, O dulcis Virgo María.
V. Ora pro nobis sancta Dei Génetrix.
R. **Ut digni efficiámur promissiónibus Christi.**

Oremus.
Omnípotens sempitérne Deus, qui gloriósæ Vírginis
Matris Maríæ corpus et ánimam, ut dignum Fílii tui
habitáculum effíci mererétur, Spíritu Sancto cooperánte, præparásti: da, ut cuius commemoratióne
lætámur, eius pia intercessióne, ab instántibus malis
et a morte perpétua liberémur. Per eúndem Christum Dóminum nostrum. R. **Amen.**

V. Divínum auxílium máneat semper nobíscum.
R. **Amen.**

HAIL HOLY QUEEN

Generally, this prayer is divided into three parts. In the first part, the soul greets the Mother of God, invoking her mercy. In the second, the soul repeats the greeting and, in the name of all people, calls to holy Mary, whom we beg to look upon us with eyes of mercy and to love us with her son, Jesus. In the third, the soul proclaims the greatest and most fundamental title (epithet) of its intercessor—that is, Mother of God.

Hail, holy Queen, mother of mercy,
our life, our sweetness, and our hope.
To you do we cry,
poor, banished children of Eve.
To you do we send up our sighs,
mourning and weeping in this valley of tears.
Turn then, most gracious advocate,
your eyes of mercy toward us,
and after this exile
show unto us the blessed fruit of your womb, Jesus.
O clement, O loving, O sweet Virgin Mary.

V. Pray for us, O holy Mother of God.

R. That we may be made worthy of the promises of Christ.

Let us pray.

Almighty and everlasting God, by the cooperation of the Holy Spirit you prepared the body and soul of Mary, glorious Virgin and Mother, to become the worthy habitation of your Son; grant that by her gracious intercession, in whose commemoration we rejoice, we may be delivered from present evils and from everlasting death. Through the same Christ our Lord. **R. Amen.**

V. May the divine assistance remain with us always.

R. Amen.

MEMORARE

Memoráre, o piísima Virgo María, non esse audítum a saéculo, quemquam ad tua curréntem præsídia, tua implorántem auxília, tua peténtem suffrágia esse derelíctum. Ego tali animátus confidéntia ad te, Virgo Vírginum, Mater, curro; ad te vénio; coram te gemens peccátor assísto. Noli, Mater Verbi, verba mea despícere, sed audi propítia et exáudi. Amen.

ALMA REDEMPTORIS MATER

HERMANN THE LAME

Alma Redemptóris Mater
quæ pérvia cæli porta manes, et stella maris,
   succúrre cadénti.

Súrgere qui curat, pópulo: tu quæ genuísti,
   natúra mochránte, tuum sanctum Genitórem,

Virgo prius ac postérius, Gabriélis ab ore
   sumens illud ave, peccatórum miserére.

AVE REGÍNA CÆLORUM

Ave, Regína cælórum,
ave, Dómina angelórum,
salve, radix, salve, porta,
ex qua mundo lux est orta.
Gaude, Virgo gloriósa,
super omnes speciósa;
vale, o valde decóra
et pro nobis Christum exóra.

THE MEMORARE

The Memorare, a prayer attributed to St. Bernard of Clairvaux, is one of the best prayers expressing our confidence in the Blessed Virgin Mary.

Remember, O most gracious Virgin Mary, that never was it known that anyone who fled to your protection, implored your help, or sought your intercession was left unaided. Inspired with this confidence, I fly unto you, O Virgin of virgins, my Mother. To you I come, before you I stand, sinful and sorrowful. O Mother of the Word incarnate, despise not my petitions, but in your mercy hear and answer me. Amen.

LOVING MOTHER OF THE REDEEMER

ATTR. TO HERMANN THELAME

Loving Mother of the Redeemer,
gate of heaven, star of the sea,
assist your people who have fallen,
    as we strive to rise again.
To the wonderment of nature,
    you bore your Creator,
yet remained a virgin after as before.
You who received Gabriel's joyful greeting,
have pity on us poor sinners.

HAIL, O QUEEN OF HEAVEN

Hail, O Queen of Heaven enthroned!
Hail, by angels mistress owned,
Root of Jesse! Gate of morn!
Whence the world's true light was born:
Glorious Virgin, joy to thee,
Loveliest whom in heaven they see.
Fairest thou where all are fair!
Plead with Christ our sins to spare.

STABAT MATER DOLOROSA

Stabat Mater dolorósa
Iuxta crucem lacrimósa,
Dum pendébat Fílius.

Cuius ánimam geméntem,
Contristátam et doléntem,
Pertransívit gládius.

O quam tristis et afflícta
Fuit illa Benedícta
Mater Unigéniti!

Quæ mærébat, et dolébat,
Pia Mater, dum vidébat
Nati pœnas ínclyti.

Quis est homo, qui non fleret,
Matrem Christi si vidéret
In tanto supplício?

Quis non posset contristári,
Christi Matrem contemplári
Doléntem cum Fílio?

Pro peccátis suæ gentis
Vidit Iesum in torméntis,
Et flagéllis súbditum.

Vidit suum dulcem natum
Moriéndo desolátum,
Dum emísit spíritum.

Eia Mater, fons amóris,
Me sentíre vim dolóris
Fac, ut tecum lúgeam.

Fac, ut árdeat cor meum
In amándo Christum Deum,
Ut sibi compláceam.

AT THE CROSS HER STATION KEEPING

At the cross, her station keeping,
stood the mournful mother weeping,
close to Jesus to the last.

Through her heart, his sorrow sharing,
all his bitter anguish bearing,
now at length the sword had passed.

Oh, how sad and sore distressed
was that mother highly blessed
of the sole begotten One!

Christ above in torment hangs,
she beneath beholds the pangs
of her dying, glorious Son.

Is there one who would not weep,
whelmed in miseries so deep,
Christ's dear mother to behold?

Can the human heart refrain
from partaking in her pain,
in that mother's pain untold?

Bruised, derided, cursed, defiled,
she beheld her tender Child,
all with bloody scourges rent.

For the sins of his own nation
saw him hang in desolation
till his spirit forth he sent.

O sweet mother! font of love,
touch my spirit from above,
make my heart with yours accord.

Make me feel as you have felt;
make my soul to glow and melt
with the love of Christ, my Lord.

Sancta Mater, istud agas,
Crucifíxi fige plagas
Cordi meo válide.

Tui nati vulneráti,
Tam dignáti pro me pati,
Pœnas mecum dívide.

Fac me tecum pie flere,
Crucifíxo condolére,
Donec ego víxero.

Iuxta crucem tecum stare,
Et me tibi sociáre
In planctu desídero.

Virgo vírginum præclára,
Mihi iam non sis amára:
Fac me tecum plángere.

Fac, ut portem Christi mortem,
Passiónis fac consórtem,
Et plagas recólere.

Fac me plagis vulnerári,
Fac me cruce inebriári,
Et cruóre Fílii.

Flammis urar ne succénsus,
Per te, Virgo, sim defénsus
In die iudícii.

Christe, cum sit hinc exíre,
Da per Matrem me veníre
Ad palmam victóriæ.

Quando corpus moriétur,
Fac, ut ánimæ donétur
Paradísi glória.
Amen. (T. P. Allelúia.)

Holy mother, pierce me through,
in my heart each wound renew
of my Savior crucified.

Let me share with you his pain,
who for all our sins was slain,
who for me in torments died.

Let me mingle tears with you,
mourning him who mourned for me,
all the days that I may live .

By the cross with you to stay,
there with you to weep and pray,
is all I ask of you to give.

Virgin of all virgins blest!
Listen to my fond request:
let me share your grief divine.

Let me to my latest breath,
in my body bear the death
of that dying Son of yours.

Wounded with his every wound,
steep my soul till it has swooned
in his very blood away.

Be to me, O Virgin, nigh,
lest in flames I burn and die,
in his awful judgment day.

Christ, when you shall call me hence,
be your mother my defense,
be your cross my victory.

While my body here decays,
may my soul your goodness praise,
safe in heaven eternally.
Amen. (Easter Time Alleluia.)

CONSECRATION TO THE BLESSED VIRGIN

My queen and my mother, I give myself entirely to you and, in proof of my affection, I give you my eyes, my ears, my tongue, my heart, my whole being without reserve. Since I am your own, keep me and guard me as your property and possession. Amen.

BLESSED BE YOUR PURITY

Purity is an eminently positive virtue, which gains the grace of God for the person who lives it. It is the virtue of the beautiful and spotless soul. It elevates us to things divine. These ten verses praise Mary. Conceived without sin, she was always pure and brighter than snow.

Blessed be your purity,
May it be blessed for ever,
For no less than God takes delight
In such exalted beauty.
To you, heavenly Princess,
Holy Virgin Mary,
I offer on this day
My whole heart, life, and soul.
Look upon me with compassion;
Do not leave me, my mother.

BLESSING AND IMPOSITION
WITH THE SCAPULAR OF
OUR LADY OF MOUNT CARMEL

There is a decree issued by Pope Paul V in 1613 stating the importance of wearing this scapular: "It is permitted to preach that the Blessed Virgin will help by her continued assistance and her merits, particularly on Saturdays, the souls of the members of the Scapular Confraternity who have died in the grace of God, if in life they had worn the scapular, observed chastity according with their state of life, and recited the Office of the Blessed Virgin Mary."

The imposition is done with a scapular of wool. Afterwards, a scapular medal could be worn. The requirements of this devotion are:

- To receive the imposition of the scapular and to wear it habitually.
- To guard one's chastity.
- To pray daily the Little Office of the Blessed Virgin. It could be substituted by praying three Hail Marys; or seven Our Fathers with Hail Mary and Glory Be; or the Divine Office.

The person who is to receive the scapular kneels, and the priest, vested in surplice and white stole, says:

V. Lord, show us your kindness and mercy.

R. **And grant us your salvation.**

V. Lord, hear my prayer.

R. **And let my cry come to you.**

V. The Lord be with you.

R. **And also with you.**

Let us pray.

O Lord Jesus Christ, Savior of mankind, by your right hand sanctify this scapular, which your servant will devotedly wear for the love of you and of your mother, the Blessed Virgin Mary of Mount

Carmel. By her intercession, may he (she) be protected from the wickedness of the enemy and persevere in your grace until death. You who live and reign for ever and ever.

R. Amen.

Then the priest sprinkles the scapular with holy water and imposes it upon the person (or upon each person), saying:

Receive this blessed scapular and ask the most holy Virgin that, by her merits, it may be worn with no stain of sin and may protect you from all harm and bring you into everlasting life.

R. Amen.

After this the priest adds:

By the power granted to me, I admit you to a share in all the spiritual works performed with the merciful help of Jesus Christ by the religious of Mount Carmel. In the name of the Father, and of the Son, and of the Holy Spirit.

R. Amen.

May almighty God, Creator of heaven and earth, bless you, whom he has been pleased to receive into the Confraternity of the Blessed Virgin Mary of Mount Carmel. We beg her to crush the head of the ancient serpent in the hour of your death and to obtain for you the palm and the crown of your everlasting inheritance. Through Christ our Lord.

R. Amen.

The priest sprinkles the person with holy water. For several persons, the prayers are said in the plural.

If the scapular is to be blessed alone, then the blessing begins with **Lord, show us your kindness and mercy** (p. 479), and concludes with the prayer **O Lord Jesus Christ**.

PRAYER TO OUR LADY OF GUADALUPE

JOHN PAUL II

In January 1979, his Holiness, pope John Paul II, in the first year of his pontificate, made the first of a long series of pastoral visits. He went to Mexico and presided over the Conference in Puebla. He visited the shrine of our Lady of Guadalupe in the new basilica built in her honor. There, in the presence of all the bishops of America, the holy Father addressed this prayer to the Blessed Virgin Mary.

O Immaculate Virgin, mother of the true God and mother of the Church! You, who from this place revealed your clemency and your pity to all those who ask for your protection, hear the prayer that we address to you with filial trust, and present it to your Son Jesus, our sole Redeemer.

Mother of mercy, teacher of hidden and silent sacrifice, to you, who come to meet us sinners, we dedicate on this day all our being and all our love. We also dedicate to you our life, our work, our joys, our infirmities, and our sorrows.

Grant peace, justice, and prosperity to our peoples, for we entrust to your care all that we have and all that we are, our lady and mother.

We wish to be entirely yours and to walk with you along the way of complete faithfulness to Jesus Christ in his Church: hold us always with your loving hand.

Virgin of Guadalupe, Mother of the Americas, we pray to you for all the bishops, that they may lead the faithful along paths of intense Christian life, of love and humble service of God and souls.

Contemplate this immense harvest, and intercede with the Lord that he may instill a hunger for holi-

ness in the whole People of God and grant abundant
vocations of priests and religious, strong in the faith
and zealous dispensers of God's mysteries.

Gain for our homes the grace of loving and respecting life in its beginnings with the same love with
which you conceived in your womb the life of the
Son of God. Blessed Virgin Mary, Mother of Fair
Love, protect our families, so that they may always
be united, and bless the upbringing of our children.

Our hope, look upon us with compassion, teach us
to go continually to Jesus, and if we fall, help us to
rise again, to return to him, by means of the confession of our faults and sins in the sacrament of Penance, which gives peace to the soul. We beg you to
grant us a great love for all the holy sacraments,
which are, as it were, the signs that your Son left us
on earth.

Thus, most holy mother, with the peace of God in
our conscience, with our hearts free from evil and
hatred, we will be able to bring to all true joy and
true peace, which come to us from your Son, our
Lord Jesus Christ, who, with God the Father and the
Holy Spirit, lives and reigns for ever and ever.
Amen.

MONTH OF MARY
(May Devotions)

*"God wills that all his gifts should come
to us through Mary"* (St. Bernard)

It was in Rome, towards the end of the eighteenth century, one fine evening in May. A child of the poor gathered his companions around him and led them to a statue of Mary, before which a lamp was burning, as is the custom in that holy city. There, these fresh young voices sang the Litany of our Lady. The next day, the little group, followed by other children, again gathered at the feet of the Mother of God. Next came their mothers, to join the little assembly. Soon, other groups were formed, and the devotion rapidly became popular. Holy souls, troubled by the disorderly conduct which always increases and becomes graver at the return of the pleasant springtime, saw in these growing practices the hand of God, and they cooperated with the designs of Providence by approving and promoting this new devotion, as a public and solemn act of reparation. The Month of Mary was founded.[5]

"This is the month in which, in the churches and individual homes, the most affectionate and fervent homage of prayers and devotions from the hearts of Christians is raised to Mary. It is also the month in which from his throne descend upon us the most generous and abundant gifts of the Divine Mercy."[6]

In our own times, we Catholics, wanting to be close to her always, offer her special presents in May: pilgrimages, visits to churches dedicated to her, little sacrifices in her honor, periods of study and well-finished work offered up to her, and a more attentive recitation of the rosary.

5. Cf. A Carthusian, *A Month with Mary,* London: Burns and Oates, 1950.
6. Paul VI, *The Month of Mary,1967.*

MARIAN READINGS

May 1
MARY: THE MOTHER OF GOD

"When the Blessed Virgin said yes, freely, to the plans revealed to her by the Creator, the divine Word assumed a human nature—a rational soul and a body—which was formed in the most pure womb of Mary. The divine nature and the human were united in a single Person: Jesus Christ, true God and, thenceforth, true man; the only-begotten and eternal Son of the Father and from that moment on, as man, the true Son of Mary. This is why our Lady is the mother of the Incarnate Word, of the second Person of the Blessed Trinity, who has united our human nature to himself for ever, without any confusion of the two natures. The greatest praise we can give to the Blessed Virgin is to address her loudly and clearly by the name that expresses her very highest dignity: 'Mother of God'."[7]

Let us offer to our Mother today:

Brief but frequent prayers of love, such as:
"Mother of God, your petitions are most powerful."

May 2

MARY: THE MOST PERFECT CREATURE

"She who is full of grace, the object of God's pleasure, exalted above all the angels and the saints, lived an ordinary life.

---

7. This excerpt and the following thirty excerpts are taken from homilies of Blessed Josemaría Escrivá in *Christ Is Passing By* (=CPB) and *Friends of God*(=FG), Princeton, N. J.: Scepter Publications, 1968/1973. This one is from "Mother of God and Our Mother," FG, 274.

"Mary is as much a creature as we are, with a heart like ours, made for joy and mirth as well as suffering and tears. Before Gabriel communicates to her God's plan, our Lady does not know that she has been chosen from all eternity to be the mother of the Messiah. She sees herself as a lowly creature. That is why she can acknowledge, with full humility, that 'he who is mighty has done great things' for her."[8]

Let us offer to our Mother today:

Many glances of affection and many words of love,
when we see her image or picture in our home,
in the church, or anywhere.

May 3

MARY AND THE BLESSED TRINITY

"Through the Incarnation of our Lord in her immaculate womb, Mary, the Daughter of God the Father, is also the Spouse of God the Holy Spirit and the Mother of God the Son."[9]

Let us offer to our Mother today:

A "Hail Mary" each time the clock strikes another hour.

May 4

MARY'S FAMILY: THE TRINITY ON EARTH

"It is only natural that the Church rejoice as it contemplates the modest home of Jesus, Mary, and Joseph. We read in the hymn from Matins on the feast of the holy Family: 'It is pleasing to recall the humble house of Nazareth and its slender resources. It is pleasing to tell again in song Jesus' hidden life.

---

8. "Cause of Our Joy," CPB, 172.
9. "Mother of God and Our Mother," FG, 274.

Jesus grows up in hidden seclusion, to be trained in Joseph's unpretentious trade. The loving mother sits beside her dear Son, the good wife by her husband, content if her loving attention can ease and comfort them in their weariness.'"[10]

Let us offer to our Mother today:
A loving review of her life with Jesus,
as we recite the Joyful Mysteries of the Rosary.

May 5

MARY: HER IMMACULATE CONCEPTION

"How would we have acted, if we could have chosen our own mother? I'm sure we would have chosen the one we have, adorning her with every possible grace. That is what Christ did. Christ being all-powerful, all-wise, Love itself, his power carried out his Will. . . . This is the clearest reason why our Lord granted his mother , from the very moment of her Immaculate Conception, all possible privileges. She was free from the power of Satan. She is beautiful, spotless and pure in soul and body."[11]

Let us offer to our Mother today:
The renewal of our baptismal vows.

May 6

THE ANNUNCIATION
MARY: THE FIRST TABERNACLE

"If you seek Mary, you will find Jesus. And you will learn a bit more about what is in the heart of God, who humbles himself, discarding all manifestations

---

10. "Marriage: a Christian Vocation," CPB, 22.
11. "Cause of Our Joy," CPB, 171.

of his power and majesty to take the form of a servant. Speaking in human terms, we could say that God outdoes himself, because he goes much further than he needs to go in order to save us. The only way to measure what he does is to say that it cannot be measured; it comes from a madness of love which leads him to take on our flesh and bear the weight of our sins."[12]

Let us offer to our Mother today:

The Angelus recited punctually
at noon and with great affection.

May 7

MARY: OUR MODEL IN ORDINARY LIFE

"We can't forget that Mary spent nearly every day of her life just like millions of other women who look after their families, bring up their children, and take care of their houses. Mary sanctifies the ordinary, everyday things—what some people wrongly regard as unimportant and insignificant: everyday work, looking after those closest to you, visits to friends and relatives. What a blessed ordinariness, that can be so full of love of God."[13]

Let us offer to our Mother today:

Affectionate details of service
and attention to those closest to us.

May 8

MARY: MOTHER OF CHRIST

"*Iesus Christus, Deus homo:* Jesus Christ, God-man. This is one of the 'mighty works of God,' which we

---

12. "To Jesus through Mary," CPB, 144.
13. "To Jesus through Mary," CPB, 148.

should reflect upon and thank him for. He has come to bring 'peace on earth to men of good will,' to all who want to unite their wills to the holy will of God—not just the rich, not just the poor, but everyone: all the brethren. We are all brothers in Jesus, children of God, brothers of Christ. His mother is our mother ."[14]

Let us offer to our Mother today:

Jesus himself, when we receive him in holy Communion.

May 9

MARY: WELCOMING THE SHEPHERDS

"You must look at the Child in the manger. He is our Love. Look at him, realizing that the whole thing is a mystery. We need to accept this mystery on faith and use our faith to explore it very deeply. To do this, we must have the humble attitude of a Christian soul."[15]

Let us offer to our Mother today:

Small hidden sacrifices,
especially those that go against the grain.

May 10

MARY: PRESENTING JESUS IN THE TEMPLE

"She teaches us to have charity. Remember the scene of the presentation of Jesus in the temple. An old man, Simeon, said to Mary, 'Behold: This child is destined to bring about the fall of many and the rise of many in Israel—and to be a sign, which people will refuse to acknowledge, so that the thoughts of many hearts shall be made manifest. As for your

---

14. "Christ Triumphs through Humility," CPB, 13.
15. "Christ Triumphs through Humility," CPB, 13.

own soul, it shall have a sword pierce it.' So great is Mary's love for all mankind that she, too, fulfilled Christ's words: 'Greater love has no man than this, that he should lay down his life for his friends.'"[16]

Let us offer to our Mother today:

A pilgrimage to one of her shrines.

May 11

MARY: WELCOMING THE MAGI

"'Going into the house, they saw the child with Mary, his mother .' Our Lady is always near her Son. The Magi are not received by a king on a high throne, but by a child in the arms of his mother . Let us ask the Mother of God, who is our mother , to prepare for us the way that leads to the fullness of love. . . . Her sweet heart knows the surest path for finding Christ."[17]

Let us offer to our Mother today:

A visit to a poor person to communicate our Lady's concern for that person.

May 12

MARY: HER FLIGHT TO EGYPT WITH JOSEPH AND THE CHILD JESUS

"The mystery of Mary helps us to see that in order to approach God, we must become little. Christ said to his disciples: 'Believe me, unless you become like little children again, you shall not enter the kingdom of heaven.'

---

16. "Mother of God and Our Mother," FG, 287.
17. "The Epiphany of Our Lord," CPB, 38.

"To become children, we must renounce our pride and self-sufficiency, recognizing that we can do nothing by ourselves. We must realize that we need grace and the help of God our Father to find our way and keep to it."[18]

Let us offer to our Mother today:

*A visit to a lonely person to share
the joy of trusting in God alone.*

May 13

MARY: HER HIDDEN LIFE WITH JESUS

"I like to go back in my imagination to the years Jesus spent close to his mother , years which span almost the whole of his life on earth. I like to picture him as a little child, cared for by Mary, who kisses him and plays with him. I like to see him growing up before the loving eyes of his mother and of Joseph, his father on earth. What tenderness and care Mary and the holy Patriarch must have shown toward Jesus, as they looked after him during his childhood, all the while, silently, learning so much from him. Their souls would become more and more like the soul of that Son, who was both man and God. This is why his mother , and after her St. Joseph, understand better than anyone the feelings of the heart of Christ; and the two of them are thus the best way, I would say the only way, to reach the Savior."[19]

Let us offer to our Mother today:

*The effort of doing our ordinary work well,
on time, with competence and finesse.*

---

18. "To Jesus through Mary," CPB, 143.
19. "Mother of God and Our Mother," FG, 281.

May 14

MARY: LOSING AND FINDING
THE CHILD JESUS

"The Mother of God, who looked for her Son so anxiously when he was lost (through no fault of her own) and experienced such great joy in finding him, will help us retrace our steps and put right whatever may be necessary when, because of our carelessness or our sins, we have been unable to recognize Christ. With her help, we will know the happiness of holding him in our arms once more and telling him we will never lose him again."[20]

Let us offer to our Mother today:

A good, sincere, sorrowful confession of our sins and failures, in the sacrament of Penance.

May 15

MARY: AT CANA

"In the Gospel, St. John has recorded a wonderful phrase of our Lady. At the wedding of Cana she turned to the waiters and said: 'Do whatever he tells you.' That is what it is all about—getting people to face Jesus and ask him: 'Lord, what do you want me to do?'"[21]

Let us offer to our Mother today:

Prompt obedience, when we are called or asked to do some errand or some act of service.

---

20. "Mother of God and Our Mother," FG, 278.
21. "To Jesus through Mary," CPB, 149.

May 16

MARY: AT THE FOOT OF THE CROSS

"We find her on Calvary, at the foot of the cross, praying. This is nothing new for Mary. She has always acted like this, in fulfilling her duties and looking after her home. As she went about the things of this earth, she kept her attention on God."[22]

Let us offer to our Mother today:

An act of contrition, said many times, asking her to offer our sorrow for our sins to Jesus crucified.

May 17

MARY: THE SORROWING MOTHER

"Our Lady is there listening to the words of her Son, united to him in his suffering, when he cried out 'My God, my God, why have you forsaken me?' What could she do? She united herself fully with the redemptive love of her Son and offered to the Father her immense sorrow, which pierced her pure heart like a sharp-edged sword."[23]

Let us offer to our Mother today:

The mortification of keeping quiet about any pain or discomfort, any inconvenience or disappointment, uniting it with her pain as she stood by her crucified Son.

May 18

MARY: THE CO-REDEMPTRIX

"It is with good reason that the popes have called Mary Co-Redemptrix. 'So fully, in union with her

---

22. "A Life of Prayer," FG, 241.
23. "Mother of God and Our Mother," FG, 288.

suffering and dying Son, did she suffer and nearly die; so fully, for the sake of the salvation of all souls, did she abdicate the rights of a mother over her Son, and immolate him, insofar as it was in her power, to satisfy the justice of God, that it can rightly be said that she redeemed mankind together with Christ.' This gives us a deeper understanding of that moment in the Passion of our Lord on which we shall never tire of meditating: *Stabat autem iuxta crucem Iesu mater eius,* 'There, standing by the cross of Jesus, was his mother.'"[24]

Let us offer to our Mother today:

*Five small hidden sacrifices in honor of
the five major wounds of our Lord.*

May 19

MARY: HER FAITH

"If our faith is weak, we should turn to Mary. St. John tells us that it was because of the miracle that Christ performed, at his mother 's request, at the marriage feast at Cana, that 'his disciples learned to believe in him.' Our Mother is always interceding with her Son, so that he may attend to our needs and show himself to us in such a way that we can cry out, 'You are the Son of God!'"[25]

Let us offer to our Mother today:

*The "Memorare" for the person in our family
who most needs the help of our Lady.*

---

24. "Mother of God and Our Mother," FG, 287.
25. "Mother of God and Our Mother," FG, 285.

May 20

MARY: OUR HOPE

"Our Lady, a full participant in the work of our salvation, follows in the footsteps of her Son: the poverty of Bethlehem, the everyday work of a hidden life in Nazareth, the manifestation of his divinity in Cana of Galilee, the tortures of his passion, the divine sacrifice on the cross, the eternal blessedness of paradise.

"All of this affects us directly, because this supernatural itinerary is the way we are to follow. Mary shows us that we can walk this path with confidence. She has preceded us on the way of imitating Christ; her glorification is the firm hope of our own salvation. For these reasons we call her 'our hope, cause of our joy.'"[26]

Let us offer to our Mother today:

A smile when we do not feel like smiling.

May 21

MARY'S PRAYER

"Let us ask the Blessed Virgin to make us contemplatives, to teach us to recognize the constant calls from God at the door of our heart. Let us ask her now: Our Mother, you brought to earth Jesus, who reveals the love of our Father God. Help us to recognize him in the midst of the cares of each day. Stir up our mind and will so that we may listen to the voice of God, to the calls of grace."[27]

Let us offer to our Mother today:

A visit to Jesus truly present in the Blessed Sacrament.

---

26. "Cause of Our Joy," CPB, 176.
27. "Cause of Our Joy," CPB, 174.

May 22
MARY: EVER VIRGIN

"The purity, humility, and generosity of Mary are in sharp contrast to our wretchedness and selfishness. To the extent that we realize this, we should feel moved to imitate her. We too are creatures of God, and if we strive to imitate her fidelity, God will surely do great things in us. Our small worth is no obstacle, because God chooses what is of little value so that the power of his love may be more manifest."[28]

Let us offer to our Mother today:

The prayer "Blessed be your purity" (p. 478).

May 23
MARY: QUEEN OF THE APOSTLES

"If we take our Lady's hand, she will make us realize more fully that all men are our brothers—because we are all sons of that God whose daughter, spouse, and mother she is. Our neighbors' problems must be our problems. Christian fraternity should be something very deep in the soul, so that we are indifferent to no one. Mary, who brought up Jesus and accompanied him through his life and is now beside him in heaven, will help us recognize Jesus as he crosses our path and makes himself present to us in the needs of others."[29]

Let us offer to our Mother today:

A kind word, a friendly conversation,
a helping hand to persons with whom we live or work.

---

28. "Cause of Our Joy," CPB, 172.
29. "To Jesus through Mary," CPB, 145.

May 24
MARY: HELP OF CHRISTIANS

"Yes, we are still pilgrims, but our Mother has gone on ahead, where she points to the reward for our efforts. She tells us that we can make it. AI we are faithful, we will reach home. Not only is the Blessed Virgin our model, but she is also the Help of Christians. And as we besiege her with our petitions— 'Show that you are our Mother'—she cannot help but watch over her children with motherly care."[30]

Let us offer to our Mother today:

In addition to the mysteries of the day, one more part (five decades) of the Holy Rosary.

May 25
MARY: OUR MOTHER

"Find out for yourself by personal experience the meaning of Mary's maternal love. It is not enough just to know that she is *our* Mother, and to think and talk about her as such. She is *your* Mother and you are her child. She loves you as if you were her only child in this world. Treat her accordingly. Tell her about everything that happens to you; honor her and love her. No one will do it for you or as well as you."[31]

Let us offer to our Mother today:

Many affectionate thoughts and prayers, by saying "Mary, my mother" each time we pause in our work.

---

30. "Cause of our Joy," CPB, 177.
31. "Mother of God and our Mother," FG, 293.

May 26
MARY: THE WAY TO JESUS

"Mary does the immense favor of bringing to the cross, of placing face to face with the example of the Son of God, those who come close to her and contemplate her life. It is in this confrontation that Christian life is decided. And here Mary intercedes for us so that our behavior may lead to a reconciliation of the younger brother—you and me—with the firstborn Son of the Father.

"Many conversions, many decisions to give oneself to the service of God have been preceded by an encounter with Mary. Our Lady has encouraged us to look for God, to desire to change, to lead a new life."[32]

Let us offer to our Mother today:

Teaching someone how to say the Holy Rosary.

May 27
MARY: MOTHER OF FAIR LOVE

"This is what explains Mary's life—her love. A complete love, so complete that she forgets herself and is happy just to be there where God wants her, fulfilling with care what God wants her to do. That is why even her slightest action is never routine or vain but, rather, full of meaning. Mary, our Mother, is for us both an example and a way. In the ordinary circumstances in which God wants us to live, we have to try to be like her."[33]

Let us offer to our Mother today:

The resolution to say,
before going to sleep every night, three Hail Marys.

---

32. "To Jesus through Mary," CPB, 149.
33. "To Jesus through Mary," CPB, 148.

May 28

THE ASSUMPTION
MARY: TAKEN UP TO HEAVEN

"Mary has gone to heaven in both body and soul, and the angels rejoice. I can imagine, too, the delight of St. Joseph, her most chaste spouse, who awaited her in paradise. Yet what of us who remain on earth? Our faith tells us that here below, in our present life, we are pilgrims, wayfarers. Our lot is one of suffering, of sacrifices, and privations. Nonetheless, joy must mark the rhythm of our steps. 'Serve the Lord with joy'—there is no other way to serve him."[34]

Let us offer to our Mother today:

A smile when someone corrects us or misjudges us.

May 29

MARY: THE QUEEN OF HEAVEN

"She lives now and is protecting us. She is there [in heaven], body and soul, with the Father and the Son and the Holy Spirit. She is the same person who was born in Palestine, who gave herself to God while still a child, who received the message from St. Gabriel the Archangel, who gave birth to our Savior, and who stood beside him at the foot of the Cross. In her, all ideals become a reality. But we should never think that this sublime greatness of hers makes her inaccessible to us. She is the one who is full of grace and the sum of all perfections . . . and she is also our Mother."[35]

Let us offer to our Mother today:

The "Hail Holy Queen" at each hour.

---

34. "Cause of our Joy," CPB, 177.
35. "Mother of God and our Mother," FG, 292.

May 30

MARY: THE CHANNEL OF GRACE

"Her power before God is such that she can obtain anything that we ask for, and, like any mother, she wants to answer our prayers. Like any mother, also, she knows and understands our weaknesses. She encourages us and makes excuses for us. She makes the way easy for us, and even when we think there is no possible solution for our worry, she always has one ready to offer us."[36]

Let us offer to our Mother today:

A visit or a conversation with a friend or relative whom we want to encourage to go to Confession.

May 31

THE VISITATION
MARY SINGS OF THE LOVE OF GOD

"God is interested in even the smallest events in the lives of his creatures—in your affairs and mine—and he calls each of us by name. This certainty that the faith gives enables us to look at everything in a new light. And everything, while remaining exactly the same, becomes different, because it is an expression of God's love. Our life is turned into a continuous prayer, we find ourselves with good humor and a peace that never ends, and everything we do is an act of thanksgiving running through all our day. 'My soul magnifies the Lord,' Mary sang, 'and my spirit rejoices in God, my Savior.'"[37]

Let us offer to our Mother today:

The Holy Rosary said with concentration and affection.

---

36. "Mother of God and Our Mother," FG, 292.
37. "To Jesus through Mary," CPB, 144.

NOVENA TO
THE IMMACULATE CONCEPTION

Pope Pius IX formally instituted the celebration of
the Immaculate Conception when he proclaimed
this dogma on December 8, 1854. Affirming the
constant faith of the Church, he expressed in that
definition the exact meaning of the truth of Mary's
Immaculate Conception: that she was conceived
free from the stain of original sin. This feast has
been celebrated in the East, and also in many places
in the West, since the eighth century. This privilege
of Mary is the most beautiful fruit of her Son's Redemption. Chosen as mother of the Savior, Mary
received the benefits of salvation from the moment
of her conception. Christ came to take away the sin
of mankind; he did not allow it to contaminate
Mary. The sanctity of our Blessed Mother is a
model for all Christians. We seek her intercession
that we may be rid of our sins and achieve sanctity.

FIRST DAY

(NOVEMBER 30)

Mary, the new Eve

Introductory Prayer

Lord God,
may our gifts be sanctified by the Holy Spirit,
who formed the Blessed Virgin Mary
to be a new creation
and sent down upon her
the dew of heavenly grace,
so that her womb might bear
    the fruit of our salvation,
Jesus Christ, your Son,
who lives and reigns for ever and ever. Amen.

Reading   Gn 3:1-6, 13-15

The serpent was more subtle than any other wild creature that the Lord God had made. He said to the woman, "Did God say, 'You shall not eat of any tree of the garden'?" And the woman said to the serpent, "We may eat of the fruit of the trees of the garden; but God said, 'You shall not eat of the fruit of the tree which is in the midst of the garden; neither shall you touch it, lest you die.'"

But the serpent said to the woman, "You will not die. For God knows that when you eat of it your eyes will be opened, and you will be like God, knowing good and evil." So when the woman saw that the tree was good for food, and that it was a delight to the eyes, and that the tree was to be desired to make one wise, she took of its fruit and ate; and she also gave some to her husband, and he ate.

Then the Lord God said to the woman, "What is this that you have done?" The woman said, "The serpent beguiled me, and I ate." The Lord God said to the serpent,

"Because you have done this,
cursed are you above all cattle,
and above all wild animals;
upon your belly you shall go,
and dust you shall eat all the days of your life.
I will put enmity between you and the woman,
and between your seed and her seed;
he shall bruise your head,
and you shall bruise his heel."

Consideration

"Mary, Mother of the Incarnate Word, is placed *at the very center of that enmity*, that struggle, that accompanies the history of humanity on earth and the history of salvation itself. In this central place, she who belongs to the 'weak and poor of the Lord' bears in herself, like no other member of the human race, that 'glory of grace' which the Father 'has bestowed on us in his beloved Son,' and this *grace determines the extraordinary greatness and beauty* of her whole being. Mary thus remains before God, and also before the whole of humanity, as the unchangeable and inviolable sign of God's election, spoken of in Paul's letter: 'in Christ . . . he chose us . . . before the foundation of the world, . . . he destined us . . . to be his sons' (Eph 1:4, 5). This election is more powerful than any experience of evil and sin, than all that 'enmity' that marks the history of man. In this history Mary remains a sign of sure hope."[38]

The Holy Rosary (p. 431 ff.) may be prayed.

Concluding Prayer

Lord God,
you prepared a worthy dwelling place for your
Son by the Immaculate Conception of the Virgin;
grant, we pray,
that, as you preserved her from all stain of sin
in your foreknowledge of his death,
so we, by her intercession,
may come to you with pure hearts.
We ask this through Christ our Lord. Amen.

---

38. John Paul II, *Mother of the Redeemer*, 11, Rome: Libreria Editrice Vaticana, 1987.

SECOND DAY

(DECEMBER 1)

Mary, full of grace

Introductory Prayer

Lord God,
in your plan for our salvation
your Word became man,
announced by an angel
and born of the Virgin Mary.
May we who believe
that she is the Mother of God
receive the help of her prayers.
We ask this through Christ our Lord. Amen.

Reading   Lk 1:26-33

The angel Gabriel was sent from God to a city of
Galilee named Nazareth, to a virgin betrothed to a
man whose name was Joseph, of the house of
David; and the virgin's name was Mary. And he
came to her and said, "Hail, full of grace, the Lord
is with you!" But she was greatly troubled at the
saying, and considered in her mind what sort of
greeting this might be.

And the angel said to her, "Do not be afraid, Mary,
for you have found favor with God. And behold,
you will conceive in your womb and bear a son,
and you shall call his name Jesus. He will be great,
and will be called the Son of the Most High; and
the Lord God will give to him the throne of his father David, and he will reign over the house of
Jacob for ever; and of his kingdom there will be no
end."

Consideration

"When we read that the messenger addresses Mary as 'full of grace,' the gospel context, which mingles revelations and ancient promises, enables us to understand that among all the 'spiritual blessings in Christ,' this is a special 'blessing.' In the mystery of Christ she is *present* even 'before the creation of the world,' as the one whom the Father 'has chosen' as *Mother* of his Son in the Incarnation. And, what is more, together with the Father, the Son has chosen her, entrusting her eternally to the Spirit of holiness. In an entirely special and exceptional way, Mary is united to Christ, and similarly she is *eternally loved in this 'beloved Son,'* this Son who is of one being with the Father, in whom is concentrated all the 'glory of grace.' At the same time, she is—and remains—perfectly open to this 'gift from above' (cf. Jas 1:17). As the Council teaches, Mary 'stands out among the poor and humble of the Lord, who confidently await and receive salvation from him.'"[39]

The Holy Rosary (p. 431 ff.) may be prayed.

Concluding Prayer

Lord God,
you prepared a worthy dwelling place for your
Son by the Immaculate Conception of the Virgin;
grant, we pray,
that, as you preserved her from all stain of sin
in your foreknowledge of his death,
so we, by her intercession,
may come to you with pure hearts.
We ask this through Christ our Lord. Amen.

---

39. Ibid., 8.

THIRD DAY

(DECEMBER 2)

Mary, the handmaid of the Lord

Introductory Prayer

Lord God,
when your Son came down from heaven,
Mary had conceived him in her heart
before she conceived him in her womb:
grant that by holy and just deeds
we may show forth in our lives the Christ whom
we have received by faith,
and who lives and reigns with you and the Holy
Spirit, one God, for ever and ever. Amen.

Reading   Lk 1:34-38

> And Mary said to the angel, "How shall this be,
> since I have no husband?"
>
> And the angel said to her, "The Holy Spirit will
> come upon you, and the power of the Most High
> will overshadow you; therefore the child to be
> born will be called holy, the Son of God. And be-
> hold, your kinswoman Elizabeth in her old age
> has also conceived a son; and this is the sixth
> month with her who was called barren. For with
> God nothing will be impossible."
>
> And Mary said, "Behold, I am the handmaid of the
> Lord; let it be done to me according to your word."
> And the angel departed from her.

Consideration

"Indeed, at the Annunciation Mary entrusted herself
to God completely, with the 'full submission of intel-
lect and will,' manifesting 'the obedience of faith' to
him who spoke to her through his messenger. She

responded, therefore, *with all her human and feminine 'I,'* and this response of faith included both perfect cooperation with 'the grace of God that precedes and assists' and perfect openness to the action of the Holy Spirit, who 'constantly brings faith to completion by his gifts.'

"The word of the living God, announced to Mary by the angel, referred to her: 'And behold, you will conceive in your womb and bear a son' (Lk 1:31). By accepting this announcement, Mary was to become the 'Mother of the Lord,' and the divine mystery of the Incarnation was to be accomplished in her: 'The Father of mercies willed that the consent of the predestined Mother should precede the Incarnation.' And Mary gives this consent after she has heard everything the messenger has to say. . . . The mystery of the Incarnation was accomplished when Mary uttered her *fiat*: 'Let it be to me according to your word,' which made possible, as far as it depended upon her in the divine plan, the granting of her Son's desire."[40]

The Holy Rosary (p. 431 ff.) may be prayed.

Concluding Prayer

Lord God,
you prepared a worthy dwelling place for your
Son by the Immaculate Conception of the Virgin;
grant, we pray,
that, as you preserved her from all stain of sin
in your foreknowledge of his death,
so we, by her intercession,
may come to you with pure hearts.
We ask this through Christ our Lord. Amen.

---

40. Ibid., 13.

FOURTH DAY

(DECEMBER 3)

Mary, blessed among women

Introductory Prayer

Lord, our God,
Savior of the human family,
you brought salvation and joy
    to the house of Elizabeth
through the visit of the Blessed Virgin Mary,
the Ark of the new Covenant.
We ask that, in obedience
to the inspiration of the Holy Spirit,
we too may bring Christ to others
and magnify your name by the praise of our lips
and the holiness of our lives.
We ask this through Christ our Lord. Amen.

Reading   Lk 1:39-44

**In those days Mary arose and went with haste into
the hill country, to a city of Judah, and she entered
the house of Zechariah and greeted Elizabeth. And
when Elizabeth heard the greeting of Mary, the
babe leaped in her womb; and Elizabeth was
filled with the Holy Spirit and she exclaimed with
a loud cry, "Blessed are you among women, and
blessed is the fruit of your womb! And why is this
granted me, that the mother of my Lord should
come to me? For behold, when the voice of your
greeting came to my ears, the babe in my womb
leaped for joy."**

Consideration

"Immediately after the narration of the Annunciation, the evangelist Luke guides us in the footsteps of the Virgin of Nazareth towards 'a city of Judah' (Lk 1:39). According to scholars, this city would be the modern Ain Karim, situated in the mountains, not far from Jerusalem. Mary arrived there 'in haste,' *to visit Elizabeth* her kinswoman. . . .

"Moved by charity, therefore, Mary goes to the house of her kinswoman. When Mary enters, Elizabeth replies to her greeting and feels the child leap in her womb, and, being 'filled with the Holy Spirit,' she *greets Mary* with a loud cry: 'Blessed are you among women, and blessed is the fruit of your womb!' Elizabeth's exclamation or acclamation was subsequently to become part of the *Hail Mary*, as a continuation of the angel's greeting, thus becoming one of the Church's most frequently used prayers. But still more significant are the words of Elizabeth in the question that follows: 'And why is this granted me, that the mother of my Lord should come to me?' (Lk 1:43). Elizabeth bears witness to Mary: she recognizes and proclaims that before her stands the mother of the Lord, the mother of the Messiah. The son whom Elizabeth is carrying in her womb also shares in this witness: 'The babe in my womb leaped for joy' (Lk 1:44). This child is the future John the Baptist, who at the Jordan will point out Jesus as the Messiah."[41]

The Holy Rosary (p. 431 ff.) may be prayed.

Concluding Prayer

Lord God,
you prepared a worthy dwelling place for your
Son by the Immaculate Conception of the Virgin;
grant, we pray,

---

41. Ibid., 12.

that, as you preserved her from all stain of sin
in your foreknowledge of his death,
so we, by her intercession,
may come to you with pure hearts.
We ask this through Christ our Lord. Amen.

FIFTH DAY

(DECEMBER 4)

Mary, Model of Faith

Introductory Prayer

All-holy Father, eternal God,
in your goodness
you prepared a royal throne for your Wisdom
in the womb of the Blessed Virgin Mary;
bathe your Church in the radiance of your
    life-giving Word,
that it may press forward on its pilgrim way
in the light of your truth,
and so come to the joy
of a perfect knowledge of your love.

God of wisdom,
in your desire to restore us to your friendship
after we had lost it by sin,
you chose the Blessed Virgin Mary
as the seat of your Wisdom.

Grant through her intercession
that we may seek not the folly of the wise
but the loving service
that marks out the poor in spirit.

We ask this through Christ our Lord. Amen.

Reading   Lk 1:45-56

[And Elizabeth exclaimed:]

"And blessed is she who believed that there
would be a fulfillment of what was spoken to her
from the Lord."

And Mary said,

"My soul magnifies the Lord,
and my spirit rejoices in God my Savior,
for he has regarded the low estate
        of his handmaiden.
For behold, henceforth all generations
        will call me blessed;
for he who is mighty
        has done great things for me,
and holy is his name.
And his mercy is on those who fear him,
from generation to generation.
He has shown strength with his arm,
he has scattered the proud
        in the imagination of their hearts,
he has put down the mighty
        from their thrones
and exalted those of low degree;
he has filled the hungry with good things,
and the rich he has sent empty away.
He has helped his servant Israel,
in remembrance of his mercy,
as he spoke to our fathers,
to Abraham and to his posterity for ever."

And Mary remained with her about three
months, and returned to her home.

Consideration

"Elizabeth's words 'And blessed is she who believed' do not apply only to that particular moment

of the Annunciation. Certainly the Annunciation is the culminating moment of Mary's faith in her awaiting of Christ, but it is also the point of departure from which her whole 'journey towards God' begins, her whole pilgrimage of faith. And on this road, in an eminent and truly heroic manner—indeed, with an ever-greater heroism of faith—the 'obedience' which she professes to the word of divine revelation will be fulfilled. Mary's 'obedience of faith' during the whole of her pilgrimage will show surprising similarities to the faith of Abraham. Just like the Patriarch of the People of God, so too Mary, during the pilgrimage of her filial and maternal *fiat*, 'in hope believed against hope.'

"In the expression 'Blessed is she who believed,' we can therefore rightly find *a kind of 'key'* that unlocks for us the innermost reality of Mary, whom the angel hailed as 'full of grace.' If as 'full of grace' she has been eternally present in the mystery of Christ, through faith she became a sharer in that mystery in every extension of her earthly journey. She 'advanced in her pilgrimage of faith,' and at the same time, in a discreet yet direct and effective way, she made present to humanity *the mystery of Christ*. And she still continues to do so. Through the mystery of Christ, she too is present within mankind. Thus through the mystery of the Son the mystery of the Mother also is made clear."[42]

The Holy Rosary (p. 431 ff.) may be prayed.

Concluding Prayer

Lord God,
you prepared a worthy dwelling place for your Son

---

42. Ibid., 14 & 19.

by the Immaculate Conception of the Virgin;
grant, we pray,
that, as you preserved her from all stain of sin
in your foreknowledge of his death,
so we, by her intercession,
may come to you with pure hearts.
We ask this through Christ our Lord. Amen.

SIXTH DAY

(DECEMBER 5)

Mary, co-redemptrix

Introductory Prayer

Lord our God,
in your eternal wisdom
you fill out the passion of Christ
through the suffering that his members endure
in the many trials of this life.

As you gave his mother strength in her agony
to stand by the cross of your Son,
grant that we too may bring loving comfort to others
in their distress of mind or body.
We ask this through Christ our Lord. Amen.

Reading　　　　　　　　　　　　　　　　　Lk 2:25-35

Now there was a man in Jerusalem whose name
was Simeon, and this man was righteous and devout, looking for the consolation of Israel, and the
Holy Spirit was upon him. And it had been revealed to him by the Holy Spirit that he should
not see death before he had seen the Lord's Christ.
And inspired by the Spirit he came into the
Temple; and when the parents brought in the
child Jesus, to do for him according to the custom

of the law, he took him up in his arms and blessed God and said, "Lord, now lettest thou thy servant depart in peace, according to thy word; for mine eyes have seen thy salvation which thou hast prepared in the presence of all peoples, a light for revelation to the Gentiles, and for glory to thy people Israel."

And his father and his mother marveled at what was said about him; and Simeon blessed them and said to Mary his mother, "Behold, this child is set for the fall and rising of many in Israel, and for a sign that is spoken against (and a sword will pierce through your own soul also), that thoughts out of many hearts may be revealed."

Consideration

"A just and God-fearing man, called Simeon, appears at this beginning of Mary's 'journey' of faith. His words, suggested by the Holy Spirit (cf. Lk 2:25-27), confirm the truth of the Annunciation. For we read that he took up in his arms the Child to whom—in accordance with the angel's command—the name Jesus was given (cf. Lk 2:21). Simeon's words match the meaning of this name, which is Savior: 'God is salvation.' Turning to the Lord, he says: 'For my eyes have seen your *salvation*, which you have prepared *in the presence of all peoples*, a light for revelation to the Gentiles, and for glory to your people Israel.' At the same time, however, Simeon addresses Mary with the following words: 'Behold, this Child is set for the fall and rising of many in Israel, and for *a sign that is spoken against*, that thoughts of many hearts may be revealed'; and he adds with direct reference to her: 'and a sword will pierce through your own soul also.'

"Simeon's words cast new light on the announcement that Mary had heard from the angel: Jesus is the Savior, he is 'a *light* for revelation' to mankind. Is not this what was manifested in a way on Christmas night, when the shepherds came to the stable (cf. Lk 2:8-20)? Is not this what was to be manifested even more clearly in the coming of the *Magi from the East* (Mt 2:1-12)? But at the same time, at the very beginning of his life, the Son of Mary, and his Mother with him, will experience in themselves the truth of those other words of Simeon: 'a sign that is spoken against.'

"Simeon's words seem like a *second Annunciation to Mary*, for they tell her of the actual historical situation in which the Son is to accomplish his mission, namely, in misunderstanding and sorrow. While this announcement on the one hand confirms her faith in the accomplishment of the divine promises of salvation, on the other hand it also reveals to her that she will have to live her obedience of faith in suffering, at the side of the suffering Savior, and that her motherhood will be mysterious and sorrowful."[43]

The Holy Rosary (p. 431 ff.) may be prayed.

Concluding Prayer

Lord God,
you prepared a worthy dwelling place for your
Son by the Immaculate Conception of the Virgin;
grant, we pray,
that, as you preserved her from all stain of sin
in your foreknowledge of his death,
so we, by her intercession,
may come to you with pure hearts.
We ask this through Christ our Lord. Amen.

---

43. Ibid., 16.

SEVENTH DAY

(DECEMBER 6)

Mary, the first of those
who heard the word of God and did it

Introductory Prayer

Lord our God,
you sent your Son from heaven
into the womb of the Blessed Virgin
to be your saving word and our bread of life:
grant that like Mary we may welcome Christ,
by treasuring his words in our hearts
and celebrating in faith
the deep mysteries of our redemption.
We ask this through Christ our Lord. Amen.

Reading   Lk 11:27-28

> As he said this, a woman in the crowd raised her
> voice and said to him, "Blessed is the womb that
> bore you, and the breasts that you sucked!" But he
> said, "Blessed, rather, are those who hear the word
> of God and keep it!"

Consideration

"The gospel of Luke records the moment when 'a
woman in the crowd raised her voice' and said to
Jesus: *'Blessed is the womb that bore you, and the breasts
that you sucked!* (Lk 11:27). These words were an expression of praise of Mary as Jesus' mother according to the flesh. . . .

"But to the blessing uttered by that woman upon her
who was his mother according to the flesh, Jesus replies in a significant way: 'Blessed, rather, are *those
who hear the word of God and keep it'* (Lk 11:28). He
wishes to divert attention from motherhood un-

derstood only as a fleshly bond, in order to direct it towards those mysterious bonds of the spirit which develop from hearing and keeping God's word. . . .

"Without any doubt, Mary is worthy of blessing by the very fact that she became the mother of Jesus according to the flesh ('Blessed is the womb that bore you, and the breasts that you sucked'), but also and especially because already at the Annunciation she accepted the word of God, because she believed it, *because she was obedient to God,* and because she 'kept' the word and 'pondered it in her heart' (cf. Lk 1:38, 45; 2:19, 51) and by means of her whole life accomplished it. Thus we can say that the blessing proclaimed by Jesus is not in opposition, despite appearances, to the blessing uttered by the unknown woman, but rather coincides with that blessing in the person of this Virgin Mother, who called herself only 'the handmaid of the Lord' (Lk 1:38). . . .

"If *through faith* Mary became the bearer of the Son given to her by the Father through the power of the Holy Spirit, while preserving her virginity intact, in that same faith she *discovered and accepted the other dimension of motherhood* revealed by Jesus during his messianic mission. One can say that this dimension of motherhood belonged to Mary from the beginning, that is to say, from the moment of the conception and birth of her Son. From that time she was 'the one who believed.' . . . Thus *in a sense* Mary as mother became *the first 'disciple' of her Son,* the first to whom he seemed to say 'Follow me,' even before he addressed this call to the apostles or to anyone else (cf. Jn 1:43)."[44]

The Holy Rosary (p. 431 ff.) may be prayed.

---

44. Ibid., 20.

Concluding Prayer

Lord God,
you prepared a worthy dwelling place for your
Son by the Immaculate Conception of the Virgin;
grant, we pray,
that, as you preserved her from all stain of sin
in your foreknowledge of his death,
so we, by her intercession,
may come to you with pure hearts.
We ask this through Christ our Lord. Amen.

EIGHTH DAY

(DECEMBER 7)

Mary, mediatrix of all graces

Introductory Prayer

God of heaven and earth,
your Son, Jesus the Lord,
while dying on the altar of the cross ,
chose Mary, his mother, to be our mother also.
Grant that we,
who entrust ourselves to her maternal care,
may always be protected
when we call upon her name.
We ask this through Christ our Lord. Amen.

Reading   Jn 2:1-11

On the third day there was a marriage at Cana in
Galilee, and the mother of Jesus was there; Jesus
also was invited to the marriage, with his disciples. When the wine failed, the mother of Jesus
said to him, "They have no wine." And Jesus said
to her, "O woman, what have you to do with me?

My hour has not yet come." His mother said to the servants, "Do whatever he tells you."

Now six stone jars were standing there, for the Jewish rites of purification, each holding twenty or thirty gallons. Jesus said to them, "Fill the jars with water." And they filled them up to the brim. He said to them, "Now draw some out, and take it to the steward of the feast." So they took it.

When the steward of the feast tasted the water now become wine, and did not know where it came from (though the servants who had drawn the water knew), the steward of the feast called the bridegroom and said to him, "Every man serves the good wine first; and when men have drunk freely, then the poor wine; but you have kept the good wine until now." This, the first of his signs, Jesus did at Cana in Galilee, and manifested his glory; and his disciples believed in him.

Consideration

"Mary is present at Cana in Galilee as the *Mother of Jesus,* and in a significant way she *contributes* to that 'beginning of the signs' which reveal the messianic power of her Son. We read: 'When the wine gave out, the mother of Jesus said to him, "They have no wine." And Jesus said to her, "O woman, what have you to do with me? My hour has not yet come"' (Jn 2: 3-4). In John's gospel that 'hour' means the time appointed by the Father when the Son accomplishes his task and is to be glorified (cf. Jn 7:30; 8:20; 12:23, 27; 13:1; 17:1; 19:27). Even though Jesus' reply to his mother sounds like a refusal (especially if we consider the blunt statement 'My hour has not yet come,' rather than the question), Mary nevertheless turns to the servants and says to them: 'Do whatever he tells you' (Jn 2:5). Then Jesus orders the servants to fill the stone jars with water, and the water becomes wine, better than the wine which has previously been served to the wedding guests."[45]

"In this passage of John's gospel we find as it were a first manifestation of the truth concerning Mary's maternal care. This truth has also found expression *in the teaching of the Second Vatican Council*. ... 'Mary's maternal function towards mankind in no way obscures or diminishes the unique mediation of Christ, but rather shows its efficacy,' because '"there is one mediator between God and men, the man Christ Jesus"' (1 Tm 2:5). ... The episode at Cana in Galilee offers us *a sort of first announcement of Mary's mediation*, wholly oriented towards Christ and tending to the revelation of his salvific power.

"From the *text of John*, it is evident that it is a mediation that is maternal. As the Council proclaims: Mary became 'a mother to us in the order of grace.' This motherhood in the order of grace flows from her divine motherhood. Because she was, by the design of divine Providence, the mother who nourished the divine Redeemer, Mary became 'an associate of unique nobility, and the Lord's humble handmaid,' who 'cooperated by her obedience, faith, hope and burning charity in the Savior's work of restoring supernatural life to souls.' And 'this *maternity of Mary in the order of grace* ... will last without interruption until the eternal fulfillment of all the elect.'"[46]

The Holy Rosary (p. 431 ff.) may be prayed.

45. Ibid., 21.
46. Ibid., 22.

Concluding Prayer

Lord God,
you prepared a worthy dwelling place for your Son
by the Immaculate Conception of the Virgin;
grant, we pray,
that, as you preserved her from all stain of sin
in your foreknowledge of his death,
so we, by her intercession,
may come to you with pure hearts.
We ask this through Christ our Lord. Amen.

NINTH DAY

(DECEMBER 8)

Mary, Mother of God and our mother

Introductory Prayer

God of mercies,
your only Son, while hanging on the cross,
appointed Mary, his mother,
to be our mother also.
Like her, and under her loving care,
may your Church grow day by day,
rejoice in the holiness of its children,
and so attract to itself all the peoples of the earth.
We ask this through Christ our Lord. Amen.

Reading   Jn 19:23-27

When the soldiers had crucified Jesus they took
his garments and made four parts, one for each
soldier; also his tunic. But the tunic was without
seam, woven from top to bottom; so they said to
one another, "Let us not tear it, but cast lots for it
to see whose it shall be." This was to fulfill the

scripture, "They parted my garments among them, and for my clothing they cast lots." So the soldiers did this.

But standing by the cross of Jesus were his mother, and his mother's sister, Mary the wife of Clopas, and Mary Magdalene. When Jesus saw his mother, and the disciple whom he loved standing near her, he said to his mother, "Woman, behold, your son!" Then he said to the disciple, "Behold, your mother!" And from that hour the disciple took her to his own home.

Consideration

"If John's description of the event at Cana presents Mary's caring motherhood at the beginning of Christ's messianic activity, another passage from the same gospel confirms this motherhood in the salvific economy of grace at its crowning moment, namely, when Christ's sacrifice on the cross, his paschal mystery, is accomplished. John's description is concise: *'Standing by the cross of Jesus* were his mother and his mother's sister, Mary the wife of Clopas, and Mary Magdalene. When Jesus saw his mother, and the disciple whom he loved standing near her, he said to his mother: "Woman, behold your son!" Then he said to the disciple, "Behold your mother!" And from that hour the disciple took her into his own home' (Jn 19:25-27).

". . . And yet the 'testament of Christ's Cross' says more. Jesus highlights a new relationship between Mother and Son, the whole truth and reality of which he solemnly confirms. One can say that if Mary's motherhood of the human race had already been outlined, now it is clearly stated and established. It *emerges* from the definitive accomplishment *of the Redeemer's paschal mystery*. The mother of Christ, who stands at the very center of this mystery—a mystery that embraces each individual and all humanity—is given as mother to every single individual and all mankind.[47]

The Holy Rosary (p. 431 ff.) may be prayed.

Concluding Prayer

Lord God,
you prepared a worthy dwelling place for your
Son by the Immaculate Conception of the Virgin;
grant, we pray,
that, as you preserved her from all stain of sin
in your foreknowledge of his death,
so we, by her intercession,
may come to you with pure hearts.
We ask this through Christ our Lord. Amen.

---

47. Ibid., 24.

DEVOTIONS TO ST. JOSEPH

God chose Joseph to be the husband of the Virgin Mary and the foster father of Jesus; he is considered the second greatest saint. He took an active part in the divine plan of redemption, as an example of humility and faith. Scripture tells us also that he was just, pure, gentle, prudent, and unfailingly obedient to the divine will. Joseph worked as an artisan and carried out his work for the glory of God—sanctifying his profession. According to tradition, he died in the presence of Jesus and Mary. We wish to imitate him by renewing our desire to be faithful. We know that the only meaning of our life is to be faithful to the Lord till the very end, as was Joseph. Pope Pius IX named him Patron of the Universal Church, and pope John XXIII included his name in the Roman Canon (Eucharistic Prayer I).

"What must Joseph have been, how grace must have worked through him, that he should have been able to fulfill this task of the human upbringing of the Son of God. For Jesus must have resembled Joseph: in his way of working, in the features of his character, in his way of speaking. Jesus' realism, his eye for detail, the way he sat at table and broke bread, his preference for using everyday situations to give doctrine—all this reflects his childhood and the influence of Joseph.

"It is not possible to ignore this sublime mystery: Jesus, who is man, who speaks with the accent of a particular district of Israel, who resembles a carpenter called Joseph, is the Son of God."[1]

---

1. Blessed Josemaría Escrivá, *Christ Is Passing By*, 55, Princeton, N.J.: Scepter Publishers, 1974.

SEVEN SUNDAYS DEVOTION

Joseph shared the happiness—but also the sufferings—of Mary. The Seven Sundays Devotion honors the seven joys and sorrows of St. Joseph. It starts on the seventh Sunday previous to March 19 (the last Sunday of January or the first Sunday of February).

FIRST SUNDAY

His sorrow when he decided to leave the Blessed Virgin;
his joy when the angel told him the mystery
of the Incarnation.

Introductory Prayer

O chaste spouse of Mary,
great was the trouble and anguish of your heart
when you were considering
quietly sending away your inviolate spouse;
yet your joy was unspeakable,
when the surpassing mystery of the Incarnation
was made known to you by the angel.

By this sorrow and this joy,
we beseech you to comfort our souls,
both now and in the sorrows of our final hour,
with the joy of a good life and a holy death
after the pattern of your own life
and death in the arms of Jesus and Mary.

Reading   Mt 1:18-25

Now the birth of Jesus Christ took place in this way. When his mother Mary had been betrothed to Joseph, before they came together she was found to be with child of the Holy Spirit; and her husband Joseph, being a just man and unwilling to put her to shame, resolved to send her away quietly.

But as he considered this, behold, an angel of the Lord appeared to him in a dream, saying, "Joseph, son of David, do not fear to take Mary, your wife, for that which is conceived in her is of the Holy Spirit; she will bear a son, and you shall call his name Jesus, for he will save his people from their sins."

All this took place to fulfill what the Lord had spoken by the prophet: "Behold, a virgin shall conceive and bear a son, and his name shall be called Emmanuel" (which means, God with us).

When Joseph woke from sleep, he did as the angel of the Lord commanded him; he took his wife, but knew her not until she had borne a son; and he called his name Jesus.

Consideration

"In the course of that pilgrimage of faith that was his life, Joseph, like Mary, remained faithful to God's call until the end. While Mary's life was the bringing to fullness of that *fiat* first spoken at the Annunciation, *at the moment of Joseph's own 'annunciation'* he said nothing; instead he simply *'did* as the angel of the Lord commanded him' (Mt. 1:24). And *this first 'doing' became the beginning of 'Joseph's way.'"*[2]

"In the words of the 'annunciation' by night, Joseph not only heard the divine truth concerning his wife's indescribable vocation; he *also heard once again the truth about his own vocation.* This 'just' man, who, in the spirit of the noblest traditions of the Chosen People, loved the Virgin of Nazareth and was bound to her by a husband's love, was once again called by God to this love.

---

2. Pope John Paul II, *Apostolic Exhortation* "Guardian of the Redeemer" (=GR), 17, 1989.

"'Joseph did as the angel of the Lord commanded him; he took his wife' into his home; what was conceived in Mary was 'of the Holy Spirit.' From expressions such as these, are we not to suppose that his *love as a man was also given new birth by the Holy Spirit?* Are we not to think that the love of God, which has been poured forth into the human heart through the Holy Spirit (cf. Rm 5:5), molds every human love to perfection?"[3]

"Through his complete self-sacrifice, Joseph expressed his generous love for the Mother of God and gave her a husband's 'gift of self.' Even though he decided to draw back so as not to interfere in the plan of God that was coming to pass in Mary, Joseph obeyed the explicit command of the angel and took Mary into his home, while respecting the fact that she belonged exclusively to God."[4]

Here the Litany of St. Joseph (p. 543 f.) may be prayed, as a conclusion. Or the following prayer may be said.

Concluding Prayer

V. Pray for us, blessed Joseph,

R. That we may be made worthy of the promises of Christ.

Let us pray.
Almighty God,
in your infinite wisdom and love
you chose Joseph to be the husband of Mary,
the mother of your Son.
As we enjoy his protection on earth,
may we have the help of his prayers in heaven.
We ask this through Christ our Lord. Amen.

---

3. GR, 19.
4. GR, 20.

SECOND SUNDAY

His sorrow when he saw Jesus born in poverty;
his joy when the angels announced Jesus' birth.

Introductory Prayer

O most blessed patriarch, glorious Saint Joseph,
who were chosen to be the foster father
    of the Word made flesh,
your sorrow at seeing the child Jesus
    born in such poverty
was suddenly changed into heavenly exultation
when you heard the angelic hymn
and beheld the glories of that resplendent night.

By this sorrow and this joy,
we implore you to obtain for us
the grace to pass over from life's pathway
to hear angelic songs of praise
and to rejoice in the shining splendor
    of celestial glory.

Reading   Lk 2:1-20

In those days a decree went out from Caesar
Augustus that all the world should be enrolled.
This was the first enrollment, when Quirinius was
governor of Syria. And all went to be enrolled,
each to his own city. And Joseph also went up
from Galilee, from the city of Nazareth, to Judaea,
to the city of David, which is called Bethlehem,
because he was of the house and lineage of David,
to be enrolled with Mary, his betrothed, who was
with child. And while they were there, the time
came for her to be delivered. And she gave birth to
her firstborn son and wrapped him in swaddling
clothes, and laid him in a manger, because there
was no place for them in the inn.

And in that region there were shepherds out in the field, keeping watch over their flocks by night. And an angel of the Lord appeared to them, and the glory of the Lord shone around them, and they were filled with fear.

And the angel said to them, "Be not afraid; for behold, I bring you good news of a great joy which will come to all the people; for to you is born this day in the city of David a Savior, who is Christ the Lord. And this will be a sign for you: you will find a babe wrapped in swaddling clothes and lying in a manger." And suddenly there was with the angel a multitude of the heavenly host praising God and saying, "Glory to God in the highest, and on earth peace among men with whom he is pleased!"

When the angels went away from them into heaven, the shepherds said to one another, "Let us go over to Bethlehem and see this thing that has happened, which the Lord has made known to us." And they went with haste, and found Mary and Joseph, and the babe lying in a manger. And when they saw it they made known the saying which had been told them concerning this child; and all who heard it wondered at what the shepherds told them. But Mary kept all these things, pondering them in her heart. And the shepherds returned, glorifying and praising God for all they had heard and seen, as it had been told them.

Consideration

"Journeying to Bethlehem for the census in obedience to the orders of legitimate authority, Joseph fulfilled for the child the significant task of officially inserting the name 'Jesus, son of Joseph of Nazareth' (cf. Jn 1:45) in the registry of the Roman Empire. This registration clearly shows that Jesus belongs to the human race as a man among men, a citizen of this world, subject to laws and civil institutions, but also *'Savior of the world.'*"[5]

"As guardian of the mystery hidden for ages in the mind of God, which begins to unfold before his eyes 'in the fullness of time,' *Joseph, together with Mary,* is a privileged witness to the birth of the Son of God into the world *on Christmas night in Bethlehem.* . . .

"Joseph was an eyewitness to this birth, which took place in conditions that, humanly speaking, were embarrassing—a first announcement of that 'self-emptying' (cf. Phil 2:5-8) that Christ freely accepted for the forgiveness of sins. Joseph also *witnessed the adoration of the shepherds,* who arrived at Jesus' birthplace after the angels had brought them the great and happy news (cf. Lk 2:15-16). Later he also *witnessed the homage of the magi who came from the East* (cf. Mt 2:11)."[6]

Here the Litany of St. Joseph (p. 543 f.) may be prayed, as a conclusion. Or the following prayer may be said.

Concluding Prayer

V. Pray for us, blessed Joseph,

R. **That we may be made worthy of the promises of Christ.**

Let us pray.
Almighty God,
in your infinite wisdom and love
you chose Joseph to be the husband of Mary,
the mother of your Son.
As we enjoy his protection on earth,
may we have the help of his prayers in heaven.
We ask this through Christ our Lord. Amen.

5. GR, 9.
6. GR, 10.

THIRD SUNDAY

His sorrow when he saw Jesus' blood shed in circumcision;
his joy in giving him the name Jesus.

Introductory Prayer

O glorious Saint Joseph,
who faithfully obeyed the law of God,
your heart was pierced
at the sight of the most precious blood
that was shed by the infant Savior during
    his circumcision,
but the name of Jesus gave you new life
and filled you with quiet joy.

By this sorrow and this joy,
obtain for us the grace
to be freed from all sin during life
and to die rejoicing,
with the holy name of Jesus in our hearts
    and on our lips.

Reading   Lk 2:21

And at the end of eight days, when he was circumcised, he was called Jesus, the name given by the angel before he was conceived in the womb.

Consideration

"A son's circumcision was the first religious obligation of a father, and with this ceremony (cf. Lk 2:21) Joseph exercised his right and duty with regard to Jesus.

"The principle that holds that all the rites of the Old Testament are a shadow of the reality (cf. Heb 9:9 f.; 10:1) serves to explain why Jesus would accept them. As with all the other rites, circumcision, too, is 'fulfilled' in Jesus. God's covenant with Abraham, of

which circumcision was the sign (cf. Gn 17:13),
reaches its full effect and perfect realization in Jesus,
who is the 'yes' of all the ancient promises (cf. 2 Cor
1:20)."[7]

"At the circumcision, Joseph names the child 'Jesus.'
This is the only name in which there is salvation (cf.
Acts 4:12). Its significance had been revealed to Joseph at the moment of his 'annunciation': 'You shall
call the child Jesus, for he will save his people from
their sins' (cf. Mt 1:21). In conferring the name, Joseph declares his own legal fatherhood over Jesus,
and in speaking the name he proclaims the child's
mission as Savior."[8]

Here the Litany of St. Joseph (p. 543 f.) may be prayed, as a
conclusion. Or the following prayer may be said.

Concluding Prayer

V. Pray for us, blessed Joseph,

R. **That we may be made worthy of the promises of
    Christ.**

Let us pray.
Almighty God,
in your infinite wisdom and love
you chose Joseph to be the husband of Mary,
the mother of your Son.
As we enjoy his protection on earth,
may we have the help of his prayers in heaven.
We ask this through Christ our Lord. Amen.

---

7. GR, 11.
8. GR, 12.

FOURTH SUNDAY

His sorrow when he heard the prophecy of Simeon;
his joy when he learned that many would be saved
through the sufferings of Jesus.

Introductory Prayer

O most faithful Saint Joseph,
who shared the mysteries of our redemption,
the prophecy of Simeon,
touching the sufferings of Jesus and Mary,
caused you to shudder with mortal dread
but at the same time filled you with a blessed joy
for the salvation and glorious resurrection
that would be attained by countless souls.

By this sorrow and this joy,
obtain for us that we may be
of the number of those who,
through the merits of Jesus
and the intercession of Mary the Virgin Mother,
are predestined to a glorious resurrection.

Reading   Lk 2:22-35

And when the time came for their purification according to the law of Moses, they brought him up to
Jerusalem to present him to the Lord (as it is written
in the law of the Lord, "Every male that opens the
womb shall be called holy to the Lord") and to offer
a sacrifice according to what is said in the law of the
Lord, "a pair of turtledoves, or two young pigeons."
Now there was a man in Jerusalem, whose name
was Simeon, and this man was righteous and devout, looking for the consolation of Israel, and the
Holy Spirit was upon him. And it had been revealed to him by the Holy Spirit that he should not
see death before he had seen the Lord's Christ. And

inspired by the Spirit he came into the Temple; and when the parents brought in the child Jesus, to do for him according to the custom of the law, he took him up in his arms and blessed God and said,

"Lord, now lettest thou thy servant depart in peace, according to thy word;
for mine eyes have seen thy salvation
which thou hast prepared in the presence
of all peoples,
a light for revelation to the Gentiles,
and for glory to thy people Israel."

And his father and his mother marveled at what was said about him; and Simeon blessed them and said to Mary his mother, "Behold, this child is set for the fall and rising of many in Israel, and for a sign that is spoken against (and a sword will pierce through your own soul also), that thoughts out of many hearts may be revealed."

Consideration

"This rite, to which Luke refers, includes the ransom of the firstborn and sheds light on the subsequent stay of Jesus in the Temple at the age of twelve.

"The *ransoming of the firstborn* is another obligation of the father, and it is fulfilled by Joseph. Represented in the firstborn is the people of the covenant, ransomed from slavery in order to belong to God. Here, too, Jesus—who is the true 'price' of ransom (cf. 1 Cor 6:20; 7:23; 1 Pt 1:19)—not only 'fulfills' the Old Testament rite, but at the same time transcends it, since he is not a subject to be redeemed, but the very author of redemption.

"The gospel writer notes that 'his father and his mother marveled at what was said about him' (Lk 2:23), in particular at *what Simeon said* in his canticle to God, when he referred to Jesus as the 'salvation which you have prepared in the presence of all peoples, a light for revelation to the Gentiles, and for glory to your people Israel' and as a 'sign that is spoken against' (cf. Lk 2:30-34)."[9]

"'It pleased God, in his goodness and wisdom to reveal himself and to make known the mystery of his will (cf. Eph 1:9). His Will was that all should have access to the Father, through Christ, the Word made flesh, in the Holy Spirit, and, thus become sharers in the divine nature (cf. Eph 2:18; 2 Pt 1:4)'[10]

"Together with Mary, Joseph is the first guardian of this divine mystery. Together with Mary, and in relation to Mary, he shares in this final phase of God's self-revelation in Christ, and he does so from the very beginning."[11]

Here the Litany of St. Joseph (p. 543 f.) may be prayed, as a conclusion. Or the following prayer may be said.

Concluding Prayer

V. Pray for us, blessed Joseph,

R. That we may be made worthy of the promises of Christ.

Let us pray.
Almighty God,
in your infinite wisdom and love
you chose Joseph to be the husband of Mary,
the mother of your Son.
As we enjoy his protection on earth,
may we have the help of his prayers in heaven.
We ask this through Christ our Lord. Amen.

---

9. GR, 13.
10. Second Vatican Ecumenical Council, *Dei Verbum*, 5.
11. GR, 5.

FIFTH SUNDAY

His sorrow when he had to flee to Egypt;
his joy in being always with Jesus and Mary.

Introductory Prayer

O most watchful guardian of the Son of God,
glorious Saint Joseph,
great was your toil in supporting
and waiting upon the Son of God,
especially during the flight into Egypt!
Yet, how you rejoiced
to have God himself always near you.

By this sorrow and this joy,
obtain for us the grace that would keep us safe
from the devil,
especially the help we need to flee
from dangerous situations.
May we serve Jesus and Mary,
and for them alone may we live and happily die.

Reading   Mt 2:13-15

Now when they had departed, behold, an angel of
the Lord appeared to Joseph in a dream and said,
"Rise, take the child and his mother, and flee to
Egypt, and remain there till I tell you; for Herod is
about to search for the child, to destroy him." And
he rose and took the child and his mother by
night, and departed to Egypt, and remained there
until the death of Herod. This was to fulfill what
the Lord had spoken by the prophet, "Out of
Egypt have I called my son."

Consideration

"Herod learned from the magi, who came from the
East, about the birth of the 'king of the Jews' (Mt 2:2).

And when the magi departed, he 'sent and killed all the male children in Bethlehem and in all that region who were two years old or under' (Mt 2:16). By killing them all, he wished to kill the newborn 'king of the Jews,' whom he had heard about."[12]

"The Church deeply venerates this Family and proposes it as the model of all families. Inserted directly in the mystery of the Incarnation, the Family of Nazareth has its own special mystery. And in this mystery, as in the Incarnation, one finds a true fatherhood: *the human form of the family of the Son of God,* a true human family, formed by the divine mystery. *In this family, Joseph is the father: his fatherhood* is not one that derives from begetting offspring, but neither is it an 'apparent' or merely 'substitute' fatherhood. Rather, it is one that *fully shares in authentic human fatherhood* and the mission of a father in the family. This is a consequence of the hypostatic union: humanity taken up into the unity of the Divine Person of the Word–Son, Jesus Christ. Together with human nature, *all that is human, and especially the family*—as the first dimension of man's existence in the world—*is also taken up* in Christ. Within this context, Joseph's human fatherhood was also 'taken up' in the mystery of Christ's Incarnation."[13]

Here the Litany of St. Joseph (p. 543 f.) may be prayed, as a conclusion. Or the following prayer may be said.

Concluding Prayer

V. Pray for us, blessed Joseph,

R. That we may be made worthy of the promises of Christ.

---

12. GR, 14.
13. GR, 21.

Let us pray.
Almighty God,
in your infinite wisdom and love
you chose Joseph to be the husband of Mary,
the mother of your Son.
As we enjoy his protection on earth,
may we have the help of his prayers in heaven.
We ask this through Christ our Lord. Amen.

SIXTH SUNDAY

His sorrow when he was afraid to return to his homeland;
   his joy on being told by the angel to go to Nazareth.

Introductory Prayer

O glorious Saint Joseph,
you marveled to see the King of heaven
obedient to your commands.
Your consolation in bringing Jesus
   out of the land of Egypt
was troubled by your fear of Archelaus.
Nevertheless, being assured by an angel,
you lived in gladness at Nazareth
with Jesus and Mary.

By this sorrow and this joy,
obtain for us that our hearts
may be delivered from harmful fears,
so that we may rejoice in peace of conscience
and may live with Jesus and Mary,
and, like you, may die in their company.

Reading   Mt 2:19-23; Lk 2:40

**But when Herod died, behold, an angel of the Lord
appeared in a dream to Joseph in Egypt, saying,
"Rise, take the child and his mother, and go to the
land of Israel, for those who sought the child's life**

are dead." And he rose and took the child and his mother, and went to the land of Israel. But when he heard that Archelaus reigned over Judaea in place of his father Herod, he was afraid to go there, and being warned in a dream he withdrew to the district of Galilee. And he went and dwelt in a city called Nazareth, that what was spoken by the prophets might be fulfilled, "He shall be called a Nazarene."

And the child grew and became strong, filled with wisdom; and the favor of God was upon him.

Consideration

"Work was the daily expression of love in the life of the Family of Nazareth. The Gospel specifies the kind of work Joseph did in order to support his family: he was a carpenter. This simple word sums up Joseph's entire life. For Jesus, these were hidden years, the years to which Luke refers after recounting the episode that occurred in the Temple: 'And he went down with them and came to Nazareth, and was obedient to them' (Lk 2:51). This 'submission' or obedience of Jesus in the house of Nazareth should be understood as a sharing in the work of Joseph. Having learned the work of his presumed father, he was known as 'the carpenter's son.' If the Family of Nazareth is an example and model for human families, in the order of salvation and holiness, so, too, by analogy, is Jesus' work at the side of Joseph the carpenter. In our own day, the Church has emphasized this by instituting the liturgical memorial of St. Joseph the Worker on May 1. *Human work,* and especially manual labor, *receives special prominence in the Gospel.* Along with the humanity of the Son of God, work, too, has been taken up in the mystery of the Incarnation, *and has also been redeemed in a special way.* At the workbench where he plied his trade together

with Jesus, Joseph brought human work closer to the mystery of the Redemption."[14]

"In the human growth of Jesus 'in wisdom, age and grace,' *the virtue of industriousness* played a notable role, since 'work is a human good,' which 'transforms nature' and makes man 'in a sense, more human.'"[15]

"What is crucially important here is the sanctification of daily life, a sanctification that each person must acquire according to his or her own state, and one which can be promoted according to a model accessible to all people: 'St. Joseph is the model of those humble ones that Christianity raises up to great destinies; . . . he is the proof that, in order to be a good and genuine follower of Christ, there is no need of great things—it is enough to have the common, simple and human virtues, but they must be true and authentic.'"[16]

Here the Litany of St. Joseph (p. 543 f.) may be prayed, as a conclusion. Or the following prayer may be said.

Concluding Prayer

V. Pray for us, blessed Joseph,

R. That we may be made worthy of the promises of Christ.

Let us pray.
Almighty God,
in your infinite wisdom and love
you chose Joseph to be the husband of Mary,
the mother of your Son.
As we enjoy his protection on earth,
may we have the help of his prayers in heaven.
We ask this through Christ our Lord. Amen.

14. GR, 22.
15. GR, 23.
16. GR, 24.

SEVENTH SUNDAY

His sorrow when he lost the Child Jesus;
his joy in finding him in the temple.

Introductory Prayer

O glorious Saint Joseph,
pattern of all holiness,
when you lost the child Jesus,
you sought him sorrowing
    for the space of three days,
until with great joy you found him again
    in the temple,
sitting in the midst of the doctors.
By this sorrow and this joy,
we ask you, with our hearts upon our lips,
to keep us from ever having the misfortune
of losing Jesus through mortal sin.
Grant also that we always may seek him
    with unceasing sorrow,
when we commit a serious sin,
until we find him again,
ready to show us his great mercy
in the sacrament of Reconciliation.

Reading   Lk 2:41-50

Now his parents went to Jerusalem every year at
the feast of the Passover. And when he was twelve
years old, they went up according to custom; and
when the feast was ended, as they were returning,
the boy Jesus stayed behind in Jerusalem. His parents did not know it, but, supposing him to be in
the company, they went a day's journey, and they
sought him among their kinsfolk and acquaintan-
ces; and when they did not find him, they returned to Jerusalem, seeking him.

After three days they found him in the Temple,
sitting among the teachers, listening to them and
asking them questions; and all who heard him
were amazed at his understanding and his answers. And when they saw him they were aston-
ished; and his mother said to him, "Son, why have
you treated us so? Behold, your father and I have
been looking for you anxiously."

And he said to them, "How is it that you sought
me? Did you not know that I must be in my
Father's house?" And they did not understand the
saying which he spoke to them.

Consideration

"Joseph, of whom Mary had just used the words
'your father,' heard this answer. That, after all, is
what all the people said and thought: Jesus was 'the
son (as was supposed) of Joseph' (Lk 3:23). Nonetheless, the reply of Jesus in the Temple brought once
again to the mind of his 'presumed father' what he
had heard on that night twelve years earlier:

'Joseph . . . do not fear to take Mary as your wife, for
that which is conceived in her is of the Holy Spirit.' From
that time onwards he knew that he was a guardian
of the mystery of God, and it was *precisely this mystery* that the twelve-year-old *Jesus brought to mind:* 'I
must be in my Father's house.'"[17]

Here the Litany of St. Joseph (p. 543 f.) may be prayed, as a
conclusion. Or the following prayer may be said.

Concluding Prayer

V. Pray for us, blessed Joseph,

R. **That we may be made worthy of the promises of
Christ.**

---

17. GR, 15.

Let us pray.
Almighty God,
in your infinite wisdom and love
you chose Joseph to be the husband of Mary,
the mother of your Son.
As we enjoy his protection on earth,
may we have the help of his prayers in heaven.
We ask this through Christ our Lord. Amen.

LITANY OF ST. JOSEPH

Lord, have mercy.	**Lord, have mercy.**
Christ, have mercy.	**Christ, have mercy.**
Holy Trinity, one God.	**Have mercy on us.**

Holy Mary,	**pray for us.**

Saint Joseph, . . .
Noble son of the House of David, . . .
Light of patriarchs, . . .
Husband of the Mother of God, . . .
Guardian of the Virgin, . . .
Foster father of the Son of God, . . .
Faithful guardian of Christ, . . .
Head of the holy family, . . .
Joseph, chaste and just, . . .
Joseph, prudent and brave, . . .
Joseph, obedient and loyal, . . .
Pattern of patience, . . .
Lover of poverty, . . .
Model of workers, . . .
Example to parents, . . .
Guardian of virgins, . . .
Pillar of family life, . . .
Comfort of the troubled, . . .
Hope of the sick, . . .
Patron of the dying, . . .
Terror of evil spirits, . . .
Protector of the Church, . . .

Lamb of God, you take away the sins of the world.	**Have mercy on us.**

Lamb of God, you take away
the sins of the world.   **Have mercy on us.**
Lamb of God, you take away
the sins of the world.   **Have mercy on us.**

V. God made him master of his household.
R. **And put him in charge of all that he owned.**

Let us pray.
Almighty God,
in your infinite wisdom and love
you chose Joseph to be the husband of Mary,
the mother of your Son.
As we enjoy his protection on earth,
may we have the help of his prayers in heaven.
We ask this through Christ our Lord.
R. **Amen.**

VARIOUS PRAYERS

PERSONAL MEDITATION

Before

My Lord and my God, I firmly believe that you are here, that you see me, that you hear me. I adore you with profound reverence; I ask your pardon for my sins and the grace to make this time of prayer fruitful. My immaculate Mother, Saint Joseph my father and lord, my guardian angel, intercede for me.

After

I thank you, my God, for the good resolutions, affections and inspirations that you have communicated to me in this meditation. I ask your help to put them into effect. My immaculate Mother; St. Joseph my father and lord, my guardian angel, intercede for me.

SPIRITUAL READING

Before

Come, O Holy Spirit, fill the hearts of your faithful and enkindle in them the fire of your love. Send forth your Spirit, and they shall be created.

R. And you shall renew the face of the earth.

Let us pray.

O God, who has taught the hearts of the faithful
by the light of the Holy Spirit,
grant that by the gift of the same Spirit
we may be always truly wise
and ever rejoice in his consolation.
Through Christ our Lord. **R. Amen.**

After

V. We give you thanks, almighty God, for all your benefits, who live and reign for ever and ever.

R. **Amen.**

V. May the Lord grant us his peace.

R. **And life everlasting.**

V. Amen.

BLESSING BEFORE A MEAL

V. Bless us, O Lord, and these your gifts, which we are about to receive from your bounty, through Christ our Lord.

R. **Amen.**

(Add for midday)

V. May the King of everlasting glory make us partakers of the heavenly table.

R. **Amen.**

(Add for evening)

V. May the King of everlasting glory lead us to the banquet of life eternal.

R. **Amen.**

THAKSGIVING AFTER A MEAL

V. We give you thanks, almighty God, for all your benefits, who live and reign for ever and ever.

R. **Amen.**

V. May the Lord grant us his peace.

R. **And life everlasting.**

V. Amen.

SOME ASPIRATIONS

Cor mundum crea in me, Deus (Ps 51:12).	A clean heart create for me, O God.
Cor contrítum, et humiliátum, Deus non despícies (Ps 51:17).	A contrite and humble heart, O God, you will not despise.
Pauper servus et húmilis.	A poor and lowly servant am I.
Deo omnis glória.	All the glory for God.
Diligéntibus Deum ómnia cooperántur in bonum (Rom 3:28).	For those who love God, all things work together for good.
Quia tu es, Deus, fortitúdo mea (Ps 43:2).	For you, O God, are my strength.
Illum oportet créscere, me autem mínui (Jn 3:30).	He must increase, but I must decrease.
Ecce ego, quia vocásti me (1 Sm 3:5).	Here I am, for you did call me.
Sancta María, spes nostra, sedes sapiéntiæ, ora pro nobis.	Holy Mary, our hope, seat of wisdom, pray for us.
Sancta María, spes nostra, ancílla Dómini, ora pro nobis.	Holy Mary, our hope, handmaid of the Lord, pray for us.
Sancta María, stella maris, filios tuos ádiuva.	Holy Mary, star of the sea, help your children.
Omnia possum in eo qui me confórtat (Phil 4:13).	I can do all things in him who strengthens me.
Credo, sed ádiuva incredulitátem meam (Mk 9:24).	I do believe; help my unbelief.

Ago tibi grátias pro univérsis benefíciis tuis, étiam ignótis.	I give you thanks for all your benefits, even the unknown ones.
In te, Dómine, sperávi; non confúndar in ætérnum (Ps 31:1).	In you, O Lord, I take refuge: let me never be put to shame.
Adauge nobis fidem (Lk 17:5).	Lord, increase our faith.
Iesu, fili David, miserére mei peccatóris (Mk 10:47).	Jesus, Son of David, have mercy on me, a sinner!
Iesu, Iesu, esto mihi semper Iesus.	Jesus, Jesus, always be Jesus to me.
Dómine, tu ómnia nosti; tu scis quia amo te (Jn 21:17).	Lord, you know all things, you know that I love you.
Dómine, ut vídeam (Lk 18:41).	Lord, that I may see.
Dómine, quid me vis fácere? (Acts 22:10).	Lord, what do you want me to do?
Mater pulchræ dilectiónis, fílios tuos ádiuva.	Mother of fair love, help your children.
Dóminus meus et Deus meus! (Jn 20:28).	My Lord and my God.
Non volúntas mea, sed tua fiat (Mt 26:39).	Not as I will, but as you will.
Regína apostolórum, ora pro nobis.	Queen of Apostles, pray for us.
Cor Iesu sacratíssimum, dona nobis pacem.	Sacred Heart of Jesus, grant us peace.
Monstra te esse matrem.	Show that you are our mother.
Cor Maríæ dulcíssimun, iter para tutum.	Sweet Heart of Mary, prepare a safe way for us.

PRAYERS
AT THE TIME OF DEATH

As death approaches, the Church stays close to the one who is dying, to give comfort and support. The family should ask that holy Communion be brought to the dying. This is Viaticum, food for the journey. Members of the local Church may wish to join the family in a vigil of prayer. After the person's death, the family is encouraged to continue in prayer, to take part in the preparation of the vigil (wake) and funeral liturgies, and to participate in the preparation of the body for burial. In all of these moments, many of the traditional prayers of the Church may be chosen.

VIATICUM [1]

Viaticum is the sacrament of the dying. In Viaticum the dying person is united with Christ in his passage out of this world to the Father. When the minister has brought holy Communion, the rite may begin with the renewal of the dying person's profession of faith.

PROFESSION OF FAITH

V. Do you reject sin, so as to live in the freedom of God's children?

R. **I do.**

V. Do you reject the glamor of evil and refuse to be mastered by sin?

R. **I do.**

---

1. National Conference of Catholic Bishops, *Catholic Household Blessings and Prayers*, 1988.

V. Do you reject Satan, father of sin and prince of darkness?

R. **I do.**

V. Do you believe in God, the Father almighty, creator of heaven and earth?

R. **I do.**

V. Do you believe in Jesus Christ, his only Son our Lord, who was born of the Virgin Mary, was crucified, died, and was buried, rose from the dead, and is now seated at the right hand of the Father?

R. **I do.**

V. Do you believe in the Holy Spirit, the holy Catholic Church, the communion of saints, the forgiveness of sins, the resurrection of the body, and life everlasting?

R. **I do.**

V. This is our faith. This is the faith of the Church. We are proud to profess it in Christ Jesus our Lord.

R. **Amen.**

Viaticum is then celebrated in the same manner as Communion of the Sick (see p. 309), but, after giving Communion, the minister says:

May the Lord Jesus Christ protect you
and lead you to eternal life.

R. **Amen.**

The concluding prayer follows:

God of peace,
you offer eternal healing to those who believe in you;
you have refreshed your servant N.
with food and drink from heaven:
lead him (her) safely into the kingdom of light.
We ask this through Christ our Lord.

R. **Amen.**

COMMENDATION OF THE DYING [2]

Through the prayers designated for the commendation of the dying, the Church helps to sustain their union with Christ to the Father until it is brought to fulfillment after death.

Christians have the responsibility of expressing their union in Christ by joining the dying person in prayer for God's mercy and for confidence in Christ. In particular, the presence of a priest or deacon shows more clearly that the Christian dies in the communion of the Church. He should assist the dying person, and all those present in the recitation of the prayers of commendation; and after the person's death, he should lead the others in the Prayers after Death (p. 557 f.). If the priest or deacon is unable to be present because of other serious pastoral obligations, other members of the community should be prepared to assist with these prayers and should have the texts readily available to them.

The minister may choose texts from among the prayers, litanies, aspirations, psalms, and readings. In the selection of these texts, the minister should keep in mind the condition and piety of both the dying person and the members of the family who are present. The prayers are best said in a slow, quiet manner, alternating with periods of silence. If possible, the minister says one or more of the brief formulas with the dying person. These may be softly repeated two or three times.

These texts are intended to help the dying person, if still conscious, to face the natural human anxiety about death by imitating Christ in his patient suffering and dying. The Christian will be helped to surmount his or her fear, in the hope of heavenly life and resurrection through the power of Christ, who destroyed the power of death by his own dying.

---

2. (ICEL), Rites of Anointing and Viaticum, *Pastoral Care of the Sick,* 1982.

[A person who appears to be unconscious may, in reality, be conscious and able to hear and join mentally the praying.] Even if the dying person is not conscious, those who are present will draw consolation from these prayers and come to a better understanding of the paschal character of Christian death. The leader may be visibly expressed this by making the Sign of the Cross on the forehead of the dying person, who was first signed with the cross at Baptism. Immediately after death has occurred, all may kneel, while one of those present leads the prayers.

SHORT TEXTS

One or more of the following short texts may be recited with the dying person. If necessary, they may be softly repeated two or three times:

Who can separate us from
the love of Christ? *Romans 8:35*

Whether we live or die,
we are the Lord's. *Romans 14:8*

We have an everlasting
home in heaven. *2 Corinthians 5:1*

We shall be with the Lord
for ever. *1 Thessalonians 4:17*

We shall see God as he really is. *1 John 3:2*

We have passed from death
to life because we love each other. *1 John 3:14*

To you, Lord, I lift up my soul. *Psalm 25:1*

The Lord is my light and my salvation. *Psalm 27:1*

I believe that I shall see the goodness
of the Lord in the land of the living. *Psalm 27:13*

My soul thirsts for the living God. *Psalm 42:2*

Though I walk in the shadow of death,
I will fear no evil, for you are with me. *Psalm 23:4*

"In my Father's home there are many
   dwelling places," says the Lord Jesus.   **John 14:2**

"Come, blessed of my Father," says
   the Lord Jesus, "and take possession
   of the kingdom prepared for you."   **Matthew 25:33**

The Lord Jesus says, "Today
   you will be with me in paradise."   **Luke 23:43**

The Lord Jesus says, "I go to prepare
   a place for you, and I will come again
   to take you to myself."   **John 14:2–3**

I desire that where I am, they also
   may be with me," says the Lord Jesus.   **John 17:24**

Everyone who believes in the Son
   has eternal life" says the Lord Jesus.   **John 6:40**

Into your hands, Lord,
   I commend my spirit.   **Psalm 31:5**

Lord Jesus, receive my spirit.   **Acts 7:59**

Holy Mary, pray for me.

Saint Joseph, pray for me.

Jesus, Mary, and Joseph, assist me in my last agony.

BIBLICAL READINGS

The word of God is proclaimed by one of those present or by the minister. Selections may be made from the following.

Isaiah 35:3-4, 6c-7, 10.1	1 John 4:16
Job 19:23-27a	Revelation 21:1-5a, 6-7
Psalm 23	Matthew 25:1-13
Psalm 25:1, 5-11	Mark 15:33-37
Psalm 91	Mark 16:1-8
Psalm 114	Luke 22:39-46
Psalm 116:3-5	Luke 23:42-43
Psalm 121:1-4	Luke 24:1-8
Psalm 123	John 6:37-40
1 Corinthians 15:1-4	John 14:1-6, 23, 27

LITANY OF THE SAINTS

> When the condition of the dying person calls for the use of brief forms of prayer, those who are present are encouraged to pray the Litany of the Saints—or at least some of its invocations—for him or her. Special mention may be made of the patron saints of the dying person, of the family, and of the parish. The litany may be said or sung in the usual way. Other customary prayers, also, may be used.

Lord have mercy.	**Lord, have mercy.**
Christ, have mercy.	**Christ, have mercy.**
Lord, have mercy.	**Lord, have mercy.**
Holy Mary, Mother of God.	**Pray for him (her).**

Holy angels of God, . . .

Abraham, our father in faith, . . .

David, leader of God's people, . . .

All holy patriarchs and prophets, . . .

Saint John the Baptist, . . .

Saint Joseph, . . .

Saint Peter and Saint Paul, . . .

Saint Andrew, . . .

Saint John, . . .

Saint Mary Magdalene, . . .

Saint Stephen, . . .

Saint Ignatius, . . .

Saint Lawrence, . . .

Saint Perpetua and Saint Felicity, . . .

Saint Agnes, . . .

Saint Gregory, . . .

Saint Augustine, . . .

Saint Athanasius, . . .

Saint Basil, . . .

Saint Martin, . . .

Saint Benedict,	**Pray for him (her).**
Saint Francis and Saint Dominic, . . .	
Saint Francis Xavier, . . .	
Saint John Vianney, . . .	
Saint Catherine, . . .	
Saint Teresa, . . .	

Other saints may be included here.

All holy men and women, . . .	
Lord, be merciful,	**Lord, save your people.**
From all evil, . . .	
From every sin, . . .	
From Satan's power, . . .	
At the moment of death, . . .	
From everlasting death, . . .	
On the day of judgment, . . .	
By your coming as man, . . .	
By your suffering and cross, . . .	
By your death and rising to new life, . . .	
By your return in glory to the Father, . . .	
By your gift of the Holy Spirit, . . .	
By your coming again in glory, . . .	
Be merciful to us sinners;	**Lord, hear our prayer.**
Bring N. to eternal life, first promised to him (her) in Baptism, . . .	
Raise N. on the last day, for he (she) has eaten the Bread of life, . . .	

Let N. share in your glory,
    for he (she) has shared in
    your suffering and death;   **Lord, hear our prayer.**
Jesus, Son of the living God, . . .
Christ, hear us.   **Christ, hear us.**
Lord Jesus,
    hear our prayer.   **Lord Jesus, hear our prayer.**

PRAYER OF COMMENDATION

   *When the moment of death seems near, the following prayer
   may be said:*

I commend you, my dear brother (sister),
    to almighty God
and entrust you to your Creator.
May you return to him
who formed you from the dust of the earth.
May holy Mary, the angels, and all the saints
come to meet you as you go forth from this life.
May Christ, who was crucified for you,
bring you freedom and peace.
May Christ, who died for you,
admit you into his garden of paradise.
May Christ, the true Shepherd,
acknowledge you as one of his flock.
May he forgive all your sins
and set you among those he has chosen.
May you see your Redeemer face to face
and enjoy the vision of God for ever.
R. Amen.

The Holy Rosary (p. 431 ff.) or the **Hail Holy Queen** (p. 471)
may be prayed

ACCEPTANCE OF DEATH (see p. 396 f.)

PRAYERS FOR THE DEAD [1]

The Church prays for the dead, and this prayer says much about the reality of the Church itself. It says that the Church continues to live in the *hope of eternal life*. Prayer for the dead is almost a battle with the reality of death and destruction that weighs down upon the earthly existence of man. This is and remains a particular *revelation of the Resurrection*. In this prayer Christ himself bears witness to the life and immortality to which God calls every human being.[2]

PRAYERS AFTER DEATH

The following prayers may be recited immediately after the person's death and may be repeated in the hours that follow.

Saints of God, come to his (her) aid!
Come to meet him (her), angels of the Lord!

R. Receive his (her) soul and present him (her) to God, the Most High.

May Christ, who called you, take you to himself;
may angels lead you to Abraham's side. **R.**

Give him (her) eternal rest, O Lord,
and may your light shine on him (her) for ever. **R.**

Let us pray.
All-powerful and merciful God,
we commend to you N., your servant.

---

1. National Conference of Catholic Bishops, *Catholic Household Blessings and Prayers* (=CHBP), 1988.

2. John Paul II, *Crossing the Threshold of Hope* (=CTH), 25, New York: Alfred A. Knopf, 1994.

In your mercy and love,
blot out the sins he (she) has committed
    through human weakness.
In this world he (she) has died:
let him (her) live with you for ever.
We ask this through Christ our Lord.

R. **Amen.**

These verses may also be used:

V. Eternal rest grant unto him (her), O Lord.

R. **And let perpetual light shine upon him (her).**

V. May he (she) rest in peace.

R. **Amen.**

V. May his (her) soul and the souls of all the faithful
    departed, through the mercy of God, rest in
    peace.

R. **Amen.**

GATHERING IN THE PRESENCE
OF THE BODY

When the family first gathers around the body, before or after it is prepared for burial, all or some of
the following prayers may be used. It is most fitting
that family members take part in preparing the
body for burial.

All make the Sign of the Cross:

In the name of the Father, and of the Son,
and of the Holy Spirit.

R. Amen.

Then one member of the family reads:

My brothers and sisters, Jesus says: "Come to me, all
you who labor and are overburdened, and I will give
you rest. Shoulder my yoke and learn from me, for I

am gentle and humble of heart, and you will find rest for your souls. Yes, my yoke is easy and my burden light."

The body may then be sprinkled with holy water.

The Lord God lives in his holy temple
yet abides in our midst.
Since in Baptism N. became God's temple,
and the spirit of God lived in him (her),
with reverence we bless his (her) mortal body.

Then one member of the family may say:

With God there is mercy and fullness of redemption.
Let us pray as Jesus taught us:

Our Father.

Then this prayer is said:

Into your hands, O Lord,
we humbly entrust our brother (sister) N.
In this life you embraced him (her)
with your tender love;
deliver him (her) now from every evil
and bid him (her) enter eternal rest.
The old order has passed away:
welcome him (her), then, into paradise,
where there will be no sorrow,
no weeping or pain,
but the fullness of peace and joy
with your Son and the Holy Spirit
for ever and ever.

R. Amen.

All may sign the forehead of the deceased with the Sign of the Cross. One member of the family says:

Blessed are those who have died in the Lord;
let them rest from their labors,
for their good deeds go with them.

V. Eternal rest grant unto him (her), O Lord.

R. **And let perpetual light shine upon him (her).**

V. May he (she) rest in peace.

R. **Amen.**

V. May his (her) soul and the souls of all the faithful departed, through the mercy of God, rest in peace.

R. **Amen.**

All make the Sign of the Cross as one member of the family says:

May the love of God and the peace
   of the Lord Jesus Christ
bless and console us
and gently wipe every tear from our eyes:
in the name of the Father,
and of the Son, and of the Holy Spirit.

R. **Amen.**

Lord Jesus, our Redeemer,
you willingly gave yourself up to death,
so that all people might be saved
and pass from death into a new life.
Listen to our prayers;
look with love on your people
who mourn and pray for their brother (sister).
Lord Jesus, holy and compassionate,
forgive N. his (her) sins.
By dying you opened the gates of life
for those who believe in you:
do not let our brother (sister) be parted from you,
but by your glorious power
give him (her) light, joy, and peace in heaven,
where you live for ever and ever. R. **Amen.**

PRAYERS AT THE GRAVESIDE

Aside from the time of mourning, the month of November, including especially All Saints' day and All Souls' day, is a traditional time for visiting graves, as is the anniversary of death. Some or all of the following prayers may be used at the graveside of a family member or friend.

All make the Sign of the Cross. The leader begins:

Praise be to God our Father, who raised Jesus Christ from the dead. Blessed be God for ever.

All respond:

Blessed be God for ever.

The following Scripture text may be read: **2 Cor 5: 1**

We know that if our earthly dwelling, a tent, should be destroyed, we have a building from God, a dwelling not made with hands, eternal in heaven.

After a time of silence, all join in prayers of intercession, or in one of the litanies or other prayers. All then join hands for the Lord's Prayer:

Our Father.

Then the leader prays:

Lord God,
whose days are without end
and whose mercies are beyond counting,
keep us mindful
that life is short and the hour of death is unknown.
Let your Spirit guide our days on earth
in the ways of holiness and justice,
that we may serve you
in union with the whole Church,
sure in faith, strong in hope, perfected in love.
And when our earthly journey is ended,
lead us rejoicing into your kingdom,
where you live for ever and ever. **R. Amen.**

or:

Lord Jesus Christ,
by your own three days in the tomb,
you hallowed the graves of all who believe in you
and so made the grave a sign of hope
that promises resurrection,
even as it claims our mortal bodies.
Grant that our brother (sister) N.
    may sleep here in peace
until you awaken him (her) to glory,
for you are the resurrection and the life.
Then he (she) will see you face to face
and in your light will see light
and know the splendor of God,
for you live and reign for ever and ever.

R. Amen.

V. Eternal rest grant unto them, O Lord,

R. And let perpetual light shine upon them.

V. May they rest in peace.

R. Amen.

V. May their souls and the souls of all the faithful
departed, through the mercy of God, rest in
peace.

R. Amen.

All make the Sign of the Cross as the leader concludes:

May the peace of God,
which is beyond all understanding,
keep our hearts and minds
in the knowledge and love of God
and of his Son, our Lord Jesus Christ.

R. Amen.

ADDITIONAL PRAYERS FOR THE DEAD

V. Do not remember my sins, O Lord,

R. **When you come to judge the world by fire.**

V. Direct my way in your sight, O Lord, my God,

R. **When you come to judge the world by fire.**

V. Give him (her) eternal rest, O Lord, and may your light shine on him (her) for ever,

R. **When you come to judge the world by fire,**

V. Lord, have mercy.

R. **Christ, have mercy, Lord, have mercy.**

All:

Our Father . . . trespass against us.

V. And lead us not into temptation,

R. **But deliver us from evil.**

V. From the gates of hell,

R. **Deliver his (her) soul, O Lord.**

V. May he (she) rest in peace.

R. **Amen.**

V. Lord, hear my prayer,

R. **And let my cry come to you.**

V. The Lord be with you.

R. **And also with you.**

Let us pray.

Lord, welcome into your presence your son (daughter) N., whom you have called from this life. Release him (her) from all his (her) sins; bless him (her) with eternal light and peace; raise him (her) up to live for ever with all your saints in the glory of the Resurrection.

We ask this through Christ our Lord. R. **Amen.**

For a parent:

Let us pray.
Almighty God, you command us to honor father and mother. In your mercy forgive the sins of my (our) parents and let me (us) one day see him (her) again in the radiance of eternal joy.
We ask this through Christ our Lord.
R. Amen.

For a brothers or sister:

Let us pray.
God, our Maker and Redeemer, in your mercy hear my (our) prayer. Grant forgiveness and peace to my (our) brother (sister) N. and N., who longed for your mercy.
We ask this through Christ our Lord.
R. Amen.

V. Give him (her) eternal rest, O Lord.

R. And may your light shine on him (her) for ever.

V. May he (she) rest in peace.

R. Amen.

V. May his (her) soul and the souls of all the faithful departed, through the mercy of God, rest in peace.

R. Amen.

BLESSINGS

BLESSING OF HOLY WATER OUTSIDE MASS [1]

On the basis of age-old custom, water is one of the signs that the Church often uses in blessing the faithful. Holy water reminds the faithful of Christ, who is given to us as the supreme divine blessing, who called himself the living water, and who, with water, established Baptism for our sake as the sacramental sign of the blessing that brings salvation.

The blessing of holy water usually takes place on Sunday, in keeping with the rite given in the Sacramentary. But when the blessing of water takes place outside Mass, the rite given here may be used by the priest or deacon. While maintaining the structure and chief elements of the rite, the celebrant should adapt the celebration to the circumstances of the place and the people involved.

ORDER OF BLESSING

Introductory Rites

The celebrant begins with these words:

In the name of the Father, and of the Son, and of the Holy Spirit.

All make the Sign of the Cross and reply:

Amen.

The celebrant greets those present, using the following or other suitable words, taken mainly from Sacred Scripture:

---

1. International Committee on English Liturgy (ICEL), Book *of Blessings* (=BB), 1990.

May God, who through water and the Holy Spirit has given us a new birth in Christ, be with you all.

All make the following or some other suitable reply:

And also with you.

As circumstances suggest, the celebrant may prepare those present for the blessing in the following or similar words:

The blessing of this water reminds us of Christ, the living water, and of the sacrament of Baptism, in which we were born of water and the Holy Spirit. Whenever, therefore, we are sprinkled with this holy water or use it in blessing ourselves upon entering the church or at home, we thank God for his priceless gift to us and we ask for his help to keep us faithful to the sacrament we have received in faith.

Reading of the Word of God

A reader, another person present or the celebrant reads a short text of sacred Scripture, such as the following:

Listen to the words of the holy gospel according to John: 7:37-39

Let anyone who is thirsty come to me.

On the last and greatest day of the feast, Jesus stood up and exclaimed, "Let anyone who thirsts come to me and drink. Whoever believes in me, as Scripture says: 'Rivers of living water will flow from within him.'"

He said this in reference to the Spirit that those who came to believe in him were to receive. There was, of course, no Spirit yet, because Jesus had not yet been glorified.

The reader concludes:

The gospel of the Lord.

All respond:

Praise to you, Lord Jesus Christ.

Alternative Readings:

You will draw water joyfully from
   the springs of salvation.   **Isaiah 12:1-6**

Oh, come to the water,
   all you who are thirsty.   **Isaiah 55:1-11**

She will give him the water
   of wisdom to drink.   **Sirach 15:1-6**

Jesus Christ came by water
   and blood.   **1 John 5:1-6**

The Lamb will lead them to
   the springs of living water.   **Revelation 7:13-17**

The river of life, rising from the
   throne of God and of the Lamb.   **Revelation 22:1-5**

You, too, are clean.   **John 13:3-15**

Prayer of Blessing

   After the reading, the celebrant says:

Let us pray.

   All pray briefly in silence; then, with hands outstretched, the
   celebrant says the prayer of blessing:

Blessed are you, Lord, all-powerful God,
who in Christ, the living water of salvation,
blessed and transformed us.
Grant that when we are sprinkled with this water
or make use of it,
we will be refreshed inwardly by the power
   of the Holy Spirit
and continue to walk in the new life
   we received at Baptism.
We ask this though Christ our Lord.
R. Amen.

or

Lord, holy Father,
look with kindness on your children
redeemed by your Son
and born to a new life by water and the Holy Spirit.
Grant that those who are sprinkled with this water
may be renewed in body and spirit
and may make a pure offering of their service to you.
We ask this through Christ our Lord.

R. **Amen.**

or the celebrant says:

O God, the Creator of all things,
by water and the Holy Spirit
you have given the universe its beauty
and fashioned us in your own image.

R. **Bless and purify your Church.**

O Christ the Lord, from your pierced side
you gave us your sacraments
as fountains of salvation.

R. **Bless and purify your Church.**

O Holy Spirit, giver of life,
from the baptismal font of the Church
you have formed us into a new creation
in the waters of rebirth.

R. **Bless and purify your Church.**

After the prayer of blessing, the celebrant sprinkles those
present with holy water, as a suitable song is sung; as circumstances suggest, he may first say the following words:

Let this water call to mind our Baptism into Christ,
who has redeemed us by his death and resurrection.

R. **Amen.**

BLESSING OF AN ADVENT WREATH [2]

The Advent wreath is made of four candles and a circle of branches. Before the first candle is lighted, the household gathers for this blessing.

All make the Sign of the Cross. The leader begins:

Our help is in the name of the Lord.

All respond:

Who made heaven and earth.

The leader may use these or similar words to introduce the blessing:

In the short days and long nights of Advent, we realize how we are always needing salvation by our God. Around this wreath, we shall remember God's promise.

Then the Scripture is read:

Listen to the words of the prophet Isaiah: 9:1-2
*The people who walked in darkness
have seen a great light.*

The people who walked in darkness have seen a great light; upon those who dwelt in the land of gloom, a light has shone. You have brought them abundant joy and great rejoicing.

The reader concludes:

The word of the Lord.

All respond:

Thanks be to God.

After a time of silence, all join in prayers of intercession and in the Lord's Prayer:

Our Father.

Then the leader invites:

Let us now pray for God's blessing upon us and upon this wreath.

2. National Conference of Catholic Bishops, *Catholic Household Blessings and Prayers* (=CHBP), 1988.

After a short silence, the leader prays:

Lord our God,
we praise you for your Son, Jesus Christ:
he is Emmanuel, the hope of the peoples,
he is the wisdom that teaches and guides us,
he is the Savior of every nation.
Lord God,
let your blessing come upon us
as we light the candles of this wreath.
May the wreath and its light
be a sign of Christ's promise to bring us salvation;
may he come quickly and not delay.
We ask this through Christ our Lord.

R. Amen.

BLESSING OF A CHRISTMAS CRÈCHE OR A MANGER SCENE [3]

The manger scene has a special place near the Christmas tree or in another place where family members can reflect and pray during the Christmas season. It is blessed each year on Christmas eve or Christmas day.

All make the Sign of the Cross. The leader begins:

Our help is in the name of the Lord.

All respond:

Who made heaven and earth.

The leader may use these or similar words to introduce the blessing:

We are at the beginning of the days of Christmas. All through the season we will look on these images of sheep and cattle, of shepherds, of Mary and Joseph and Jesus.

Then the Scripture is read:

---

3. CHBP.

Listen to the words of the holy gospel
according to Luke: 2:1-7

The birth of Jesus

In those days a decree went out from Caesar Augustus
that all the world should be enrolled. This was the first
enrollment, when Quirinius was governor of Syria.
And all went to be enrolled, each to his own city. And
Joseph also went up from Galilee, from the city of
Nazareth, to Judaea, to the city of David, which is
called Bethlehem, because he was of the house and lineage of David, to be enrolled with Mary, his betrothed,
who was with child. And while they were there, the
time came for her to be delivered. And she gave birth
to her firstborn son and wrapped him in swaddling
clothes, and laid him in a manger, because there was
no place for them in the inn.

The reader concludes: **The gospel of the Lord.**

All respond: **Praise to you, Lord Jesus Christ.**

The figures may be placed in the crèche. After a time of silence,
all join in prayers of intercession and in the Lord's Prayer. Then
the leader invites:

Pray now for God's blessing as we look on these
figures.

After a short silence, the leader prays:

God of every nation and people,
from the very beginning of creation
you have made manifest your love.
When our need for a Savior was great,
you sent your Son to be born of the Virgin Mary.
To our lives he brings joy and peace,
justice, mercy, and love.
Lord,
bless all who look upon this manger;
may it remind us of the humble birth of Jesus

and raise our thoughts to him,
who is God-with-us and Savior of all,
and who lives and reigns for ever and ever. **R. Amen.**

or

God of Mary and Joseph, of shepherds and animals,
bless us whenever we gaze on this manger scene.
Through all the days of Christmas
may these figures tell the story
of how humans, angels, and animals
found the Christ in this poor place.
Fill our house with hospitality, joy,
gentleness, and thanksgiving,
and guide our steps in the way of peace.
Grant this through Christ our Lord. **R. Amen.**

The leader says: Let us bless the Lord.

All respond, making the Sign of the Cross:

Thanks be to God.

Then Christmas songs and carols are sung; for example:

It came upon a midnight clear,
That glorious song of old,
From angels bending near the earth
To touch their harps of gold:
"Peace on the earth, good will to all
From heaven's all-gracious King";
The world in solemn stillness lay,
To hear the angels sing.

Yet with the woes of sin and strife,
The world has suffered long;
Beneath the heavenly hymn have rolled
Two thousand years of wrong.
And warring humankind hears not
The tidings which they bring;
O hush the noise and cease your strife
And hear the angels sing.

BLESSING OF A CHRISTMAS TREE [4]

When the tree has been prepared, the household gathers around it. All make the Sign of the Cross. The leader begins:

Blessed be the name of the Lord.

All respond:

Now and for ever.

The leader may use these or similar words to introduce the blessing:

This tree is a blessing to our home. It reminds us of all that is beautiful, all that is filled with the gentleness and the promise of God. It stands in our midst as a tree of light, that we might promise such beauty to one another and to our world. It stands like that tree of paradise that God made into the tree of life, the cross of Jesus.

Then the Scripture is read:

Listen to the words of the apostle Paul to Titus: 3:4-7

His own compassion saved us

But when the kindness and generous love of God our Savior appeared, not because of any righteous deeds we had done but because of his mercy, he saved us through the bath of rebirth and renewal by the Holy Spirit, whom he richly poured out on us through Jesus Christ our Savior, so that we might be justified by his grace and become heirs in the hope of eternal life.

The reader concludes:

The word of the Lord.

All respond:

Thanks be to God.

After a time of silence, all join in prayers of intercession and in the Lord's Prayer. Then the leader invites:

---

4. CHBP.

Let us now pray for God's blessing upon all who
gather around this tree.

After a short silence, the leader prays:

Lord our God,
we praise you for the light of creation:
the sun, the moon, and the stars of the night.
We praise you for the light of Israel:
the Law, the prophets, and the wisdom
    of the Scriptures.
We praise you for Jesus Christ, your Son:
he is Emmanuel, God-with-us, the Prince of Peace,
who fills us with the wonder of your love.
Lord God,
let your blessing come upon us
as we illumine this tree.
May the light and cheer it gives
be a sign of the joy that fills our hearts.
May all who delight in this tree
come to the knowledge and joy of salvation.
We ask this through Christ our Lord. **R. Amen.**
    or

God of all creation,
we praise you for this tree
which brings beauty and memories
    and the promise of life to our home.
May your blessing be upon
all who gather around this tree,
all who keep the Christmas festival by its lights.
We wait for the coming of the Christ,
the days of everlasting justice and of peace.
You are our God, living and reigning,
    for ever and ever.

R. Amen.

The lights of the tree are then turned on.

BLESSING OF A NEW HOME [5]

When any of the faithful wish to mark their moving into a new home with a religious celebration, the parish priest (pastor) and his associates should gladly cooperate. The occasion provides a special opportunity for a gathering of the members of the community to mark the joyful event and to thank God, from whom all blessings come, for the gift of a new home.

The present order may be used by a priest or deacon. It may also be used by a lay person, who follows the rites and prayers designated for a lay minister. While maintaining the structure and chief elements of the rite, the minister should adapt the celebration to the circumstances of the place and the people involved.

There is to be no blessing of a new home unless those who will live in it are present.

Introductory Rites

When the family members and their relatives and friends have gathered in a convenient place, the minister says:

In the name of the Father, and of the Son, and of the Holy Spirit.

All make the Sign of the Cross and reply:

Amen.

A minister who is a priest or deacon greets those present in the following or other suitable words, taken mainly from sacred Scripture.

Peace be with this house and with all who live here.

All make the following or some other suitable reply:

And also with you.

---

5. BB.

A lay minister uses the following greeting:

May the God whom we glorify with one heart and voice enable us, through the Spirit, to live in harmony as followers of Christ Jesus, now and for ever. **R. Amen.**

In the following or similar words, the minister prepares those present for the blessing.

When Christ took flesh through the Blessed Virgin Mary, he made his home with us. Let us now pray that he will enter this home and bless it with his presence. May he always be here with you, share in your joys, comfort you in your sorrows. Inspired by his teachings and example, seek to make your new home before all else a dwelling place of love, diffusing far and wide the goodness of Christ.

Reading of the Word of God

A reader, another person present, or the **minister** reads a text of sacred Scripture.

Listen to the words of the holy gospel
according to Luke: 10:5-9

Peace to this house.

The Lord said to the seventy-two: "Into whatever house you enter, first say, 'Peace to this household.' If a peaceful person lives there, your peace will rest on him; but if not, it will return to you. Stay in the same house and eat and drink what is offered to you, for the laborer deserves his payment. Do not move about from one house to another. Whatever town you enter and they welcome you, eat what is set before you, cure the sick in it, and say to them, 'The kingdom of God is at hand for you.'"

Alternative Readings:

Lord, do not pass your servant by.	Genesis 18:1-10a
Jesus went straight to Simon's house.	Mark 1:29-30
Martha welcomed Jesus into her house.	Luke 10:38-42
Today salvation has come to this house.	Luke 19:1-9
Stay with us.	Luke 24:28-32

As circumstances suggest, the following responsorial psalm or some other suitable song may be sung or said.

R. **Happy are those who fear the Lord.** Psalm 112

Happy the man who fears the Lord,
who greatly delights in his commands.
His posterity shall be mighty upon the earth;
the upright generation shall be blessed. R.

Wealth and riches shall be in his house;
his generosity shall endure for ever.
He dawns through the darkness,
    a light for the upright;
he is gracious and merciful and just. R.

Well for the man who is gracious and lends,
who conducts his affairs with justice;
He shall never be moved;
the just man shall be in everlasting remembrance. R.

An evil report he shall not fear;
his heart is firm, trusting in the Lord.
His heart is steadfast; he shall not fear
till he looks down upon his foes. R.

Lavishly he gives to the poor;
his generosity shall endure for ever;
his horn shall be exalted in glory. R.

Alternative Responsorial Psalms:

Psalm 127: 1. 2. 3-4. 5

R. **The Lord will build a house for us.**

Psalm 128: 1-2. 3. 4-6a

R. **See how the Lord blesses those who fear him.**

As circumstances suggest, the minister may give those present a brief explanation of the biblical text, so that they may understand through faith the meaning of the celebration.

Intercessions

The intercessions are then said. The minister introduces them, and an assisting minister or someone else announces the intentions. From the following intentions, those best suited to the circumstances may be used or adapted, or other intentions that apply to the particular circumstances may be composed.

The minister says:

The Son of God, Lord of heaven and earth, made his home among us. With thankfulness and gladness let us call upon him, saying:

R. **Stay with us, Lord.**

or

R. **Lord, hear our prayer.**

Assisting minister:

Lord Jesus Christ, by your life with Mary and Joseph you sanctified the life of the home; dwell with us in our home, so that we may have you as our guest and honor you as our Head. (For this we pray:) R.

Assisting minister:

In you every dwelling grows into a holy temple; grant that those who live in this house may be built up together into the dwelling place of God in the Holy Spirit. (For this we pray:) R.

Assisting minister:

You taught your followers to build their houses upon solid rock; grant that the members of this family may hold fast to your teachings and, free of all discord, serve you with their whole heart. (For this we pray:) **R**.

Assisting minister:

You had no place to lay your head, but in uncomplaining poverty you accepted the hospitality of your friends; grant that through our help people who are homeless may obtain decent housing. (For this we pray:) **R**.

Prayer of Blessing

A minister who is a priest or deacon says the prayer of blessing with hands outstretched; a lay minister says the prayer with the hands joined.

Lord,
be close to your servants
who move into this home (today)
and ask for your blessing.
Be their shelter when they are at home,
their companion when they are away,
and their welcome guest when they return.
And at last receive them
into the dwelling place you have prepared for them
in your Father's house,
where you live for ever and ever. **R. Amen.**

After the prayer of blessing, the minister sprinkles those present and the new home with holy water and, as circumstances suggest, during the sprinkling may say:

Let this water call to mind our Baptism into Christ, who has redeemed us by his death and resurrection.

Concluding Rite

The minister concludes the rite by saying:

May the peace of Christ rule in our hearts |, and may the word of Christ in all its richness dwell in us, | so that whatever we do in word and in work, | we will do in the name of the Lord. **R. Amen.**

It is preferable to end the celebration with a suitable song.

BLESSING FOR A PLACE OF WORK [6]

When a place of work is to be blessed, both those who labor there and those who share the fruit of that labor should be invited to the ceremony.

All make the Sign of the Cross. The leader begins:

Blessed be God, who has begun a good work in us. Blessed be the name of the Lord.

All respond:

Now and for ever.

The leader may use these or similar words to introduce the blessing:

Jesus showed us the dignity of labor. He was known as the carpenter's son, and he willingly worked with the tools of his trade. Through the labor of our hands, we bring God's blessing upon ourselves and others. Let us pray for all who will work here and for those who will share the fruit of their labor.

Then the Scripture is read:

Listen to the words of the apostle Paul
to the Thessalonians: 1 Thes 4:10-12

We urge you, brothers [and sisters], to progress even more, and to aspire to live a tranquil life, to mind your own affairs, and to work with your [own] hands, as we instructed you, that you may conduct yourselves properly toward outsiders and not depend on anyone.

The reader concludes:

The word of the Lord.

All respond:

Thanks be to God.

---

6. CHBP.

After a time of silence, all join in prayers of intercession and in the Lord's Prayer. A cross or other symbol may then be reverenced with a kiss and put in a place of honor. The leader then speaks the prayer of blessing; one of the following may be used or adapted as needed.

OF AN OFFICE

O God, | in your wise providence | you are glad to bless all human labor, | the work of our hands and of our minds. | Grant that all who plan and conduct business in this office | may, through your guidance and support, | come to right decisions and carry them out fairly. | We ask this through Christ our Lord.

R. Amen.

OF A SHOP OR FACTORY

God, our all-provident Father, | you have placed the earth and its fruits under our care, | so that by our labor we will endeavor | to ensure that all share in the benefits of your creation. | Bless all those who will use this building | either as buyers or sellers, | so that by respecting justice and charity | they will see themselves as working for the common good | and find joy in contributing to the progress of the earthly city. | We ask this through Christ our Lord.

R. **Amen.**

Then holy water may be sprinkled on the office, shop, or factory, and on the participants.

All make the Sign of the Cross, as the leader concludes:

May God, the Father of goodness, | who commanded us to help one another as brothers and sisters, | bless this building with his presence | and look kindly on all who enter here. R. Amen.

And may almighty God bless you,
the Father, and the Son, ✠ and the Holy Spirit.

R. Amen.

BLESSING OF TRAVELERS (SHORTER RITE)[7]

The minister says: Our help is in the name of the Lord.

All reply: **Who made heaven and earth.**

Someone reads a text of sacred Scripture, such as the following.

Listen to the words of the book of Tobit:　　5:17–18

[Tobit] called his son and said to him: "My son, prepare whatever you need for the journey, and set out with your kinsman. May God in heaven protect you on the way and bring you back to me safe and sound; and may his angel accompany you for safety, my son."

Then the minister says the prayer of blessing:

All-powerful and ever-living God,
when Abraham left his own land
and departed from his own people,
you kept him safe all through his journey.
Protect us, who also are your servants:
walk by our side to help us;
be our companion and our strength
　　[as we travel] on the road
and our refuge in every adversity.
Lead us, O Lord,
so that we will reach our destination in safety
and happily return to our homes.
We ask this through Christ our Lord. R. **Amen.**

or

May God bless you with every heavenly blessing
and give you a safe journey;
wherever life leads you,
may you may find him there to protect you.
We ask this through Christ our Lord. R. **Amen.**

The blessing may conclude with a song, such as "Now Thank We All Our God."

7. BB.

BLESSING OF A MOTHER BEFORE CHILDBIRTH (SHORT FORMULARY) [8]

As circumstances suggest, a priest or deacon may use the following short blessing formulary:

God has brought gladness and light to the world | through the Virgin Mary's delivery of her child. | May Christ fill your heart with his holy joy | and keep you and your baby safe from harm. | In the name of the Father, ✠ and of the Son, and of the Holy Spirit. R. **Amen.**

BLESSING OF A MOTHER AFTER CHILDBIRTH (SHORT FORMULARY) [9]

As circumstances suggest, a priest or deacon may use the following short blessing formulary:

May the Lord God almighty, | who through the earthly birth of his own Son | has filled the whole world with joy, so bless ✠ you | that the child he has given you | will always bring joy to your heart. R. **Amen.**

BLESSING AND IMPOSITION WITH THE SCAPULAR OF OUR LADY OF MOUNT CARMEL
(See p. 479.)

BLESSING AND THANKSGIVING AT MEALS
(See p. 546.)

---

8. BB.
9. BB.

BLESSING OF ROSARIES
(SHORTER RITE) [10]

To begin, the celebrant says:

Lord, show us your mercy and love.

All reply:

And grant us your salvation.

As circumstances suggest, the celebrant may begin with an explanation of the blessing.

Someone reads a text of sacred Scripture, such as the following.

Lk 2:51b-52

Mary, his mother, kept all these things in her heart. And Jesus advanced in wisdom and age and favor before God and man.

or   Acts 1:14

All these devoted themselves with one accord to prayer, together with some women and Mary, the mother of Jesus, and his brothers.

With his hands outstretched, the celebrant says the prayer of blessing:

**Blessed be our God and Father,
who has given us the mysteries of his Son
to be pondered with devotion
and celebrated with faith.
May he grant us, his faithful people,
that by praying the rosary we may,
with Mary, the Mother of Jesus,
seek to keep his joys, sorrows,
and glories in our minds and hearts.
We ask this through Christ our Lord.**

R. **Amen.**

---

10. BB.

or
In memory of the mysteries
of the life, death, and resurrection of our Lord
and in honor of the Virgin Mary,
Mother of Christ and Mother of the Church,
may those who devoutly use this rosary
    to pray be blessed,
in the name of the Father, and of the Son, ✠ and
    of the Holy Spirit.
R. **Amen.**

BLESSING OF ROSARIES
(SHORT FORMULARY)

In special circumstances, a priest or deacon may use the following short blessing formulary:

May this rosary and the one who uses it be blessed,
in the name of the Father, and of the Son, ✠ and
    of the Holy Spirit.

R. **Amen.**

BLESSING OF RELIGIOUS ARTICLES
(SHORT FORMULARY) [11]

To be used to bless medals, small crucifixes, statues, or pictures that will be displayed elsewhere than in a church or chapel; scapulars, rosaries, and other articles used for religious devotions.

In special circumstances, a priest or deacon may use the following short blessing formulary.

May this (name of article) and the one who uses
    it be blessed,
in the name of the Father, and of the Son, ✠ and
    of the Holy Spirit. R. **Amen.**

---

11. BB.

BLESSING OF MEANS OF TRANSPORTATION (SHORTER RITE) [12]

At the beginning of the celebration, the minister says:

Our help is in the name of the Lord.

All reply:

Who made heaven and earth.

Someone reads a text of sacred Scripture, such as the following.

Listen to the words of the holy gospel according to John: **14:6**

Jesus said to Thomas: "I am the way and the truth and the life. No one comes to the Father except through me."

Prayer of Blessing

A minister who is a priest or deacon says the prayer of blessing with hands outstretched; a lay minister says the prayer with the hands joined.

All-powerful God,
Creator of heaven and earth,
in the rich depths of your wisdom
you have empowered us to produce great and
    beautiful works.

Grant, we pray, that those who use this vehicle
may travel safely, with care
    for the safety of others.

Whether they travel for business or pleasure,
let them always find Christ
    to be the companion of their journey,

who lives and reigns with you for ever and ever.

R. Amen.

As circumstances suggest, the minister may sprinkle those present and the vehicle with holy water.

---

12. BB.

RECEPTION OF SACRAMENTS BY A PERSON IN DANGER OF DEATH

CHRISTIAN INITIATION FOR THE DYING

BAPTISM [1]

In the case of a person who is at the point of death, or in imminent danger of death, the minister, omitting all other ceremonies, pours water (not necessarily blessed, but real and natural water) on the head of the person, while saying:

N., I baptize you in the name of the Father, ✠

The minister pours water the first time.

and of the Son, ✠

The minister pours water the second time.

and of the Holy Spirit. ✠

The minister pours water the third time. It is desirable that should be one or two witnesses. If able to do this, an adult candidate is required to make a profession of faith, such as the Apostles' Creed, p. 45, before the Baptism,.

CONFIRMATION [2]

When circumstances permit, the entire rite is followed. *In case of urgent necessity*, the minister of Confirmation lays his hands upon the sick person, as he says:

All-powerful God, Father of our Lord Jesus Christ,
by water and the Holy Spirit
you freed your son (daughter) from sin
and gave him (her) new life.

---

1. Cf. *The Rites of the Catholic Church* (=RCC), Rite of Baptism for Children, 21.1, 160, 164; Rite of Christian Initiation of Adults, 373. New York: Pueblo Publishing Co., 1990.
2. Cf. RCC, Rite of Confirmation, 53, 54, and 56.

Send your Holy Spirit
upon him (her) to be his (her) Helper and Guide.
Give him (her) the spirit of wisdom and understanding,
the spirit of right judgment and courage,
the spirit of knowledge and reverence.
Fill him (her) with the spirit of wonder
　　　and awe in your presence.
We ask this through Christ our Lord.

R. Amen.

Then the minister dips his right thumb in the chrism and with
it makes the Sign of the Cross on the forehead of the one to be
confirmed, as he says:

N., be sealed with the Gift of the Holy Spirit. ☩

The newly confirmed responds, if able: **Amen.**

Other parts of the preparatory and concluding rites [from the
Rite of Confirmation] may be added in individual cases, de-
pending on the circumstances.

In case of extreme necessity, it is sufficient that the anointing
be done with the sacramental form:

N., be sealed with the Gift of the Holy Spirit. ☩

SACRAMENTAL RITES FOR THOSE BAPTIZED

SACRAMENTAL ABSOLUTION [3]

When pastoral need dictates, the priest may omit or shorten
some parts of the rite but must always retain in their entirety
the penitent's confession of sins and acceptance of the act of
penance, the invitation to contrition, and the formularies of absolution and dismissal. In [the case of] *imminent danger of death,
it is sufficient for the priest to say the essential words of the form of
absolution, namely*:

I absolve you from your sins
in the name of the Father, and of the Son, ☩
and of the Holy Spirit.

The penitent answers: **Amen.**

---

3. Cf. RCC, *Rite of Penance,* 21 and 44.

ABSOLUTION OF CENSURES [4]

The [external] form of absolution is not to be changed when a priest, in keeping with the provision of law, absolves a properly disposed penitent within the sacramental forum [sacrament of Reconciliation; Confession] from a censure *latæ sententiæ*. It is enough that the confessor [when giving the sacramental absolution] intends to absolve also from censures. When a priest, in accordance with the law, absolves a penitent from such a censure outside the sacrament of Reconciliation, he uses the following formula:

By the power granted to me, I absolve you from the bond of excommunication (or suspension or interdict). In the name of the Father, and of the Son, ✠ and of the Holy Spirit.

The penitent answers: **Amen.**

DISPENSATION FROM IRREGULARITY [5]

When, in accordance with the law, a priest dispenses a penitent from an irregularity, either during sacramental Confession, after absolution has been given, or outside the sacrament of Reconciliation, he says:

By the power granted to me, I dispense you from the irregularity which you have incurred. In the name of the Father, and of the Son, ✠ and of the Holy Spirit.

The penitent answers: **Amen.**

ANOINTING OF THE SICK [6]

When a priest has been called to attend a person who is already dead, he is not to administer the sacrament of Anointing. Instead, he should pray for the dead person, asking that

---

4. Cf. RCC, *Rite of Penance*, Appendix I, 1-2.
5. Cf. RCC, *Rite of Penance*, Appendix I, 1-2.
6. Cf. *Pastoral Care of the Sick* (=PCS), 124, 263-264, New York:Catholic Book Publishing, 1983. The sacrament is to be conferred upon sick persons who requested it at least implicitly when they were in control of their faculties, or when there is a doubt whether the person is de: *Codex Iuris Canonici*, 1005-1006.

God forgive his or her sins and graciously receive him or her into the kingdom.

If the priest has reason to believe that the person is still living, he anoints him or her.

First he anoints the forehead, saying:

Through this holy anointing,
may the Lord in his love and mercy help you
with the grace of the Holy Spirit. ✠

R. Amen.

Then he anoints the hands, saying:

May the Lord who frees you from sin
save you and raise you up.

R. Amen.

The sacramental form is said only once, for the anointing of the forehead and hands, and is not repeated.

APOSTOLIC PARDON [7]

At the conclusion of the sacrament of Penance or the penitential rite, the priest may give the Apostolic pardon for the dying, with plenary indulgence, using one of these forms:

Through the holy mysteries of our redemption,
may almighty God release you from all punishments
in this life and in the life to come.

May he open to you the gates of paradise
and welcome you to everlasting joy. **R. Amen.**

or

By the authority which the Apostolic See has given me,

I grant you a full pardon and the remission
of all your sins

the name of the Father, and of the Son, ✠
of the Holy Spirit.

INDEX